D1320989

£ 4-00

£ 4-00

THE
TEDDY BEAR
ENCYCLOPEDIA

THE
TEDDY BEAR
ENCYCLOPEDIA

PAULINE COCKRILL

FOREWORD BY PAUL AND ROSEMARY VOLPP

PHOTOGRAPHY BY PETER ANDERSON AND JIM COIT

COVENT
GARDEN
BOOKS

A DORLING KINDERSLEY BOOK

PROJECT EDITOR Irene Lyford
PROJECT ART EDITOR Peter Cross

EDITOR HelenTownsend
DESIGNER Deborah Myatt

MANAGING EDITOR Mary-Clare Jerram
MANAGING ART EDITOR Gill Della Casa

PRODUCTION Helen Creeke

First published in Great Britain in 1993
by Dorling Kindersley Limited, 9 Henrietta Street,
London WC2E 8PS
Reprinted 1993

COPYRIGHT © 1993
DORLING KINDERSLEY LIMITED, LONDON

A CIP catalogue record for this book is available
from the British Library.

ISBN 1- 85605453- 5

Computer page make-up by The Cooling Brown
Partnership, London
Text film output by The Right Type, London
Reproduced by Colourscan, Singapore
Printed and bound in Spain
D.L.TO:736-1998

CONTENTS

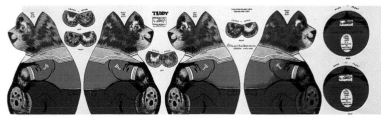

FOREWORD

PAUL AND ROSEMARY VOLPP

W HAT A PRIVILEGE AND PLEASURE to introduce you to another beautiful Dorling Kindersley book written by best-selling author Pauline Cockrill. If you are already acquainted with *The Ultimate Teddy Bear Book*, and with the *The Little Books of Traditional Bears*, *of Celebrity Bears*, and *of Bear Care*, you will know that you are holding a feast of reading and viewing in your hands.

Our introduction to the teddy-bear world happened over a decade ago, in an enchanting store called The Teddy Bear Station in Yorba Linda, California. We were browsing, just killing time until a restaurant opened, when Rosemary was captivated by a blue bear in an aviator suit looking down from a shelf. The sales lady came over and said, "If you like that bear, you'd better take it now. It's the last one in southern California, and there won't be any more." Rosemary replied that that was very interesting, but she wasn't a bear collector. Famous last words! A friend who accompanied us to dinner kept teasing Rosemary that she would regret not buying the bear for the rest of her life, until she got so excited that she went back to the store between the main course and dessert and bought her. She was a North American Bear Company Amelia Bearhart. Although her original price was under $40.00, Amelias now sell for over $1,000.00 *(see p.146)*.

Very important bear
Amelia Bearhart launched the North American Bear Company's V.I.B. (Very Important Bear) range of costumed teddy characters with punning names (see pp.146–47).

Paul caught bear fever, too, and then we were off and running to every bear store we could find. That was the beginning of a hobby that has taken the two of us all over the world. In a remarkably short time, Amelia became part of a collection of about 5,000 teddy bears, of every description imaginable. We often say we don't know whether we are bragging or complaining when we admit to the size of our collection. But one thing is certain: the bears have led us to meet some unforgettable people, and this is a bonus of collecting. We have happy memories of having been twice in Minneapolis at the Teddy Tribune Convention, and

Bear-happy author
Teddy-bear historian and author Pauline Cockrill signs a copy of The Ultimate Teddy Bear Book, *watched by Paul and Rosemary Volpp's world-famous Steiff bear "Happy".*

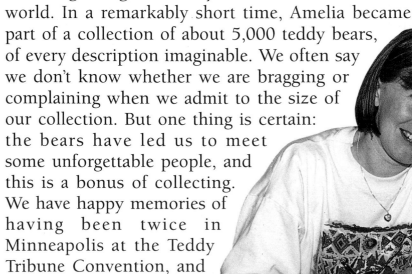

enjoying the company of Mr. Peter Bull, the British actor and author, who has been credited with revitalizing the teddy-bear phenomenon. Sadly, Peter died in May 1984, but the world is still enjoying the legacy of his remarkable contribution. In our own home, we have Peter's bear "Delicatessen" – or "Aloysius" as he is known in the British TV series *Brideshead Revisited* (*see p.147*).

Along with our bear "Happy" (*see p.37*), we were invited to take part in a week-long, fund-raising effort in England by Action Research – an event rather similar to our March of Dimes in the United States. During the week, we had the pleasure of spending an evening with Michael Bond, the creator of that marvellous character Paddington Bear, and we also experienced the thrill of being presented to Her Royal Highness, Princess Margaret. Today's collectors are drawn from every age group and from every corner of the globe. We recently received a letter from a ten-year-old collector in South Africa, and in our files we have copies of three doctoral dissertations on teddy bears sent to us by Ph.D. researchers. At the same time, bears and related items have become a part of almost every avenue of commerce.

One for the album
Paul and Rosemary Volpp, who have one of the largest collections of teddy bears in the world, shown here with their Steiff bear "Happy"; together they have raised large sums of money for charity.

Peter Bull once confessed that he was somewhat confused by the "sudden and quite sensational" popularity of the teddy bear. Unlike the majority of toys and dolls – the novelties that come and go along with the latest children's crazes – teddies seem to be with us permanently. But what is the reason for their triumphant survival? We agree with Peter Bull who tried to explain the phenomenon, saying, "The mystique lies in the faces of the bears themselves." It is true; every teddy is, indeed, unique. Therefore, it is with the greatest of pleasure that we urge you on to read this book: look at the bears' faces; enjoy their faces. Don't you agree? The enchantment and the mystique will last forever!

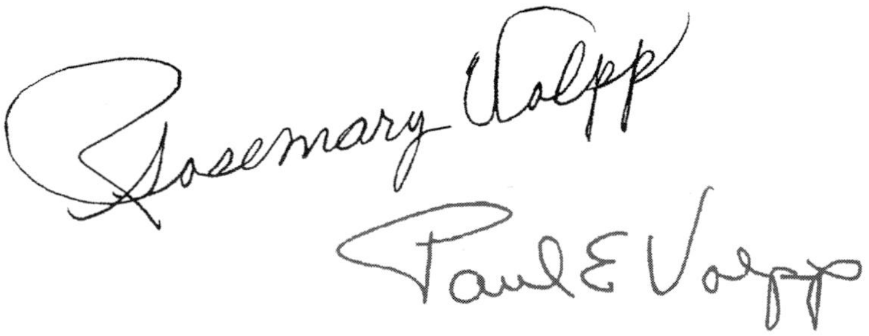

Rosemary Volpp

Paul E Volpp

First choice
"Lindy", a 1909, golden mohair-plush Steiff, was the first traditional bear in the Volpps' collection.

Introduction

FROM POLITICAL MASCOT TO TREASURED TOY AND WORK OF ART

From wild carnivore to much-loved children's toy may seem an unlikely leap for a bear to make. However, from the late nineteenth century, bears (or "bruins") were common in the nursery, both as characters in books and as playthings. Performing bears were well known in Europe and North America, travelling around with their itinerant trainers. These bears were imitated by French toy manufacturers, such as Décamps or Martin, whose clockwork models could dance, growl, or drink from bottles. At the same time, German, Swiss, and Russian toy-makers were producing carved, wooden bears.

The teddy bear's immediate ancestor was the realistic soft-toy bear on all fours, produced in Germany from the late nineteenth century. Already world leaders in all aspects of the toy industry, from porcelain dolls, wooden animals and printed games, to tin boats and trains, Germany soon became the leading manufacturer of soft toys as well. For these toys, they used mohair plush – a new fabric that had been developed to resemble real fur, woven from mohair, the wool of angora goats. Reinhold Schulte founded his Duisberg weaving mill in 1901, importing spun mohair from the north of England – hence the descriptive term "Yorkshire cloth".

In 1901, Theodore Roosevelt (nick-named "Teddy") became President of the United States. In November 1902, he embarked on a four-day hunting expedition in Mississippi, during which he refused to shoot a bear that had been cornered for him. The incident prompted a cartoon by Clifford K. Berryman which appeared in the *Washington Post* on 16 November 1902; the title of the cartoon, "Drawing the Line at Mississippi", also referred to a boundary dispute which the President had set out to resolve.

Teddy-bear ancestor
Soft-toy bears, sometimes set on cast-iron wheels (above), *and popular from the late nineteenth century, were made in Germany before World War I.*

Theodore Roosevelt (1858–1919)
Dressed (left) *as a pioneer in hunting attire, Roosevelt loved the outdoor life.*

"Drawing the Line..."
The original Berryman cartoon (below) *from the* Washington Post *of 16 November 1902.*

THE TEDDY CRAZE BEGINS
Soon after Berryman's cartoon appeared, Morris Michtom, a Russian emigré, displayed a plush bear, made by his wife Rose and labelled "Teddy's Bear", in the window of his New York store. It was an instant success. The wholesalers Butler Brothers eventually bought the Michtom's entire stock and, helped by the backing of Butler Brothers, Mitchom established the Ideal Novelty and Toy Company, reputed to be the first US teddy-bear manufacturer *(see pp.24–25)*.

As interest in the teddy was developing in the United States, a German company founded by Margarete Steiff *(see pp.38–39)* to make felt clothes and toys, was making plush toys and developing a

Billy Possum
The plush opossum (above), *named after US president William Taft, was intended to rival the teddy bear. Steiff made a version from 1909 until 1914 and, in the US, H. Fisher & Co., Hahn & Amberg, and Harman Manufacturing Co. also made versions.*

DRAWING THE LINE IN MISSISSIPPI

jointed bear-doll. Although these were unpopular at first, Hermann Berg of the New York wholesalers George Borgfeldt & Co. – prompted by the "Teddy" mania sweeping the US – bought 3,000 of these bear-dolls at the March 1903 Leipzig Toy Fair. Over the next five years, the Steiff business expanded dramatically.

US RIVALS STEIFF

The height of the teddy craze coincided with Roosevelt's second administration (1905–09). Several shortlived American companies were formed to compete with Steiff, producing teddy-related novelties (*see pp.26–27*). In 1906, the US toy trade catalogue *Playthings* first referred to "Teddy's Bears" and this was soon abbreviated to "Teddy Bear".

In 1908, an enterprising American asked the Karl Hofmann company, in the Sonneberg-Neustadt area of Germany, to make teddy bears, thereby launching a cottage industry largely devoted to US exports. This later evolved into various successful businesses, including the Hermann factories (*see pp.94–95*). It is said that in the same year, J.K. Farnell & Co. produced the first British teddy bear on the advice of German exporters, Eisenmann & Co. Prompted by the increased competition, manufacturers turned to novelty bears:

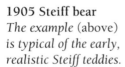

1905 Steiff bear
The example (above) is typical of the early, realistic Steiff teddies.

Steiff factory
Steiff was founded in 1893 as The Felt Toy Factory (below).

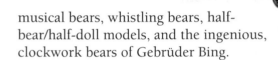

musical bears, whistling bears, half-bear/half-doll models, and the ingenious, clockwork bears of Gebrüder Bing.

CHARACTER BEARS

Probably conceived as a bear-doll for boys, the design of the teddy-bear was ideal for dressing-up. Teddies in masculine costume began to appear, influenced by Seymour Eaton's poems about the Roosevelt Bears. From 1907, Kahn & Mossbacher of New York and Steiff produced outfits embroidered with "Teddy B" or "Teddy G", while D.W. Shoyer & Co. produced knitted sweaters and hats for bears. Women's magazines published patterns for teddy outfits.

In 1909, Roosevelt lost the election to William Taft, and new mascots were made, trying, unsuccessfully, to overthrow Teddy's Bear. One was Billy Possum, a reference to Taft's love of "possum and 'taters" (once served to him at a banquet in Georgia). The popular, but shortlived, Billiken also dates from 1909; other rivals included W.J. Terry's Billy Owlett, a patriotically dressed owl, which the manufacturer predicted "may challenge the supremacy of the teddy bear". But the confidence was unfounded – and the teddy bear still reigns supreme.

Bear wardrobe
Produced for a US department store c.1906, this Steiff bear's possessions (above) include denim overalls and a knitted one-piece swimsuit, as well as a case of toys complete with skipping rope, train, and American football.

Electric-eye bear
From 1907, novelties abounded; the bulbs in this bear's eyes light up when its chest is squeezed (above).

EFFECTS OF WORLD WAR I

In 1913, German toy output was six times that of Great Britain. However, following the outbreak of World War I, the importation of German goods into Great Britain was designated an "act of treason" (according to a 1914 British trade journal), so launching Britain's own soft-toy industry. W.J. Terry, J.K. Farnell, and the British United Toy Manufacturing Co. were already making teddies, and other toy firms seized the opportunity to begin production. Dean's Rag Book Co. Ltd. (who had produced printed, cloth, cut-out "Knockabout" teddy bears in 1908) and Johnson Brothers of Birmingham, makers of "Chad Valley" board-games, are two such examples.

Several shortlived soft-toy firms were established, such as the Wholesale Toy Company, the Worthing Toy Factory, and the South Wales Toy Manufacturing Co., as well as pioneers W.H. Jones and the Teddy Toy Company. Many novelties were introduced, such as the British Doll and Novelty Company's Teddy Bear Exerciser, with expandable arms, or Isaac & Company's Isa spring-leg teddy bear. Also popular were uniformed mascots such as Harwin's Ally Bears (see p.29); Dean's printed Bear of Russia, Germany Crusher; the London Toy Company's Ivan the Russian Tommy; and Britannia Toy Works' Cossack.

From 1919, France also developed its teddy-bear industry and the companies Thiennot, Pintel, and F.A.D.A.P. were formed (see pp.48–49). In Australia, Charles Jensen patented a jointed bear in 1916, and the first commercially made Australian teddy bears were produced by Joy-Toys of Victoria (see pp.58–59) in the 1920s.

THE EVOLUTION OF THE BRITISH TEDDY

The 1920s and 1930s were the boom years for British teddy-bear manufacturers, with old-established firms, such as Farnell, Chad Valley, and Dean's, and new firms like H. G. Stone and Merrythought, becoming world leaders. The teddy bear acquired a new look: previously, the traditional stuffing was wood-wool – fine, wood shavings used as packing material for china etc., known in the United States by its nineteenth-century name "excelsior". Pieces of cork and horsehair were also used sometimes as stuffing. Now manufacturers turned to the lighter, softer, and more hygienic kapok – a fine cottonlike material, harvested from the seed-pod of the tropical tree *Ceiba pentandra*, and originally used as a stuffing for cushions and life-jackets. British manufacturers, in particular, preferred it as it could be purchased cheaply from within the Empire. The Teddy Toy Company patented its kapok-stuffed

Teddy parade
The 1920s catalogue page (above) of the Sonneberg-based company Max Hermann (later Hermann-Spielwaren), shows their 112 range in 10 sizes. The design was reproduced as their 1990 German Unification Bear.

1920s J.K. Farnell
The golden mohair bear (above) was made by J.K. Farnell, one of Britain's first teddy-bear manufacturers. The bear has five "webbed" claws on its paws with two dots behind, a distinctive Farnell feature.

Final grooming
Young girls working in a British teddy-bear factory during World War I (below); while the girls groom finished bears with large, scrubbing brushes, a pile of legs and arms lies on the floor awaiting assembly.

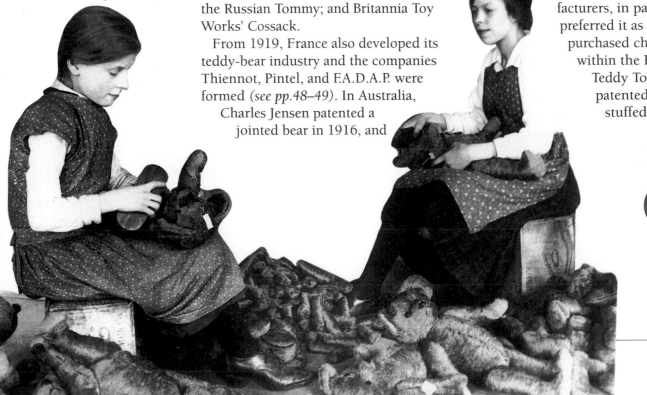

Stuffing funnels
Tin funnels (above), used in German factories to prevent the plush fraying while bears are being stuffed with wood-wool, are still in use today.

Softanlite bears in 1920, followed by Chad Valley's Aerolite (see p.52), and W.J. Terry's Ahsolite bears. Boot buttons, made of moulded, compressed wood pulp, were traditionally used for teddy bears' eyes, but after the war the blown-glass type of eye used by taxidermists came into favour.

Artificial-silk plush (woven from a fibre made from reconstituted wood pulp, or other form of cellulose) became a popular alternative; it first appeared in Britain in 1929 on Farnell's Silkalite and Chiltern's Silky Bear, in several fashionable colours.

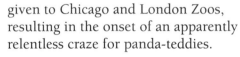

1930s Chad Valley
The bear (above) has a horizontally stitched nose, and the typical, Chad Valley red, embroidered label.

NOVELTY AND LITERARY BEARS
Mass-produced teddy bears, with rod-jointed, straight bodies and limbs, became increasingly popular. Novelties included the famous Yes/No bears made by Schuco (see pp.42–43); the London-based Wholesale Toy Company's 1921 Blinka rolling-eyed bears, which were similar to Gebrüder Süssenguth's Peter (see p.31); Swiss squeeze-type musical bears; and Gross & Schild's 1926 Bruno the Talking Bear of 1926, which emitted a growl from its mouth.

Tipped mohair plush became fashionable, as did clown bears with ruffs and pierrot's hats. Influenced by Steiff's 1930 Teddy Baby (see p.37), teddies with open mouths were made, some with pacifiers and bibs: the Commonwealth Toy & Novelty Company's 1937 Feed Me bear, produced for the National Biscuit Co., had a back zip to allow the retrieval of items fed into its jaws.

This period also saw the emergence of bears based on contemporary literary characters, including Rupert, Winnie the Pooh, and Mary Plain in the United Kingdom, and, in France, the character Prosper from Alain Saint-Ogan's 1933 comic strip.

In 1936, New York dress designer Ruth Harkness brought the first giant panda to the West; specimens were subsequently given to Chicago and London Zoos, resulting in the onset of an apparently relentless craze for panda-teddies.

AT WAR AGAIN
Hitler's rise to power in 1933, and the resulting world war, had a dramatic effect on industry. From 1939, toy production was severely reduced to give priority to munitions and uniforms. Raw materials required for making teddy bears, such as cloth, card, and metal, were rationed. "Sub" (textile industrial waste) was substituted for kapok stuffing. In the UK, leathercloth or oilcloth (a painted woven fabric with tradenames such as "Rexine" and "Duxeen", and made in Manchester) replaced the previously preferred pad fabrics of felt and velveteen.

Many children suffered the traumas of wartime evacuation, often with only their teddies for comfort. Poignant stories abound: in Austria, for example, a child's precious teddy bear was given to farmers in exchange for food, and in Croatia it is reported that a mother hid her jewellery in her daughter's Steiff bear.

Sheepskin bear
1940s Australian bear (above) with leather pads, "sub" stuffing, and unjointed neck.

Flat-face Hugmee
In the 1940s, Chiltern redesigned its Hugmee range (above) to use less mohair plush.

Final details
A Peacock range bear is fitted with eyes at Chad Valley's factory in the 1930s (above).

Teddy gas-mask
The cover of the British child's gas-mask (above) is decorated with a fully featured, mohair teddy head and felt clothes.

Jester Bear

Made by Beverly Port, doll-maker and pioneer bear artist, this porcelain-faced bear (left) is an early example of bear artistry incorporating doll- and soft-toy-making techniques. Beverly's bear-making workshops created a huge following on the West Coast of America. Her daughter and son are also bear artists.

Flexible knees

This little girl bear (below), by Florida artist Donna Claustre, has "ball-and-socket" knee joints allowing human-like flexibility.

POST-WAR PRODUCTION

The aftermath of World War II resulted in several German companies moving from the Russian to the US Zone. At the same time, new firms were established, such as Clemens in Germany, and Fechter and Berg in Austria. In the UK, sheepskin continued to be popular during the years of rationing and beyond, with manufacturers using descriptive tradenames such as "Lamkin" and "Cuddlam".

Synthetic fibres, such as nylon, were increasingly employed in the teddy-bear industry after the war. Patented by Du Pont or Monsanto in the US, by Courtaulds in the UK, or by the Farben Bayer companies in Germany, these synthetic materials included Orlon, Acrilan, Dacron, Courtelle, and Dralon. Moulded vinyl muzzles first appeared in the early 1950s; later, rubber or plastic noses were used. 1955 heralded the introduction of the first fully washable, unjointed teddy bear produced by Wendy Boston in the UK, using the company's patented, safe, screw-in eyes and foam rubber stuffing. The latter was considered to be the perfect filling, until its capacity to disintegrate and its potentially toxic fume emission were later discovered. With the introduction of tougher legislation on toy safety, all teddy bears, by the late-1960s, were fitted with safe, locked-in, plastic eyes.

WIDENING HORIZONS

Just as books and radio influenced the early teddy-bear manufacturers, so too did television and cinema from the early 1960s. TV and film bear characters appeared in various related merchandise; literary heroes such as Paddington were reproduced later, in the 1970s and 1980s.

The declining birth rate, and the rise of cheap imports from East Asia during the late 1960s and 1970s, caused the demise of several leading soft-toy companies, such as Schuco, J.K. Farnell, Chiltern, Chad Valley, and Wendy Boston.

New US manufacturers, such as Dakin, Russ Berrie, and Applause, launched the trend to manufacture in countries, such as Korea, Taiwan, China, the Philippines, and Haiti where production costs were cheaper. The advent of the microchip in the 1980s opened up a whole new world of novelties: Teddy Ruxpin, with moving facial features synchronized with a taped story, and Musical Tubby Bear, of Dandee Imports, whose plastic heart flashes in time to the 14 electronically produced, popular lullabies, were two examples.

THE RISE OF BEAR ARTISTRY

In the meantime, the concept of bear artistry was emerging amongst dollmakers in the US; Beverly Port introduced her Theodore B. Bear at the 1974 International Doll Makers' Convention in Reno, Nevada, while Carol-Lynn Rössel Waugh was producing porcelain bears in Maine. In the early days, other dollmakers such as the UK's Carol Ann Stanton and Anne Keane from Australia. produced porcelain-headed bears. In 1981, an article in the

No Frills Bear

This unusual, printed calico bear, was produced in Korea in 1985 for US manufacturer R. Dakin & Co.

Bear Ritz

The 100% natural mink bear (above), made in 1983, is the work of Californian bear artists Charlotte Holst and Shawn Frey.

"Sewn in Haiti"

A typical post-1970s label (above).

Teddies' picnic
Typical 1960s, fully washable, Wendy Boston bears with patented, safe, screw-in eyes (above).

US magazine *Doll Reader* used the term "bear artist", and in 1984 Carol-Lynn Rössel Waugh published *Teddy Bear Artists: Romance of Making and Collecting Bears*.

During the 1980s, bear artistry developed throughout the UK, closely followed by Australia. By the late 1980s, other European countries had joined the movement, including Elke Kraus and Rotrau Ilisch in Germany. The Netherlands boasts many artists, and has hosted an annual bear artist convention since 1991. Bear artistry is now thriving in many far-flung places: Victoria Marsden in the Outer Hebrides of Scotland; Amy Shukuya in Hawaii; Margaret York in Australia's Alice Springs; Shelly Armstrong-Plaunt in Canada's Yukon Territory; and Eunice Beaton in Durban, in the Republic of South Africa. There is also a burgeoning movement in Japan.

1992 replica "Alpha"
Bears Paw Collectables of Leicester, England, made this replica (above) of a Farnell "Alpha" bear.

FANTASY AND NOSTALGIA
Two major styles have emerged within bear artistry; the first stems from its origins in dollmaking, with the teddy as a vehicle for fantasy, recreating past historical and literary figures, or in the guise of other creatures. The second responds to the steady

demand for old bears, and businesses have emerged that reproduce old-style teddies in antique fabrics or "distressed" mohair. Many bear-artists' bears are specifically designated "not for children" because their construction does not comply with the current safety regulations; others are exhibited as "soft sculpture" in art galleries – such as Kimberlee Port's Christmas Tree Bear in New York, and the Hanton's Edwardian Bears *(see p.185)* in Wellington, New Zealand.

LIMITED-EDITIONS AND REPLICAS
With the growth of arctophily in the 1980s, many firms turned to producing special limited-edition teddy bears; some older companies followed Steiff's example and produced limited-edition replicas of past models. Other manufacturers created dressed, adult-orientated collectables, such as the North American Bear Company's VIB series *(see pp.146–47)*, or Gabrielle Designs' Henry and Caroline series, and the Lakeland Bears, in the UK.

The introduction of the prestigious Golden Teddy and TOBY awards has done much to encourage and inspire quality in the design of teddy bears amongst both bear artists and manufacturers.

Christmas Tree Bear
Barbara McConnell's musical bear (above) has battery-operated lights inside the green, mohair-plush body.

Original and replica
The c.1904 rod-jointed Steiff bear (below, left) is shown along-side Bärle, the company's 1992 replica of a similarly jointed bear (below, right).

1960s KNICKERBOCKER
JOY OF A TOY PRINTED LABEL

c.1956–57 MERRYTHOUGHT
PRINTED LABEL

1970s DEAN'S CHILDSPLAY
TOYS PRINTED LABEL

1980s–90s GEBRÜDER HERMANN
EMBROIDERED LABEL

1925–30s FARNELL ALPHA TOY
EMBROIDERED LABEL

1980s HOUSE OF NISBET
EMBROIDERED LABEL

1964–70s ACTON TOYCRAFT
TWYFORD PRINTED LABEL

1945–67 CHILTERN PRINTED
LABEL

1930s–40s JOY-TOYS
EMBROIDERED LABEL

1950s Steiff
The hole in the left ear
indicates the position of
the former trademark.

1946–71 PEDIGREE SOFT TOYS
(BELFAST) PRINTED LABEL

GUND

1980s GUND EMBROIDERED
LABEL

Pre-1914 Steiff
Even if it did not have
its "button in ear"
trademark (*see p.21*),
this teddy would still
be clearly identifiable
as a pre-World War I
Steiff bear, every
feature helping to
confirm its origins.

1950s SCHUCO
PLASTIC CHEST-TAG

1930s CHAD
VALLEY CELLULOID
ON METAL BUTTON

1980s LENCI
EMBROIDERED LABEL

1980s DORIS & TERRY
MICHAUD CARROUSEL
PRINTED LABEL

1980s APPLAUSE
PRINTED LABEL

1980s DAKIN
EMBROIDERED LABEL

1960s Knickerbocker
The soft-stuffed, nylon-plush body, safe, spangle-effect plastic eyes, and printed, New York label determine the age of this bear.

POST-1986 STEIFF
METAL BUTTON AND
PRINTED EAR-TAG

c.1990 ROMSEY BEAR COMPANY
EMBROIDERED LABEL

1980s REAL
SOFT TOYS
PRINTED CARD
SWING-TAG

1991 CANTERBURY BEARS
EMBROIDERED LABEL

UK bear artist
Liz Carless achieved novelty appeal with this toddler bear, which contains a unique, internal frame that allows realistic positioning of the limbs.

THE CATALOGUE

THE MAJOR TASK FOR teddy-bear collectors, and for many owners of old or unlabelled teddy bears, is to establish the pedigree of their bears. This catalogue will help you in your research. It is set out chronologically, with each double-page spread representing either a manufacturer or a trend within a country during a certain period in the history of the teddy bear. The work of bear artists is featured at the end of the catalogue, where the teddies are grouped according to the artists' nationality.

I have chosen five representative bears for each spread, and describe each of these fully, with their key features clearly annotated. Wherever possible, I have selected bears with their original trademarks intact as these provide the most positive form of identification. When trying to identify a bear, always check for traces of a trademark – it may be hidden between limb and body, for example. Even a few, remaining, coloured threads from a tattered label are useful for comparing with the photographs of labels illustrated in the catalogue. A hole in the ear, or a faded area on a foot-pad, will also provide evidence of the former presence of a trademark.

Remember that wear and tear or repair-work can alter a bear considerably, and you should keep this in mind when trying to establish a pedigree. Anecdotes by the original or previous owners will also provide clues. Review all the relevant factors in the context of the information provided in the *Encyclopedia* and you will then be well on the way to establishing the identity of your bear.

Steiff: 1902–05

EXPERIMENTAL PERIOD; INTRODUCTION OF "BUTTON IN EAR"

I n 1902, Richard Steiff began experimenting to invent a satisfactory, flexible jointing system. He devised a series of simple, string-jointed animals, one of which was the brown *Bär 55 PB* – so called because it was 55cm (22in) high (seated), made of *Plusch* (plush), and *Beweglich* (movable). The bear was in a crate of toys sent to New York in February 1903, but was initially unsuccessful. A month later, however, US wholesalers Geo. Borgfeldt & Co. ordered 3,000 at the Leipzig Spring Fair. Steiff patented four designs, culminating in the rod-jointed *Bär 28 PB*. Made for only one year, it is now highly prized.

1904–05 ROD JOINTED; ELEPHANT LOGO

Richard Steiff's bear evolved further in 1904: a card-disc and string-jointed *Bär 35 PB* was registered on 5 March, and a double-wire-jointed bear was registered later that year, on 6 December. The teddy bear illustrated is rod-jointed like *Bär 28 PB* (registered 8 June 1905), but is larger. The rodded bears were given a new trademark in November 1904 – a nickel-plated button, with Steiff's elephant and S-shaped trunk logo.

Height: 50cm (20in)

Embossed button

Ears: *the small, rounded ears are sewn across the facial seams.*

Eyes: *the eyes are probably replacement (but authentic) black boot-buttons.*

Muzzle: *the plush on the thin, elongated muzzle is worn.*

Nose/mouth: *the replacement shield-shaped nose and Y-shaped mouth are stitched in thick, black, embroidery thread.*

Fur: *the fur is beige mohair plush.*

Pads/claws: *the beige, felt pads are replacements; five brown claws are stitched across the plush.*

BEAR PROFILE
In profile, you can clearly see the typical characteristics of early Steiff bears: the elongated, pointed muzzle; the hump; the rounded lower back; the large feet; and the long arms, which extend beyond the legs when the bear is seated.

Feet: *the oval feet are typically large and narrow.*

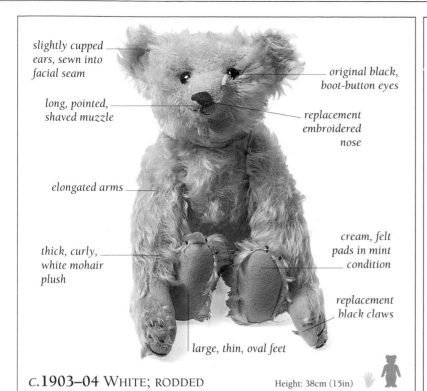

slightly cupped ears, sewn into facial seam

original black, boot-button eyes

long, pointed, shaved muzzle

replacement embroidered nose

elongated arms

thick, curly, white mohair plush

cream, felt pads in mint condition

replacement black claws

large, thin, oval feet

C.1903–04 WHITE; RODDED

Height: 38cm (15in)

This rodded bear, with an elephant button, is probably a prototype – this colour does not appear on any known production bear. Its crooked, cinnamon-coloured, embroidered nose is a replacement; the original beige stitching for the mouth is just visible.

Embossed button

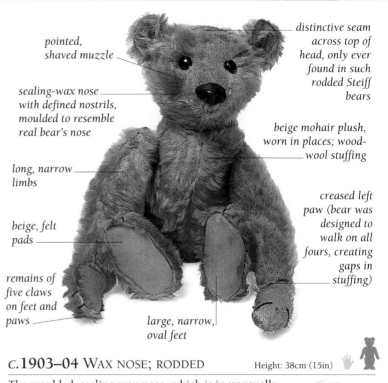

pointed, shaved muzzle

distinctive seam across top of head, only ever found in such rodded Steiff bears

sealing-wax nose with defined nostrils, moulded to resemble real bear's nose

beige mohair plush, worn in places; wood-wool stuffing

long, narrow limbs

creased left paw (bear was designed to walk on all fours, creating gaps in stuffing)

beige, felt pads

remains of five claws on feet and paws

large, narrow, oval feet

C.1903–04 WAX NOSE; RODDED

Height: 38cm (15in)

The moulded, sealing-wax nose, which is in unusually excellent condition and is particularly realistic, with well-defined nostrils, makes this rodded bear highly collectable. (Sealing wax is a mixture of shellac, rosin (natural resins), turpentine, and pigment.)

Embossed button

original black, boot-button eyes

horizontal seam across top of head

dark stain marks position of original sealing-wax nose

remnants of inverted-Y-shaped, brown thread, double-stitched mouth

shaved, pointed, protruding muzzle

elongated, curved, tapering arms

golden mohair plush; wood-wool stuffing throughout

remains of black claws on paw

slim legs with large, narrow feet

C.1903–04 GOLDEN; RODDED

Height: 45cm (18in)

The typical, elongated shape of this bear can still be discerned despite extensive repair work. Rodded bears tend to suffer sagging and splitting at the wrists because of their ability to stand on all fours. A dark stain is all that remains of the sealing-wax nose.

Embossed button

horizontal seam across top of head

black, sealing-wax nose with realistically defined nostrils

original black, boot-button eyes

elongated, shaved, worn muzzle

long, curved, tapering arms extend beyond legs

golden mohair plush

large, narrow feet

worn, beige, felt pads; five claws on paws

1905 BÄR 28 PB; RODDED

Height: 40cm (16in)

Unfortunately, this bear has lost its elephant button, but it clearly resembles Richard Steiff's 28 PB model in overall shape and height. It is in relatively good condition apart from some holes in the plush and pads. It still retains its sealing-wax nose.

Embossed button

Steiff: 1905–World War I

DESIGN PERFECTED; TRIANGULAR NOSE FOR SMALL SIZES

Richard Steiff perfected his plush bear-doll, patenting the design on 12 February 1905. The new bear had card disc-joints and was made in white, and light or dark brown mohair plush (although the prototype, a 32cm (13in) example now in the Steiff archives, was grey). Known as "*Bärle*" in catalogues, its code name was "*PAB*": *Plusch* (plush), *Angeschiebt* (disc-jointed), and *Beweglich* (movable). Steiff patented its "button in ear" trademark on 13 May 1905, replacing the embossed elephant with the word "Steiff". In 1908–09, the company introduced linen ear-tags printed with product numbers.

1909 LIGHT BROWN MOHAIR

Seven sizes of this bear were produced in 1905, and two sizes were added a year later. By 1910, the range had increased to thirteen: from 10cm (4in) to 115cm (45in). Bears under 40cm (16in) had a distinct triangular, horizontally stitched nose. The example illustrated here probably dates from 1909 when the 30cm (12in) height was introduced. The boot-button eyes indicate a pre-World War I date; other design features and the trademark remained virtually unchanged until 1950.

Height: 30cm (12in)

Embossed button

Ears: *the ears are small, cupped, and set wide apart, with the inside edges caught in the facial seams.*

Eyes: *the eyes are original, small, black boot-buttons.*

Nose/mouth: *the horizontally stitched, black nose is outlined with two stitches that converge at the base to join an inverted-Y-shaped mouth.*

Fur: *the fur is short, light brown mohair plush; the bear is stuffed with wood-wool.*

Feet: *the thin ankles end in large, narrow feet.*

Claws: *each paw and foot has four black, stitched claws.*

BEAR PROFILE
In profile, you can see the slightly shaved, protruding, blunted muzzle; a plump body still retaining a suggestion of a humped back; elongated arms with curved, spoon-shaped paws; and large feet with narrow ankles. Notice the trademark in the left ear.

Pads: *the beige, felt pads are in perfect condition (except for a small hole in the left foot).*

horizontally stitched, triangular, black nose

small, black, boot-button eyes

original orange, cossack-style tunic and trousers

unique rust-red mohair plush, worn in places

four black claws on each paw and foot

damaged beige, felt pads reveal wood-wool stuffing

1908 RED MOHAIR

Height: 33cm (13in)

"Alfonzo" was commissioned by the Grand Duke of Russia for his daughter Princess Xenia Georgievna, and accompanied her on her visit to Buckingham Palace in London in 1914. The Russian Revolution meant that neither princess nor bear ever returned home.

Embossed button

brown mohair pile

original small, black, boot-button eyes

triangular nose with replacement stitching

protruding muzzle

elongated arms and curved paws

large feet

replacement woven fabric pads; originals would have been beige felt

five claws indicate early origins

1905 BROWN MOHAIR

Height: 33cm (13in)

This bear, bought in Europe by a sea captain and taken home for his daughter in Australia, is now virtually bald and has replacement pads. The left arm sags at the wrist as the wood-wool stuffing has disintegrated – probably because the bear was regularly held by this paw.

Embossed button

horizontally stitched, triangular, black nose

original black, boot-button eyes

light brown mohair plush; internal squeaker

long arms with curved paws

hand-embroidered, black claws

hole in pad reveals wood-wool stuffing

replacement beige, felt pad

C.1905 BLANK BUTTON

Height: 33cm (13in)

Although identical in design to others illustrated here, this bear possesses the rare, early Steiff, blank button in its left ear. The trademark dates from the 1903–04 experimental days, but old stock was used for a short time after the embossed Steiff button was introduced.

Blank button

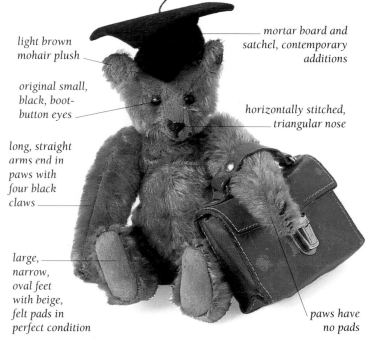

light brown mohair plush

mortar board and satchel, contemporary additions

original small, black, boot-button eyes

horizontally stitched, triangular nose

long, straight arms end in paws with four black claws

large, narrow, oval feet with beige, felt pads in perfect condition

paws have no pads

C.1910 SMALL; NO PAW PADS

Height: 22cm (8½in)

In 1909, Steiff added three smaller sizes to its range: 22cm (8½in), 18cm (7in), and 10cm (4in). In 1910, a 15cm (6in) size was added. The basic design was much the same, but the three shortest in height had straighter arms and, like this bear, had no felt pads on their paws.

Embossed button

Steiff: 1903-World War I

ALTERNATIVE NOSE DESIGN USED ON LARGER BEARS

T he demand for teddies, particularly in the US, soared between 1903 and 1908, the period that the Steiff company called the *Bärenjahre* (*see p.38*), when production increased from 12,000 to about 975,000. To use materials economically, Steiff cut six complete teddy-bear heads from one length of mohair plush; a seventh head was cut in two pieces, so creating the "centre-seam" teddy bear, which is now greatly prized. By 1905, seven sizes were available; this increased to fourteen by 1910. Bears over 40cm (16in) tall had a different nose design from smaller bears – shield shaped, vertically stitched, with a felt underlay.

1905 CINNAMON; CENTRE SEAM

This is an excellent example of a teddy bear with a centre seam, which is clearly visible along the length of the long, shaven muzzle. The bear is made from shaggy, cinnamon-coloured mohair plush, a colour much prized by collectors. The original shield-shaped nose has been repaired with black wool, but you can still make out the felt underlay.

Height: 55cm (22in)

Embossed button

Face: *the central seam indicates that this bear's head was the seventh to be cut from one length of mohair plush; the other six would have been cut in one piece.*

Fur: *the curly, cinnamon-coloured mohair plush is in mint condition; the bear is stuffed with wood-wool throughout.*

Arms: *the arms are long with brown, felt paw-pads; the remains of the black, embroidered claws are visible.*

Feet: *the feet are long and narrow, with thin ankles; originally, there would have been four claws on each foot and paw.*

Ears: *the small, unstuffed, cupped ears are placed high on the head.*

Eyes: *the eyes are large, black boot-buttons.*

Muzzle: *the mohair plush on the muzzle has been clipped.*

Nose/mouth: *both the nose and the mouth have been replaced in black wool, similar to the original thread.*

BEAR PROFILE

Seen from the side, this bear demonstrates all the features of a traditional, pre-World War I Steiff teddy: a realistic, protruding, shaved muzzle; a slightly humped back; elongated arms and legs, with curved, spoon-shaped paws; and large feet with narrow ankles.

Pads: *the pads have been replaced; the originals would have been beige.*

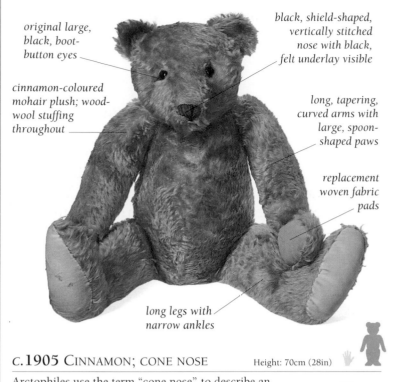

original large, black, boot-button eyes

cinnamon-coloured mohair plush; wood-wool stuffing throughout

black, shield-shaped, vertically stitched nose with black, felt underlay visible

long, tapering, curved arms with large, spoon-shaped paws

replacement woven fabric pads

long legs with narrow ankles

c.1905 CINNAMON; CONE NOSE
Height: 70cm (28in)

Arctophiles use the term "cone nose" to describe an early experimental phase in Steiff's history when the bear's muzzle, in profile, appears more cone-shaped than on other early examples. This bear would originally have had felt pads on its feet and paws.

Embossed button

original black, boot-button eyes

shaved muzzle

double-stitched, inverted-V-shaped, smiling mouth

black, vertically stitched nose; central five stitches dropped to meet mouth

shaggy, beige mohair plush in excellent condition; wood-wool stuffing through-out

unworn beige, felt pads; four black thread claws on each paw

1908 SHAGGY, BEIGE MOHAIR
Height: 50cm (20in)

Known to date from 1908, this bear is in excellent condition. It has typical pre-World War I features, including a prominent hump, and well-defined, narrow feet with small ankles. It is the fourth largest in the range of sizes available at the time.

Embossed button

large, black, boot-button eyes

vertically stitched, black thread nose

four black claws on paws and feet, stitched across plush

Steiff button, with raised lettering, in left ear

well-worn, pointed muzzle

slightly worn, beige mohair plush

large, narrow feet; dark brown, felt underlay revealed

1909 LARGE; BEIGE MOHAIR
Height: 70cm (28in)

This bear, which arrived in the US as padding around an English family's best china, is an example of one of the larger Steiff teddy bears, making it highly collectable; the next size up (115cm/45in), is very rare. Holes in the foot-pads reveal the felt underlay.

Embossed button

original large, black, boot-button eyes

beige thread claws to match nose and mouth

very long, thin feet with narrow ankles

large, flat ears set on sides of head

beige nose over felt underlay; five stitches dropped to meet mouth

felt pads worn and darned; red, felt underlay beneath

1903–05 WIDE-EAR DESIGN
Height 63cm (25in)

Some very early Steiff bears have been found with this head design – ears wide apart and set low down on the sides of the head – indicating an experimental period for Steiff. Although this bear has lost its Steiff "button in ear", similar bears exist with the trademark intact.

Embossed button

Steiff: 1908–World War I

INTRODUCTION OF NOVELTY DESIGNS TO RETAIN MONOPOLY

In 1908, Steiff tried to regain its monopoly on teddy-bear manufacture by producing a number of novelties; in 1909, it added bright gold to its natural range of brown, beige, and white; and in 1912, it produced a special black bear for the British market. The Dolly bear of 1913 was produced for the US election, in red, white, and blue. Other novelties included the 1909 Roly Poly bear; the clockwork somersaulting teddy (*opposite*); and the 1913 Record Teddy (seated on a wooden-wheeled metal chassis). The latter was copied by several British manufacturers, including J.K. Farnell & Co. Ltd.

1908 *MAULKORB BÄR*

This bear was first introduced by Steiff in 1908. It wears a leather muzzle and leading-rein, inspired by the popular dancing bears that performed in the town squares of central Europe. Available in brown or white mohair plush and in ten sizes, this bear is one of the smaller examples. It is basically the same Richard Steiff design as that shown on pp.18–19, with the leather muzzle added for novelty value. Steiff made a replica of this bear in 1990.

Height: 25cm (10in)

Embossed button

Eyes: *the black, boot-button eyes are original.*

Nose: *the triangular nose is horizontally stitched in black thread, like those of the bears on pp.18–19.*

Muzzle: *the muzzle, made of leather, with studs like the blank Steiff buttons, has darkened with age.*

Fur/stuffing/growler: *the fur is brown mohair plush; the bear is stuffed with wood-wool; there is an internal squeaker.*

Feet: *the large feet have replacement beige, felt pads in a colour similar to that of the originals.*

BEAR PROFILE
From this angle you can see clearly the typical, pointed muzzle and accentuated limbs of this bear. The long, tapering arms with curved paws are considerably longer than the legs. The leather muzzle and the leading-rein, which would originally have ended in a loop like a dog's lead, are also visible.

Claws: *four claws are embroidered, in black thread, across the mohair plush only.*

black, bead eyes

brown thread, horizontally stitched nose; inverted-V-shaped mouth

fully jointed limbs and head

central seam along each foot; no pads

raised lettering on Steiff "button in ear"; cloth label still, unusually, in place

each digit of product number on label is significant: 5 means jointed; 3 means mohair plush; 07 means sitting height of 7cm

white mohair plush, highly prized by collectors

1909 MINIATURE; WHITE

Height: 10cm (4in)

Originally introduced in 1909, this is an early example of the smallest bear produced by Steiff; a larger, 15cm (6in), version became available a year later. In addition to the "button in ear", the bear still carries a cloth label showing the product number – a feature introduced in 1908–09.

Embossed button/label

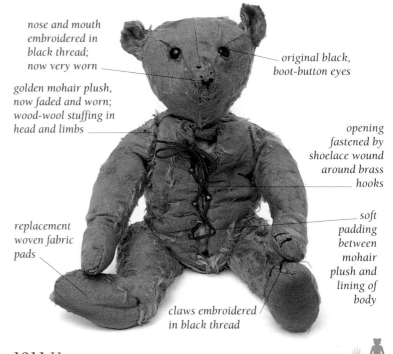

nose and mouth embroidered in black thread; now very worn

golden mohair plush, now faded and worn; wood-wool stuffing in head and limbs

replacement woven fabric pads

original black, boot-button eyes

opening fastened by shoelace wound around brass hooks

soft padding between mohair plush and lining of body

claws embroidered in black thread

1911 HOT-WATER BOTTLE

Height: 25cm (10in)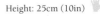

This bear was bought in the north of England for the present owner's uncle's first birthday on 11 February 1911. It is a rare find, for only 90 examples were made during the years of production, 1907–14. Its padded body would originally have housed a tin for hot water.

Embossed button

triangular, horizontally stitched nose, as used on all traditional bears up to 40cm (16in) in height

black, boot-button eyes

golden mohair plush (only colour in which this bear was produced)

beige, felt pads

c.1910 PANTOM BÄR

Height: 40cm (16in)

This bear was produced, as part of a marionette range, from 1910 to 1918 in two sizes, 35cm (14in) and 40cm (16in); only 6,268 were manufactured. The range was developed by Albert Schlopsnies, an East Prussian artist who worked as a freelance designer for Steiff.

Embossed button

nose horizontally stitched in black thread

right arm acts as key for clockwork mechanism; when rotated, bear tips forward and turns somersaults

Steiff button in left ear

celluloid high collar added by present owner

light brown mohair plush

beige, felt pads in mint condition

c.1915 PURZEL BÄR

Height: 26cm (10½in)

Introduced in 1909 in various colours and sizes, this teddy bear has a clockwork mechanism developed by Richard Steiff's brother, Hugo, a trained engineer. From 1911 to 1915, Steiff was involved in a legal battle with Bing who produced a similar toy (*see p.35*).

Embossed button

Ideal: 1903-World War I

BIRTH OF TEDDY'S BEAR AND FIRST US MANUFACTURER

The story of the original teddy bear, hand-sewn by Rose Michtom and sold as Teddy's Bear at her husband Morris's New York novelty and stationery store, is now legendary (*see pp.8–9*). In 1903, the Michtoms – having sold their entire stock of bears to the wholesale firm Butler Brothers, who then guaranteed their credit with the plush-producing mills – established the Ideal Novelty and Toy Company. The company moved to larger premises in 1907, and a year later its first advertisement appeared in the US trade journal *Playthings*, in which they claimed to be "the largest bear manufacturers in the country".

c.1905 LARGE; GOLDEN MOHAIR

Early Ideal bears were not labelled and can be identified only by their general shape and by certain design details. (One of the first teddies produced by the company was presented to the Smithsonian Insitute, Washington DC, in 1964, and is a useful reference.) These pre-World War I bears typically have triangular heads and pointed foot-pads.

Height: 49cm (19½in)

Ears: *the large ears are sewn from just inside the facial seams, down the sides of the head.*

Eyes: *shiny, black, boot-button eyes were in general use during this period.*

Face: *this is a classic, triangular, Ideal face shape.*

Nose: *the black nose is horizontally stitched across the junction of the muzzle seams.*

Arms: *the long, tapering arms, like those on early Steiffs, have spoon-shaped, curved paws with beige, felt pads.*

Legs: *the thighs are slightly rounded, with ankle definition; the feet have rounded heels and distinct, pointed toes.*

Fur/stuffing: *the short, golden mohair plush is typical of early Ideal bears; the stuffing is wood-wool.*

BEAR PROFILE
This bear exhibits several, classic Ideal features: the wedge-shaped muzzle; the plump, humped-back torso; the long, curved, tapering arms; and the unique, pointed, oval toes.

Claws: *there are five claws on the feet, and four on the paws.*

black, boot-button eyes, sewn just inside facial seams

large ears, placed wide apart and low on sides of head

long arms tapering to curved paws

rust-coloured, triangular, broadcloth nose may be repair work

short, beige mohair plush; wood-wool stuffing throughout

feet rounder than usual Ideal style; pads reinforced with card

four beige claws on paws; five on feet

C.1904 BEIGE MOHAIR
Height: 43cm (17in)

This bear is said to be one of the early prototypes produced by Ideal, and is known to have belonged to its previous owner from 1904. Although the feet are not typically Ideal, the bear exhibits the characteristic, triangular Ideal head with large ears set low down on the sides. Early American bears often had broadcloth noses like the one on this example.

small, black, boot-button eyes

ears wide apart; left ear has bogus Steiff button

black, triangular, horizontally stitched nose

beige mohair plush; stuffed with wood-wool throughout

five black, slightly converging claws on paws and feet

beige, felt pads on slightly pointed feet

1904–05 SMALL; BEIGE MOHAIR
Height: 28cm (11in)

This bear demonstrates many classic Ideal features: a triangular face with a broad forehead; large ears set wide apart; elongated, curved arms; and, in particular, distinct, egg-shaped feet. However, a Steiff button has been fraudulently placed in the left ear – presumably before early Ideal bears, such as this, had gained popularity or high prices in the marketplace.

blue, glass eyes with black pupils

ears set wide apart, on corners of head

distinctly triangular face with broad forehead

black, triangular, horizontally stitched nose

three black claws on each paw and foot

long, curved arms with beige, felt pads

slightly pointed feet with beige, felt pads

C.1914 GLASS EYES
Height: 40cm (16in)

Glass eyes became common on Ideal bears after World War I; before the war, Ideal – like most other teddy-bear manufacturers – used boot-button eyes. This bear, with its attractive and unusual blue, glass eyes, also exhibits a slightly more slender torso and shorter arms than the earlier Ideal bears, offering a preview of the new, slimmer designs of the 1920s.

slightly cupped ears, sewn down sides of head from facial seams

black, boot-button eyes with white, painted rims

very worn, short, tan mohair plush

black, triangular, horizontally stitched nose, with border stitches along two diagonal edges

long, curved arms

five black claws on paws and feet

beige, felt pads on pointed feet

1904–12 CARTOON-STYLE EYES
Height: 30cm (12in)

With its characteristic Ideal face and feet, this bear has rare, painted, white-rimmed, black, boot-button eyes, possibly intended to imitate Clifford T. Berryman's *Washington Post* cartoon bear. Ideal teddies of an unusual 15cm (6in) size, with similar but more "googly" eyes, were handed out during Roosevelt's 1904 election campaign.

US: *c.*1907–14

SHORT-LIVED FIRMS; TRADITIONAL AND NOVELTY DESIGNS

Theodore Roosevelt's second term in office (1905–09) saw the teddy-bear craze at its peak, with the establishment of numerous manufacturers. These included the American Doll and Toy Manufacturing Co. and the Miller Manufacturing Co. Many non-toy-making companies began to make teddy bears as well at this time: in 1907 the Fast Black Skirt Company's Electric Bright Eye and Hahn & Amberg's cork-filled teddy bears came on the market. Other novelties included Harman's 1908 Teddy Bear Purse and the Dreamland Doll Company's topsy-turvy, half-teddy/half-doll of 1905–08.

c.1910–15 POSSIBLY STRAUSS

Although the glass eyes may indicate a later date, this example is reminiscent of illustrations of bears by Strauss (reputedly the Toy King of New York) seen in trade journals. Known principally for his 1907 Self-Whistling Bear, whose mechanism was activated by tipping the bear upside down, Strauss also produced a clockwork musical bear, which was wound up at the back.

Height: 43cm (17in)

Ears: *the fairly large ears are set wide apart, on the corners of the triangular head.*

Eyes: *the reddish brown paint on the backs of the clear, glass eyes has partially worn off.*

Nose: *the wide, black nose is vertically stitched, bordered by horizontal stitches; a few stitches are dropped in the centre to meet the wide, smiling mouth.*

Fur/stuffing: *shaggy, tan mohair plush; the bear is stuffed mainly with wood-wool, with some kapok in the head, body, and paws.*

Pads: *the beige, felt pads are in good condition.*

Claws: *there are five black, almost converging claws on paws and feet.*

Feet: *the large, oval feet narrow towards the "heels".*

BEAR PROFILE

Like many early American bears, this example has very long arms, a protruding muzzle, and large feet – all an attempt to copy the Steiff look. At this angle, however, you can see the unusual, squared shoulders, unshaven muzzle, and the wedge-shaped, more American-style head.

brown and black, glass eyes; the left eye is a replacement

small, rounded ears, set wide apart on head

inverted-Y-shaped, smiling mouth

rectangular, black, vertically stitched nose, with horizontal borders

shaggy, golden mohair plush

long, tapering arms, curving into long, spoon-shaped paws

well-worn, beige, felt pads

large, narrow, oval feet

five claws on paws and feet

*c.*1907 BRUIN MANUFACTURING CO.

Height: 35cm (14in)

A few, tell-tale strands of red and gold thread left in the seam of the right foot confirm that this bear was made by the Bruin Manufacturing Co., a short-lived firm based at 497 Broome Street, New York. Early advertisements described their trademark "BMC" as being stamped on the foot; the later, woven, label was probably preferred for its permanence.

triangular face with expansive forehead

large, flat ears, set on corners of head, across facial seams

black, vertically stitched, triangular nose; inverted-V-shaped mouth

brown, glass eyes with black pupils

beige mohair plush

wide, squared-off shoulders; arms taper to curved paws

Aetna trademark, with oval outline, stamped on right foot

large, oval feet with beige, felt pads, reinforced with card

insect damage pinholes on left foot

*c.*1907 AETNA TOY ANIMAL CO.

Height: 50cm (20in)

Aetna bears (formerly known as Keystone Bears) featured largely in early trade journals, but appear to have been produced for only a short period. It is rare to find an example such as this with some of the blue, stamped name remaining on the right foot. Aetna also made an unusual bear, with a two-colour body, a wide, pinked collar, and a dunce's cap.

ears set wide apart on corners of head

triangular face with wide forehead

rectangular, black, vertically stitched nose; horizontal stitch along bottom edge

black, boot-button eyes

wide, square shoulders with long, tapering arms, curved at paws

four short claws on each paw and foot-pad

woven label stitched across foot

beige, felt pads in good condition

*c.*1907 BRUIN MANUFACTURING CO.

Height: 33cm (13in)

A rare find, this bear retains its original trademark – a silky, blue and red, woven label with the letters "BMC" in gold thread. Bruin claimed that their bears contained "imported voices" – referring to the growler mechanisms imported from Germany.

Woven label

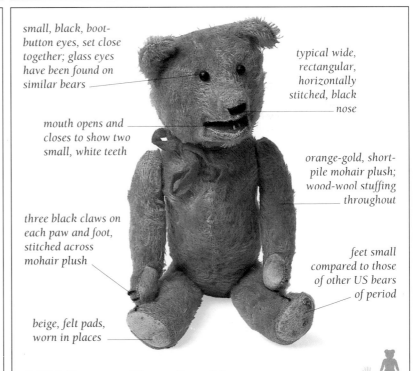

small, black, boot-button eyes, set close together; glass eyes have been found on similar bears

typical wide, rectangular, horizontally stitched, black nose

mouth opens and closes to show two small, white teeth

orange-gold, short-pile mohair plush; wood-wool stuffing throughout

three black claws on each paw and foot, stitched across mohair plush

feet small compared to those of other US bears of period

beige, felt pads, worn in places

1907 COLUMBIA TEDDY BEAR MFRS.

Height: 45cm (18in)

When the stomach is squeezed, a string mechanism opens the mouth of this Laughing Roosevelt Bear, revealing two pointed teeth made of white glass. When closed, the teeth rest in holes inside the wooden upper jaw. The manufacturers, based at 145–49 Center Street, New York, also made traditional, jointed, mohair-plush teddy bears.

Great Britain: 1908–c.1920

BIRTH OF BRITISH SOFT-TOY INDUSTRY; FIRST BRITISH BEARS

The teddy-bear craze reached Britain around 1908, fuelled perhaps by the fact that the country had its own "Teddy", Edward VII. Most teddy bears available in the early years were German, though made from mohair spun in English mills. A few soft-toy manufacturers existed, such as W.J. Terry and Dean's Rag Book Company, but it is J.K. Farnell & Co. that take the credit for making the first British, jointed, plush teddy bear, in 1908. World War I had a significant effect on the manufacture of teddy bears in Great Britain, many new factories being established as a result of the ban on German imports.

1912 BRITISH PROTOTYPE

Although imitating the German teddy-bear design to a large extent, British manufacturers tended to shorten the limbs – a characteristic that was to become truly British by the 1930s. They also preferred glass, and sometimes metal, eyes to the traditional boot-buttons used by German manufacturers during this period.

Height: 48cm (19in)

Ears: *the fabric is gathered and pushed into the facial seams – usually the mark of a cheaper bear.*

Eyes: *the painted, metal eyes are stuck into the face like carpet tacks.*

Nose/mouth: *a few horizontal stitches suggest the nose; the mouth is an inverted Y shape.*

Limbs: *the limbs, particularly the arms, are very short.*

BEAR PROFILE
This bear clearly illustrates the short limbs, the long, thin body, and the absence of a hump that were all distinguishing features of British bears at this time. However, the pointed muzzle still follows the German style.

Claws: *some remains of the original black, thread claws are visible on the feet and paws.*

Pads: *the beige, felt pads are pear-shaped; the bear's right foot-pad is a replacement.*

Fur: *the short-pile mohair plush is golden in colour.*

golden mohair plush

boot-button eyes

shaved muzzle

fully jointed head and limbs

khaki, felt, British army officer's uniform

pale peach, felt pads on paws and feet

four claws on each paw and foot

1916 ALLY BEAR; HARWIN & CO.   Height: 29cm (11½in)

This teddy bear was designed by Dorothy Harwin of the north London firm Harwin & Co. (est. 1914) as part of its World War I series of mascots, dressed in uniforms of the Allied Forces. It is similar in design to Steiff bears; interestingly, Harwin's sales manager, Fred Taylor, had previously been a travelling salesman for the German company.

large ears, flat on sides of head

unusual vertical centre-seam meets horizontal seam halfway down face

vertically stitched, square-shaped nose

wide, smiling, embroidered mouth; small, pink tongue below

bulbous, opaque, brown, glass eyes; black pupils sewn in

blue, felt trousers with red, felt patch; webbing braces

pink and white checked shirt

very worn, light brown mohair plush

1915 MASTER TEDDY; CHILTERN   Height: 20cm (8in)

Manufactured at the Chiltern Toy Works in Chesham, Bucks. (later H.G. Stone & Co. Ltd.), Master Teddy was available in five sizes. His googly eyes are typical of the period, and mimic the popular animal caricatures of the day.

Card chest-tag

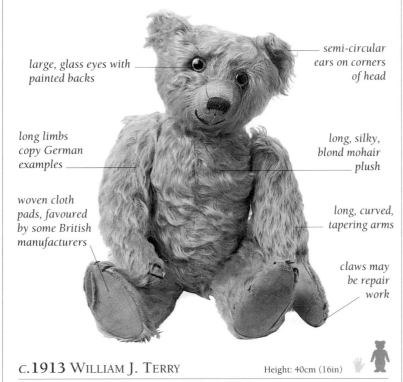

large, glass eyes with painted backs

semi-circular ears on corners of head

long limbs copy German examples

long, silky, blond mohair plush

woven cloth pads, favoured by some British manufacturers

long, curved, tapering arms

claws may be repair work

C.1913 WILLIAM J. TERRY   Height: 40cm (16in)

It is thought that this bear was made by William J. Terry of east London (one of the forerunners of the British soft toy industry) because of its resemblance to a photograph of similar bears for sale in the London department store Whiteleys. The bear's straight, tubular body and unusual hump make it unique. The growler is no longer working.

two new ears made by cutting one remaining original ear in half

large, clear, glass eyes with brown, painted backs

shaved muzzle

black, vertically stitched, shield-shaped nose; central stitches dropped to meet inverted-V-shaped mouth

light brown, brushed cotton pads with card reinforcement

front final seam, as on Steiff bears

golden mohair plush

C.1920 WEBBED CLAW   Height: 46cm (18½in)

This bear has the typical paws associated with several of the early, British teddy-bear manufacturers, including W.J. Terry, J.K. Farnell, and, much later, Merrythought. The paws are stuffed with kapok, whereas wood-wool has been used elsewhere. The five, black claws are linked by four, short, horizontal stitches over the pads only.

Germany: 1920s–30s

HERMANN FAMILY AND OTHER NEUSTADT/SONNEBERG COMPANIES

The teddy-bear industry in the Neustadt/Sonneberg area of Germany, the traditional toy-making region, began in 1907–08 in response to the US demand for bears, and in direct competition with Steiff. By 1930, the industry was fully developed: Artur, Bernhard, and Max, sons of Johann Hermann (*see pp.94–95*) founded three major factories during this period, and even established doll companies, such as Gebrüder Süssenguth and Ernst Liebermann, turned to making bears. The bears of this region often had inset, contrasting muzzles, a style that endured after World War II (*see pp.114–115*).

1933 MAX HERMANN

This example, part of a group of dressed bears made for a large toy show held in Sonneberg in 1933, is in perfect condition, as it has been kept in the Sonneberg Toy Museum ever since. The bear is shown standing, as originally displayed, based on a photograph of a tableau that had paired teddies positioned as if dancing around a maypole. The original triangular swing-tag is the rare, earliest known trademark, featuring a bear and running dog with the words "Maheso" (from the first two letters of the words, Max Hermann Sonneberg) and "Erzeugnis" (product).

Height: 18cm (7in)   Printed label

Hat: *the traditional German hat has a turned-up brim and "feather" trim.*

Eyes: *the eyes are original black, boot-buttons.*

Nose/mouth: *the shield-shaped nose is horizontally stitched in light brown embroidery thread; the mouth is an inverted Y shape.*

Claws: *the claws are stitched in dark brown embroidery thread. There are three on each paw and foot.*

BEAR PROFILE

In profile you can see the elongated features typical of traditional bears; these include the protruding, pointed muzzle, the long, curved arms, spoon-shaped paws, and large feet. A silver-coloured metal button, clearly visible on the shoulder, is one end of the simple rod joint connecting the arms; the same system is used on the legs.

Shorts: *this bear wears a crocheted version of the traditional lederhosen.*

Pads: *the pads are made from a distinctive red felt.*

Fur/stuffing: *the fur is white, artificial-silk plush; the bear is stuffed with wood-wool.*

Limbs: *the limbs and head are fully jointed.*

hollow, moulded composition head

"googly" glass eyes set in eye sockets and attached to tongue

painted, moulded composition teeth with movable, pink tongue

black, painted, moulded composition nose

fully jointed limbs and head

thread on centre of chest marks position of original trademark

curved, tapering arms with slightly hooked paws

blond-tipped, dark brown mohair plush; wood-wool stuffing

beige, felt pads in mint condition

1925 GEBRÜDER SÜSSENGUTH
Height: 35cm (14in)

This rare model originally came with a chest-tag reading: "'Peter' Ges Gesch" (legally protected); with the number Nr 895257. The "googly" glass eyes and moulded composition tongue move from side to side when the head is turned. Existing "Peters" are mostly in mint condition: it is likely that the toy was too frightening for children and was never sold.

sewn-in, amber, glass eyes with black pupils

distinctive ears

slightly shaggy, brown-tipped blond mohair; wood-wool stuffing; internal voice box

horizontally stitched, shield-shaped, black nose; inverted-Y-shaped mouth

remains of black, stitched claws on paws and feet

replacement pads; originals would have been felt

1925–29 MAX HERMANN
Height: 30cm (12in)

Max Hermann founded his company in 1920 at the Hermann family home in the village of Neufang, then moved to nearby Sonneberg in 1923. A friend of Max's wife Hilde bought this unmarked bear from the Sonneberg factory as a present for her daughter, Elfriede Müller, born in 1922. The bear remains in the daughter's possession at her Coburg home.

slightly shaggy, brown-tipped, blond mohair on blond woven backing; wood-wool stuffing

horizontally stitched, oval, black nose; inverted-Y-shaped mouth

fully jointed limbs and head

replacement beige, felt pad on left paw

curved, tapering paws

relatively straight legs with small, narrow, oval feet

1927 BERNHARD HERMANN
Height 35cm (14in)

This brown-tipped blond, mohair-plush bear, typical of the era, hails from the Gebrüder Hermann archives. It was made at Bernhard Hermann's factory in Sonneberg, where he had been based since 1920. The original swing-tag would have read: "Marke Beha Teddy Bürgt Für Qualität" (Beha mark guaranteed for quality). A replica of this design was made in 1986.

horizontally stitched, triangular, black nose; inverted-Y-shaped mouth

large, flat ears

inset muzzle of clipped, contrasting, pale golden plush

short-pile, beige mohair plush; wood-wool stuffing

original beige, felt pads

three black, stitched claws

holes in foot-pad reveal wood-wool

1930s BERNHARD HERMANN
Height: 50cm (20in)

This bear has an inset muzzle of clipped, golden mohair plush, and slender limbs – a style adopted since the 1920s. The 1950s label, although historically incorrect, was recently added by the company to this archive sample to indicate its origins.

Printed tag

Bing: 1909–32

TRADITIONAL DESIGN; BUTTON DISPUTE WITH STEIFF

Gebrüder Bing, a Nuremberg-based tinware company, turned to toymaking in the 1880s, and quickly established a reputation for its fine-quality, mechanical tin toys. Bing then set out to challenge Steiff's monopoly on teddy bears by introducing teddies into its programme in the early 1900s.

Originally, Bing copied Steiff's overall design, differing only in small details; for example, by attaching a metal arrow to the right ear of its bears. Steiff's objection to this, however, led to Bing fixing a button (at first incised, later painted) to the left side of the bears; this was subsequently moved to the right arm.

c.1911 BUTTON UNDER ARM

Early Bing teddy bears had a metal arrow trademark clipped to the right ear. This was replaced in 1909, as a result of Steiff's protests, by a metal button fixed under the arm – permitted provided the word "button" was not used in the trademark. The "GBN" incised on the metal button is identical to that painted on the original, metal, arrow trademark.

Height: 53cm (21in)

Incised metal button

Ears: *the ears are set wide apart.*

Eyes: *boot-button eyes were used before World War I.*

Nose: *the black, triangular nose is vertically stitched; smaller Bing bears had horizontally stitched, triangular noses.*

Fur/stuffing/growler: *the mohair plush is dark chocolate-brown (Bing used similar natural colours to Steiff). This bear is stuffed throughout with wood-wool, and has a tilt growler.*

Arms: *the long arms end in curved, Steiff-like paws.*

Feet: *the large feet are similar to those of Steiff bears.*

BEAR PROFILE
You can see more easily, in profile, this bear's pointed muzzle, hump back, and extremely long arms – all features that Bing borrowed from Steiff. The metal trademark button is clearly visible under the bear's left arm.

Pads: *the original felt pads have been replaced by leather ones.*

black, vertically stitched nose

replacement brown, plastic eyes

orange painted, metal button trademark

closely shaved, mohair-plush muzzle

replacement beige, felt pads

long, silky, silver-tipped mohair plush

EARLY 1920s BUTTON ON THE ARM
Height: 58cm (23in)

This bear carries the later 1919–32 Bing metal button, painted orange, with the letters "BW" (standing for *Bing Werke*) in black. The button is attached to the right arm. The lettering on the buttons of pre-1919 bears read "GBN" (for *Gebrüder Bing Nuremberg*).

Painted button

typical post-World War I glass eyes

vertically stitched nose over felt

long, shaved muzzle

final seam at front

shaggy, gold mohair plush on dark brown, woven backing

repaired felt pads

1919–32 ELONGATED DESIGN
Height: 59cm (23½in)

Experts generally agree that the use of shaggy mohair plush, coupled with more elongated features, such as a pointed muzzle and a wide, smiling mouth, are characteristics of post-World War I Bing bears. Although this example has no surviving trademark, its resemblance to the bear *(left)* suggests that it was made by Bing between 1919 and 1932.

vertically stitched nose, similar to those of large, Steiff bears

boot-button eyes

final seam at front (a feature also found on early Steiff and J.K. Farnell bears)

long arms, longer than legs, a feature of early bears

long, narrow feet

felt pads

c.1910 ALL-IN-ONE EARS
Height: 48cm (19in)

Some early Bing bears, bearing the silver-coloured button with incised "GBN" diamond design, have been found with the head and ears cut all-in-one: the ear is formed by folding the extension of mohair plush forward, and over-sewing the edges into the inside of the ear. This bear has no button, but the all-in-one ears indicate its manufacturing origins.

small ears and wide forehead, typical of Bing bears from this period

boot-button eyes

vertically stitched nose with border stitches

final front seam, a common Bing feature

very long arms

replace-ment felt under worn areas of foot-pads

replacement woven cotton paw-pads

c.1910 BUTTON UNDER ARM
Height: 50cm (20in)

Like Steiff, Bing used beige thread for the embroidered features on light-coloured, mohair-plush bears. The nose design in this example is typical of that used by Bing for larger bears. The silver-coloured button, with incised "GBN" diamond design, is under the left arm.

Incised metal button

Gebrüder Bing: c.1910–32

ADDITION OF CLOCKWORK MECHANISMS TO TEDDY-BEAR RANGE

Gebrüder Bing, already established as the world's largest mechanical tin-toy maker, soon introduced clockwork mechanisms into its teddy bears, with a wind-up key at the side or front. Later bears, such as the somersaulting and skating bears, were dressed in felt outfits. Bing bears usually had a metal arrow (pre-World War I), a silver "GBN" button (*Gebrüder Bing Nürnberg*, pre-1919), or a red "BW" button (*Bing Werke*, post-1920). Some had a red, metal button with "DRPa div DRGM" (*Deutsches Reichs Patent/Deutsches Reichs Gebrauchmuster*). The company went into receivership in 1932.

c.1910 MOVING HEAD

A key to activate the clockwork mechanism inside this bear's body is concealed under its right arm. The mechanism moves the bear's head from side to side. Bing produced similar 28cm (11in) and 50cm (20in) bears of brown and white mohair plush. A pre-1919, silver-coloured, incised metal button, with "GBN" inside the diamond pattern, is located under the left arm, and the letters "DRPa" and "DRGM" are incised around the metal keyhole.

Height: 40cm (16in)

Incised metal button

Eyes: *the eyes are original black, boot buttons.*

Nose/mouth: *the vertically stitched, shield-shaped, black nose, with double stitch borders, is a typical Bing design. It has five long, central stitches extending down to meet an inverted-V-shaped mouth.*

Fur: *the fur is light brown mohair plush. The bear is stuffed with wood-wool. A clockwork mechanism inside the body controls the movement of the head.*

Legs: *the legs are rounded at the thighs, tapering to narrow ankles, with large, slender, oval feet.*

Pads: *the beige, felt pads are worn. The new felt and oversewing are visible on the left foot.*

BEAR PROFILE

At this angle, you can see that the bear follows the traditional early Bing design with its protruding but blunt muzzle, slight hump, elongated arms extending beyond the legs, narrow ankles, and large feet. The patching on the left paw-pad is clear, and the key is visible under the right arm.

Arms: *the very long arms curve upwards at the paws.*

1912 ROLLER-SKATING BEAR

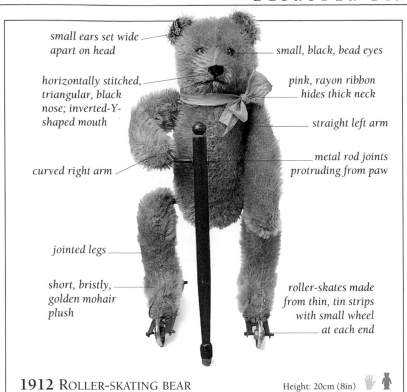

small ears set wide apart on head

small, black, bead eyes

horizontally stitched, triangular, black nose; inverted-Y-shaped mouth

pink, rayon ribbon hides thick neck

straight left arm

metal rod joints protruding from paw

curved right arm

jointed legs

short, bristly, golden mohair plush

roller-skates made from thin, tin strips with small wheel at each end

Height: 20cm (8in)

When you wind up the key under the left arm, this bear lurches back and forth while the curved arm moves up and down. There is a metal arrow in the right ear. Other examples of this bear have an added orange "patent" button near the keyhole.

Metal arrow

c.1910 SOMERSAULTING BEAR

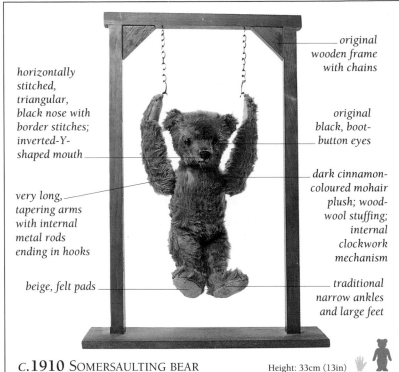

original wooden frame with chains

horizontally stitched, triangular, black nose with border stitches; inverted-Y-shaped mouth

original black, boot-button eyes

dark cinnamon-coloured mohair plush; wood-wool stuffing; internal clockwork mechanism

very long, tapering arms with internal metal rods ending in hooks

beige, felt pads

traditional narrow ankles and large feet

Height: 33cm (13in)

Steiff claimed that this bear copied their 1909 "Purzel-Bär"; the resulting lawsuit continued from 1911 to 1915, during which time Bing continued to produce their bear who turns somersaults after his arms have been rotated a few times. Some examples with the red, "patent" button exist, as well as a later example dressed in felt clothes.

c.1913 MOVING ARMS

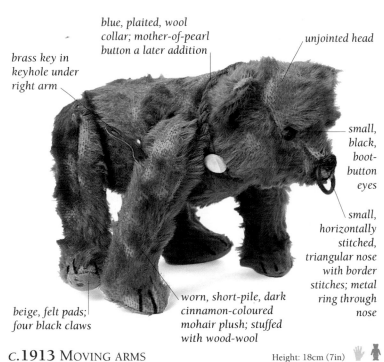

blue, plaited, wool collar; mother-of-pearl button a later addition

unjointed head

brass key in keyhole under right arm

small, black, boot-button eyes

small, horizontally stitched, triangular nose with border stitches; metal ring through nose

beige, felt pads; four black claws

worn, short-pile, dark cinnamon-coloured mohair plush; stuffed with wood-wool

Height: 18cm (7in)

This small bear, made of dark cinnamon-coloured mohair plush (much favoured by Bing) can stand on all fours, as here, or sit upright. When wound up, the front legs move back and forth. It has a red-painted metal button under its left front arm.

Metal button

c.1913 FOOTBALLER BEAR

horizontally stitched, triangular, black nose with border stitches; inverted-Y-shaped mouth

small, cupped ears

small, black, boot-button eyes

fixed head

curved right arm with internal rod protruding from paw

straight left arm

short-pile, dark cinnamon-coloured mohair plush; wood-wool stuffing

jointed legs with small feet

tin ball made in two halves, containing clockwork mechanism with key

Height: 20cm (8in)

When wound up, the mechanism inside the ball makes it turn. The wheeled bear, joined to the ball by a rod protruding from its slightly curved arm, follows as if pushing it. The trademark is a red, painted, "patent" button, printed with "DRPa div DRGM".

Metal button

Steiff: 1920s-30s

TRADITIONAL AND NOVELTY BEARS; INTRODUCTION OF GLASS EYES

During World War I, the Steiff factory was turned over to making war supplies, and in the post-war period, when materials were rationed, teddies were made from reconstituted wood fibre. The 1920s saw a different style of Steiff teddy emerge, with glass eyes and kapok stuffing, and the introduction of new colours of plush. Teddy Clown arrived in 1926, followed by Teddybu, dressed in a felt waistcoat. In 1928, a squeeze-type musical teddy was made. Unique designs included Petsy, Teddy-Baby, and Dicky. In 1938, after the arrival of the first pandas in Western zoos, Steiff introduced their Panda-Bear.

1921 MEDIUM; WHITE

This is a beautiful example of a white Steiff bear, its colour and condition making it very collectable. The glass eyes and partial kapok stuffing date it to post-1920, when these features became part of the Steiff Original Teddy design. The white label indicates a pre-1926 date. The shield-shaped nose is vertically stitched; smaller bears in the range had triangular, horizontally stitched noses.

Height: 38cm (15in)

Embossed button

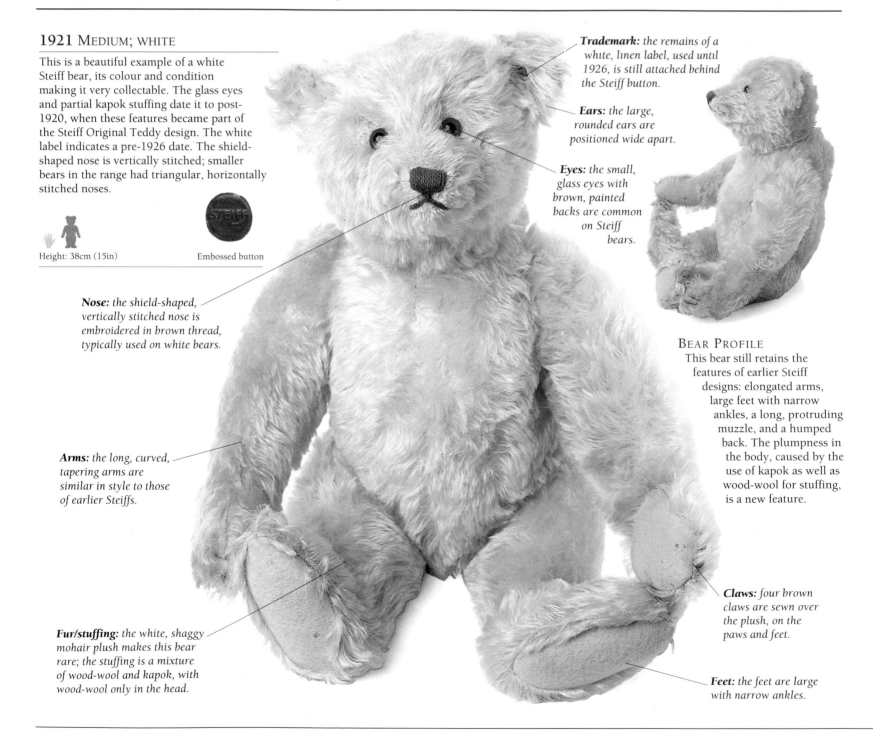

Trademark: *the remains of a white, linen label, used until 1926, is still attached behind the Steiff button.*

Ears: *the large, rounded ears are positioned wide apart.*

Eyes: *the small, glass eyes with brown, painted backs are common on Steiff bears.*

Nose: *the shield-shaped, vertically stitched nose is embroidered in brown thread, typically used on white bears.*

Arms: *the long, curved, tapering arms are similar in style to those of earlier Steiffs.*

Fur/stuffing: *the white, shaggy mohair plush makes this bear rare; the stuffing is a mixture of wood-wool and kapok, with wood-wool only in the head.*

BEAR PROFILE
This bear still retains the features of earlier Steiff designs: elongated arms, large feet with narrow ankles, a long, protruding muzzle, and a humped back. The plumpness in the body, caused by the use of kapok as well as wood-wool for stuffing, is a new feature.

Claws: *four brown claws are sewn over the plush, on the paws and feet.*

Feet: *the feet are large with narrow ankles.*

large ears, with internal wire armature, are fully "poseable"

remains of red thread nose and mouth

shaggy, "dual" mohair plush

bulbous, blue, glass eyes with black pupils, sewn in on wire shanks

pointed muzzle with unusual, central seam down front of head

sweater is not original

1927–28 BLUE-EYED PETSY
Height: 34cm (13½in)

This is the more unusual and collectable of the two Petsy designs; the other one has brown eyes and a black, embroidered nose. Produced in ten sizes, the design was also available as a glove puppet, and on a wheeled chassis, as part of the Record series.

Embossed button

large, brown, vertically stitched, shield-shaped nose, over brown felt underlay; central stitches dropped

long, narrow feet with beige, felt pads, reinforced with card; narrow ankles

large, clear, glass eyes with brown, painted backs and black pupils, sewn in on wire shanks

shaggy, white mohair plush; internal tilt-growler

four brown claws on paws and feet

EARLY 1920s LARGE, WHITE
Height: 73cm (29in)

This bear is a larger version of the example opposite but, unlike the smaller bear, it has beige, felt pads and the foot-pads have card reinforcements. It has a slightly corroded "button in ear" trademark with the remains of a white linen tag, which effectively dates it to pre-1926.

Embossed button

large, rounded ears set wide apart on sides of head

brown, vertically stitched, shield-shaped nose

long, tapering arms with curved paws

large, clear glass eyes, with brown, painted backs

"dual" or "tipped" plush, popular in the 1920s, created by brushing surface of mohair with darker dye

large feet with narrow pads

C.1926 "DUAL" MOHAIR PLUSH
Height: 60cm (24in)

This bear is cited in *The Guinness Book of Records* as the most expensive teddy bear ever bought at auction. It was sold at Sotheby's in 1989 for £55,000. Once thought to be unique, one or two bears with the same "dual" mohair plush and large eyes have since been found.

Embossed button

small, stiff ears; right ear has collapsed with age

clipped, mohair plush muzzle; brown, vertically stitched nose

card-tag design dates from 1928–50

peach-coloured cotton plush; internal squeaker

large, flat, pink, cotton pads, reinforced with card

brown, glass eyes with black pupils, set into muzzle seam

open, flesh-coloured, felt palate

blue, leatherette collar, fastened at back with metal button; card tag and bell attached

four brown claws on paws and feet

1930 TEDDY BABY
Height: 30cm (12in)

Steiff's successful Teddy Baby series was designed in 1929 and marketed the following year. The bear was produced in different sizes, materials, and colours, always with the large, flat feet and curved "begging" arms. It remained popular well into the 1950s.

Embossed button

Steiff: In the Beginning...

THE STORY OF STEIFF AND THE "BUTTON IN EAR" TEDDY BEAR

Margarete Steiff was born on 24 July 1847 in Giengen, southern Germany. Although she was confined to a wheelchair as a result of polio contracted in infancy, she bought herself a sewing-machine and proceeded to earn her living as a seamstress. In 1877, Margarete established the Felt Mail Order Co., making felt clothing, and by 1880 she was also selling stuffed felt toy animals, adapted from patterns in magazines. With the help of her brother Fritz, Margarete's toy-making enterprise flourished and, in March 1893, the business became the Felt Toy Company. Margarete assembled all the samples herself, and extended the range to include toy animals in velvet, burlap, and even in real fur, all stuffed with wood-wool. She registered patents, appointed a travelling salesman, and, by 1897, was employing 10 factory workers and 30 home workers.

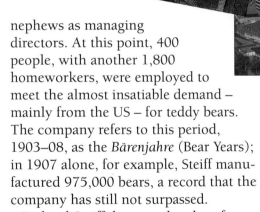

Steiff factory
The iron and glass buildings, seen in 1912 (left) and in the 1980s (below), are renowned for their modernistic design that pre-dated the later Bauhaus movement.

Richard Steiff, Margarete's nephew and the second of her brother Fritz's six sons, joined the business in 1897 after graduating from Art School in Stuttgart. He devoted himself to soft-toy design and manufacture, using sketches he had made earlier at Stuttgart Zoo and Hagenbeckschen Animal Circus. Richard's unique, string-jointed *Bär 55 PB* caught the attention of Hermann Berg, of the New York wholealers George Borgfeldt & Company, and at the Leipzig Fair in March 1903, Berg ordered 3,000 of these bears, so beginning Steiff's teddy-bear industry. In the following year, both Margarete and Richard were awarded gold medals at the World Fair in St. Louis, Missouri, USA, and the company itself gained the Grand Prix award. By the end of the year, Steiff had sold 12,000 teddy bears. Richard Steiff registered his disc-jointed teddy-bear design on 12 February 1905.

Margarete Steiff (1847–1909)
Despite her handicap, Margarete Steiff (above) founded the company whose name is now synonymous with teddy bears.

THE BÄRENJAHRE
On 6 July 1906, the Felt Toy Factory was renamed Margarete Steiff GmbH, with Margarete as owner, and her three nephews as managing directors. At this point, 400 people, with another 1,800 homeworkers, were employed to meet the almost insatiable demand – mainly from the US – for teddy bears. The company refers to this period, 1903–08, as the *Bärenjahre* (Bear Years); in 1907 alone, for example, Steiff manufactured 975,000 bears, a record that the company has still not surpassed.

Richard Steiff drew up the plans for a new factory in 1902: the east wing was completed in 1903, the west wing in 1905, and the north wing in 1908. The later work was overseen largely by Richard's brother, Hugo, who had studied engineering in Mannheim.

FRESH HORIZONS
From early on, Steiff sought to develop overseas markets; Paul ran a New York showroom during his year's visit to the city in 1902 and, in 1911, Otto founded

1903–04 Bärle
This rare, rod-jointed bear (left), with its long muzzle and sealing-wax nose, dates from Richard Steiff's experimental period.

Metal buttons
The first Steiff button, in 1904, was blank, then with an elephant logo; "Steiff", with stylized final "F", was used from 1905–06; a blank button was used from 1948–50; and raised, cursive script from the 1950s.

Richard Steiff and prototype teddy
This 1909 photograph (right) shows Richard Steiff holding his prototype teddy, which remained virtually unchanged until 1950. Richard died in Michigan in 1939, having gone to the US in 1923 as Steiff's New York representative.

Factory workers
Women did most of the work, from cutting out or stuffing (above), to adding details such as the nose and mouth.

Labels
Steiff used side-seam labels (top) in 1947–53, when the factory was in the US Occupied Zone. Printed linen tags (middle) were used in 1960–72, and folded tags (bottom) from 1980.

Steiff Frères in Paris. By 1913, there were Steiff agents all over the world. In 1910, a young Prussian artist, Albert Schlopsnies, joined Steiff as a designer; he introduced elaborate displays – scenes from everyday life, staged with Steiff dolls and animals – which were set up in shop windows, exhibitions, and trade fairs. These became one of Steiff's unique specialities.

THE WAR YEARS AND BEYOND
During World War I, Steiff's toy production decreased to a minimum: the three company directors went into the army, materials such as felt, which was used for military uniforms, were in short supply, borders were closed preventing trade, and the factory was turned over mainly to the manufacture of war supplies such as gas masks, feed bags for horses, ammunition, and aeroplane parts.

For a short period after the war, Steiff made teddies from reconstituted nettle plant, as mohair plush was still unavailable. By the early 1920s, however, despite Richard's emigration to the US as the New York representative, the company was back on its feet, helped by the introduction of the conveyer-belt system, which speeded up production considerably. In 1927, Ernst, the youngest Steiff brother, joined the company. The decade following Hitler's rise to power in 1933 was difficult for the Steiff factory; toy production finally ceased in 1943, and the factory reverted to manufacturing munitions. At the

1953 Jackie-Baby
The 50th anniversary of the first Steiff teddy bear was celebrated with this bear cub (left).

end of World War II, Giengen was occupied by American troops who stormed the factory in the hope of finding souvenirs to send home. However, all the samples and archives had been safely packed away and stored.

BACK IN BUSINESS
In October, 1945, Steiff manufactured a few toys for American troops, and started exporting again in January 1947. Low-quality plush had to be used at first, often in conjunction with blank tin buttons. The company resumed its high profile during the 1950s, when the workforce increased from 550 to 2,000, but in the 1970s, Steiff, like other soft-toy manufacturers, suffered from the competition of cheap imports from East Asia, and from the decrease in the birthrate in the West.

BEARS FOR COLLECTORS
The teddy-bear renaissance of the late 1970s in the US prompted Steiff to start producing limited-edition replicas of archive samples, heralding a period of renewed growth. Today, production methods continue on traditional lines, although some processes have been modernized (bears are now usually machine-stuffed). Collectors' bears however, are still stuffed by hand, using the traditional spiked stick and mallet.

Anniversary replica
In 1983, Steiff created a replica of Richard Steiff's 1905 design to mark the 100th anniversary of Margarete Steiff's first soft toy. The original is made of an unusual grey mohair plush, which was used only for the prototype. The example (below) has been signed on the right foot by Hans Otto Steiff, with "1983" on the left.

Schuco: 1920s–30s

SCHUCO MINIATURES AND NOVELTIES

In 1912, Heinrich Müller, a former employee of Gebrüder Bing, founded Schreyer & Co. (usually known as Schuco) with his partner, Heinrich Schreyer, in Nuremberg. After World War I, when both men were conscripted, Schreyer left the firm and Müller took on a new business partner, Adolf Kahn. Since the company's inception, the registered trademark had been a little, tumbling man clasping his feet. In 1921, "Schuco" was officially added to this logo. Müller concentrated primarily on ingenious novelties, many of which were clockwork, including a uniformed marching bear and a bear with a football.

1927 PICCOLO; *PUDER-BÄR* (COMPACT BEAR)

In 1924, Schuco introduced its 9cm–15cm (3½in–6in) Piccolo series of miniature, jointed, mohair-plush toy animals, including teddy bears, in various colours. In 1925, the company produced a small teddy bear with sparkling, diamond-like eyes. In 1927, Schuco made this novelty bear – designed to fit into a lady's handbag – containing a mirror, compact, lipstick, and powder puff.

Height: 9cm (3½in)

Nose/mouth: *a few horizontal stitches of black thread form the narrow, rectangular nose, ending in an inverted-Y-shaped mouth.*

Ears: *the ears are small half-circles, stiffened with card inside.*

Lipstick: *the metal tube still contains its red lipstick.*

Fur: *the bear is constructed of a unique internal metal frame, covered in lilac-coloured, short-pile mohair plush.*

Eyes: *the eyes are painted, black, metal beads.*

Limbs: *the short, straight limbs do not have pads or claws.*

BEAR PROFILE
In profile, you can clearly see the typical Schuco features: the straight back and limbs, and the triangular, blunted muzzle that projects straight out from the forehead.

Compact: *the bear's torso contains a hinged compact, with powder on one side and a mirror on the other.*

painted, black,
metal bead eyes

semi-circular
ears stiffened
with card

horizontally stitched,
black, narrow, rectangular
nose with inverted-Y-
shaped mouth

original green,
rayon, ribbon
bow, now faded

short-pile,
golden mohair
plush

cream, felt pads

internal metal frame

c.1924 PICCOLO; MINIATURE
Height: 6cm (2¼in)

Schuco intended the tiniest jointed bears to be given away free of charge, as a publicity gimmick, but they resulted in the Piccolo series. Pre-1930 examples had felt paws and feet attached to the ends of the internal metal frame, which is made up of various sections shaped by stamping and bending machines. The external jointing system used thin, metal rods.

painted, black,
metal eyes

horizontally stitched,
black, rectangular nose;
long, vertical stitch
leads to inverted-Y-
shaped mouth

short-pile
golden mohair,
on head only

metal body frame
covered by felt
jacket and
trousers; black,
felt buttons

metal rod projects
from clockwork
mechanism,
allowing wind-up
by key

when wound
up, arms go
over head;
legs follow
arms

black, painted
paws and feet
are continuation
of metal frame

c.1920–30s TUMBLING BEAR
Height: 10cm (4in)

This miniature bear with a patented, internal metal frame, tumbles when the clockwork mechanism is wound up. Schuco also manufactured an unclothed example with a blunter muzzle, which continued to be made after World War II until 1965. The firm made larger, non-mechanical tumbling bears from 1920, including one on a metal trapeze.

painted, black,
metal eyes

ears, reinforced with card,
inserted into head-seam

glass bottle inserted into
hollow body; hollow head
conceals top of bottle

short-pile, golden
mohair plush

straight arms
with no pads
or claws

limbs jointed
with patented
Schuco external
metal pin method

straight legs
with small feet

1920s PICCOLO; PERFUME BOTTLE
Height: 13cm (5in)

Part of a series, this bear contains a corked, glass, perfume bottle designed for ladies' handbags. Contemporary advertisements also describe versions containing jam. It was available in two other sizes, 9cm (3½in) and 11cm (4¼in) and also as a brooch, with a safety-pin on the back. A prototype of a similar bear containing a cigarette lighter exists in the Schuco archive.

mouth has short, metal
nozzle with central hole
for perfume spray

painted, black,
metal eyes

short, stubby,
unjointed legs
and arms
sewn onto
corners of fat,
round body,
containing
bellows

short-pile,
golden mohair
plush (red
example also
exists)

round, metal,
screw cap between
legs gives access to
perfume container

1920s MINIATURE ATOMIZER BEAR
Height: 10cm (4in)

This little bear sprays perfume from its mouth when the flattened body is pressed. The bottle could be filled by unscrewing the round, metal cap at the base of the torso. By squeezing the internal bellows, the liquid is forced up a tube to the small, metal nozzle in the face. Its ingenious design reflects the excellence of Schuco craftsmanship.

Schuco: 1920s–30s

INTRODUCTION OF SCHUCO PATENTED YES/NO BEARS

I n 1921, Schreyer and Company's famous patented Yes/No bears appeared for the first time at the Leipzig Spring Toy Fair in Germany. Their heads could be turned from left to right, as well as nodded up and down, by moving the tail, which acted as a lever connected to a metal rod running up through the body to a ball-and-socket neck joint. The bears, with disc-jointed limbs and silk bows, were available in six sizes, from 25cm to 60cm (10in to 24in), in short, shaggy, and extra-shaggy mohair plush. The two larger sizes had tilt-growlers, whereas the rest contained squeakers.

1930S PICCOLO; YES/NO BEAR

This Yes/No bear is part of the Piccolo series of miniature bears, and is very similar in design to the perfume bear and the miniature compact bear *(see pp.40–41)*, although it is a fraction larger. Another example exists that was once attached to a tiny piano stool and which, when its head was moved back and forth using the tail lever, would appear to play a miniature piano.

Height: 13cm (5in)

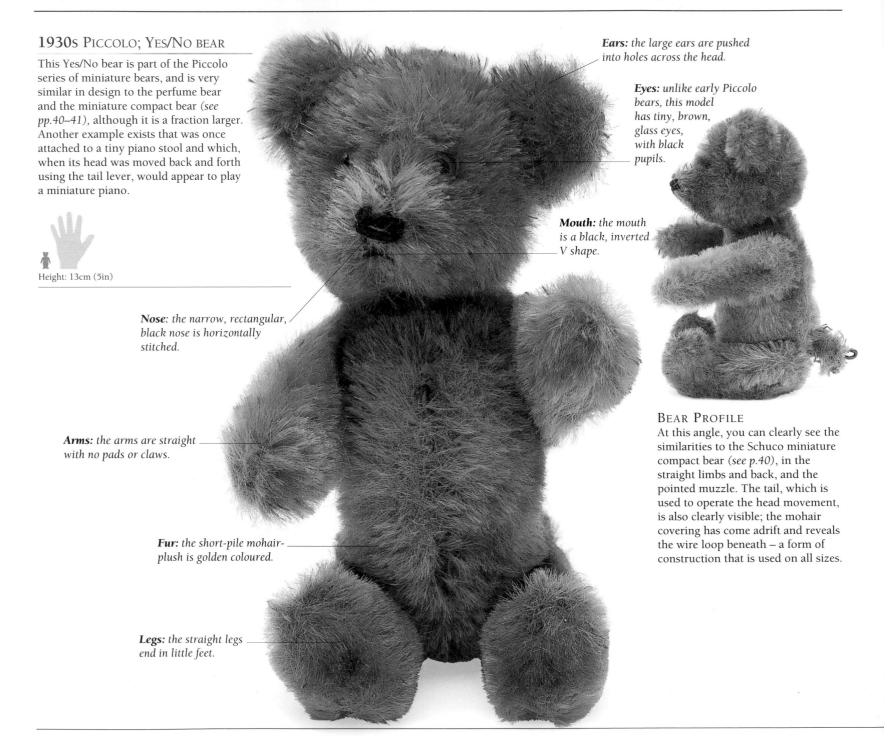

Nose: *the narrow, rectangular, black nose is horizontally stitched.*

Arms: *the arms are straight with no pads or claws.*

Fur: *the short-pile mohair-plush is golden coloured.*

Legs: *the straight legs end in little feet.*

Ears: *the large ears are pushed into holes across the head.*

Eyes: *unlike early Piccolo bears, this model has tiny, brown, glass eyes, with black pupils.*

Mouth: *the mouth is a black, inverted V shape.*

BEAR PROFILE
At this angle, you can clearly see the similarities to the Schuco miniature compact bear *(see p.40)*, in the straight limbs and back, and the pointed muzzle. The tail, which is used to operate the head movement, is also clearly visible; the mohair covering has come adrift and reveals the wire loop beneath – a form of construction that is used on all sizes.

1930s YES/NO BEAR

large, slightly cupped ears

shaved muzzle reveals woven backing beneath

beige, felt pads on paws and feet; black, embroidered claws

vertically stitched, square nose with inverted-Y-shaped mouth

soft, shaggy, honey-coloured mohair plush in excellent condition; wood-wool stuffing

large, oval feet

1930s YES/NO BEAR   Height: 53cm (21in)

One of the larger Yes/No bears, this example is made of soft, shaggy, honey-coloured mohair plush and has translucent brown and black, glass eyes with unusual opaque white surrounds. The bear's eyes, and its chubby arms and legs with big feet, suggest its later date – the earlier 1920s examples have long, tapering limbs, and black, boot-button eyes.

1930s YES/NO CLOWN

brown, glass eyes with large, black pupils

silk ruff

shaggy, beige mohair plush in excellent condition; wood-wool stuffing throughout

silk hat in perfect condition, except for faded rosettes

vertically stitched, square-shaped nose on shaved muzzle; inverted-Y-shaped mouth

beige, felt pads in mint condition

1930s YES/NO CLOWN   Height: 50cm (20in)

This rare bear is similar to the previous example (left) but has more usual brown, glass eyes, and wears a cream, silk, pierrot's hat and ruff trimmed with frills and pink rosettes – a popular costume for teddy bears of this period. It has large, stiffened feet and its paws are turned down, features that anticipate the later Tricky post-war series (see p.112).

1930s BABY-BÄR

glass rims of eyes painted, mustard colour on backs; maroon pupils; white surrounds

open mouth lined with felt, with separate felt tongue

pale pink, velveteen pads; airbrushed heels, toes, and paw tips

vertically stitched, oval nose

original pale blue, silk bow

beige wool plush; wood-wool stuffing; plush-covered metal tail

1930s BABY-BÄR   Height: 35cm (14in)

This is probably the largest of the four sizes of Baby Bear design, which ranged from 20cm to 35cm (8in to 14in). Made of shaggy, beige wool plush, with unusual side-glancing eyes, open mouth, and a squeaker, it wears either a silk bow, or a bib with a feeding bottle.

Card tag

c.1923 MESSENGER-BÄR

narrow, oval nose horizontally stitched in black thread; inverted-Y-shaped mouth

leather bag and strap

black, felt trousers

long paws and feet, with three black claws; woven, cream, fabric pads

red, felt, pill-box hat with leather chin strap

clear, glass eyes with brown, painted backs and black pupils

red, felt jacket with yellow braid trimming and black, felt buttons

feet, paws, head and tail of golden mohair plush

c.1923 MESSENGER-BÄR   Height: 36cm (14½in)

The second of three sizes of this Bellhop bear, produced from 1921, its arms contain bent, metal rods and its feet are stiffened with card. Earlier models had black, boot-button eyes. This bear has a squeaker; the larger size had a tilt-growler but smaller sizes were voiceless.

Card tag

Helvetic: mid-1920s

SWISS-MADE, SQUEEZE-TYPE, MUSICAL-BOX TEDDIES

Experts have identified a range of unmarked bears – produced *c.*1925 and containing squeeze-type musical boxes – as the work of the Helvetic Company. A 1928 issue of the US trade journal *Toy World* reported that the Helvetic Company held the exclusive manufacturing rights to teddy bears containing such mechanisms, but it is not known whether Helvetic was a US company importing the mechanisms from Switzerland, or a Swiss company exporting musical teddies. The name Helvetic is derived from *Helvetia*, the Latin name for Switzerland, where the clockwork musical box was invented.

*c.*1925 SHAGGY, BLOND/PINK MOHAIR

This bear possesses typical Helvetic features: large, glass eyes; distinctive, pear-shaped feet; and four black claws embroidered very close together at the ends of the paws. At the base of the right ear, you can just detect the original pastel pink, woven backing. Blue, gold, and green were other colours favoured by this manufacturer. The wide torso stores the music-box cylinder and comb mechanism which, for this large bear, has 32 teeth.

Height: 48cm (19in)

Ears: *the large ears are sewn across the facial seams.*

Eyes: *the large, brown eyes have a thick, white backing that renders them opaque.*

Nose: *the triangular, vertically stitched, black nose is very similar to those of early Steiff designs.*

Muzzle: *the protruding muzzle, with a long, pointed tip, is completely shaved.*

Arms: *the curved arms, tapering from wide shoulders to very narrow paws, are longer than the legs.*

Fur: *the woven backing of the blond, shaggy mohair plush, was originally pink, but this is now faded; the bear is stuffed with wood-wool throughout.*

Claws: *four black claws are embroidered very close together, across the plush, in a typical Helvetic design.*

BEAR PROFILE

From the side, you can clearly see this bear's narrow, pointed muzzle projecting from the shaggy mohair plush. The unusual curved, narrow paws and compact claw markings are also more evident at this angle, as are the bulbous, over-sized eyes, the expansive chest, and the strange, angular, humped back.

Feet: *the large feet have distinctive, narrow, pear-shaped pads, squared off at the toes.*

large eyes set wide apart, typical of Helvetic bears

large, round ears, sewn across facial seams

wide torso, containing bellows-operated musical box

worn nose repaired with vertical stitches; mouth missing

replacement dark brown, felt pads, oversewn in place

curved, thin, tapering paws; remains of black claws at ends

large, narrow, pear-shaped feet

c.1925 SHAGGY, BLOND/BLUE MOHAIR   Height: 38cm (15in)

This bald and badly stained bear was originally a stunning blue, a popular colour with the Helvetic Company; tinges of blue are still visible in areas of the body protected from light. The brown, glass eyes are fused onto a slightly smaller, white glass backing (creating the darker rim), each with an integral shank that is pushed into the head and glued in place.

large, brown, glass eyes with dark, outer rims

beige, felt hat, reinforced with card; two pink pompoms

narrow, pointed, slightly up-turned muzzle

small, black, horizontally stitched, triangular nose; inverted-Y-shaped mouth

two layers of rayon gathered into ruff

narrow, up-turned paws, with beige, felt pads

four black claws on each paw and foot

beige, felt pads repaired with new felt on right foot

large, narrow feet, slightly pear-shaped and squared off at ends

c.1925 BLOND/GREEN MOHAIR   Height: 38cm (15in)

Although in near-perfect condition, the original green, woven backing on this bear's fur has faded to yellow (the original colour is still visible beneath the pierrot's hat). The blond mohair pile is very short, but this bear possesses all other major Helvetic attributes. The woven, rayon ruff appears orange but is actually made up of pink and yellow threads.

large, rounded ears, sewn over facial seams

replacement translucent, amber, glass eyes; originals would have been larger

triangular, black, horizontally stitched nose; inverted-Y-shaped mouth

pointed, shaved, protruding muzzle

replacement cream, felt pads, oversewn around edges

large, pear-shaped feet

c.1925 BLOND/BLUE MOHAIR   Height: 30cm (12in)

Much of the long pile has worn away from the original blue backing, especially above the region of the musical box. The latter consists of a toothed cylinder and comb and a coiled spring, all enclosed in a round, wooden and oilcloth container. When the spring is pressed, it activates a lever, which turns the cylinder, causing the comb to strike the teeth.

large, rounded, slightly cupped ears, sewn over facial seams

replacement black, boot-button eyes

triangular nose at tip of muzzle; slightly lop-sided, inverted-Y-shaped mouth

wide chest contains round musical box

beige, felt pads; damaged left paw reveals wood-wool stuffing

beige, felt pads damaged by insects and wear and tear

large, narrow feet

c.1925 GOLDEN SHAGGY MOHAIR   Height: 30cm (12in)

Little of the original long pile remains on this bear's head or body, and this emphasizes its classic, Helvetic features: the narrow, pointed, slightly up-turned muzzle with horizontally stitched nose, and the curved, tapering arms, with slender paws and four-claw arrangement. Most Helvetic bears are between 30cm (12in) and 38cm (15in) high.

US: 1914–20s

CHEAP QUALITY "STICK" BEARS; TRADITIONAL AND NOVELTY

During the early craze in the United States (*c.*1907), the American teddy bear acquired realistic bear features, such as an elongated muzzle, long limbs, and a hump, copying the example set by Steiff and other German manufacturers. From the end of World War I onwards, however, inferior quality, US-made teddy bears were developed. Now known in American arctophilic circles as "US stick bears", because of their reduced features, these bears were produced for the masses by many small, now-forgotten, soft-toy factories. Unfortunately, these companies did not attach labels to their products.

1920s SMALL; SHORT, GOLDEN MOHAIR

This small bear demonstrates all the features of a typical "stick" bear, both in shape – with its oversized head, elongated muzzle, puny body, noticeable hump, and short, stiff limbs – and in the overall quality of the materials and the workmanship. The mohair plush, for example, has a sparse pile, indicating its inferior quality.

Height: 28cm (11in)

Ears: *the mohair-plush ears are gathered and pushed into the seam openings at the back of the head – the mark of a cheap bear.*

Eyes: *the boot-button eyes are sewn inside the two facial seams.*

Mouth: *the vertical stitch of the inverted-Y-shaped mouth is slightly awry, giving the bear a comical expression.*

Nose: *the small, elongated, triangular nose, embroidered in black, horizontal stitches across the end of the muzzle where the facial seams meet, is a typical feature of early American bears.*

Limbs: *the arms and legs are fully jointed.*

Arms: *the short, stubby, slightly curved arms taper towards the paws. The pads extend almost halfway up the arm.*

Legs: *the legs are different lengths, demonstrating poor workmanship.*

Pads: *the beige, woven cloth pads are badly stained, especially on the right paw.*

Claws: *three short, black claws are embroidered at the end of each limb.*

BEAR PROFILE
At this angle you can see the bear's "stick-like" features quite clearly: the large head with a flattened muzzle; the upright, narrow body; the short, slightly curved arms; and the thin, sausage-like legs with only the merest indication of feet.

Fur: *the bristly, golden mohair plush is very worn, especially on the chest where the squeaker has been pressed frequently.*

Foot-pads: *the legs end in small, circular pads.*

nose and mouth embroidered in black thread

small, rounded ears, gathered and sewn into seams at back of head – typical of poor quality bear

pointed paws stick out almost at right angles to arm

three black claws sewn across plush to edges of pads

small, rounded feet with three black claws

straight legs

1920s ORANGE, BRISTLY MOHAIR
Height: 48cm (19in)

This bear is made from short, bristly mohair plush (sometimes known as "sealskin" in the trade because of its texture), consisting of sparse, golden pile on an orange, woven backing. Although the body and legs are stick-like, the bear has a traditional, pronounced muzzle and slightly upturned, strangely curved arms, which are almost S-shaped.

large, flat, floppy ears oversewn across corners of almost square head

short, beige mohair plush, worn in places, particularly to right of chest

slightly curved arms

small eyes sewn into facial seams

inverted-Y-shaped mouth, embroidered in black thread, gives glum expression

straight legs

small, tear-shaped pads

1920s BEIGE MOHAIR; CLOTH NOSE
Height: 58cm (23in)

This bear has a particularly large head with a wide forehead, a typical feature of early American bears. The black, woven broadcloth nose, sewn onto the end of the muzzle between the two facial seams, is another characteristic of early bears made in the United States. The slightly asymmetrical shape of the nose indicates a teddy bear of poor quality.

small, rounded ears, gathered at base and badly sewn onto head; left ear has been attached too close to left eye

spherical head, with upturned, slightly pointed muzzle

small, embroidered, black nose at junction of facial seams, on tip of muzzle

inverted-V-shaped mouth, often found on cheap bears

brown, cloth pads on straight paws

sausage-shaped body has no shoulders, so arms seem to be attached halfway down body

1927 US "STICK" BEAR
Height: 55cm (22in)

Virtually shapeless when lying flat, this teddy bear's limbs are straight, sausage-like appendages attached, by traditional disc joints, to a similarly straight, humpless body. Both the body and the limbs are cut as almost identical oblong shapes – an easier, and therefore cheaper, procedure than that required to make the more curved, traditional design.

triangular nose of faded, black broadcloth stitched onto end of muzzle

leatherette collar around neck

short, almost straight arms, jointed to body

miniature electric light bulbs connected to battery inside body, and held in place by compact wood-wool

body made from sections of red, blue, and white, cheap quality plush; stuffed with wood-wool throughout

off-white, felt pads

unjointed legs made of same piece of fabric as body

1917 THE NATIONAL BEAR
Height: 45cm (18in)

This unusual "electric-eye" bear of patriotic red, white, and blue plush, was manufactured by the American Made Stuffed Toy Company of New York. Made in three sizes: 40cm (16in), 45cm (18in), and 55cm (22in), it retailed at $1, $1.50, and $2. This type of bear, with stiff neck and legs, was also made in traditional gold mohair plush, with electric eyes.

France: 1920s–30s

BIRTH OF FRENCH SOFT-TOY INDUSTRY; ROD-JOINTED BEARS

A lthough already renowned for its mechanical bears, France did import teddy bears from Germany during the early years of the craze. However, the 1914–18 war and the resulting border closures led to the establishment of a French teddy-bear industry. Generally of lower quality than their German counterparts, French bears were often made of short, bristly mohair or of coloured rayon plush. Manufacturers often employed cheaper methods of attaching eyes and ears (they pushed them into holes in the sides of the head, for example), as well as an unsophisticated, exterior jointing system.

1920s M. PINTEL FILS & CIE.

This Paris firm manufactured a range of soft toys, including animals, caricatures, and dolls. In the early 1920s, its lines were displayed in the London showrooms of Messrs. Ellis & Amiet. Pintel also manufactured mechanical bears including, later on, a dressed bear on a clockwork tricycle. The logo on the button trademark, showing two embracing bears, copied an illustration from pre-World War I Steiff catalogues. Pintel Fils always marked their bears with a chest-button.

Height: 38cm (15in)

Brass-plated button

Eyes: *the small, clear, glass eyes, with remains of paint on the backs, are sewn into the face on wire shanks.*

Nose: *this is a typical Pintel nose, vertically stitched in black thread, with the two outer stitches dropped.*

Arms: *the long, thin, tapering arms end in small, narrow paws with three claws on each; they are jointed in the traditional way using card discs.*

Fur/stuffing/squeaker: *the short, cinnamon-coloured, mohair-plush body is stuffed throughout with wood-wool. An oval squeaker in the body is still in working condition.*

Feet: *the feet are relatively large with thin, Steiff-like ankles.*

BEAR PROFILE
The side view demonstrates how slender and elongated this bear is in comparison with the more rounded German and British bears of the same period. There is the merest indication of a hump, and the muzzle is not very pronounced. The limbs are relatively long, with narrow ankles and slightly curved, pointed paws.

Claws: *the claws are stitched, in black thread, across both the plush and the pads.*

Pads: *the brown felt on the foot-pads is different from that on the paws, indicating that one set is a replacement.*

black, boot-button eyes

card tag attached with metal button

vertically stitched, cinnamon-coloured nose

faded pink artificial-silk plush, in very good condition

long, slender body fully jointed in traditional manner

beige, felt pads on paws and feet; no claws

long, slim, tapering legs

big feet and narrow ankles

1930s F.A.D.A.P.
Height: 43cm (17in)

This bear was made by a company based in Divonne-les-Bains, near the Swiss border. The Steiff-like button in the left ear indicates the company name in raised lettering, and the card tag behind is reminiscent of Steiff's 1928–50 circular chest-tags.

Embossed button

light golden mohair plush, slightly shaved around muzzle

clear, glass eyes with traces of paint on backs, sewn into face with knot at back

traditionally jointed head; fairly inflexible

black, vertically stitched, rectangular nose

original price-tag

long, thin torso

curved arms tapering to thin paws

beige, woven twill pads

straight legs

1920s ROD-JOINTED
Height: 38cm (15in)

This bear is a typical example of the inferior-quality teddy bears produced in France in the 1920s. The work is not of a high standard – for example, the left ear is slightly larger than the right, and the jointing system is fairly crude. Thin, metal rods run through the body and into the arms and legs, where they emerge and form a final loop on the outside of each limb.

small, black, boot-button eyes, sewn into face

vertically stitched, black, rectangular nose

slightly shaved muzzle, pointing upwards

short, straight arms; no pads

pale golden mohair plush

straight legs with pointed feet; no pads

original price-tag

1920s STIFF NECK; ROD-JOINTED
Height: 25cm (10in)

A smaller version of the rod-jointed bear (above right), this example shares similar characteristics, determined largely by economy measures. It is also rod-jointed, with the loop of wire visible at the top of each limb; the neck is unjointed, as the head and body have been cut, all-in-one, from the same piece of fabric. The facial features are asymmetrical.

large, cupped ears, set over facial seams

black, horizontally stitched, rectangular nose; small, vertical stitch in centre dropped to meet inverted-V-shaped mouth

original faded blue rayon ribbon, tied in bow

three black claws on hands

blue artificial-silk plush; wood-wool stuffing throughout

white, felt pads slightly discoloured; otherwise in good condition

1920s BLUE ARTIFICIAL-SILK PLUSH
Height: 43cm (17in)

This tall, slender bear demonstrates several features typical of French bears of the inter-war period. Artificial-silk (rayon) plush became popular, and the French seem to have favoured it in pastel shades. Boot-button eyes were used in France well into the 1920s and 1930s, although other countries had, by then, turned wholly to glass eyes.

J.K. Farnell: 1920s–30s

ALPHA BEARS AND OTHER TRADITIONAL NOVELTY RANGES

Henry and Agnes Farnell, whose earlier family business made small textile items, established a soft-toy firm in their Acton home in west London after the death of their father, John Kirby Farnell, in 1897. J.K. Farnell made its name with the Alpha trademark after World War I, building a factory and becoming a private limited company in 1921. By the end of the decade, the company had showrooms in London, Paris, and New York. Despite a fire that destroyed the factory in 1934, J.K. Farnell was operating again the following year with new lines and billing itself as the "world's premier soft-toy manufacturers".

1930s ALPHA BEAR; LARGE

Farnell's famous Alpha Bear range, made with Yorkshire mohair, was first advertised in trade journals in the early 1920s. Farnell introduced a swing-tag with the words "Alpha Make" in 1925; a permanent embroidered label was used until *c.*1945. The inspiration for Winnie the Pooh was probably an Alpha Bear, bought by A.A. Milne's wife in 1921.

Height: 55cm (22in)

Embroidered label

Ears: *the slightly cupped ears are sewn over the facial seams.*

Eyes: *the amber, glass eyes with black pupils may be replacements.*

Mouth: *the inverted-Y-shaped mouth is possibly a replacement.*

Nose: *the wide, vertically stitched, rectangular nose is a typical Farnell design.*

Fur/stuffing: *the fur is high-quality, golden mohair plush; the head is stuffed with wood-wool, the body with a mixture of kapok and wood-wool, and the limbs with kapok.*

Arms: *the very long arms have curved, tapering, spoon-like paws.*

Legs: *the legs taper to narrow ankles, with large, slender, oval feet.*

Final seam: *the final, central chest-seam is a typical Farnell feature that copies the style of Steiff and Bing.*

BEAR PROFILE
This J.K. Farnell bear clearly resembles its early Steiff counterpart, with a realistic, protruding muzzle, a humped back, long, tapering arms with upward curving, spoon-shaped paws, and legs with rounded thighs, narrow ankles, and large, slender feet.

Trademark: *the embroidered label is stitched to the left foot-pad.*

amber, glass eyes with black pupils

cupped ears, sewn across facial seams

inverted-Y-shaped, single-stitched mouth

wide, rectangular, embroidered, black nose of typical Farnell design

curly, golden mohair plush; kapok stuffing; internal squeaker

embroidered trademark, machine-stitched to foot-pad

final, central chest-seam

long, thin, Rexine pads

1930s GOLDEN MOHAIR; SMALL
Height: 34cm (13½in)

This bear is possibly one of Farnell's cheap Unicorn range launched in 1931, which included Cuddle Bear in four sizes and colours. It has Rexine pads, without any claws, and its foot-label has the alternative wording "A Farnell Alpha Toy".

A FARNELL ALPHA TOY MADE IN ENGLAND

Embroidered label

cinnamon-tipped, white mohair plush; wood-wool and kapok stuffing in head; kapok in body; internal squeaker

large, brown, glass eyes with black pupils

wide, black, vertically stitched nose, with black, felt underlay

long arms with spoon-shaped paws; cream, felt pads

five black claws stitched over plush and pad

thick thighs; large, slender feet

embroidered label

c.1926 ALPHA BEAR; "DUAL" MOHAIR
Height: 65cm (26in)

As one of the earliest British teddy-bear manufacturers, J.K. Farnell rivalled Steiff, with many similarities between their designs. This bear, with its curly mohair plush and large, glass eyes, is reminiscent of the 1926 Steiff (*see p.37, bottom left*).

FARNELL'S ALPHA TOYS MADE IN ENGLAND

Embroidered label

white, artificial-silk plush; kapok stuffing with wood-wool in muzzle

clear, glass eyes with blue, painted backs

black, vertically stitched nose; inverted-Y-shaped, single-stitched mouth

original card swing-tag with company name and address

pale pink, velour jacket with powder-blue, felt edging

unjointed limbs in permanent seated position

pink, artificial-silk feet

base of body reinforced with card on which internal music box rests

c.1937 MUSICAL BEAR
Height: 30cm (12in)

In 1937, J.K. Farnell advertised a range containing the Swiss-made Thorens "Stop and Go" musical movement (Farnell held the sole rights). This example is made of artificial-silk plush, a fabric Farnell introduced with their 1929 Silkalite teddy bear.

Embroidered label

small, cupped ears

black, felt, circular eyes

vertically stitched, black, oblong nose with few stitches extending to meet inverted-Y-shaped mouth

short, white, woollen plush on woven backing; stuffed with kapok; wood-wool in head

short, tapering arms

pale peach, felt pads

small, slender, oval feet

embroidered trademark

1930s WHITE WOOL; SMALL
Height: 23cm (9in)

This wool-plush bear with felt eyes may be part of Farnell's Alpac range of alpaca toys for babies. Introduced in 1935, the range included pink, blue, gold, and white teddy bears. By that time, bears in a wide choice of quality and colour were available.

Embroidered label

Chad Valley: 1920s–30s

EARLY TRADITIONAL BEARS; BUTTON AND LABEL TRADEMARKS

T he first Chad Valley traditional, jointed, plush teddy bears were manufactured in 1915–16, following the ban on German imports into Britain. "Chad Valley" was the trademark of Johnson Brothers who made stationery and board games at their works in Harborne, Birmingham. By 1920, the company had so expanded that soft-toy production was moved to a separate factory, the Wrekin Toy Works in Wellington, Shropshire; the business became known as The Chad Valley Co. Ltd. The teddy bears of the 1920s–30s were marked by a printed, celluloid-covered, metal button and/or a woven label.

1923–26 AEROLITE BUTTON

The early years were an experimental period for Chad Valley; some bears have been found with a stuffing of cork chippings and others with wire jointing. From 1920 onwards, Chad Valley used kapok stuffing; the company's 1923–26 Aerolite trademark refers to the soft, light nature of this material.

Height: 40cm (16in)

Aerolite button

Ears: *the large, flat ears are set on the sides of the head.*

Eyes: *the amber, glass eyes, with black pupils, are stitched into place on wire shanks.*

Nose: *the triangular nose is vertically stitched, with some horizontal stitches along the top.*

Fur: *the long, silky, golden mohair plush is clipped on the muzzle, and quite worn in places.*

Arms: *the arms are long and curved, with velveteen pads.*

Feet: *the large feet have oval, brown, velveteen pads.*

BEAR PROFILE
The protruding, rounded forehead and prominent, clipped muzzle, along with the less accentuated hump, shorter limbs, and smaller feet, illustrate the new, developing shape of the British teddy bear.

Pads: *there are five claws on each foot and four on the paws.*

flat, triangular head

large, triangular nose; smiling, inverted-Y-shaped mouth

pale golden mohair plush; shaved muzzle

foot-pads reinforced with card

large ears sewn over facial seams

clear, glass eyes with remains of brown paint on right eye; sewn in place and fastened off at back of head

beige, brushed-cotton pads

C.1920s BUTTON UNDER CHIN

Height: 73cm (29in)

Chad Valley generally placed its trademark button on the bear's right ear, but buttons are occasionally found on a bear's upper chest, as here, or on the upper back. Problems with Steiff's patent "button in ear" may have prompted these alterations.

Celluloid button

typical 1920s–30s triangular nose; vertical stitching with horizontal stitches across top

shaved muzzle

original felt pad; the others are replacements

celluloid missing from button; metal corroded

glass eyes on wire shanks, sewn in and finished off at back

unusual, wine-coloured mohair plush on brown woven backing

1930s WINE-COLOURED PLUSH

Height: 53cm (21in)

From 1930 until the 1940s Chad Valley attached a white woven label with red lettering to each of its bears. This was in addition to the celluloid-covered metal button, and was machine-stitched onto the foot-pad, or to the leg on smaller bears.

Embroidered label

amber, glass eyes on wire shanks, sewn and glued in position

long, curly, golden mohair plush; largely kapok-stuffed

long, curved, tapering arms

brown, brushed-cotton pads

large, flat ears set across top and sides of head

vertically stitched nose with horizontal stitch across top; shaved muzzle

foot-pads reinforced with card

C.1930 BUTTON IN EAR

Height: 43cm (17in)

The most common Chad Valley buttons are those with this wording, printed in black on a celluloid-covered metal stud. All Chad Valley buttons are larger than the early Steiff buttons. The nose is typical of those of Chad Valley bears produced during this period.

Celluloid button

replacement glass eyes; left eye larger than right

shaved muzzle, with wood-wool stuffing

golden mohair plush; kapok stuffing in body and limbs; hardboard joints

brushed-cotton pads on paws and feet

foot-pads reinforced with card (card in right foot broken)

thick thighs

C.1920s BUTTON IN EAR

Height: 73cm (29in)

This is yet another form of the Chad Valley trade-mark, with different wording and print colour, indicating an experimental phase in the company's history. This very large bear is stuffed with kapok, apart from the muzzle which contains wood-wool.

Celluloid button

Chad Valley: 1920s–30s

TRADITIONAL BEARS WITH ALTERNATIVE NOSE DESIGNS

Chad Valley expanded rapidly throughout the 1920s and 1930s, taking over five companies, including Isaacs & Co. and Peacock & Co. (*see pp.70–71*). By the early 1930s, the company was advertising bears in fourteen sizes, including three that were available either "hard or soft stuffed". By the end of the decade, however, only kapok was being used. During this period, also, nose designs were modified: the rectangular, horizontally stitched nose and the triangular, vertically stitched nose developed into the thickly bound, oval shape that is now often referred to as the "typical Chad Valley nose".

*c.*1930 HORIZONTAL NOSE

Although similar in body shape to others of the period, this bear has the horizontal nose design usually associated with the Magna series (*p.55, bottom right*). Its short, bristly mohair plush also suggests it belonged to the "A" range, one of five different qualities of fur used by Chad Valley in the early years. The bear is entirely stuffed with wood-wool, which the company continued to offer as an alternative to kapok.

Height: 25cm (10in)   Embroidered label

Button: *the metal button in the right ear is corroded.*

Ears: *the large, flat, slightly cupped ears are sewn over the facial seams.*

Eyes: *the clear, glass eyes, painted bright cinnamon on the backs, may be replacements.*

Nose: *the horizontally stitched nose is reminiscent of those of Peacock bears of the period (see pp.70–71).*

Muzzle: *narrow in shape, but prominent, the muzzle is completely shaved, revealing the woven fabric.*

Fur: *the short, slightly bristly mohair plush is of inferior quality. The bear is stuffed with wood-wool throughout, and has a tilt-growler.*

Pads: *the nutmeg-brown, felt pads have been extensively repaired with a different shade of brown felt. There are no claws.*

Feet: *the pads on the large, rounded feet are reinforced with thick card.*

Trademark: *the red and white label is machine-stitched to the left foot-pad.*

BEAR PROFILE

This teddy still demonstrates some characteristics usually associated with early, traditional-style teddy bears: a slight hint of a humped back; relatively long, curved arms; and large feet. An endearing feature is the smiling, embroidered mouth, which spans the width of the distinct, protruding, shaved muzzle.

flat, relatively large ears, sewn over facial seams

small, translucent, amber, glass eyes, sewn in on wire shanks

shaggy, light golden mohair plush; kapok stuffing

slightly protruding, shaved muzzle

short, straight, jointed arms; no pads

short, straight, jointed legs

feet only slightly indicated

1930s SMALL; WIDE, BOUND NOSE
Height: 20cm (8in)

This little bear has the button trademark fixed into its upper back. Although the smallest in the traditional range, it still demonstrates many archetypal Chad Valley characteristics, such as the thickly bound, vertically stitched, oval nose with horizontally stitched borders.

Celluloid button

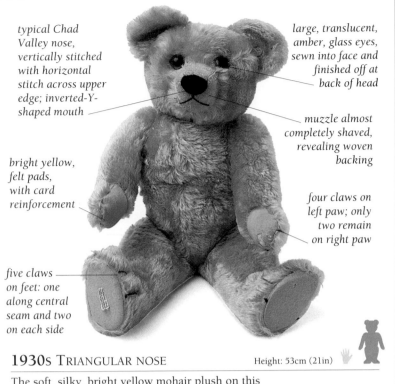

typical Chad Valley nose, vertically stitched with horizontal stitch across upper edge; inverted-Y-shaped mouth

large, translucent, amber, glass eyes, sewn into face and finished off at back of head

muzzle almost completely shaved, revealing woven backing

bright yellow, felt pads, with card reinforcement

four claws on left paw; only two remain on right paw

five claws on feet: one along central seam and two on each side

1930s TRIANGULAR NOSE
Height: 53cm (21in)

The soft, silky, bright yellow mohair plush on this bear is different from that of the bear opposite, and shows the range of quality offered by Chad Valley. This design was produced in white and in wine-coloured mohair as well as in artificial-silk plush.

HYGIENIC TOYS MADE IN ENGLAND BY CHAD VALLEY CO. LTD

Embroidered label

Chad Valley button in right ear

amber, glass eyes, on wire shanks, sewn into face and fastened off at back of head

black, vertically stitched, wide, bound nose, with horizontal stitch across upper edge

three black, embroidered claws on paws and feet, barely visible through plush

embroidered label stitched onto foot-pad

1930s SHAGGY, DARK BROWN MOHAIR
Height: 30cm (12in)

With its tightly bound nose, this bear demonstrates yet another quality of mohair plush available in the Chad Valley range, as well as an alternative colour to the usual gold. Its mint condition, light brown, appealing face, and surviving trademarks make it highly collectable.

Celluloid button

brown, glass eyes with black pupils, set rather wide apart

narrow, rectangular nose consists of several horizontal stitches; inverted-Y-shaped mouth

muzzle of same plush as body, not shaved as in other Chad Valley designs

mid-brown, brushed-cotton pads; paw-pads repaired with new fabric

light golden mohair plush

c.1930 MAGNA SERIES
Height: 38cm (15in)

This bear dates from around 1930 and possesses the unusual, blue and white Magna label, as well as the horizontally stitched nose generally associated with it. "Harborne" refers to the part of Birmingham where Chad Valley had its main toy factory.

CHAD VALLEY "MAGNA" SERIES HARBORNE ENGLAND

Embroidered label

Chiltern: 1920s–40s

DEVELOPMENT OF FAMOUS CHILTERN HUGMEE RANGE

Leon Rees inherited the Chiltern Toy Works from his father-in-law, Josef Eisenmann, in 1919. In 1920, he collaborated with Harry Stone, formerly of J.K. Farnell, to form H.G. Stone and Co., which became one of the foremost British soft-toy manufacturers of the time. The trademark "Chiltern Toys" referred to the company's location in Chesham, in the Chiltern Hills. Bears were made there until 1940 when the factory was turned over to war work. One of Chiltern's earliest teddy bears was Baby Bruin, the Bear Cub, of 1922. In 1937, the Wagmee series – similar to Schuco's Yes/No bear – was introduced.

LATE 1920s HUGMEE; "DUAL" PLUSH

The mainstay of the company's soft-toy business was the Hugmee teddy bear which began to appear in trade journals in 1923. Permanent, cloth Chiltern labels did not appear until the 1940s; earlier bears would have possessed an orange, circular, card chest-tag, with the words "Chiltern Toys Trademark/Made in England".

Height: 58cm (23in)

Fur/stuffing/squeaker: *"dual" mohair plush was popular in the 1920s – this example has dark roots with blond tipping although the reverse was also used. There is wood-wool stuffing in the head and around the squeaker, and kapok in the limbs and body.*

Eyes: *the clear, glass eyes are sewn in, with a final diagonal stitch at the back of the head – a typical Chiltern trait.*

Nose: *the oblong nose is vertically stitched with raised outer stitches, typical of the Hugmee range.*

BEAR PROFILE
At this angle you can see the typical Hugmee features of this period – long arms with spoon-like paws, thick thighs with large feet, an extended muzzle, and an embroidered nose with raised outer stitches.

SQUEAKER
The squeaker, which no longer works, is oval with a double reed (a reed at the end of each cardboard pipe) and oilcloth bellows that are now torn. The spring is rusty.

Claws: *there are four converging claws on the paws, and five on the feet.*

Pads: *the beige, velveteen foot-pads are reinforced with card.*

white mohair plush; kapok stuffing, with wood-wool in head and around squeaker

original large, clear glass eyes with black pupils; sewn in and tied with knot at back of head

remains of typical, pre-war Hugmee nose and mouth

curved arms with spoon-shaped paws; same size as legs

four black claws over plush on each foot and paw

beige, velveteen pads; foot-pads reinforced with card

drumstick-shaped legs; fat thighs, narrow ankles, and large feet

1938 HUGMEE; WHITE MOHAIR   Height: 58cm (23in)

This bear has all the pre-war Hugmee features: the shaved, pointed muzzle; the distinct nose design, with two extended outer stitches; the remains of a typical, wide smile; long, curved arms; and "drumstick" legs with velveteen pads. Only 1,000 of these unusual white, mohair-plush teddies, advertised in Hamleys' 1938 catalogue, were made.

glass eyes

shaved muzzle

wide, enigmatic smile

oblong nose with outer stitches extended upwards

long arms

spoon-like hands with velveteen pads

large feet; pads reinforced with card

thick "drumstick" thighs

c.1930 GOLD MOHAIR   Height: 65cm (26in)

Although this particular bear is unmarked, it has many characteristics of the early Hugmee bears. This design was also available in other colours, including pink and blue, and a rare white. Hugmee bears were usually fitted with a squeaker, and originally had a chest tag reading "I Growl"; some early Hugmees contained squeeze-type musical boxes.

reddish brown, glass eyes

shield-shaped nose

indentation around waist caused by wearing elasticated trousers

golden mohair plush

small, pointed feet with Rexine pads and four claws in two-by-two arrangement

Rexine pads are typically British feature of period

1940s HUGMEE; FLAT FACE   Height: 50cm (20in)

During World War II and the years of rationing that followed, a new-look Hugmee evolved. Due to the lack of materials available, a pattern was designed that required less fabric, and so the Hugmee bear acquired a shortened muzzle and mouth, giving it a glum expression. The absence of claws on the paws was another economy measure.

translucent, reddish brown, glass eyes; sewn in and finished off at back of head

almost circular ears with inner edge caught into facial seam

shield-shaped nose embroidered in black thread

pink artificial-silk plush on woven backing

four black claws across pads and plush in two-by-two arrangement

small feet with beige, velveteen pads in perfect condition; four claws across pads and plush

1940s ARTIFICIAL SILK; MUSICAL   Height: 40cm (16in)

The Chiltern Silky Bear of 1929 was Chad Valley's first artificial-silk teddy bear. The bear illustrated (a flat-face, glum design similar to the previous bear) contains a key-operated, wind-up musical box in the small of the back, which plays Brahms' *Lullaby*. The bear is stuffed throughout with a light, soft cotton waste, known in the trade as "sub".

JOY-TOYS: 1920s–60s

BIRTH OF FIRST AUSTRALIAN SOFT-TOY MANUFACTURER

Joy-Toys was founded in the 1920s by Mr. and Mrs. Gerald Kirby of South Yarra, Victoria, and was probably the first Australian commercial teddy-bear manufacturer. Before this, teddies were imported from Europe or they were home-made. After the Kirbys' departure to London in 1937 to form the soft-toy company, G.L. Kirby Ltd., Joy-Toys expanded under the leadership of Maurice Court, gaining the sole Australian franchise for Walt Disney characters and opening a factory at Whangarei, New Zealand. In 1966, the firm was bought out by the British-owned company, Cyclops, and ceased business in the 1970s.

LATE 1920s–30s FULLY JOINTED

Pre-World War II Joy-Toys bears are made of mohair plush with wood-wool stuffing and have a distinctive nose shape, which imitates the Chiltern design (see pp.56–57) of the same period. Chiltern's Hugmee range was exported to Australia from Britain around 1930, according to advertisements in Grace Brothers department-store catalogues, and it is possible that Joy-Toys based its bears' nose design on that of the Hugmee bears.

Height: 50cm (20in)

Embroidered label

JOY-TOYS
MADE IN AUSTRALIA

Ears: *the ears are set wide apart at the back of the head and sewn across the facial seams.*

Eyes: *made of translucent, amber glass, the eyes are sewn into the face on wire shanks.*

Nose: *two stitches extend upwards from the vertically stitched, black nose.*

Mouth: *the inverted-T-shaped mouth is stitched in black.*

Arms: *the arms are short and fixed high on the body, giving the impression that the bear has no neck; the paws are tapered and curved.*

Body: *the body is long and thin.*

Fur/stuffing: *the fur is shaggy, golden mohair plush, worn in places, exposing the woven backing beneath; the bear is stuffed with wood-wool throughout.*

Pads: *the beige coating on the original Rexine pads is worn away, revealing the off-white, woven backing.*

Legs: *the legs are short and straight; they are slightly wider at the thighs.*

BEAR PROFILE

This bear borrows many characteristics from the typical British bears of the period, with its relatively short limbs and curved paws, plump thighs and small feet, and its straight back. The protruding muzzle projects straight out from the bear's forehead; the long, outer stitch of the distinctive nose is clearly visible.

Feet: *the feet are short and stumpy; there are no claws.*

Trademark: *an embroidered cloth label is stitched onto the left foot-pad.*

unusual glass eyes with painted, amber backs and black pupils, set wide apart

flat ears, set wide apart across facial seams, at back of head

no neck joint

vertically stitched, square, black nose; inverted-T-shaped mouth

short, coarse, golden mohair plush

short, curved, tapering arms with wide shoulders

short, stumpy, oval feet

beige, felt pads with no claws

1940s SQUARE NOSE

Height: 38cm (15in)

Perhaps as a result of wartime shortages, this bear is made from short, coarse mohair plush and has no neck joint, a feature that was to become a characteristic of Joy-Toys and other Australian bears. The nose design is a simple square shape.

Embroidered label

brown, glass eyes with black pupils sewn in on long, wire shanks

unusual triangular nose

vertical stitch is all that remains of mouth

worn, shaggy, blond mohair plush; kapok or "sub" stuffing

fur worn away by frequent use of squeaker

short, tapering arms end in pointed paws

short, straight legs with pointed feet

1940s–50s SEMI-JOINTED; NO PADS

Height: 25cm (10in)

This small, well-worn, shaggy, blond mohair-plush bear has no neck joint. The body and head are all-in-one, being cut from the same piece of fabric. Like many small bears, it lacks foot-pads. A label is machine-stitched to the heel.

Embroidered label

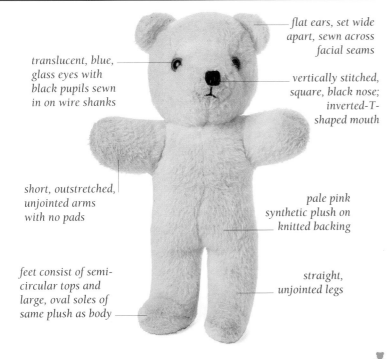

flat ears, set wide apart, sewn across facial seams

translucent, blue, glass eyes with black pupils sewn in on wire shanks

vertically stitched, square, black nose; inverted-T-shaped mouth

short, outstretched, unjointed arms with no pads

pale pink synthetic plush on knitted backing

feet consist of semi-circular tops and large, oval soles of same plush as body

straight, unjointed legs

c.1960 UNJOINTED; MOULDED FILLING

Height: 30cm (12in)

This unjointed bear has a complete foam-rubber filling, moulded into a bear shape, and then inserted via the back-seam into the outer covering of pale pink synthetic plush. It has a German-made, clear vinyl, concertina squeaker.

Printed label

vertically stitched, square, brown nose; inverted-T-shaped mouth

large, amber and black, glass eyes

stiff neck

jointed limbs

brown, velveteen pads

bright golden synthetic plush; foam-rubber stuffing

1960s SEMI-JOINTED; FOAM FILLING

Height: 38cm (15in)

The Joy-Toys shape did not generally change during the late 1950s and 60s. The square nose design and large, glass eyes continued to be used, and the body was semi-jointed with the characteristic stiff neck. However new synthetic fabrics were used for plush and filling, and the printed label was folded and often sewn into the leg- or pad-seam.

Merrythought: 1930s

EARLY DEVELOPMENT OF TWO TRADITIONAL BRITISH DESIGNS

I n 1930, W.G. Holmes and G.H. Laxton opened a soft-toy factory in a building originally leased from the Coalbrookdale Company, in Ironbridge, Shropshire, *(see pp.66–67)*. They registered their trademark Merrythought (a 17th-century English word meaning wishbone, and a symbol of good luck) that same year. In 1931, they produced their first catalogue, advertising two golden mohair teddy-bear designs: the Magnet range, which was designed, in four sizes, to "attract" the cheaper end of the market; and the Merrythought range, which evolved later into their key pattern, the M line.

EARLY 1930s TRADITIONAL DESIGN

This early design combines features associated with Chad Valley (printed, celluloid-covered, metal, button trademark, and large, flat ears) and J.K. Farnell (webbed claw markings). This may be because the new directors of Merrythought, C.J. Rendle and H.C. Janisch, had previously worked for these two well-established, soft-toy firms. Most Merrythought bears were made from golden mohair plush, but a dark-brown-tipped, biscuit-coloured, mohair-plush bear was produced from 1936 to 1938.

Height: 58cm (23in)

Celluloid/metal button

Button: *the printed, celluloid button, with wishbone trademark, was used during the 1930s; it is fixed to this bear's left ear.*

Eyes: *the amber, glass eyes, sewn into the face on wire shanks, are set wide apart and low down.*

Nose: *the outer two stitches of the vertically stitched nose are dropped; the mouth is an inverted Y shape.*

Fur/stuffing: *the fur is golden mohair plush; the bear is stuffed with a wood-wool and kapok mixture, apart from the limbs, which are stuffed with kapok.*

Claws: *the webbed claws on the paws, typical of early Merrythought bears, consist of four stitches across each felt pad, with the inner ends joined by horizontal stitches.*

Legs: *the fully jointed legs end in small, rounded feet; the fat thighs are typical of British bears of this period.*

Pads: *the deep orange, felt pads complement the golden mohair plush.*

Trademark: *the embroidered label, machine-stitched to the right foot, dates the bear to pre-World War II; Merrythought later used printed labels.*

BEAR PROFILE

The nose formation, clearly visible at this angle, and consisting of two, dropped, outer stitches, is typical of the early Merrythought design. The protruding, shaven muzzle emulates the traditional, realistic, Steiff design.

large, flat ears, sewn across the facial seams

large, amber, glass eyes with black pupils, set wide apart

completely shaved, protruding muzzle

shaggy, blond mohair plush; wood-wool stuffing in muzzle, kapok elsewhere

webbed claws on paws

beige, felt pads

label machine-stitched to foot-pad

four claws across plush only

EARLY 1930s SHAGGY MOHAIR

Height: 50cm (20in)

Early Merrythought bears were made in varying grades of plush. This example is made from a luxurious, long-pile mohair plush. The original golden colour has faded with time, but you can still see it inside the ears and around the joints.

Embroidered label

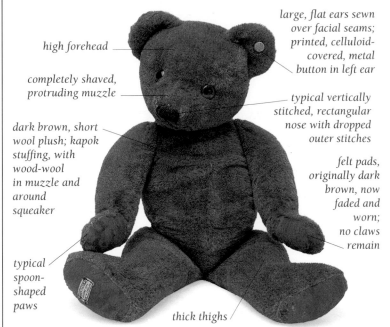

high forehead

large, flat ears sewn over facial seams; printed, celluloid-covered, metal button in left ear

completely shaved, protruding muzzle

typical vertically stitched, rectangular nose with dropped outer stitches

dark brown, short wool plush; kapok stuffing, with wood-wool in muzzle and around squeaker

felt pads, originally dark brown, now faded and worn; no claws remain

typical spoon-shaped paws

thick thighs

1930s DARK BROWN, SHORT PILE

Height: 48cm (19in)

This bear is similar to other 1930s Merrythought bears, but is made from a shorter pile, soft wool plush in an unusual chocolate-brown colour. The webbed claws have disappeared, but unfaded areas on the paw-pads indicate their original position.

Embroidered label

nose and mouth have been repaired but follow original design: dropped outer stitches on nose; inverted-Y-shaped mouth

amber, glass eyes with black pupils, sewn in and finished off at back of head

four webbed claws on paws; three straight claws on feet

golden mohair plush; wood-wool stuffing in muzzle and head, wood-wool/kapok mix in body, kapok in limbs

1930s GOLDEN MOHAIR

Height: 45cm (18in)

The shaved muzzle, high forehead, large, flat ears, webbed claws, and thick thighs are all typical features of a 1930s Merrythought bear. The pads, however, are made from dark brown velveteen, rather than from the more usual felt.

Embroidered label

rectangular, vertically stitched nose, without dropped outer stitches; inverted-Y-shaped, double-stitched mouth

bulbous, brown and black, glass eyes

slender torso; curved arms with thin paws

golden mohair plush, slightly worn on chest

beige, woven-twill pads; five claws on paws; four on feet, across plush only

short legs with slightly stumpy feet

woven label machine-stitched to left foot-pad

EARLY 1930s ALTERNATIVE DESIGN

Height: 50cm (20in)

This design was also available in eight fashionable shades of artificial-silk plush: "Salmon", "Ciel", "Myosotis", "Iris", "Canary", "Crimson", "Copper-glow", and "Jade". It still has its celluloid-covered, metal button on the back, behind the left arm joint.

Embroidered label

Chad Valley: 1938–50s

ROYAL WARRANT LABEL; TRADITIONAL TEDDY BEARS

By the end of the 1930s, The Chad Valley Company was recognized as one of the world's leading toy manufacturers. It had expanded greatly and, in 1938, was granted the British Royal Warrant of Appointment. From that time, all of the firm's toys carried a label with the declaration "Toymakers to Her Majesty the Queen", referring to Queen Elizabeth, the wife of the monarch, King George VI. The wording changed in 1953 with the coronation of the present Queen Elizabeth II, when "the Queen" became "the Queen Mother" – a detail that is helpful when trying to date Chad Valley bears.

1938–52 LARGE; GOLDEN MOHAIR

The basic, traditional teddy-bear design did not change greatly during this period. The nose shape, however, developed from the typical triangular form of the 1920s and 1930s to a tightly bound, wide, rectangular shape. Rexine, a treated buckram, became a popular fabric for the paw- and foot-pads, replacing the flannelette and velveteen that were previously preferred.

Height: 73cm (29in)   Printed label

Ears: the large, flat ears, sewn across the top and sides of the head, are typical of Chad Valley bears.

Eyes: the large, reddish brown, translucent, glass eyes are sewn in on wire shanks.

Nose: the wide, rectangular nose is composed of closely bound, vertical, black stitches, with horizontal stitches across the top edge, as on the company's earlier, triangular nose design.

Trademark: the blue, printed label is sewn into the chest seam.

Fur/stuffing: the particularly beautiful, golden mohair plush is in mint condition, with no worn patches. The bear is stuffed with kapok.

Feet: the feet are long and narrow.

BEAR PROFILE
This side view shows the typical emerging British bear shape, with its straight back, flattened muzzle, and particularly wide thighs. The arms are extremely long and curved at the paws. Notice the Royal Warrant label on the left foot.

Pads: the Rexine pads are slightly worn, revealing the woven backing fabric. There are no claws.

1938–52 BLUE MOHAIR

typical Chad Valley flat ears sewn across facial seams

brown, glass eyes sewn off at back of head

black, bound nose

blue mohair plush, with soft stuffing

printed label sewn into chest-seam

pre-1953 Royal Warrant label sewn onto foot-pad

blue, felt pads

Height: 35cm (14in)

Chad Valley was well known for its colourful bears, and blue was a popular choice. This bear lacks the round plumpness of earlier Chad Valley teddies – a result of the war-time rationing that reduced the materials available for making teddy bears.

Printed label

POST-1953 SHAGGY, GOLDEN MOHAIR

reddish brown, translucent, glass eyes

large, flat ears

shaved muzzle; wood-wool stuffing in head

wide, bound nose is characteristic of this period

shaggy, golden mohair; kapok stuffing in body and limbs

dark brown, suede-like, Rexine pads

Height: 44cm (17½in)

The Royal Warrant label, both pre- and post-coronation, was usually square (but sometimes oblong), with the Royal Warrant, coat-of-arms, and company name printed in blue. The label was usually zigzag-stitched onto the bear's foot.

Printed label

POST-1953 WHITE WOOL

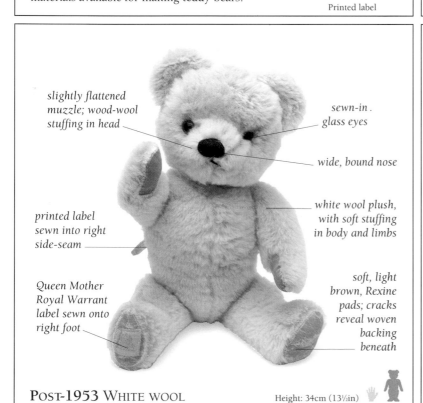

slightly flattened muzzle; wood-wool stuffing in head

sewn-in glass eyes

wide, bound nose

printed label sewn into right side-seam

white wool plush, with soft stuffing in body and limbs

Queen Mother Royal Warrant label sewn onto right foot

soft, light brown, Rexine pads; cracks reveal woven backing beneath

Height: 34cm (13½in)

This bear shares many of its Chad Valley characteristics with the earlier, golden bear (opposite), although it is made of a cheaper plush. The Rexine pads are light brown, to complement the colour of the wool plush.

Printed label

1940s LARGE; GOLDEN MOHAIR

large, soft ears in excellent condition

large, wide head

compact, vertical stitching on nose

original, amber and black, glass eyes

shiny, brown, leather-like, Rexine pads on paws and feet; no claws indicated

short arms compared to those of German bears

good quality, golden mohair plush

Height: 107cm (42in)

This exceptionally large bear has hardboard-reinforced foot-pads. A printed label is sewn into a side-seam, the usual positioning, although Chad Valley labels are often found in the chest-seam or near the leg joint.

Printed label

Chad Valley: 1930s–40s

NOVELTIES; INTRODUCTION OF ALTERNATIVE PLUSH FABRICS

The Chad Valley Company produced a number of novelty items, beginning with its 1926 Rainbow Tubby Bear, with ruff and pierrot's hat. Its most popular novelty in the 1930s was Cubby Bear, which was made of brown and fawn alpaca plush and available in three sizes. This endearing bear was possibly the Chad Valley equivalent of Merrythought's Bingie (*see pp.68–69*). Cubby's baby brother Sonny Bear was made from biscuit-coloured plush and wore a bib. In 1934, Chad Valley produced Winnie the Pooh and various other A.A. Milne characters, popularized by the BBC radio's *Children's Hour* programme.

1930s BLUE; MUSICAL

Blue was a popular colour for British teddy bears from the late 1930s to the early 1950s. The squeeze-type musical mechanism found in this bear was one favoured by British manufacturers such as Chiltern and Chad Valley from the mid-1920s to the early 1930s, when it was superseded by the key-wound, clockwork variety.

Height: 55cm (22in)

Embroidered label

Trademark: *the celluloid button in the left ear has the wording: "Chad Valley British Hygienic Toys".*

Eyes: *the large eyes are made of glass.*

Nose: *the triangular nose is typical of the period.*

Muzzle: *the protruding, shaved muzzle is stuffed with wood-wool.*

Fur/stuffing/musical mechanism: *the curly, blue mohair plush is badly worn in places, especially in the centre of the chest above the squeeze-type musical mechanism. The body and limbs are stuffed with a mixture of wood-wool and kapok.*

Pads: *the light brown, felt pads were originally reinforced with card; (now missing from the right foot-pad).*

Label: *the red and white label is sewn onto the left foot-pad.*

BEAR PROFILE
The side view illustrates the larger feet, fatter thighs, and shorter arms of the British teddy bear compared to German bears, as well as clearly showing the protruding, shaven muzzle.

amber and black, glass eyes may be replacements

large, cupped ears

shaved muzzle, stuffed with wood-wool

black, vertically stitched nose with two horizontal stitches across top

original golden-coloured artificial silk, now dirty

original golden, felt foot-pads repaired with woven fabric

paw-pads repaired with beige kid leather; three claws on left paw

five claws on each foot

c.1930 GOLDEN ARTIFICIAL SILK
Height: 33cm (13in)

The main British manufacturers began making artificial-silk plush teddy bears in 1929. Chad Valley used a variety of colours, usually with felt pads in a matching colour. Originally this bear was a pale golden colour, but it is now discoloured.

Embroidered label

amber and black, glass eyes

small ears sewn across facial seams

original pink, vertically stitched nose with horizontal stitch across top

shaved muzzle

soft, short-pile alpaca plush in cream and brown

short arms with replacement beige, felt pads

brown, artificial-silk pompoms on central seam

fully jointed limbs

c.1945 CLOWN BEAR
Height: 28cm (11in)

This soft alpaca plush teddy bear was illustrated on the front cover of a toy-trade journal in 1945. It is stuffed with kapok, except for the muzzle, which is stuffed with wood-wool. There is a red and white, embroidered label on each foot-pad.

Embroidered label

black, horizontally stitched nose with inverted-Y-shaped mouth

tiny, glass eyes with brown-painted backs; sewn in with knot at back of head

dark brown, felt ears

beige, alpaca plush

fully jointed limbs; head unjointed

flattened, shaved muzzle

dark brown, felt foot-pads

blue, felt jacket and yellow, felt waistcoat

c.1938 THREE BEARS
Height: 10cm (4in)/baby 7cm (3in)

These three little bears, a mother, father, and baby, were advertised in a 1938 catalogue as the "Bears' Tea Party", complete with a wooden table and three chairs. Baby Bear holds a handkerchief to his eyes, crying as in the story of The Three Bears.

Embroidered label

small, flat ears sewn across facial seams

fully jointed head and limbs

small, amber and black, glass eyes, sewn in at back

white sheepskin; soft stuffed apart from head, which is quite solid

black, vertically stitched, oblong nose

long legs with well-defined feet

black, leather pads

1940s WHITE SHEEPSKIN
Height: 28cm (11in)

This bear was probably made during the war years when mohair plush was difficult to purchase. As is traditional with sheepskin teddies, it has black, leather pads. The blue label of the 1940s–50s period is sewn to the inside of the right leg.

Printed label

Merrythought Magic

BRITAIN'S OLDEST FAMILY-OWNED, SOFT-TOY COMPANY

In 1919, W.G. Holmes and G.H. Laxton opened a small spinning mill in Yorkshire to weave yarns from raw mohair imported from countries such as Turkey and South Africa. During the 1920s, the partnership bought Dyson Hall and Co. Ltd., a mohair-plush weaving factory in Huddersfield. Seeking an outlet for their plush fabric, they decided to establish a soft-toy factory: Merrythought Ltd. was founded in 1930. The following year they leased one of the buildings belonging to the Coalbrookdale Co. in Ironbridge, Shropshire, on the banks of the River Severn.

1989 CHEST-TAG

Once known as "Little Switzerland", with hamlets nestling on the banks of the River Severn, the area around Ironbridge is also referred to as the "cradle of the Industrial Revolution" as it was here, in 1709, that Abraham Darby first smelted iron ore with coke. The first iron bridge, built in 1779 by Abraham Darby III, is about one kilometre (half a mile) away from the Merrythought factory, and its shape is echoed in the design of the word

the pre-World War II bears. C.J. Rendle, a former Chad Valley manager, was hired to take charge of production. The company also employed H.C. Janisch, a sales manager at J.K. Farnell, to run the sales operation at the company's London showroom at 113 Holborn. With 20 workers, Rendle began manufacturing in temporary premises in September 1930, moving into the permanent factory in February 1931. The area had excellent transport facilities, with the two main railway lines a short distance away.

Main factory
The main factory at Ironbridge, built in 1898, is guarded by two life-size "London Bears". Merrythought leased the factory in 1931–56 then bought it. The gates carry the word "Merrythought".

A GROWING BUSINESS
In early 1931 the company rented larger factory space from the iron foundry, the main workshop then measuring 40x16m (135x52ft). It also employed more people: by 1932, numbers had risen to nearly 200. An article in a trade magazine of the same year reported that Merrythought possessed an ideal work space for toy production, describing the factory as being extremely light, unobstructed by pillars or columns, with two rows of roof lights on each side of the pitch of the roof, and large windows along one wall. At one end there were benches of power-driven sewing-machines, operated by a large, light-oil engine; by the end of 1932, electric motors were installed, with a special feed line run by West Midlands Electrical Commission. Outside, there were sheds for the storage of packing

1932 Factory floor
In the 1930s, the workers and the supervisors (centre left, standing) wore neat uniforms. The work area (above) is still used today for soft-toy production.

"Merrythought" on the company's labels. The reasoning behind the "Merrythought" name is now unknown, although it is derived from the old English word for wishbone, the forked bone in birds that is traditionally a symbol of good luck. It was registered as the company's trademark in 1930 and illustrated on buttons marking

Traditional methods
An employee hand-sews the nose of a 60th anniversary bear; two modern "M" bears sit in the background. Much of the work is still done traditionally.

Early catalogues
Catalogues from the Merrythought archives.

1931 catalogue
An illustration of the early Magnet and Merrythought lines.

PRE-WORLD WAR II, EMBROIDERED, WOVEN LABEL

C.1945–C.1956, PRINTED, WOVEN LABEL

C.1957–91, PRINTED, WOVEN LABEL

1992–PRESENT, EMBROIDERED, WOVEN LABEL

1931 BINGIE

cases and crates, bales of wood-wool, and huge sacks of kapok.

Manufacture began with cutting out the plush, followed by sewing the pieces together; the bears were then stuffed, assembled, and finished off (adding features and ribbons, etc.). The bears were then packed in boxes and sent to the stock rooms.

Florence Atwood, the chief designer employed from 1930 until her death in 1949, was deaf and had learned her trade at the Deaf and Dumb School in Manchester. She created bears from her own designs and also transformed the work of other artists, such as Lawson Wood's caricatured orang utan, Gran'pop. She designed Merrythought's first panda bear, following the panda cub Ming's arrival at London Zoo in 1939.

By 1935, the company had acquired 3,865 square metres (41,600 square feet) of work space, making it the largest soft-toy factory in the United Kingdom.

WORLD WAR II

During World War II, the British Admiralty and the Ministry of Aircraft Production took over the Merrythought factory to produce maps and to store plywood. Merrythought continued to manufacture a few toys at temporary premises in near-by Wellington, however, later undertaking Government contracts for the production of gaberdine and velour items. Toy production was reinstated at Ironbridge in 1946, although flooding of the Severn that year destroyed all pre-war samples and much of the company's supplies.

Following C.J. Rendle's death in April 1949, B.T. (Trayton) Holmes, son of the founder, W.G. Holmes, joined the company. In 1952, he employed Jimmy Matthews, now Sales Director, to boost sales after the lean post-war years. The following year, the designer Jean Barber joined the company and in October 1955 she

created the popular Cheeky (*see pp.120–21*). Barber was succeeded by various designers after 1965; Jackie Harper took over from 1967–69. The post-war era saw the introduction of new, synthetic fabrics, such as nylon and Dralon, many coming from East Asia. The company also acquired new machinery: in 1955, a stuffing machine using compressed air was introduced from the US, and hydraulic press cutters were later installed.

The 1970s saw major changes in personnel. In 1970, Jacqueline Revitt, now the Design Director, joined the company; the present Managing Director, Oliver Holmes, Trayton's son, joined two years later.

LIMITED EDITIONS AND REPLICAS

In 1982, the company introduced a traditional range of limited-edition mohair teddy bears for import by Tide-Rider Inc. of New York. In 1986, Merrythought provided a giant bear, ordered by H.R.H. Prince Edward, to ride in a royal coach at his brother Prince Andrew's wedding. Also in 1986, the publication of John Axe's history, *The Magic of Merrythought*, inspired the manufacture of the first replica – the Magnet bear (*see p.161*) – followed by Bingie (*see p.68*), Mr Whoppit (*see p.121*), and a reproduction of the Bing bear "Gatti" (*see p.193*).

In 1988, Merrythought opened a shop and museum next to the factory, run by the Ironbridge Gorge Museum Trust. In 1992, the company's high quality workmanship was acknowledged with a TOBY award for its character bear Master Mischief.

Diamond jubilee
Merrythought launched a limited edition of 2,500 bears for its 60th anniversary in June 1990.

1984 catalogue
This features the Champagne Luxury Bear (see p.135).

Limited editions
Since the 1980s, the company has turned its attention to the collectors' market, introducing special commissions and replicas. This unique greenish blue, pure mohair-plush bear was made in 1983. Its foot is signed by Chairman, Trayton Holmes.

Merrythought: 1930s

BINGIE FAMILY SERIES AND OTHER PRE-WAR NOVELTIES

Soon after its foundation, Merrythought began making novelty teddy bears. The company made several soft alpaca bear-cub ranges ideal for young children, such as the very early Tumpy, and the later Chubby Bear of the mid-1930s; both are reminiscent of Chad Valley's Cubby Bear (*see p.105*).

Bobby Bruin (*opposite*) and Teddy Doofings were a new departure. The latter, available in brown, blue, pink, and green plush, with sleeping eyes, was Mickey-Mouse-like and fully "poseable". The Bingie family – introduced at the firm's outset, and available throughout the 1930s – was especially popular.

1931 BINGIE

Part of a family of novelty teddies made from 1931–38, Bingie represents a sitting bear cub with soft kapok filling and unjointed legs. It was made in seven sizes, with two extra-small sizes for babies, known as Baby Bingie. This bear possesses a rare example of Merrythought's earliest label, used only in the first year of production, omitting the words "Hygienic Toys".

Height: 35cm (14in)

Embroidered label

Ears: *the ears are lined with white, artificial-silk plush.*

Eyes: *the large, amber, glass eyes are positioned low on the face.*

Arms: *the short, stocky arms end in rust-coloured, felt pads with brown, double-stitched claws over the plush and pads.*

Legs: *the short, stocky, unjointed legs are designed so that the bear adopts a sitting position.*

Feet: *the feet are particularly long and large. The rust-coloured, felt pads are wider at the heels and toes, with four claws, double-stitched in brown thread to match the nose and mouth.*

Fur: *the brown-tipped, cream, shaggy mohair plush is now worn in places. Bingie is stuffed with kapok, and with fine wood-wool in the feet.*

Trademark: *the woven label is attached to the inside of the left foot.*

BEAR PROFILE
From this angle you can see the pronounced muzzle, which is constructed from a separate piece of clipped plush. The large head, rounded back, and huge feet are all features reminiscent of a real bear cub.

bulbous, dark brownish black eyes

ears placed wide apart on sides of head

unusual bend at elbow

unusual, round, felt paws, machine-stitched onto arms

very stiff, card-reinforced foot-pads, allowing bear to stand up; internal metal rods end in rings around outer edges of feet

legs cut all-in-one with body

woven label stitched to left foot-pad

1936 BOBBY BRUIN

Height: 65cm (26in)

Said to be "designed from nature", according to a 1936 catalogue, this large bear had patent "movie" joints – thin, metal rods in his legs to enable him to pose in various positions. He was available in three sizes, of which this was the largest.

Embroidered label

ears lined with artificial-silk plush

black, mohair-plush busby

dropped outer stitches on nose – a Merrythought design feature

celluloid button in left ear

red, felt jacket, now faded and worn

three, brown claws across pads and plush

faded, cinnamon-coloured, tipped mohair plush on head, paws, and fronts of arms

worn, knitted socks, without toes; original shoes missing

black, felt trousers

c.1933–38 BINGIE GUARDSMAN

Height: 50cm (20in)

Bingie, dressed in a Grenadier Guardsman's uniform, was first introduced in 1933. The original, cinnamon-tipped mohair plush has faded to a dirty white. The parts of the body under the clothes are made of flesh-coloured brushed cotton.

MERRYTHOUGHT HYGIENIC TOYS MADE IN ENGLAND

Embroidered label

only the head is jointed

flat ears

amber and black, glass eyes

brown, vertically stitched nose with inverted-Y-shaped mouth

pale pink, corduroy trousers, now discoloured with age

beige mohair plush; kapok stuffing in body and limbs, and wood-wool elsewhere

card-reinforced feet with three claws over plush and pads

cream, tear-shaped paw-pads, machine stitched around edge

1938 DUTCH TEDDY

Height: 30cm (12in)

Merrythought introduced eight sizes of Dutch Teddy in 1938, all wearing wide, Dutch-style, all-in-one trousers with patch pockets. Dutch motifs were particularly popular in toys, games, and childhood ephemera during the 1930s.

MERRYTHOUGHT HYGIENIC TOYS MADE IN ENGLAND

Embroidered label

inset muzzle, similar to those of Bingie and the guardsman

slightly bulbous, brown, glass eyes

typical Merrythought nose with dropped outer stitches

flesh-coloured, brushed-cotton body and limbs

three claws on pads

stiffened foot-pads, with woven trademark stitched in place

1931 BARE BINGIES

Height: 38/50cm (15/20in)

The dressed Bingie family series was introduced in 1933 and included a girl, a boy, a sailor, a guardsman, a Highlander, and a ski girl. These two bears show the flesh-coloured, brushed-cotton bodies and limbs found beneath the clothes.

MADE IN ENGLAND BY MERRYTHOUGHT LTD.

Embroidered label

UK: 1930s–50s

MINOR BRITISH COMPANIES; UNMARKED, LOWER QUALITY EXAMPLES

S everal minor soft-toy manufacturers were in operation in the UK during the 1930s, many founded during World War I, but later forced into liquidation during the lean years of the late 1930s to the early 1950s. For example, W.H. Jones, a pioneering British soft-toy manufacturer, established in 1914, went into liquidation in 1937. The Teddy Toy Company, also established at the outbreak of World War I, became famous for its Softanlite teddies of the 1920s and 1930s, but eventually wound up business in 1951. Many manufacturers did not attach permanent trademarks, making identification difficult.

1930s PEACOCK & CO. LTD.

Several teddy bears with the Peacock trademark have come to light, all dating from around the 1930s; they have horizontally stitched noses similar to those of Chad Valley's Magna Series bears. Chad Valley bought Peacock & Co. in 1931, and we now know that this well-established manufacturer produced a range of bears with the new label.

Height: 68cm (27in)

Embroidered label

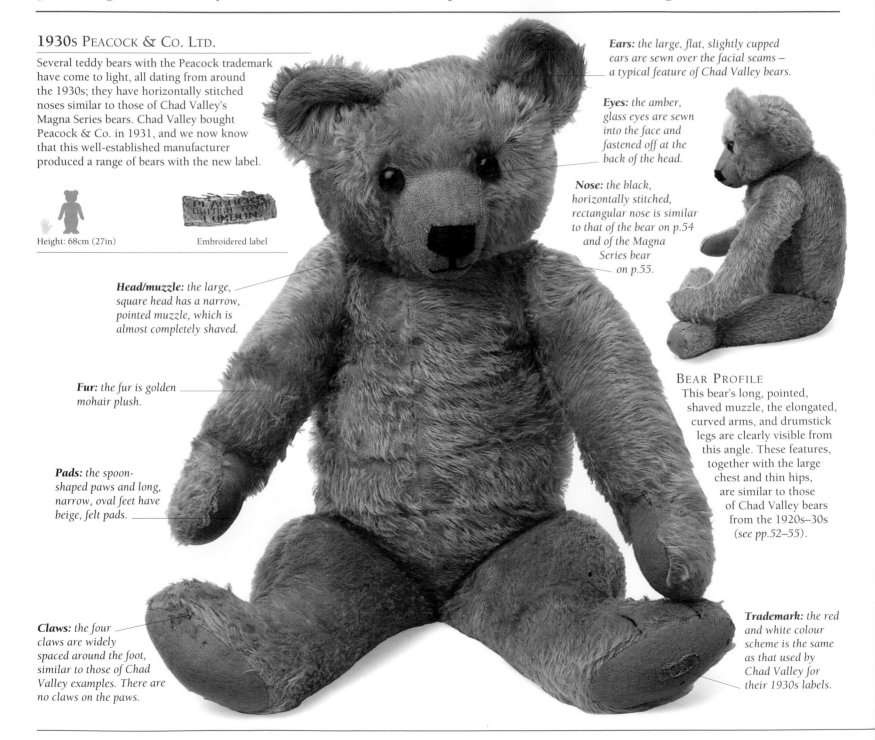

Ears: *the large, flat, slightly cupped ears are sewn over the facial seams – a typical feature of Chad Valley bears.*

Eyes: *the amber, glass eyes are sewn into the face and fastened off at the back of the head.*

Nose: *the black, horizontally stitched, rectangular nose is similar to that of the bear on p.54 and of the Magna Series bear on p.55.*

Head/muzzle: *the large, square head has a narrow, pointed muzzle, which is almost completely shaved.*

Fur: *the fur is golden mohair plush.*

Pads: *the spoon-shaped paws and long, narrow, oval feet have beige, felt pads.*

Claws: *the four claws are widely spaced around the foot, similar to those of Chad Valley examples. There are no claws on the paws.*

BEAR PROFILE

This bear's long, pointed, shaved muzzle, the elongated, curved arms, and drumstick legs are clearly visible from this angle. These features, together with the large chest and thin hips, are similar to those of Chad Valley bears from the 1920s–30s (see pp.52–55).

Trademark: *the red and white colour scheme is the same as that used by Chad Valley for their 1930s labels.*

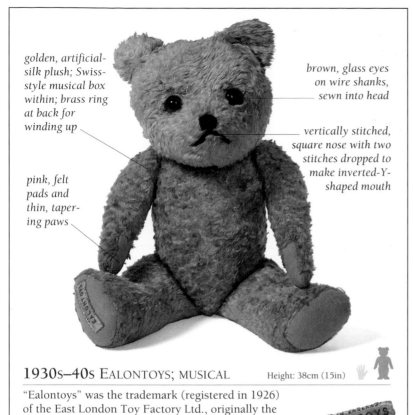

golden, artificial-silk plush; Swiss-style musical box within; brass ring at back for winding up

brown, glass eyes on wire shanks, sewn into head

vertically stitched, square nose with two stitches dropped to make inverted-Y-shaped mouth

pink, felt pads and thin, tapering paws

1930s–40s EALONTOYS; MUSICAL   Height: 38cm (15in)

"Ealontoys" was the trademark (registered in 1926) of the East London Toy Factory Ltd., originally the East London Federation Toy Factory, established in 1914 by Sylvia Pankhurst. Its other novelties included a teddy-bear hot-water-bottle cover.

Printed label

square, vertically stitched nose and long, inverted-V-shaped mouth, both features of Ealontoys bears

small, brown, glass eyes with black pupils sewn into face on wire shanks

shaggy, golden mohair plush

nightshirt not original

pointed paws; no pads

pink, felt pads on feet

c.1940s EALONTOYS; MOHAIR   Height: 30cm (12in)

In 1948 the East London Toy Factory Ltd. changed its name to Ealontoys Ltd., but still operated from the same premises. A 1950 advertisement described the company as "The Teddy Bear People" but, sadly, they went out of business in the early 1950s.

Printed label

black, vertically stitched, long, slender nose; mouth indicated by curved line

brown, glass eyes with black pupils, set low down

low-grade, blue artificial-silk plush; wood-wool stuffing throughout

light brown Rexine pads, slightly cracked to reveal woven fabric beneath; no claws

short, stumpy arms

short, stocky feet

LATE 1930s ARTIFICIAL SILK   Height: 70cm (28in)

This teddy bear is typical of the many cheap bears manufactured in Britain and sold in chain stores from the 1930s. It was made from cheap-quality, artificial-silk plush with Rexine pads. This design – with its large head and jutting-out chin – carried on into the 1950s, making such teddy bears difficult to date precisely. Blue was a popular colour at this time.

short, golden orange mohair plush; wood-wool stuffing in head and around squeaker, with kapok elsewhere

amber, glass eyes with black pupils, sewn into face on wire shanks

relatively straight arms and legs, similar to those of Magna Series bears

woven fabric pads, similar to those used on Magna Series bears

three long, black claws on feet

1930s PEACOCK; ALTERNATIVE LABEL   Height: 53cm (21in)

This bear, made by Chad Valley for Peacock & Co., is reminiscent of the Magna Series bear on p.55. The label features Peacock's original trademark – an open-tailed peacock. The significance of the word "Stores" is unknown.

Embroidered label

Dean's: 1920s–50s

DEVELOPMENT OF TRADITIONAL BRITISH BEAR; TWO FACTORY MOVES

Dean's produced their first catalogued teddy bears at their Elephant and Castle factory in London in 1915, although the company may have been making bears for other firms prior to this. By 1922–23 Dean's had registered its tradename "A1 Toys", observed in catalogues as triangular, card swing-tags. The bears came in three grades of plush, stuffed with wood-wool, and with either a squeaker or growler. From 1937–55 Dean's teddies were made at the new, purpose-built factory at Merton, Surrey, but few were produced during World War II, when the factory concentrated on producing war materials.

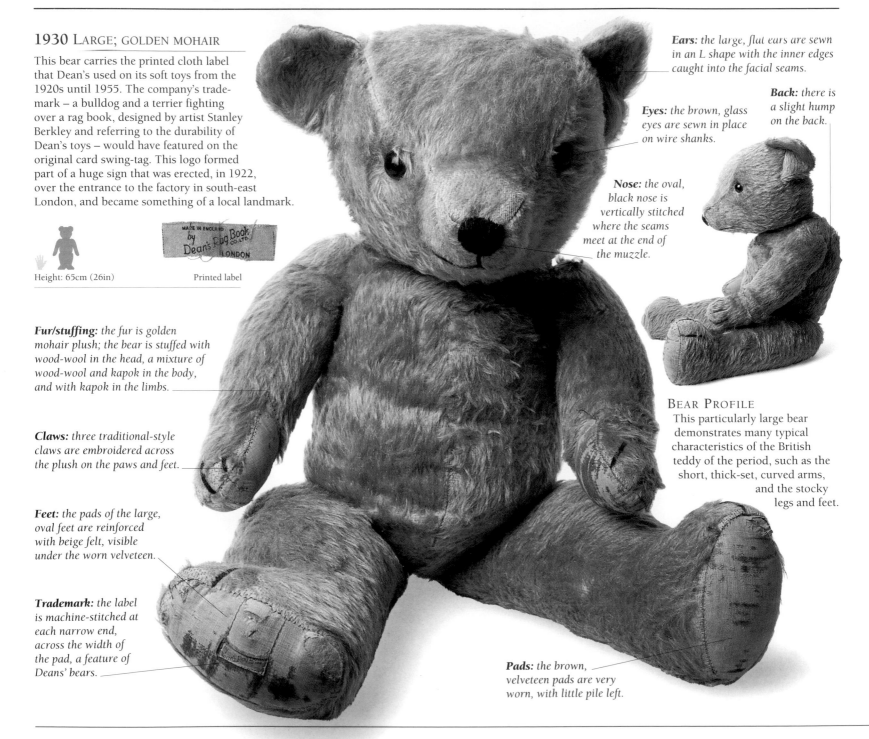

1930 LARGE; GOLDEN MOHAIR

This bear carries the printed cloth label that Dean's used on its soft toys from the 1920s until 1955. The company's trademark – a bulldog and a terrier fighting over a rag book, designed by artist Stanley Berkley and referring to the durability of Dean's toys – would have featured on the original card swing-tag. This logo formed part of a huge sign that was erected, in 1922, over the entrance to the factory in south-east London, and became something of a local landmark.

Height: 65cm (26in)   Printed label

Ears: *the large, flat ears are sewn in an L shape with the inner edges caught into the facial seams.*

Back: *there is a slight hump on the back.*

Eyes: *the brown, glass eyes are sewn in place on wire shanks.*

Nose: *the oval, black nose is vertically stitched where the seams meet at the end of the muzzle.*

Fur/stuffing: *the fur is golden mohair plush; the bear is stuffed with wood-wool in the head, a mixture of wood-wool and kapok in the body, and with kapok in the limbs.*

Claws: *three traditional-style claws are embroidered across the plush on the paws and feet.*

Feet: *the pads of the large, oval feet are reinforced with beige felt, visible under the worn velveteen.*

Trademark: *the label is machine-stitched at each narrow end, across the width of the pad, a feature of Deans' bears.*

BEAR PROFILE
This particularly large bear demonstrates many typical characteristics of the British teddy of the period, such as the short, thick-set, curved arms, and the stocky legs and feet.

Pads: *the brown, velveteen pads are very worn, with little pile left.*

brown, plastic eyes with black pupils, sewn into face and finished off at back of head; may be replacements

flat ears, sewn in L shape, with inner edges caught into facial seams

black, oblong, vertically stitched nose, with inverted-T-shaped mouth

attractive, golden mohair plush; backing slightly darker than pile

pink, felt pads; other pink fabric used to repair paws

three black claws across plush

label stitched to pad at narrow ends

1930s MOHAIR; WOOD-WOOL STUFFING   Height: 40cm (16in)

The bear's shape and wood-wool stuffing indicate pre-World War II origins. By 1931, artificial-silk plush was preferred by Dean's; there was no mohair in the 1935 range, but gold, pink, and blue mohair plush was reintroduced in 1936.

Printed label

ears placed towards back of head; inner edges sewn into facial seam

expansive forehead with plastic eyes placed wide apart, set into facial seams

only one vertical, black stitch remains of original mouth

golden mohair plush; soft-stuffed, except for wood-wool around tilt-growler

remains of black, embroidered claws on paws and feet

well worn, dark brown, velveteen pads

long, narrow feet and paws

MID-1950s PLASTIC EYES   Height: 44cm (17½in)

The sewn-in plastic eyes (fastened off at the back of the head with a horizontal stitch) confirm this bear's age. The dark stain on the muzzle-tip suggests that the bear may originally have had a typical Dean's, sewn-on, moulded rubber nose.

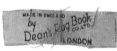

Printed label

large ears with inner edges caught into facial seams

brown and black, plastic eyes, with integral short shank, sewn into face

very worn, golden mohair plush

small, square, vertically stitched nose; inverted-Y-shaped mouth with left half missing

short, curved arms with pointed paws

three black claws remain on right foot

cotton-waste stuffing evident

pink, felt pads, repaired by darning

MID-1950s "SUB" STUFFING   Height: 35cm (14in)

This bear is almost bald and is bursting at the seams, so you can see clearly the cotton-waste stuffing. Known in the industry as "sub" (substitute), it was an alternative to kapok, which was in short supply in the post-war years.

Printed label

sewn-in, clear, glass eyes with black pupils are probably replacements

cupped ears, set over facial seams

shaggy golden mohair plush, bald in places

unusual black, shield-shaped, vertically stitched nose in V shape, meets inverted-V-shaped mouth

long, slender body with arms set low down

replacement brown, woven fabric pads; reinforced with card

five black claws on paws and feet

long, narrow feet

EARLY 1920s GOLDEN MOHAIR   Height: 37cm (14½in)

Although much repair work has been carried out on this bear's essential features, its slender shape and wood-wool filling match illustrations of early A1 bears. The pads are replacements, but the label is from the original pad.

Printed label

Knickerbocker: 1920–30s

TRADITIONAL MOHAIR PLUSH; POINTED MUZZLE DESIGN

The Knickerbocker Toy Company was first established in Albany, New York during the mid-nineteenth century, producing typical educational toys of the period, such as lithographed alphabet blocks. The unusual name "Knickerbocker" was derived from the traditional nickname for New York inhabitants, a reference to the original Dutch settlers' baggy breeches. A 1980 Knickerbocker label states that the company had been making soft toys for more than half a century. Certainly today the earliest bears attributable to Knickerbocker date from the 1920s when permanent labels were introduced.

c.1935–36 CINNAMON MOHAIR

Although not in possession of a trademark, this bear demonstrates many characteristics typical of American bears; it also resembles other Knickerbocker bears of the period. It can be accurately dated, as it is known to have been one of two identical bears belonging to twin boys; the other bear is still in existence, but has unfortunately lost its eyes. The crayoned "L" on the foot-pads helped the brothers to identify their teddies.

Height: 45cm (18in)

Nose: the narrow, rectangular nose is vertically stitched in black thread across the muzzle seam.

Paws: the paws are long, curved, and tapering.

Fur/stuffing/squeaker: the mohair plush is a rich, cinnamon colour, much favoured by US manufacturers. The bear is soft-stuffed throughout. There is an internal squeaker.

Pads: the discoloured pads are made of tan velveteen, a fabric typically used by Knickerbocker.

Feet: the large, oval feet are slightly pointed, with no claws.

Ears: the large, slightly cupped ears are typical of those of Knickerbocker bears in size and shape.

Eyes: the translucent, amber, glass eyes, with black pupils, are sewn in on wire shanks.

Mouth: the black, inverted-V-shaped mouth is almost entirely worn away.

BEAR PROFILE

From the side, you can see clearly the shape of the head, with its shaved, elongated, but blunt muzzle. Although the curved, tapering arms and large feet, with narrow ankles, follow the traditional teddy-bear design, the thin, straight body and lack of hump is typical of American bears of the interwar period.

large, rounded, cupped ears, sewn across facial seams

broad, Knickerbocker head; pointed muzzle, with fur slightly worn at tip

black, vertically stitched, narrow, oval nose (typical Knickerbocker shape)

translucent, amber, glass eyes with black pupils, set wide apart

low-set shoulders (typical Knickerbocker feature)

silky, shaggy, cinnamon-coloured mohair plush; kapok stuffing in body and limbs; wood-wool in head; internal squeaker

long paws

large, oval feet; replacement felt pads

1933 CINNAMON MOHAIR
Height: 55cm (22in)

This teddy was given to its present owner for Christmas 1933 and was later a favourite toy of her son, until attacked by an English setter who chewed the nose and removed the head! Thanks to early photographs, it was possible to restore the bear to almost its original state. The owner recalls that a white label was removed from the centre front body-seam.

translucent, amber, glass eyes with black pupils, sewn in on wire shanks

cupped ears; slightly smaller than usual Knickerbocker ears

long, oval, black, vertically stitched nose; inverted-Y-shaped mouth

long, silky, white mohair plush; wood-wool stuffing in head; kapok elsewhere

inset, clipped muzzle

paws curve upwards from wrist, and widen slightly

white, velveteen pads; no claws

long, oval feet

LATE 1930s INSET MUZZLE; MUSICAL
Height: 35cm (14in)

This bear has a slightly pointed muzzle, like those of the other bears illustrated here, but it is cut from a separate piece of slightly clipped plush – a typical Knickerbocker design feature that is believed to have been introduced by the late 1930s. The internal musical box, wound up by a key in the lower back, plays the waltz from *The Merry Widow*.

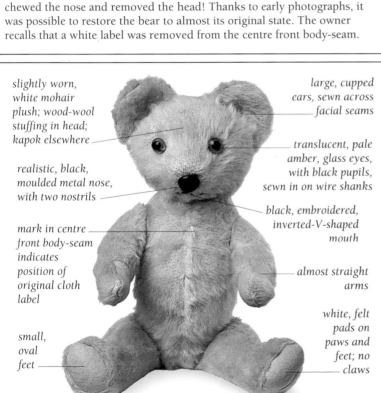

slightly worn, white mohair plush; wood-wool stuffing in head; kapok elsewhere

large, cupped ears, sewn across facial seams

realistic, black, moulded metal nose, with two nostrils

translucent, pale amber, glass eyes, with black pupils, sewn in on wire shanks

mark in centre front body-seam indicates position of original cloth label

black, embroidered, inverted-V-shaped mouth

almost straight arms

white, felt pads on paws and feet; no claws

small, oval feet

LATE 1920s WHITE; METAL NOSE
Height: 30cm (12in)

Although unmarked, this bear demonstrates several typical Knickerbocker features of the period: a flat face; a straight, slender back; ears positioned straight across the head; and arms set low. It also possesses an unusual, moulded metal nose, heavier than tin, and possibly with some iron content, judging by the rust stains around the muzzle.

translucent, brown, glass eyes with black pupils, sewn in on wire shanks

head and limbs jointed, possibly with hardboard

shaggy mohair plush, worn or clipped on muzzle; wood-wool stuffing in head; kapok elsewhere

rectangular, black, vertically stitched nose; black, inverted-Y-shaped mouth

long, curved, tapering arms; shoulders set low down

stiff button-up collar not original

long paws

tan, felt pads; no claws

large, oval feet

c.1930 DARK BROWN; LARGE EARS
Height: 50cm (20in)

This bear, made of rich, dark brown mohair plush, has the typical, broad, triangular head of pre-war Knickerbocker bears, with a pointed muzzle, widely spaced eyes, narrow, rectangular nose, and, most particularly, large, rounded ears sewn across the facial seams. The tan felt pads suggest a slightly earlier date than that of other bears shown with velveteen pads.

Knickerbocker: post-World War II

TRADITIONAL DESIGN WITH INSET MUZZLE, AND NOVELTIES

The post-war, Knickerbocker traditional design was typified by the inset, rounded muzzle of clipped plush, chubby body, and round head with high forehead, although still retaining the large ears seen on some pre-war bears. As well as beginning to use synthetic fabrics at this time, the company also adopted "spangle" eyes – of glass, and later of plastic – as well as felt noses and tongues. Knickerbocker's pre-war "Animals of Distinction" logo was joined by the new registered "Joy of a Toy" trademark in the 1950s. The company regained the license for making "Smokey Bear" from Ideal from the 1960s until the late 1970s.

1940s SHAGGY, WHITE MOHAIR

Many examples of white Knickerbocker bears have been found, suggesting that this was a popular colour. This bear is made of a particularly luxurious, shaggy-pile mohair plush that is still in mint condition, and has a typical shaved, rounded muzzle. The satinized cloth label shows a figure standing inside a lucky horseshoe with the words "Made under sanitary laws", indicating the hygienic nature of the plush and stuffing.

Height: 38cm (15in)

Printed label

Ears: *the large ears are sewn across the facial seams.*

Eyes: *the dark amber, glass eyes, with black pupils, are sewn in on wire shanks.*

Nose/mouth: *the black, oval nose is vertically stitched across the horizontal muzzle seam; the mouth is an inverted Y shape.*

Muzzle: *the inset, rounded, blunt muzzle is made of the same mohair plush as the body, but clipped short to appear bristly.*

Fur/stuffing: *the good quality, white mohair plush is shaggy and slightly curly. The length of pile and the woven backing can be seen on the right ear. The body and limbs are stuffed with kapok and the head with wood-wool.*

Pads: *the white, velveteen pads are in mint condition.*

BEAR PROFILE

From this angle, you can see clearly the typical Knickerbocker shape of this bear's rounded, flattened muzzle. Unlike those of earlier examples, the arms and legs are of similar length; the latter are particularly straight, with little ankle definition. The printed label, placed (unusually for Knickerbocker) under the left arm, is clearly visible.

Feet: *the slightly squared-off, oval feet have no claws.*

large, cupped ears

inset, protruding, rounded muzzle of brown, short-pile mohair plush

slightly curved, tapering arms

tan, velveteen pads

large, squared-off, oval feet; no claws

large, amber, glass eyes with black pupils, set wide apart; sewn in on wire shanks

dark brown, vertically stitched, oval nose; inverted-Y-shaped mouth

shaggy, long-pile, dark brown mohair plush on woven backing

1950s SHAGGY, BROWN MOHAIR   Height: 43cm (17in)

This bear demonstrates many Knickerbocker characteristics, including the large, broad head and the shape and fabric of the pads. The printed label features the company's new "Joy of a Toy" trademark, registered in the 1950s.

Printed label

amber, glass, "spangle" eyes

brown, vertically stitched nose; wide, smiling mouth

dark brown woollen plush; wood-wool stuffing in head; kapok elsewhere

pale golden, velveteen pads

very large ears with golden, velveteen lining

inset, rounded, pale golden, velveteen muzzle

wide, rounded body, with low-set shoulders

curved arms

wide thighs; narrow ankles

large, oval feet

1950s "BAT" EARS; "SPANGLE" EYES   Height: 50cm (20in)

Although this particular bear is unmarked, it possesses several, typical Knickerbocker features, such as the glass "spangle" eyes and "bat" ears – so-called because of their large, flat design. The general shape of the bear, and particularly its expansive, almost oval, head, and the contrasting muzzle, anticipates the company's Teddy Kuddles of the 1960s.

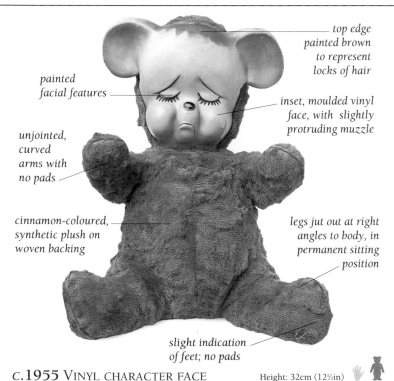

painted facial features

unjointed, curved arms with no pads

cinnamon-coloured, synthetic plush on woven backing

top edge painted brown to represent locks of hair

inset, moulded vinyl face, with slightly protruding muzzle

legs jut out at right angles to body, in permanent sitting position

slight indication of feet; no pads

C.1955 VINYL CHARACTER FACE   Height: 32cm (12½in)

This unusual bear is characteristic of both its era and its country of origin – vinyl-faced bears were being produced by other US companies at this time (see pp.85; 86). Its unjointed body and cinnamon-coloured, synthetic plush are also typical. Only a fragment remains of the original white cloth label, printed in navy-blue, which is sewn into the left side-seam.

good quality, soft, bright golden mohair plush

amber, glass eyes with black pupils

black, vertically stitched nose – rounder than usual Knickerbocker shape

pale golden, velveteen pads with no claws

large, rounded ears; inner edges sewn into facial seams

large, rounded head with expansive forehead

inset, clipped muzzle of same plush as body

narrow, pointed, oval paws

squared-off, oval feet

1940s BRIGHT GOLDEN MOHAIR   Height: 50cm (20in)

This cuddly bear, with its rounded head, inset muzzle, and chubby limbs, is stuffed with kapok. It still has its printed label sewn into the front central seam. The glass eyes may be replacements – the originals are likely to have been larger.

Printed label

Japan: 1945–90s

SYNTHETIC MATERIALS; ROD JOINTING; MECHANICAL BEARS

T he Japanese had produced moulded, bisque and celluloid teddy bears from the 1920s; the post-war era saw Japan leading the technological field (from 1945 to 1950 the "Made in Japan" label changed to "Made in Occupied Japan"). From *c.*1950 to 1970 Japanese manufacturers produced clockwork and battery-operated tin bears. They also made traditional teddies with mechanical devices, such as the Kamar Toy Company's Dear Heart with a battery-operated "beating" heart. In the 1980s, Tokyo's First Corporation described itself as Japan's premier supplier of quality stuffed animals to the world.

1940S KAMAR TOY COMPANY

This bear's distinctive, airbrushed paw design has been attributed to the Kamar Toy Company, although airbrushing was common among other Japanese firms. This bear is typical of those made by Japanese manufacturers at the time, being made of synthetic plush, with "sliced-in" ears, a stiff neck, and rod jointing. Some contained musical boxes, while a unique example from *c.*1960, marked "Jestia/Made in Japan", accommodated a radio, with a tuning dial on the chest.

Height: 70cm (28in)

Ears: *the fabric is gathered at the base and pushed into a hole in the head, in a cheap method known as "sliced-in ears".*

Eyes: *the eyes are clear glass, with orange, painted backs and black pupils.*

Muzzle: *the inset, white, velveteen muzzle is now discoloured with age.*

Nose/mouth: *the design of the nose and mouth is typically Japanese: the nose is vertically stitched in black, cotton thread made up of several strands; the mouth is an inverted Y shape.*

Limbs: *the jointed arms have fat shoulders and taper to small, curved, squared-off paws; the legs and head are also jointed.*

Fur/stuffing: *the fur is white, nylon plush on a woven backing, now discoloured; the bear is stuffed with wood-wool.*

Feet: *the feet are small and rounded.*

BEAR PROFILE

From this angle, you can see this bear's rounded, "drumstick" arms and legs. The hole in the shoulder indicates where the round piece of plush, which disguises the end of the external wire and washer jointing system, has come away. The large left ear, with its internal wire frame missing, has come away slightly from the head opening, revealing some original white plush.

Pads/claws: *the pads are made from yellow, woven velveteen with black, painted claws.*

vertically stitched, narrow, oblong nose, with inverted-V-shaped mouth

large, cloth ears stiffened with wire and pushed into holes at top of head

large, reddish brown glass eyes with black pupils

pink, nylon plush on knitted backing

inset, pale golden, velveteen muzzle

four short claws embroidered in black thread across seam

large feet reinforced with thick card; black, embroidered/airbrushed claws

pale golden, velveteen pads

inset, white, nylon-plush feet

1940s EMBROIDERED/AIRBRUSHED PAWS   Height: 38cm (15in)

Of a similar design to the bear (*opposite*), this example is in near-mint condition, with its original rayon ribbon and bell intact. Black claws are embroidered close together on the narrow paws; the claws are airbrushed onto the foot-pads, and embroidered over the pads and plush. The knitted backing of the nylon plush indicates a post-war date.

small, black, plastic, button eyes

hole for plastic nose

muzzle and fronts of ears in cream, flannel-like fabric

round, red, woven fabric mouth, secured with glue

head, shoulders, arms, and backs of ears in brown-beige nylon plush on knitted backing

glued-on, brown, woven fabric buttons

internal frame of moulded tin, in two sections

tin book printed with coloured pictures of farm animals with names in English

red, woven fabric overalls glued onto body

feet printed to resemble shiny brogues

1950s CLOCKWORK READING BEAR   Height: 16cm (6½in)

This unjointed, standing bear appears to read the book it holds. When wound up with a key in its back, the clockwork mechanism moves the right arm up and down. The magnet under the right hand attracts the metal page, causing it to flip back and forth. This is a simple, inexpensive toy; later Japanese battery-operated tin bears were often more complex.

soft, brown, acrylic plush; soft-stuffed throughout

two pieces of contrasting plush make up ears

large, bulbous, black, safe, plastic eyes

stylized, triangular, dark brown, safe, moulded, plastic nose

unjointed, short, stubby arms; no pads

Japanese wording on swing-tag translates "Merry-go-round Dreams"

short, thick legs with white, acrylic-plush foot-pads

1980s UNJOINTED; SYNTHETIC   Height: 23cm (9in)

This is a typical example of the safe, cuddly, unjointed bears made by Japanese manufacturers from the 1970s to the 1990s. It has locked-in, plastic eyes and nose, and wears a sewn-on outfit of a brown, gingham, short-sleeved shirt with a white collar, and brown, corduroy trousers. A stubby, brown plush tail protrudes from a hole at the back of the trousers.

contrasting plush ears sewn side-by-side on top of large, bulbous head with high forehead

large, black, safe, plastic eyes

inset, protruding, white, vinyl muzzle

stylized, black, safe, moulded, plastic nose

pink, nylon plush on woven backing; stuffed with wood-wool

stiff, unjointed neck; plastic limb joints show on outside of body

short, stubby arms; no pads or claws

1960s PINK NYLON   Height: 29cm (11½in)

This bear, with its expansive forehead, is a later version of the lower-quality, rod-jointed Japanese bears (*above left and opposite*). Made of pink, nylon plush with an inset, white, vinyl muzzle, it has plastic rods that allow the limbs to move up and down – the ends of the rods are visible at the shoulders and thighs. Like the earlier bears, the head is not jointed.

Australia: 1930s–60s

DEVELOPMENT OF AUSTRALIAN-MADE TRADITIONAL BEAR

S everal Australian soft-toy manufacturers were established in the 1930s, but the scarcity of traditional materials limited teddy production during World War II. Sheepskin bears with leather or suede pads and noses date from this period, when the stiff-necked Australian bear (without a neck joint) was developed, saving on card and metal (*see p.11*). Some new companies emerged in the 1950s, such as Parker Toys of Brunswick, Victoria, and Barton Waugh Pty. Ltd. of Hurstville, New South Wales, but by the 1970s, many established firms had gone out of business, unable to compete with cheap imports from East Asia.

c.1960 JAKAS SOFT TOYS

This fully-jointed bear, produced by Jakas, is the precursor of the machine-washable Australian teddy bear. Joe and Marion Stanford, an English couple, first established the Melbourne-based company in 1954. They later manufactured unjointed bears similar in construction to Wendy Boston's in the UK. The printed, satinized label includes the instructions "Wash in Lux", just as Wendy Boston's bears of a similar vintage had recommended the detergent "Persil".

Height: 70cm (28in)   Printed label

JAKAS TOYS

Ears: *the large, flat, slightly cupped ears are sewn across the facial seams.*

Eyes: *the translucent, brown, glass eyes with black pupils are sewn into the plush.*

Nose/mouth: *the square, black nose is vertically stitched; the smiling, single-stitched mouth is an inverted T shape.*

Fur/stuffing: *the fur is a blend of beige wool and synthetic plush on a woven backing; the stuffing is granulated foam-rubber.*

Bow: *the pink satin bow is a later addition.*

Arms: *the arms, short in comparison to the legs, end with slightly curved paws.*

Pads: *the long, clawless pads are made from woven, beige fabric.*

Feet: *the feet are large and stumpy.*

Label: *the satinized label is machine-stitched to the foot-pad.*

BEAR PROFILE

This bear has traditional features with its protruding, blunted muzzle and humped, rounded back. It is fully jointed, in contrast to the later unjointed, flat-faced bears that are more commonly associated with Jakas (see p.136). The long, thin legs have unusually narrow thighs, and the arms are positioned towards the front, accentuating the hump.

Legs: *the legs are thin with narrow thighs.*

brown, glass eyes with black pupils

typical Emil nose with two outer, raised stitches

shiny, Rexine pads, slightly cracked revealing woven backing beneath

golden mohair plush; wood-wool stuffing in head, and kapok elsewhere

LATE 1930s–40s EMIL TOYS

Height: 58cm (23in)

Emil Toys made teddy bears from the 1930s to the 1970s. Although this example possesses no label, it does have the typical black, square nose and shiny, Rexine pads. The white, cloth labels were usually stitched into a seam and had "Emil Toys" written in script, with a bear sitting, clutching the upright of the capital "E", and "Made in Australia" printed in blue.

flat ears sewn across facial seams

amber and black, plastic eyes

golden mohair plush, stuffed with solid, shaped pieces of foam-rubber

black, felt nose and embroidered mouth

fully jointed limbs and head

fawn, vinyl pads in very good condition

1950s VERNA TOYS

Height: 75cm (30in)

This firm was established in Victoria by Eve Barnett in 1941, but after 1948 it made teddy bears under the ownership of Arthur Eaton. Black, felt noses were a particular feature of the bears. Embroidered labels were replaced by printed labels in the 1980s.

Embroidered label

slightly cupped ears with inner edges caught into facial seams

round, moulded, hard rubber nose; black, embroidered, inverted-Y-shaped mouth

sewn-in, brown, glass eyes with black pupils

golden mohair plush; cotton wadding stuffing in body, wood-wool in head; internal musical box

black, Rexine pads, cracked revealing woven backing beneath

typical, pointed Lindee feet

c.1960 LINDEE TOYS

Height: 53cm (21in)

This Sydney-based company manufactured teddy bears from 1944 to 1976. Its white, satinized label, with an outline of a reclining deer and the red print lettering "Lindee Toys" and "Made in Australia" beneath, was usually found in a foot-pad seam. This bear has a hard rubber nose and contains a musical box that plays Brahms' *Lullaby*.

brown, glass eyes with black pupils

vertically stitched, triangular, black nose with inverted-Y-shaped, smiling mouth

well-worn golden mohair plush

swivel-jointed, short arms

cream, vinyl pads

1950s BERLEX TOYS

Height: 55cm (22in)

This Melbourne company produced bears from the 1930s to the 1970s. The bear shown here has a distinctive triangular nose and cream-coloured, vinyl paws, typical of Berlex bears. Labels have either "Berlex", in script, with "Melbourne" beneath and "Made in Australia" on the reverse, or simply "Berlex Melbourne" printed in capital letters.

Character: 1945–83

DEVELOPMENT OF TRADITIONAL AND UNJOINTED DESIGN BEARS

Two New Yorkers, Caesar Mangiapani and Jack Levy, established the Character Novelty Co. in 1932, at 14 South Main Street, Norwalk, Connecticut. The business really began to develop after World War II, when it started to produce a wide range of soft toy animals, including teddy bears. The toys were designed by Caesar Mangiapani, and his partner managed the sales side of the business. The company sold to all the major department stores, including Bloomingdales, and had a showroom in New York. Jack Levy retired in about 1960, but the business continued until 1983, when Caesar Mangiapani died.

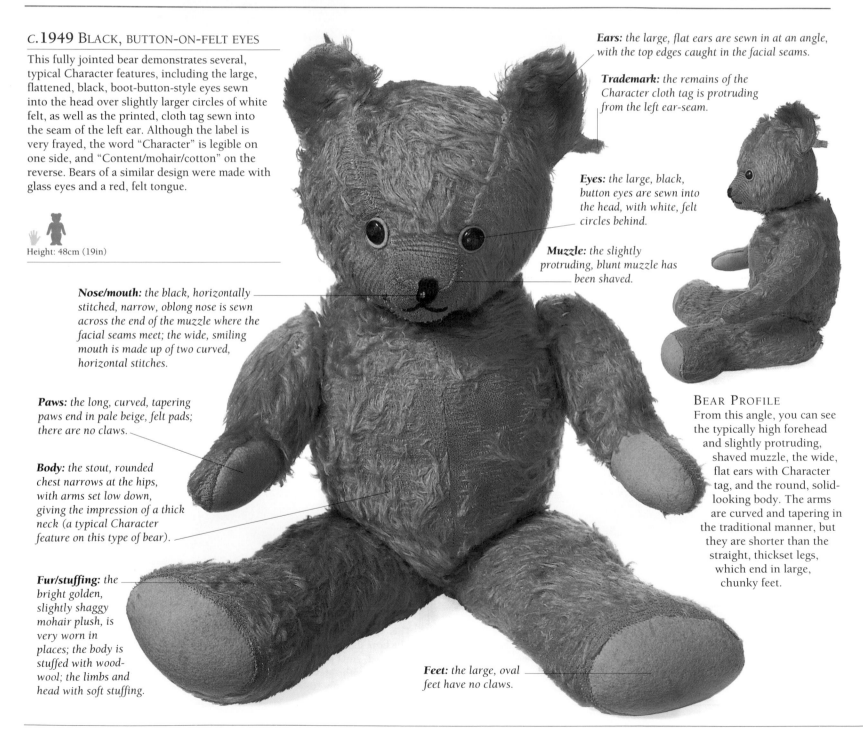

c.1949 BLACK, BUTTON-ON-FELT EYES

This fully jointed bear demonstrates several, typical Character features, including the large, flattened, black, boot-button-style eyes sewn into the head over slightly larger circles of white felt, as well as the printed, cloth tag sewn into the seam of the left ear. Although the label is very frayed, the word "Character" is legible on one side, and "Content/mohair/cotton" on the reverse. Bears of a similar design were made with glass eyes and a red, felt tongue.

Height: 48cm (19in)

Ears: *the large, flat ears are sewn in at an angle, with the top edges caught in the facial seams.*

Trademark: *the remains of the Character cloth tag is protruding from the left ear-seam.*

Eyes: *the large, black, button eyes are sewn into the head, with white, felt circles behind.*

Muzzle: *the slightly protruding, blunt muzzle has been shaved.*

Nose/mouth: *the black, horizontally stitched, narrow, oblong nose is sewn across the end of the muzzle where the facial seams meet; the wide, smiling mouth is made up of two curved, horizontal stitches.*

Paws: *the long, curved, tapering paws end in pale beige, felt pads; there are no claws.*

Body: *the stout, rounded chest narrows at the hips, with arms set low down, giving the impression of a thick neck (a typical Character feature on this type of bear).*

Fur/stuffing: *the bright golden, slightly shaggy mohair plush, is very worn in places; the body is stuffed with wood-wool; the limbs and head with soft stuffing.*

Feet: *the large, oval feet have no claws.*

BEAR PROFILE

From this angle, you can see the typically high forehead and slightly protruding, shaved muzzle, the wide, flat ears with Character tag, and the round, solid-looking body. The arms are curved and tapering in the traditional manner, but they are shorter than the straight, thickset legs, which end in large, chunky feet.

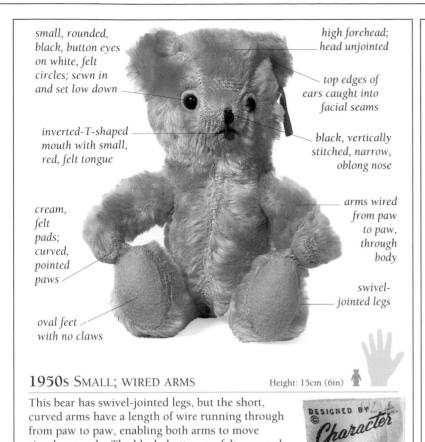

small, rounded, black, button eyes on white, felt circles; sewn in and set low down

high forehead; head unjointed

top edges of ears caught into facial seams

inverted-T-shaped mouth with small, red, felt tongue

black, vertically stitched, narrow, oblong nose

cream, felt pads; curved, pointed paws

arms wired from paw to paw, through body

oval feet with no claws

swivel-jointed legs

1950s SMALL; WIRED ARMS

Height: 15cm (6in)

This bear has swivel-jointed legs, but the short, curved arms have a length of wire running through from paw to paw, enabling both arms to move simultaneously. The black, button-on-felt eyes and the red tongue are both typical Character features.

DESIGNED BY Character

Printed label

large, round head with flattened muzzle and extensive forehead

large, flat ears; back section made of body plush; lined with rust-brown felt

round, red, felt tongue

triangular, black, felt nose

unjointed, square body

long, curly, brown nylon plush with white flecks

short, stubby limbs with rounded ends; no pads or claws

c.1960–70 NYLON

Height: 48cm (19in)

The safe, plastic eyes, nylon plush, and synthetic foam stuffing of this unjointed bear indicate a probable 1960–70 date. The large, orange and black, spangle-effect eyes were also used by rivals, Knickerbocker, at the same time.

DESIGNED BY Character

Printed label

typically high, extensive forehead with eyes set low down towards beginning of pointed muzzle

large ears, with inner edge caught into facial seam

folded, printed, cloth ear-tag sewn into left ear-seam

white, mohair plush; soft stuffing

three long, black claws across plush and felt

pale peach, felt pads

c.1955–60 WHITE MOHAIR; JOINTED

Height: 43cm (17in)

This fully jointed bear still retains the remnants of its typical Character, red, felt tongue. The clear, glass eyes, with painted backs of brown enamel, are less typical. The ear-tag mentions "rubber contents" – probably a granulated, foam-rubber stuffing.

Printed label

large, flat ears; inner edges caught in facial seams; printed, cloth ear-tag attached to left ear

large, brown eyes with black pupils

narrow, black, vertically stitched nose; inverted-Y-shaped mouth

original yellow, satin bow

square body with short, stubby limbs

pads are made of same plush as body; no claws

LATE 1940–50s TIMME; UNJOINTED

Height: 20cm (8in)

This bear is made of a new fabric, containing some mohair, which was invented for children's toys after World War II, and carries the trademark Timme. The bear is unjointed and floppy, and originally wore a card swing-tag describing the new plush.

CHARACTER NOVELTY CO., INC. So. Norwalk, Conn.

Printed label

Gund: 1930s–60s

TRADITIONAL AND UNJOINTED DESIGNS

German emigrant Adolph Gund established Gund Manufacturing Co. in Norwalk, Connecticut in 1898, moving to New York City in the early 1900s. The firm produced novelties, including soft toys, and added teddy bears in 1906. Jacob Swedlin, a Russian emigré and Adolph Gund's aide,

bought the firm after Gund retired in 1925. He was responsible for the firm's expansion and procured the license to produce Walt Disney characters. Until 1971, the factory was sited in Brooklyn, and the offices in New York City, moving to Edison, New Jersey in 1973. Today, some of Gund's teddies are made in East Asia.

c.1948 TEDDIGUND

This fully jointed, good-quality mohair-plush bear follows the traditional design. The capital "G" on its label mimics a rabbit's head; this label was first used c.1948. After World War II the firm introduced new lines that broke away from traditional design, including unjointed teddies made from modern synthetic materials, such as their 1940s–1950s Dreamies series. These culminated in Gund's revolutionary ultra-soft toys of the 1970s–1980s made of multifilament, modacrylic fibres.

Height: 38cm (15in)

Printed label

Ears: the ears are large and slightly cupped, with their inner edges caught into the facial seams.

Eyes: the amber, glass eyes have black pupils.

Nose/mouth: the black, shield-shaped nose is vertically stitched; the inverted-T-shaped mouth forms a smile.

Muzzle: the inset, protruding muzzle, originally of short-pile mohair plush, is now very worn, revealing the discoloured, white, woven backing.

Fur: the golden mohair plush is in very good condition.

Stuffing: the kapok stuffing is visible through the worn foot-pads.

BEAR PROFILE
In profile, you can see all the main characteristics of a traditional teddy bear: the large head; the pointed, clipped, mohair-plush muzzle (now very worn); tapering, curved arms with spoon-shaped paws; relatively long legs with large feet; and a very slightly humped back.

Pads: the white, felt pads are worn, particularly on the feet.

cinnamon- and gold-coloured, rayon plush; foam-rubber stuffing

inset, protruding, vinyl muzzle with moulded grooves representing fur

white, plastic, "joggle" eyes with loose, black, plastic disc in clear, plastic covering

simple, unjointed, short and stubby limbs

round pads of contrasting plush on paws and feet

1952 CUBBIGUND CUDDLE BEAR
Height: 43cm (17in)

The round, contrasting plush pads on the paws and feet make Cubbigund a "four circle" bear. The head and ears are also circular. Other US manufacturers produced similar flat, floppy bears. The vinyl muzzle was introduced in 1952.

Printed label

horizontally stitched, narrow, rectangular, black nose, and inverted-Y-shaped mouth

small, amber glass eyes with black pupils

unjointed arms wired for posing

white, twill fabric hands, with thumbs indicated

removable waistcoat of mustard-coloured leatherette with studded black trim

white, twill fabric legs beneath leatherette "chaps"; kapok stuffing throughout

tartan, cotton fabric shirt; red and white polka-dot kerchief around neck

1940s COWBOY
Height: 30cm (12in)

Cinnamon-coloured, artificial-silk (rayon) plush was popular with US firms from the late 1930s to the 1950s, and is therefore a good indicator of this unmarked bear's origins. Gund produced unjointed, dressed bears and rabbits during this time, with plush heads and bodies formed by the clothes. Paper tags stating "A Gund Animal" exist on similar soft toys.

flat, rounded ears

rounded head

slightly protruding muzzle

composition face with painted features

circular pads with no claws

brown and cream, shaggy, synthetic plush; soft stuffing

"Sitting Bear" printed label

c.1950 SITTING BEAR
Height: 40cm (16in)

This floppy, stylized bear is another "four circle" example (see above), made of contrasting plushes. It has a small tail and an inset, moulded, composition face, a precursor of the vinyl-faced bears popular among US firms in the early 1950s (see pp.75 and 86).

Printed label

rounded ears of black plush

clamped-in, plastic, "joggle" eyes

inset, white, woven fabric muzzle

vertically stitched, square, black nose with inverted-V-shaped mouth

black and white, rayon plush

"four-circle" paw- and foot-pads

1947 JUMBO CUDDLE PANDA
Height: 69cm (27½in)

Su-Lin, the West's first giant panda, arrived in the US in 1936, and was sent to Brookfield Zoo, Chicago, a year later. In 1938, New York Zoo obtained its first panda, Pandora, inspiring many US soft-toy manufacturers to produce panda teddy-bears. Like many panda toys, this example is simply a teddy-bear design manufactured in black and white plush.

Ideal: 1930s–50s

In the years before World War II, Ideal bears differed little from their earlier designs and they were not permanently marked, so dating and positive identification can be difficult for collectors. Ideal's founder Morris Michtom died in 1938 but, under the leadership of his son Benjamin, the post-war era was a highly productive one, with the introduction of new designs and materials, a permanent trademark, as well as the new name of Ideal Toy Corporation. The company was granted the licence for the first Smokey Bear soft toy (promoting the US Forest Fire Prevention Campaign), which was introduced in 1953.

c.1950s VINYL CHARACTER FACE

Bears with soft, moulded vinyl faces were introduced by Ideal and other US companies (*see p.77*) in the early 1950s, but not all of these had realistic, moulded paws and feet like this example. The "spangle" eyes are typical of this type of bear, although some were equipped with "sleeping" dolls' eyelids. The remains of the label reads: "It's Ideal". Some of these vinyl-faced bears have been found with a tag reading: "Ideal, recommended by Miss Francis' Ding Dong School".

Height: 30cm (12in)   Printed label

Ears: *the large, floppy ears, made in two sections of contrasting plush, are sewn into the facial seams.*

Eyes: *the "spangle" amber eyes with brown pupils are made of plastic.*

Face: *the soft, pink, moulded vinyl face is inset into the plush head; facial features are painted on.*

Body: *the body is made of brown plush with the rounded, protruding stomach in white; brown limbs project from the body, in a permanently seated position.*

Fur: *dark cinnamon-coloured mohair plush was favoured by US manufacturers during the 1950s.*

Paws: *the paws are made of soft, pink, realistically moulded vinyl. The slightly cupped paws have five fingers, each with a tiny finger nail.*

Feet: *the top surface of each soft, pink, vinyl foot is moulded to resemble fur, with five claws pointing upwards, and realistic moulded foot-pads beneath.*

BEAR PROFILE
From this angle you can see the rounded, squat features, particularly the large head, pug nose, bulging stomach, and short, chubby legs, of a design that caricatures the attributes of a bear cub, and probably owes much to the work of Walt Disney. The small, stubby tail is a typical feature.

large, cupped ears at corners of triangular head

fully jointed head and limbs

white, embroidered, horizontal stitches form nose

unusual small, yellow, glass eyes with black pupils, sewn in

black mohair plush on woven backing; limbs re-covered with grey fabric

long, slender torso

long, thin limbs with no feet, typical of US "stick" bears

remains of white, felt pads visible on left paw; wood-wool stuffing

C.1930 BLACK MOHAIR

Height: 65cm (26in)

Although unmarked, as was typical of pre-World War II Ideal bears, this example has many characteristics associated with Ideal, particularly its large, triangular head. The slender body and limbs, however, suggest a date during the interwar period. Of rare black mohair, this bear is quite a collector's item, despite much wear and tear and partial restoration.

rounded head stuffed with wood-wool

round, hard, moulded resin nose

black, glass eyes

original ribbon bow around neck

short, curved arms

straight, stubby legs; no pads

long, cinnamon-coloured mohair plush; kapok stuffing in body and limbs

1940S SMALL; UNJOINTED

Height: 25cm (10in)

This small, unjointed bear, with large ears on a rounded head, is made of cinnamon-coloured mohair plush, a colour popular with US manufacturers at this time. In mint condition, the bear possesses a rare, printed, circus-wagon card swing-tag.

Card swing-tag

large, swivel-jointed head

large, slightly cupped ears

round, hard, moulded resin nose

brown, glass eyes with black pupils

cinnamon-coloured mohair plush

small, round, protruding muzzle of clipped mohair

straight, unjointed legs with small feet; no pads

curved, tapering arms with no pads; unjointed

1940S MEDIUM; UNJOINTED

Height: 38cm (15in)

This is a larger version of the previous example, the design being available in a range of sizes. Made of a similar, cinnamon-coloured mohair plush, it also has unjointed arms and legs, although the large, rounded head is swivel-jointed in the traditional way.

Card swing-tag

brown, glass eyes with black pupils

small, rounded muzzle of shaved mohair

hard, moulded plastic nose

curved, tapering arms; fully jointed limbs and head

cinnamon-red mohair plush in mint condition

felt pads in perfect condition; no claws

small feet

1940S LARGE; JOINTED

Height: 43cm (17in)

This fully jointed, cinnamon-red bear with felt pads was also available in a smaller size. It possesses its original card swing-tag, shaped like a circus wagon with "Ideal Novelty & Toy Co. (Stuffed Toy Division) Long Island City NY" printed in small lettering.

Card swing-tag

Merrythought: 1940s–50s

POST-WAR TRADITIONAL BEARS AND REDESIGNED LABEL

D uring World War II, Merrythought made few bears, as the Ironbridge factory was taken over by the British Admiralty for map-making and storage purposes. A room in nearby Wellington was·rented for toy production, but eventually all work turned to the war effort (*see pp.66–67*). The traditional bear design remained unaltered after the war, except for the effects of rationing on the quality and quantity of fabric. The button trademark was phased out, but the foot-label was still used, with the words printed on instead of being embroidered, as before the war; in 1957, "Ironbridge, Shrops." replaced "Hygienic Toys".

1940s ORANGE MOHAIR

This uniquely coloured, bright orange bear is typical of its era: Merrythought produced teddies in "burnished bronze" mohair plush from 1939, and introduced "amber" mohair plush to its range in 1947–48. Despite extensive repairs to its felt paw-pads, this bear still possesses its printed, foot-label with the earlier wording, "Hygienic Toys", which dates it to the period soon after World War II. In 1957 the wording on the label was changed to "Ironbridge, Shrops." (*see opposite, bottom left*).

Height: 55cm (22in)

Printed label

MERRYTHOUGHT HYGIENIC TOYS MADE IN ENGLAND

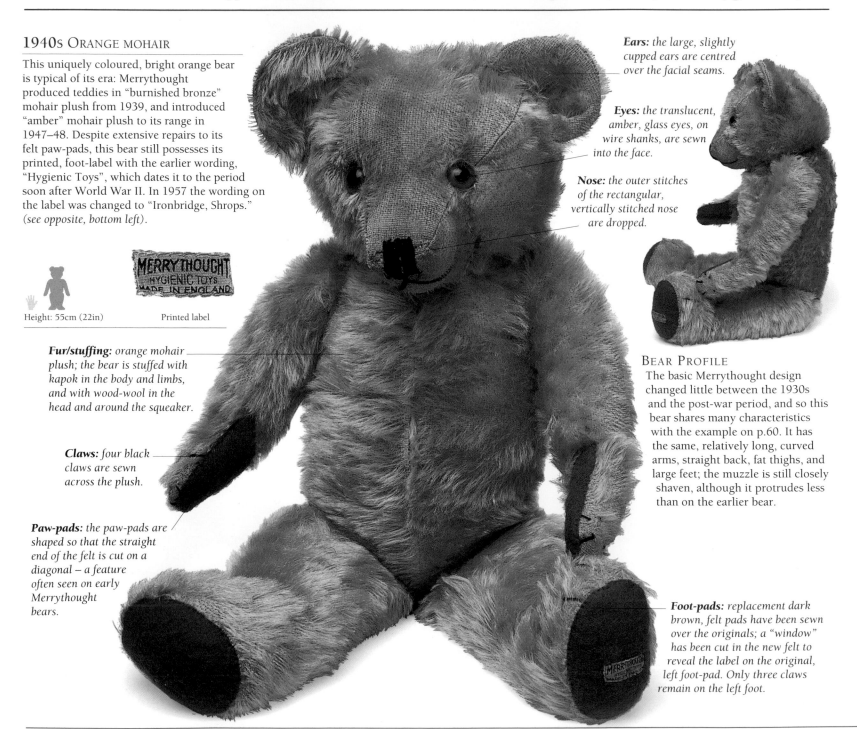

Ears: *the large, slightly cupped ears are centred over the facial seams.*

Eyes: *the translucent, amber, glass eyes, on wire shanks, are sewn into the face.*

Nose: *the outer stitches of the rectangular, vertically stitched nose are dropped.*

BEAR PROFILE

The basic Merrythought design changed little between the 1930s and the post-war period, and so this bear shares many characteristics with the example on p.60. It has the same, relatively long, curved arms, straight back, fat thighs, and large feet; the muzzle is still closely shaven, although it protrudes less than on the earlier bear.

Fur/stuffing: *orange mohair plush; the bear is stuffed with kapok in the body and limbs, and with wood-wool in the head and around the squeaker.*

Claws: *four black claws are sewn across the plush.*

Paw-pads: *the paw-pads are shaped so that the straight end of the felt is cut on a diagonal – a feature often seen on early Merrythought bears.*

Foot-pads: *replacement dark brown, felt pads have been sewn over the originals; a "window" has been cut in the new felt to reveal the label on the original, left foot-pad. Only three claws remain on the left foot.*

closely shaved, slightly protruding muzzle

translucent, amber, glass eyes, with black pupils, on wire stalks

brown, vertically stitched, square nose with outer dropped stitches

inverted-Y-shaped, double-stitched mouth

beige, twill pads

short, blond mohair plush; kapok stuffing throughout, with wood-wool in muzzle and around squeaker

1940s SHORT, GOLDEN MOHAIR
Height: 38cm (15in)

Both the printed label and the less rounded features of this bear suggest that it was made during the period when material were rationed. The claws on the paws (three stitches across the tips of the pads) are noticeably curtailed.

Printed label

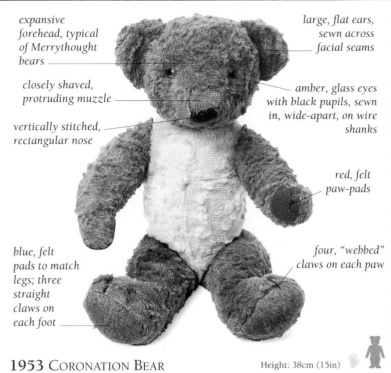

expansive forehead, typical of Merrythought bears

large, flat ears, sewn across facial seams

closely shaved, protruding muzzle

amber, glass eyes with black pupils, sewn in, wide-apart, on wire shanks

vertically stitched, rectangular nose

red, felt paw-pads

blue, felt pads to match legs; three straight claws on each foot

four, "webbed" claws on each paw

1953 CORONATION BEAR
Height: 38cm (15in)

This bear has all the classic Merrythought features, although it lacks a label. Made in red, white, and blue mohair plush, it was produced to commemorate the coronation of Queen Elizabeth II. According to trade catalogues, similar, patriotic teddies, made of artificial-silk plush, were designed in 1937 by J.K. Farnell for the coronation of King Edward VIII.

small, amber, glass eyes with black pupils, sewn into face

large, rounded ears sewn flat across corners of head

black, vertically stitched, rectangular nose, with one horizontal stitch across top edge

fixed head, with no neck joint

single-stitched, Y-shaped mouth

straight legs with small, pointed feet

straight arms; no paw-pads

traditional, card disc-joints in limbs

LATE 1950s SMALL; GOLDEN MOHAIR
Height: 23cm (9in)

Until the mid-1950s, the minimum size in the traditional range was 30cm (12in), but a smaller size was introduced in 1955–56. This bear has jointed limbs, but the head is fixed. The label, with new wording, is sewn into the back seam.

Printed label

translucent, orange, glass eyes, with black pupils, sewn in

relatively large, flat ears, sewn across corners of head

single-stitched, inverted-Y-shaped mouth

black, vertically stitched, square nose; horizontal stitch along upper edge

pink, artificial-silk plush; wood-wool stuffing

pointed paws with no pads or claws

short, slightly curved arms

short, straight legs; small feet with pointed toes

fully jointed limbs

c.1955–56 SMALL; PINK, ARTIFICIAL SILK
Height: 23cm (9in)

Merrythought first introduced a small, traditional bear in artificial-silk plush in 1954. This example, along with a "twin", was bought as a Christmas present from Harrods c.1955–56. The label, with old wording, is sewn along the bear's back.

Printed label

J.K. Farnell: 1945-68

TRADITIONAL AND NOVELTY BRITISH BEARS; REDESIGNED LABEL

The embroidered Farnell label was replaced, after World War II, by a printed, satinized label, with "Alpha" in a shield shape – a shape also used for swing-tags at this time. Although Alpha teddy bears remained Farnell's major line, the company also advertised La Vogue nightdress cases,

and, in 1960, it registered Mother Goose as the tradename for a range of washable soft toys. In 1959, the head office and some production was transferred to Hastings, Sussex; in 1964 the lease for the Acton Alpha Works terminated and all production was then moved to Hastings. The business was sold in 1968.

MID-1960s GOLDEN MOHAIR

This appealing, small bear possesses the last label used by J.K. Farnell & Co. Ltd. before the company ceased production in 1968. Slightly frayed, the satinized label is printed in the same colours as the earlier shield label (see opposite) but reads: "This is a Farnell Quality Soft Toy; Made in Hastings, England", with no mention of their original tradename Alpha. The safe, plastic eyes also indicate an early 1960s date; these came into general use from the mid-1960s because of the new toy safety laws.

Height: 33cm (13in)   Printed label

Ears: the flat ears are sewn centrally across the facial seams.

Eyes: the amber and black, safe, plastic, lock-in eyes are set low down, giving the forehead a large, expansive look.

Muzzle: the fur on the protruding muzzle is worn.

Nose/mouth: the square, black nose is vertically stitched; the mouth is a double-stitched, inverted T shape.

Fur/stuffing/squeaker: the fur is golden mohair plush; the bear is stuffed with soft stuffing, probably kapok or "sub" (see p.205). The squeaker feels like the plastic, concertina type.

Limbs: the arms and legs are short and stubby.

Pads: the Rexine pads are quite worn, revealing the woven fabric beneath.

Trademark: the satinized, printed label is sewn into the left side-seam.

BEAR PROFILE

At this angle, you can see the thin, straight body, and the short, stubby arms and legs, ending in slightly rounded feet. The ears are sewn centrally across the facial seams and down the sides of the relatively large head; the eyes are positioned low, in line with the appealing, pert, protruding muzzle.

Feet: the feet are slightly rounded.

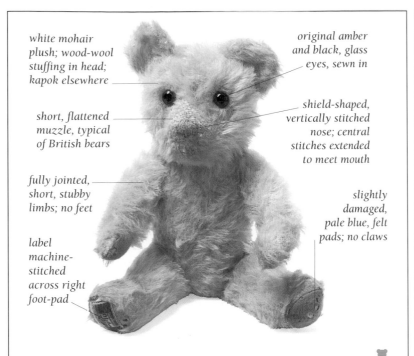

white mohair plush; wood-wool stuffing in head; kapok elsewhere

original amber and black, glass eyes, sewn in

short, flattened muzzle, typical of British bears

shield-shaped, vertically stitched nose; central stitches extended to meet mouth

fully jointed, short, stubby limbs; no feet

slightly damaged, pale blue, felt pads; no claws

label machine-stitched across right foot-pad

1940s WHITE MOHAIR; SHIELD LABEL   Height: 33cm (13in)

This small, white, mohair-plush bear has a pale cinnamon-coloured nose and mouth, typical of white Farnell bears of this era. The shortened muzzle and stubby limbs suggest that the bear was made during, or just after, World War II.

Printed label

brown, glass eyes with black pupils

large, slightly cupped ears, sewn over facial seams

square, black, vertically stitched nose; mouth missing

golden mohair plush; wood-wool stuffing in head; soft stuffing elsewhere

bear in permanently seated position

slightly worn, brown, Rexine pads

short, straight, unjointed legs

1950s NIGHTDRESS CASE   Height: 50cm (20in)

Farnell started making nightdress cases in the 1930s, but this example has the later, shield label stitched to its leg. The bear, with unjointed limbs and swivel head, contains a flexible, internal wire frame and a pink, quilted, rayon lining.

Printed label

small ears, set low down on sides of head, and caught into side-seams

orange, knitted, bobble hat and scarf (may not be original)

flattened muzzle and large, bulbous forehead – typical Toffee shape

amber, glass eyes with black pupils, sewn in with knot at back of head; set low down and wide apart

golden mohair plush; wood-wool stuffing in head; kapok elsewhere

square, black, vertically stitched nose; inverted-T-shaped mouth

worn, brown, Rexine pads; no claws

short, stumpy limbs

1960 TOFFEE; RADIO CHARACTER   Height: 25cm (10in)

Toffee is a character from the 1950s BBC radio programme *Listen with Mother*. The company first advertised an undressed version in 1960 – this outfit may be a later addition. Chad Valley also produced a version, in 1953 *(see p.104)*.

Printed label

dark amber, glass eyes with black pupils, sewn in on wire shanks

large, cupped ears, centred over facial seams

square muzzle

black, vertically stitched, oblong nose

black, double-stitched, inverted-Y-shaped mouth; long, vertical stitch meets nose

dense, short-pile, white mohair plush; soft stuffed throughout

spoon-shaped paws with no claws

large, oval feet; narrow ankles

c.1960–64 WHITE MOHAIR; RED PADS   Height: 48cm (19in)

This bear resembles later, red-padded examples by Acton Playcraft Ltd. *(see p.125)*, suggesting that the latter company used Farnell designs after they moved into the Alpha works in 1964. Although the label has been cut short, "Farnell" is still legible.

Printed label

Pedigree: 1937–50s

TRADITIONAL BRITISH BEARS FROM MERTON AND BELFAST FACTORIES

Pedigree Soft Toys Ltd. was a subsidiary of Lines Bros., the largest toy manufacturer in the world in the 1930s–50s; it originally operated from Lines' Triang Works in Merton, Surrey. The first catalogue offering Pedigree Soft Toys was produced in 1937, although the tradename had been used since the early 1930s for Lines' pram range. Soft and chassis toys continued to be made in Merton until the 1950s when production was transferred to the company's Castlereagh factory in Belfast, N. Ireland. Pedigree bears were also made in factories around the world including one in Auckland, New Zealand.

c.1955 "MADE IN IRELAND" LABEL

This bear demonstrates one of the two Pedigree teddy-bear designs that existed during this period *(see also opposite, bottom left)*. The front of the face has a vertical, central seam with a second seam running horizontally across the top of the head. The ears, with the edges folded over, are sewn into this horizontal seam. The printed label is attached at the top of the back seam. The plush is described in Pedigree catalogues as "super quality 'London Gold' mohair plush".

Height: 45cm (18in)

Printed label

Ears: *the entire ear, with the inner edge folded over, is sewn into the seam across the top of the head.*

Eyes: *these are early examples of the plastic, lock-in type of eye.*

Nose: *the square, black nose is vertically stitched.*

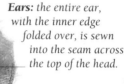

Ribbon: *the red ribbon is not the original, but the bear would have left the factory with a similar bow around its neck.*

BEAR PROFILE

This bear's classic Pedigree, bulbous head has little muzzle definition; the eyes are set low down towards the nose, creating a large, rounded forehead. The straight body, arms, and legs, which make the bear more doll-like than bear-like, are also typical of Pedigree teddy bears.

Fur/stuffing/squeaker: *The fur is golden mohair plush; the bear is stuffed with wood-wool in the head and body, and with kapok in the limbs. There is an internal squeaker.*

Pads: *the beige, velveteen pads are well worn, showing the woven backing beneath. There are no claws.*

Feet: *the little feet have round pads, a feature of this particular Pedigree design.*

typical Pedigree, amber and black, two-part, plastic eyes

inner edges of ears folded and sewn into horizontal head-seam

straight arms with pointed paws, a Pedigree feature

small piece of stiffened black felt cupped over muzzle to represent nose (may be repair work)

straight legs with small, round feet

dirty, well-worn, beige, velveteen pads; no claws

1950s "MADE IN ENGLAND" LABEL
Height: 33cm (13in)

Although the label sewn into the back seam is almost unreadable, it is just possible to make out the letters "Eng" of England as opposed to "Ire" of Ireland, effectively dating the bear to the period before all production was moved to Belfast.

Printed label

high forehead

inner edges of ears folded inwards, and caught into horizontal seam

square, black, vertically stitched nose with inverted-T-shaped mouth

golden mohair plush; wood-wool stuffing in body and muzzle, kapok in limbs and rest of head

short, slightly curved arms

straight legs with small feet and round pads; no claws

EARLY 1950s GLASS EYES
Height: 45cm (18in)

Although this bear has no label, its rounded head, with centre seams and a horizontal seam running from ear to ear, make it almost identical in design to the model on p.92. However, it has amber, glass eyes, with black pupils, sewn into the face and tied off at the back, suggesting that it was made slightly earlier, before plastic, lock-in eyes became the norm.

realistic, black, moulded plastic nose

typical Pedigree, black, single-stitch, inverted-T-shaped mouth

golden mohair plush; wood-wool stuffing around tilt-growler and muzzle; kapok elsewhere

typical Pedigree, two-part, safe, plastic eyes with opaque, black pupil forming shank

bow-tie is not original (bear would have left factory with ribbon bow)

LATE 1950s PLASTIC NOSE
Height: 54cm (21½in)

This example demonstrates Pedigree's second teddy-bear design of the period. The bear has a central, triangular section inserted into the head pattern to create a more protruding and traditional muzzle shape. Similar bears with plastic noses were advertised in the mid-1950s, including an example in coloured silk plush with a squeaker in each leg.

large ears with inner edges folded over and caught in horizontal head seam

two-part, amber and black, safe, plastic eyes, with centre forming integral shank

black, moulded plastic, slightly off-centre nose; inverted-T-shaped mouth

short, straight arms with slightly pointed paws; swivel-jointed

short, straight, stumpy legs with little foot definition

golden mohair plush; soft stuffing throughout, except for wood-wool around squeaker

LATE 1950s PLASTIC NOSE; STIFF NECK
Height: 30cm (12in)

According to a 1950s catalogue, this was the smallest bear in Pedigree's centre-seam range, described as "number 014: teddy bear with squeak". It is identical to the other centre-seam examples represented here, except for the addition of a moulded plastic nose, indicating a later date, and its fixed head, which was cut, all-in-one, from the same fabric as the body.

The Hermann Dynasty

THREE GENERATIONS OF TEDDY-BEAR MANUFACTURERS

Two German soft-toy factories bearing the Hermann name are currently in production, both producing highly collectable teddy bears: Gebrüder Hermann GmbH & Co. KG and Hermann-Spielwaren GmbH. The present owners of these family firms are distant cousins, descended from Johann Hermann, a Sonneberg toymaker, and moved to their present factories in the West following World War II. German reunification on 3 October 1990 made access to the family records possible, enabling a complete picture of the Hermann dynasty and its place in the teddy-bear story to emerge.

Family portrait
The 1910 photograph (above) shows Johann and Rosalie Hermann with their children, who created the first Hermann teddy bears.

Johann Hermann (1854–1919) founded a toy business *c.*1907 in Neufang, near Sonneberg, at that time the worldwide centre of the toy industry. Johann specialized in children's miniature wooden fiddles, but was also a "jobber", buying toys from home-workers to sell at markets. He and his wife Rosalie Suffa (1867–1933) had six children who all became involved in teddy-bear manufacture, a fast-growing industry in this part of Germany. Johann's second son, Artur (1894–1989), worked for Neufang teddy-bear manufacturer, Ernst Siegel. He married Siegel's daughter, Viktoria, and left the company to start his own business with his elder sister, Adelheid (1891–1939) and young brother, Max (1899–1955) in the attic room of their father's house. Max left school at the age of 14 to help his family make teddy bears.

THE FIRST HERMANN BEAR
According to family letters, the first Hermann bear was made here on 24 October 1913, when the business was operating as Johann Hermann Spielwarenfabrik. Johann sold the bears locally and to the large Sonneberg jobbers, such as Lindner, Gebrüder Fleischmann, and Escher & Son, who exported them to Britain and the United

Max Hermann factory
Stuffing soft toys at the Sonneberg factory in the 1930s (above).

States. At the start of World War I, Artur was drafted into the army. Max and Adelheid continued the business until 1917 when Max, too, went to war.

NAME CHANGES
In 1919, Johann Hermann died; Artur moved to Sonneberg to start his own firm, called Artur Hermann, but by 1929 he had renamed it "J.Hermann Nachf. Inh. Artur Hermann" (meaning Johann Hermann follower, owned by Artur Hermann). Artur recognized that the key to his success lay in his father's reputation. His trademark was a walking teddy bear leading a bear on all fours, carrying a monkey, and later a crown with "Rex" on the rim. Artur moved from Sonneberg to Munich in 1940, selling up to the Anker Plush Toy Company (*see p.114*) in 1954, and founding the toy shop Teddy: Haus des Kindes (House of the Child).

Adelheid, co-creator of the first Hermann teddy bear, married Neufang-born Hermann Baumann. They had four children, including Franz (born 1919). In 1946, he founded his own small arts and crafts toy factory (Kunstgewerbliches Spielzeug) in Flensburg. He returned home to Rodach in 1951 and, with his old friend Franz Kienel, founded the plush toy company, Baumann & Kienel OHG, today known as Baumann & Kienel KG trading under the tradename "Baki" (*see p.116*).

Bears in the attic
Artur, Adelheid, and Max made their first teddy in the attic of their father's Neufang house (above). From 1920 to 1923, Max operated his own business from there.

Sonneberg, 1930
The small boy (above, centre) is Max's son Rolf-Gerhard who later helped his father to run the business, taking over after his death. Rolf-Gerhard now heads Hermann-Spielwaren GmbH.

Bear in *lederhosen*
The little bear (above) is one of a set of Max Hermann bears made for a Sonneberg toy exhibition in 1933. The bears were originally arranged as if dancing around a maypole.

Traditional, jointed range
Hermann & Co. developed a range of teddies in both mohair and Dralon plush in the 1950s and 60s (left).

ORIGINS OF HERMANN-SPIELWAREN

After World War I, Max Hermann remained in Neufang, founding his own firm in 1920 at the family home. In 1923, he moved to Sonneberg with his wife Hilde Stammberger (1898–1985) and their son Rolf-Gerhard (born 1922). He used the trademark "Maheso", derived from the first two letters of the words "Max Hermann Sonneberg", and later added a teddy-bear and the running-dog logo. In 1947, Rolf-Gerhard joined the firm. Two years later, father and son founded Hermann & Co. KG, in Coburg, in the US Occupied Zone, about 15km (9 miles) east of Soviet-occupied Sonneberg. On 22 February 1953, fearing the emerging Communist regime in East Germany, Max and his family fled across the border to Coburg where they relocated Max Hermann Sonneberg. When Max died in 1955, Rolf-Gerhard took over the firm, still operating in Coburg. The firm became a public limited company, Hermann-Spielwaren GmbH, in 1979. Until her death in 1992, Rolf-Gerhard's wife, Dora-Margot designed many of the bears which have won awards in Germany and the US. In 1992 they were nominated for a TOBY award. Rolf-Gerhard and his daughter Dr Ursula Hermann now run the company.

Modern techniques
Workers inserting joints (above) at the Hermann-Spielwaren factory in Coburg.

Green triangle
The running teddy and dog logo (above) was used by Max Hermann and his descendents.

Late 1920s bear
The mohair bear (left), typical of its time, was produced by Bernhard Hermann's company, and would have borne the trademark "Beha Quality Germany". From 1930 to 1939, this wording was changed to "Marke Beha Teddy bürgt für Qualität".

GEBRÜDER HERMANN

In 1912, Johann Hermann's eldest son Bernhard (1888–1959) married Ida Jäger. After World War I, they moved to Sonneberg, where Bernhard founded his own small business specializing in teddies and dolls. Factory workers made the better quality mohair-plush bears, while local piece-workers made the cheaper models. Bernhard and Ida had four sons, all of whom helped in the business: Hellmut (1909–85), Artur (1912–90), Werner (born 1917), and Horst (1920–37). When Sonneberg came under Russian occupation after the war, Bernhard sent Werner to establish a factory in the US Zone. For over two years, Werner cycled back and forth from Sonneberg to Hirschaid, carrying machinery and tools, to set up a workshop in an abandoned bicycle factory. Finally, in 1953, both family and production were relocated in Hirschaid, with Hellmut, Artur, and Werner as partners and trading as Gebrüder Hermann KG. Following Bernhard's death in 1959, Artur became business manager with Hellmut the director of operations, and Werner responsible for design and production. Today, the firm is run by Hellmut's daughter Isabella, Werner's daughter Marion, and Artur's daughters Margit and Traudel.

Family group
Bernhard Hermann in 1929 (above, centre) with his wife Ida and their sons (from left to right) Horst, Artur, Hellmut and Werner.

New wording on tags
The wording (above) has been in use since 1952.

1986 Celebration bear
This bear (below) celebrated the foundation of Bernhard Hermann's business.

Replica of 1929 design
Hermann-Spielwaren won a gold medal in the 1992 "Eurodoll" contest for this bear.

Gebrüder Hermann: 1948–c.1970

TRADITIONAL AND NOVELTY BEARS; NEW POST-WAR FACTORY

After World War II, when Sonneberg became part of the Soviet Occupied Zone of Germany, Bernhard Hermann, fearing the communist regime, sent his son Werner to the small town of Hirschaid, in the American Occupied Zone, to set up a new factory there. By 1951, the whole family had been relocated and the business, owned by the three brothers, became known as Gebrüder Hermann KG. Hellmut was director of operations, Artur was business manager, and Werner was product manager and designer. The company thrived, reproducing traditional designs and introducing novelty ranges.

1960s INSET MUZZLE

This bear shares characteristics with pre-World War II Gebrüder Hermann bears, retaining the traditional long, curved arms and paws, and the typical inset muzzle of contrasting, short-pile mohair plush. Other German manufacturers followed this design, so possession of a trademark is the only guarantee of a bear's origination. This bear still has its swing-tag, attached by a gold cord to the original green, ribbon bow. Hermann used green and gold, printed, paper swing-tags from 1952 until the 1970s, when the company introduced red and gold paper, or red, plastic tags.

Height: 43cm (17in)

Printed paper swing-tag

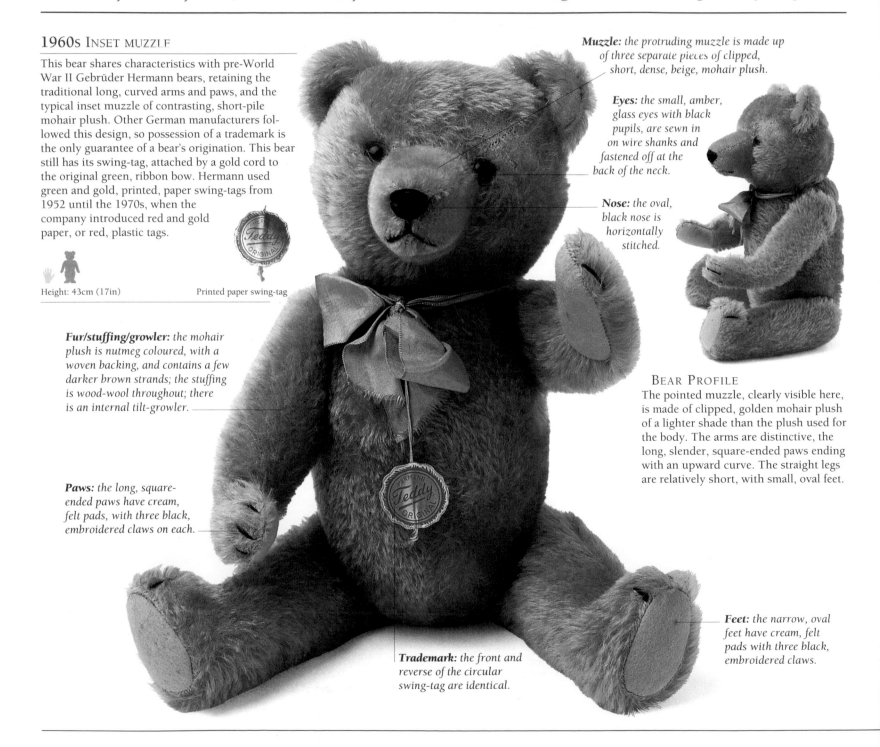

Muzzle: the protruding muzzle is made up of three separate pieces of clipped, short, dense, beige, mohair plush.

Eyes: the small, amber, glass eyes with black pupils, are sewn in on wire shanks and fastened off at the back of the neck.

Nose: the oval, black nose is horizontally stitched.

Fur/stuffing/growler: the mohair plush is nutmeg coloured, with a woven backing, and contains a few darker brown strands; the stuffing is wood-wool throughout; there is an internal tilt-growler.

Paws: the long, square-ended paws have cream, felt pads, with three black, embroidered claws on each.

Trademark: the front and reverse of the circular swing-tag are identical.

BEAR PROFILE

The pointed muzzle, clearly visible here, is made of clipped, golden mohair plush of a lighter shade than the plush used for the body. The arms are distinctive, the long, slender, square-ended paws ending with an upward curve. The straight legs are relatively short, with small, oval feet.

Feet: the narrow, oval feet have cream, felt pads with three black, embroidered claws.

short, golden mohair plush; length of pile clearly seen on tops of ears

small, amber, glass eyes with black pupils, set wide apart; sewn into face on wire shanks

three black, embroidered claws across tips of paws

short, stubby, curved arms

pointed feet with central seam along length; no pads

fabric label sewn into left side-seam

POST-1953 MINIATURE
Height: 13cm (5in)

This tiny, fully jointed bear was produced in Gebrüder Hermann's Hirshaid factory. The wording on the green, fabric label, which is sewn into the left side-seam, indicates a date of manufacture following the division of Germany into the Democratic and Federal Republics.

Printed label

shaggy, dark brown, Zotty mohair plush with blond-tipped shaggy pile; wood-wool stuffing in head; soft stuffed elsewhere

short, clipped, beige mohair muzzle

vertically stitched, brown, embroidered nose with two outer stitches dropped

inverted-Y-shaped mouth along top edge of peach, felt, open mouth, with pink, air-brushed, tongue

downward-curved arms with tear-shaped paws

large, slim, oval feet with three black claws on each

peach, felt pads

1960s ZOTTY TYPE
Height: 29cm (11¼in)

Several German manufacturers imitated the Zotty design first created by Steiff in 1951, and examples are hard to differentiate if, as in this case, no trademark exists. The main distinguishing Gebrüder Hermann features are the lack of a chest plate, and the embroidered nose with two outer, dropped stitches – the Steiff bears had shield-shaped noses.

brown, glass eyes with black pupils

short, clipped muzzle of lighter mohair plush; open mouth lined with peach felt

curved arms in begging attitude

shaggy, Zotty mohair on dark, woven backing; internal squeaker

three brown, embroidered claws on each paw

1950s ZOTTY TYPE
Height: 25cm (10in)

This is an earlier version of the Zotty type than the previous example. It has a typical 1950s circular, metal tag. The essential Gebrüder Hermann, dropped, outer stitches on the nose, and the inverted-Y-shaped mouth are missing, having been damaged by wear and tear.

Metal tag

brown, glass eyes with black pupils – one a replacement

short, golden plush ears, set over facial seams

black, oval, horizontally stitched nose; inverted-Y-shaped mouth

shaggy, honey-coloured mohair plush; internal tilt-growler

oval feet; pads repaired with woven fabric

curved, slender paws; pads repaired with woven fabric

1940s–50s SHAGGY, HONEY MOHAIR
Height: 55cm (22in)

This bear shows much wear and tear, and its colour has faded, with a richer, golden-coloured plush visible in the joint areas, where it is protected from light. There is no trademark, and the inset muzzle is uncharacteristic of Hermann bears. However, evidence in the Gebrüder Hermann factory archives confirms its pedigree.

Hermann & Co: 1940s–60s

TRADITIONAL INSET MUZZLE AND NOVELTIES

In 1947, Max Hermann's son, Rolf-Gerhard, joined the family business, which then took on the name, Max Hermann & Sohn. In 1949, they founded the subsidiary company, Hermann & Co. KG, in Coburg, Bavaria, in what was then the US Occupied Zone of Germany, about 15km (9 miles)

from Sonneberg. Fearing the Communist regime, they moved Max Hermann & Sohn and the family home to Coburg in 1953, joining Hermann & Co. KG there. Max died in 1955, leaving the business in the hands of Rolf and his wife, Dora-Margot. The company eventually became known as Hermann-Spielwaren.

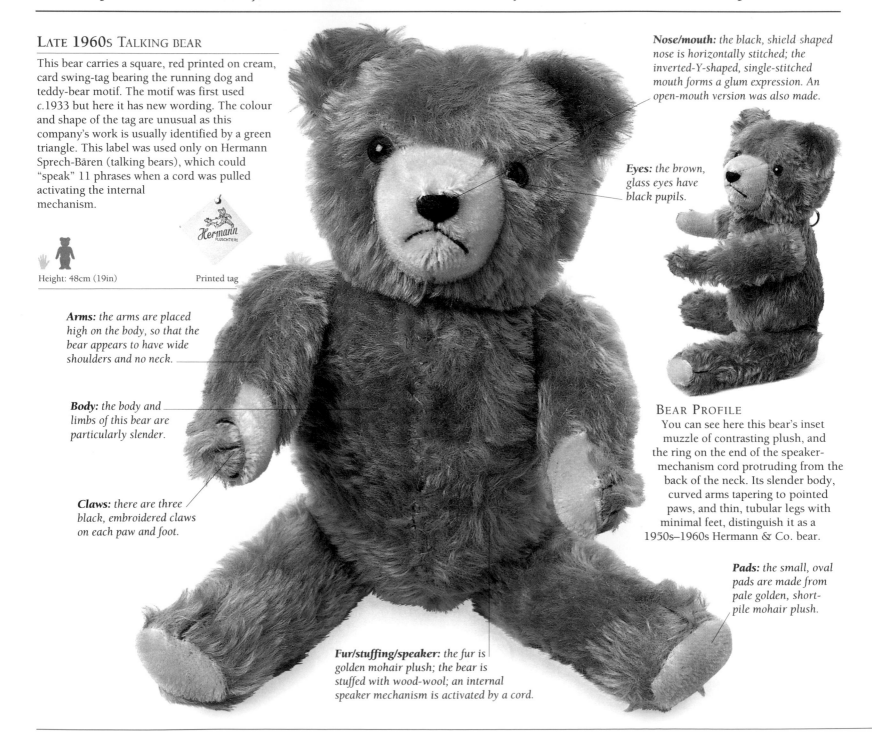

LATE 1960s TALKING BEAR

This bear carries a square, red printed on cream, card swing-tag bearing the running dog and teddy-bear motif. The motif was first used *c.*1933 but here it has new wording. The colour and shape of the tag are unusual as this company's work is usually identified by a green triangle. This label was used only on Hermann Sprech-Bären (talking bears), which could "speak" 11 phrases when a cord was pulled activating the internal mechanism.

Height: 48cm (19in)

Printed tag

Arms: *the arms are placed high on the body, so that the bear appears to have wide shoulders and no neck.*

Body: *the body and limbs of this bear are particularly slender.*

Claws: *there are three black, embroidered claws on each paw and foot.*

Fur/stuffing/speaker: *the fur is golden mohair plush; the bear is stuffed with wood-wool; an internal speaker mechanism is activated by a cord.*

Nose/mouth: *the black, shield shaped nose is horizontally stitched; the inverted-Y-shaped, single-stitched mouth forms a glum expression. An open-mouth version was also made.*

Eyes: *the brown, glass eyes have black pupils.*

BEAR PROFILE

You can see here this bear's inset muzzle of contrasting plush, and the ring on the end of the speaker-mechanism cord protruding from the back of the neck. Its slender body, curved arms tapering to pointed paws, and thin, tubular legs with minimal feet, distinguish it as a 1950s–1960s Hermann & Co. bear.

Pads: *the small, oval pads are made from pale golden, short-pile mohair plush.*

horizontally stitched, triangular, black nose with outer vertical stitches; inverted-Y-shaped mouth

brown, glass eyes with black pupils

inset muzzle of shorter pile, cream mohair plush

arms attached high up on body

triangular, metal chest-tag

three black, stitched claws

shaggy, brown-tipped, cream mohair plush; wood-wool stuffing

beige, felt pads

1948–52 BROWN-TIPPED MOHAIR
Height: 80cm (31½in)

This brown-tipped mohair-plush bear with inset, contrasting muzzle and ears was manufactured by Hermann & Co., Coburg. Although it resembles those produced by Gebrüder Hermann, the triangular "Hermann Plüschtiere" tag confirms its origins.

Printed tag

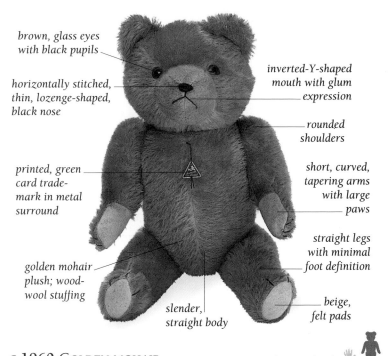

brown, glass eyes with black pupils

inverted-Y-shaped mouth with glum expression

horizontally stitched, thin, lozenge-shaped, black nose

rounded shoulders

printed, green card trade-mark in metal surround

short, curved, tapering arms with large paws

golden mohair plush; wood-wool stuffing

straight legs with minimal foot definition

slender, straight body

beige, felt pads

C.1960 GOLDEN MOHAIR
Height: 48cm (19in)

This bear with high shoulders, inset muzzle, and small feet possesses its original triangular, metal tag. The label design was introduced in the early 1950s; from the mid-1950s to the early 1960s the words "Hermann Plüschtiere" were incised on the back.

Printed tag

horizontally stitched, lozenge-shaped, black nose

brown, glass eyes with black pupils

shaggy, brown Dralon plush; wood-wool-stuffed head; soft-stuffed body; internal squeaker

open mouth with peach-coloured, felt palate and airbrushed tongue

original lilac, satin, ribbon bow

green and gold, scalloped, circular, chest-tag

C.1960 ZOTTY-TYPE
Height: 25cm (10in)

This bear, produced when the firm was known as Hermann & Co. KG, resembles Steiff's Zotty. It carries a large label indicating, on the reverse, that it is made of Dralon. Throughout the 1960s, only soft-stuffed, Dralon toys bore this tag.

Printed tag

horizontally stitched, lozenge-shaped, black nose; inverted-Y-shaped mouth

amber, glass eyes with black pupils

green and white patterned ruff around neck

golden, artificial-silk plush, in perfect condition

fully jointed with Yes/No mechanism; small tail operates head movement

pink, felt pads

three black, stitched claws across plush

narrow, oval-shaped feet

1948–52 YES/NO BEAR
Height: 26cm (10½in)

This Yes/No bear, with original price and product number tag, was produced by Max Hermann & Sohn in Sonneberg and then sold to Hermann & Co. KG in Coburg. The two firms operated simultaneously in Sonneberg and Coburg between 1948 and 1953, when the family left East Germany, unable to return until the 1990 reunification.

Steiff: 1940s–early 1960s

POST-WAR, REDESIGNED, TRADITIONAL ORIGINAL TEDDY

R aw materials became increasingly difficult to obtain from 1939, and in 1943 Steiff ceased toy production, becoming a munitions factory for the rest of World War II. After the war, the firm made small quantities of bears, often from low-quality fabrics. Steiff remodelled their Original Teddy design in 1950; the new version had shorter limbs and was available in 23cm (9in) and 35cm (14in) sizes, in caramel-coloured and dark brown mohair. A year later, the range increased to ten sizes and included white and beige mohair plush. The bears also carried newly designed buttons and printed card chest-tags.

c.1950 NEW ORIGINAL TEDDY DESIGN

Although its original "button in ear" trade-mark is missing, this bear still possesses the printed, cloth label sewn into its right side-seam, which was used by Steiff from 1947–53, following World War II and the subsequent division of Germany into separate military zones. The new Original Teddy design saw the end of the typical, horizontally stitched, triangular nose previously used on smaller Steiff bears; the shield-shaped nose now applied to the whole range.

Height: 35cm (14in)

Printed label

Eyes: the eyes are brown glass, with black pupils. They are sewn into the face.

Nose/mouth: the nose is shield shaped and vertically stitched in brown (a feature of most white bears). The mouth is an inverted V shape.

Fur: the short, white mohair plush is discoloured, but is otherwise in good condition.

Paws: the ends of the paws are squarer than those of earlier bears.

Claws: four claws on each foot and paw are stitched in brown.

Pads: the foot-pads are made of cream felt, and are in perfect condition.

BEAR PROFILE

The slightly shorter, blunter muzzle, and significantly less elongated limbs, are features of the Original Teddy's new design. The arms, however, are still longer than the legs, so retaining the traditional teddy-bear shape. Notice how the curved, spoon-like paws of its predecessor (see pp.18–19) are replaced by a squarer version.

Feet: the feet are long and narrow.

horizontally stitched, triangular, black nose; inverted-Y-shaped mouth

discoloured, pale golden, cotton plush

clear, glass eyes, with flaking, painted, brown backs, sewn into face

off-white, cloth pads (felt was unobtainable after the war)

elegant clothing added by pre-vious owner

four black claws stitched on each foot and paw

large, narrow, oval feet

*c.*1949 BLANK BUTTON

Height: 33cm (13in)

Produced in the post-war years, when materials were scarce, this bear is made of low-quality cotton plush; it has a blank, tin-plate button, typical of the period. A blue-painted, blank button, and one embossed with "Steiff", in capital letters, were also used at this time.

Blank button

small, brown and black, glass eyes sewn in on wire shanks

small ears, sewn over facial seams; button and remains of original tag in left ear

fur slightly worn on muzzle

shield-shaped, vertically stitched, brown nose; inverted-V-shaped mouth

square-ended paws with four stitched claws

beige, felt pads in good condition

short, beige mohair plush

1950s ORIGINAL TEDDY; BEIGE

Height: 35cm (14in)

This bear exemplifies the remodelled Original Teddy pattern that was to remain in circulation until the introduction of the 1966 design (*see p.128*). It retains its button with "Steiff" in raised, cursive script, a design that was used from 1952/53 until 1977.

Embossed button

brown, glass eyes with black pupils, sewn into face

original yellow, printed ear-tag records product number 5318, 03

straight arms slightly longer than legs; no paw-pads; four claws stitched in black

short, dark brown mohair plush; wood-wool stuffing throughout; internal squeaker

long, narrow feet with beige, felt pads

1950s ORIGINAL TEDDY; BROWN

Height: 18cm (7in)

This is an example of one of the smaller Original Teddy designs. Like its pre-war predecessors, it has straighter arms than the larger bears and lacks felt paw-pads. Its card chest-tag features the redesigned bear's head, first introduced in 1950.

Embossed button

brown, glass eyes with black pupils; originally sewn in, but right eye glued by repairer

shield-shaped, vertically stitched, brown nose; inverted-V-shaped mouth

curly, blond mohair plush on beige, cloth backing

wood-wool stuffing sagging near top of shoulder

long, slightly curved arms

holes in beige, felt pads reveal wood-wool stuffing

square-ended paws with four brown claws

1950s ORIGINAL TEDDY; CURLY

Height: 53cm (21in)

This bear possesses the unmistakable shape and features of a post-war Original Teddy and although it does not display a Steiff button, a small hole in the ear indicates its Giengen factory origins. Plastic eyes replaced glass eyes in early 1960s models.

Embossed button

Dean's: 1950s

The first Dean's catalogue after World War II appeared in 1949, offering a much reduced range due to the shortage of raw materials. However the company, with a reorganized sales force, was soon back on its feet. A further boost to business was provided by the birth of London Zoo's first polar bear cub Brumas in 1949, generating great demand for white bears. In 1952 a new assistant designer, Sylvia R. Willgoss, joined Dean's and introduced many novel designs. She succeeded Richard Ellett as head designer in 1956 when the company moved from Merton, Surrey, to new premises in Rye, Sussex.

MID-1950S TRU-TO-LIFE

This black, North American bear was available in three sizes. It has realistic, pink, moulded rubber paws and foot-pads, with five claws on each. A white version (a polar bear) was first advertised in trade catalogues in 1955. Sylvia Wilgoss designed these unjointed bears to sit, stand upright, or walk on all fours, aided by a collar and chain lead, which have been found on similar examples.

Height: 48cm (19in)

Printed label

Ears: the large, rounded ears are set wide apart on the sides of the head.

Eyes: the brown, glass eyes are placed inside rubber sockets, cut into the rubber face mask.

Nose: the large, black, moulded rubber nose and mouth protrude through the end of the muzzle.

Muzzle: the white, acrylic plush muzzle contrasts with the black mohair plush of the body.

Arms: the long, unjointed, soft-filled arms are particularly floppy because of the lack of stuffing at the shoulders.

Fur/growler: the fur is black, shaggy, acrylic plush; the bear is stuffed with wood-wool and kapok, and has a tilt-growler.

Legs: the unjointed legs are stuffed with wood-wool and sewn to the front of the body, giving a permanent sitting position.

Paws: the foot-pads and paws are made of pink rubber moulded into five claws, some of which have been bent and damaged.

BEAR PROFILE
Notice how life-like this teddy is with its pointed muzzle and outlined, slightly curled, bottom lip. The back is rounded, the limbs are long and floppy, and the feet are splayed outwards in the typical fashion of a real seated bear.

wide-apart, amber, glass eyes with black pupils, sewn in, with knot at back of head

large, flat ears sewn to sides of head

black, horizontally stitched, triangular nose; inverted-T-shaped mouth

original pink, rayon ribbon tied in bow around neck

straight, stubby arms and legs; no pads or claws

blue wool plush; wood-wool stuffing in muzzle, soft stuffing elsewhere

EARLY 1950S WOOL

Height: 14cm (5½in)

Bought in a bankruptcy sale, this tiny, unjointed bear still carries its original, circular, card swing-tag – a lucky find for any collector. It was probably designed as a baby's plaything, although the glass eyes would not pass today's toy safety standards.

Printed label

wide-apart, amber, glass eyes with black pupils, sewn in, with knot at back of head

small, cupped ears, with inner edges caught into facial seams

black, vertically stitched, rectangular nose; inverted-T-shaped mouth

original yellow ribbon tied in bow; original card tag with pre-1956 Merton address

short, light brown wool plush (probably alpaca) on woven backing

short, straight arms

short, straight legs with small feet

pale peach, felt pads in perfect condition; no claws

EARLY 1950S SEATED; WIRE JOINTING

Height: 20cm (8in)

Although this small bear is not jointed in the traditional fashion, an internal wire frame enables the limbs to move up and down in unison, as well as to bend in a variety of poses. The printed fabric label is sewn into the back of the neck.

Printed label

ears placed wide apart, with inner edges caught into facial seams

brown, plastic eyes with integral shank, sewn into face and fastened off at back

head and paws of golden mohair plush

rectangular, black, vertically stitched nose; inverted-T-shaped mouth

blue, velvet shirt with three, orange, plastic buttons

red, velvet, jodhpur-style trousers

original, card swing-tag with Merton address: reverse reads "Velvet Bear T272/1"

blue, velvet shoes

MID-1950S VELVET BEAR

Height: 35cm (14in)

Under the designer Richard Ellett, Dean's was renowned for its velvet toys. Unjointed bears with all-in-one clothes were made from the 1930s, but remained popular in the years following World War II, when traditional materials were still scarce.

Printed label

small ears with inner edges caught into facial seams

brown, plastic eyes with short, integral, plastic shanks, sewn into face and fastened off at back of head

pointed muzzle

black, vertically stitched, rectangular nose

upward-stretching arms

soft, white, woollen plush (possibly alpaca), on woven backing

MID-1950S WHITE; GLOVE-PUPPET

Height: 25cm (10in)

All the major soft-toy manufacturers made teddy-bear glove-puppets. This white, woollen-plush example may have been produced as a result of the British post-1949 Brumas craze. The printed label is stitched across the lower back of the glove.

Printed label

Chad Valley: 1950s–60s

NOVELTIES, AND DEVELOPMENTS IN TRADITIONAL DESIGN

Post-war advances in the plastics industry had their effect on teddy bears. During the 1950s, Chad Valley gradually replaced glass eyes with plastic ones and produced some teddy bears with realistic, moulded plastic noses. The company also began to introduce nylon and other synthetic fabrics into its range, although the basic bear design remained the same. Radio had influenced the toy industry since the early days, but in the 1950s Chad Valley obtained the sole rights to manufacture Harry Corbett's mischievous Sooty glove puppet, which featured in a popular children's television programme from 1952.

1953 TOFFEE

Toffee was a character from the 1950s–60s BBC children's radio programme *Listen with Mother*. Jane Alan later published a book of stories about his adventures with a little girl called Lulupet. Here, Toffee wears his original red hat and scarf. J.K. Farnell also made a Toffee teddy bear (without clothes) in the 1960s (*see p.91*).

Height: 25cm (10in)

Printed label

Ears: *the typical Chad Valley, large, flat ears are set on the sides of the head.*

Eyes: *the amber and black, glass eyes are sewn in place.*

Nose: *this is a typical Chad Valley bound nose, with black vertical stitches.*

Fur: *the dark beige mohair plush is quite long, but worn in places.*

Trademark: *the Queen Mother Royal Warrant label is zigzag-stitched onto the right foot-pad. The bear would also originally have had a card tag with "Toffee, the Teddy with a Personality" printed in red and blue.*

BEAR PROFILE

In profile, the most noticeable feature is the particularly high, domed forehead and the flat muzzle. The arms are very short, with Rexine pads. The legs are also short and quite fat with small feet. The red, knitted, woollen hat with a pompom is sewn onto the back of the head.

Pads: *the Rexine pads are worn. The left pad is torn, revealing the wood-wool stuffing that is used throughout.*

large ears sewn into slits on head

brown and black, safe, plastic eyes

light brown mohair plush; particularly worn on right arm

realistic, black, moulded plastic nose

straight arms with up-curved paws; no claws

fully jointed head and limbs

worn, Rexine pads reveal "sub" stuffing

fat thighs and big, stumpy feet

LATE 1950s PLASTIC NOSE; SAFE EYES
Height: 38cm (15in)

This bear has brown and black, safe, plastic eyes, and a realistic, black, moulded plastic nose – both new developments in teddy-bear design. The printed, blue and white, cloth label is sewn into the side-seam under the arm.

Printed label

amber and black, glass eyes on wire stalks, sewn in and finished off at back of head

high forehead with central seam; ears set into seam

short, white and light brown, alpaca wool plush

black, vertically stitched nose; horizontal stitching across top

three, long, black claws on each paw

fully jointed head and limbs

oblong feet; five claws on corners

POST-1953 CUBBY BEAR
Height: 30cm (12in)

This Cubby Bear, made of alpaca plush, is less shaggy than the original 1930s version. Originally also available in artificial-silk plush, by the 1950s it was being manufactured in various colours of nylon plush. This example has a Queen Mother Royal Warrant label.

Printed label

large, flat ears, typical of Chad Valley bears

flattened face with high forehead

black, vertically stitched, tightly bound nose

pale golden mohair plush, worn in places

fully jointed head and limbs

label under right arm

short arms

slightly cracked, Rexine pads

short legs with little feet

1950s PLASTIC EYES ON WIRE SHANKS
Height: 30cm (12in)

By the late 1950s, Chad Valley was using orange, plastic eyes on wire shanks, which were sewn in and finished off at the back of the head like glass eyes. The next stage in the development of a safer Chad Valley teddy was to attach plastic eyes with washers.

Printed label

wide, black, vertically stitched nose

brown and black, glass eyes; sewn in and finished off at back

fully jointed head and limbs

inset muzzle; head stuffed with wood-wool

upwardly curved arms

golden mohair plush, lined with artificial silk; opening closed by zip fastener

chunky thighs and big feet

worn, soft, Rexine pads; reinforced with card

POST-1953 NIGHTDRESS CASE
Height : 49cm (19½in)

Nightdress cases and other containers in the shape of teddy bears and animals became popular in the soft-toy trade from the 1930s. Other major manufacturers, including J.K. Farnell (see p.91), H.G. Stone, and Merrythought, also produced such teddy bears.

Printed label

Chiltern: post-World War II – 1950s

POST-WAR CHILTERN HUGMEE AND NOVELTY TEDDY BEARS

Towards the end of World War II, it became clear that H.G. Stone's factories in Tottenham, north London, and Chesham, Bucks., would never be able to meet the demand for Chiltern toys, and so in 1945 the company obtained a site near Pontypool, in south Wales, to build a new and larger factory with modern facilities. The company set up a school to train young girls and women in soft-toy production techniques in readiness for the factory's opening in 1947. The new factory was extended on several occasions during the highly productive, post-war period, when up to 300 workers were employed.

1956–57 HUGMEE; CHILTERN LABEL

H.G. Stone continued to make Hugmee bears during the 1950s, with little change to the original pre-war design; the company used good quality mohair plush, and velveteen pads reinforced with card on the feet. For the first time, however, they used a new, permanent, printed label.

Height: 53cm (21in)

Printed label

Eyes: *the reddish brown, translucent, glass eyes with black pupils are sewn in on wire shanks, and finished off with a diagonal stitch at the back of the head.*

Nose: *the shield-shaped nose is similar to those of the flat-face Hugmees (see p.57).*

Fur/stuffing: *this light golden, mohair-plush bear is stuffed with kapok in the body and limbs; wood-wool is used in the head and around the squeaker.*

BEAR PROFILE
This bear shares many similarities with the earlier Hugmee design (*see pp.56–57*): thick thighs, large, slightly pointed feet, extended muzzle, and relatively long arms.

Trademark: *the new, printed label is attached to the right foot-pad.*

Pads: *the light rust-coloured, velveteen pads, are reinforced with thin card; the feet have five claws, whereas the paws have four.*

small, L-shaped ears, caught into facial seams

brown and black, glass eyes, sewn in place

light golden mohair plush; soft stuffing in body and limbs, with wood-wool in head and around squeaker and joints

triangular, black, vertically stitched nose

rust-coloured, velveteen pads with four claws over pads and plush

four claws on each foot

1950s HUGMEE; MEDIUM
Height: 35cm (14in)

The Hugmee range came in various sizes; this is a smaller version of the large Hugmee (opposite). This bear no longer possesses a trademark, but the discoloured area on the right foot-pad indicates where the original, printed label was attached.

CHILTERN HYGIENIC TOYS MADE IN ENGLAND

Printed label

amber and black, glass eyes, sewn in and finished off at back of head

short-clipped mohair plush on fronts of ears

black, shield-shaped, vertically stitched nose

separate section of clipped mohair plush forms muzzle

dark brown, shiny, Rexine pads

beige mohair plush; wood-wool and kapok stuffing in body and limbs; wood-wool in head

foot-pads reinforced with card

1953 TING-A-LING BRUIN BEAR
Height: 29cm (11½in)

This fully jointed teddy bear contains a mechanism (now inoperative) that was common in 1950s toys – a cardboard tube fitted with an internal metal ring of metal teeth arranged around its inner circumference. A metal clapper suspended from the top of the tube strikes each tooth when the toy is shaken or tipped up, making the teddy bear tinkle musically.

ears sewn into facial seams and into darts down sides of head

typical Chiltern, reddish brown, glass eyes, sewn in and finished off with knot at top of head

paws stuffed with wood-wool

wide, vertically stitched, black nose

golden mohair plush; head stuffed with wood-wool; finger-space inside head lined with green Rexine

unusual red on white, printed label, sewn into hem inside base of glove

1950s GLOVE PUPPET
Height: 20cm (8in)

Teddy-bear glove puppets have been made since before World War I, but in the 1950s all the major British soft-toy manufacturers, including Dean's (see p.103), J.K. Farnell, H.G. Stone, and Chad Valley, produced their own versions.

CHILTERN HYGIENIC TOYS MADE IN ENGLAND

Printed label

vertically stitched, oblong nose; inverted-Y-shaped mouth

woven fabric, pill-box hat, originally blue but now faded

brown, glass eyes

all-in-one, long-sleeved blue mohair plush "sweater"

artificial-silk plush stuffed with wood-wool and kapok

pads on feet only

LATE 1930s–50s SKATER
Height: 40cm (16in)

This artificial-silk-plush bear, with all-in-one, long-sleeved, blue, mohair-plush sweater, originally had a white, mohair-plush muff to match the hood. The model was illustrated in a 1937 toy-trade journal but is known to have been made after World War II as well. This bear is unmarked, but others exist with a printed Chiltern label on the foot.

Chiltern: c.1958–early 1960s

INTRODUCTION OF MOULDED PLASTIC NOSE AND WASHABLE TEDDY BEARS

The company H.G. Stone first used moulded plastic noses on its Chiltern bears in about 1958. Originally sewn on, the noses were later locked-in with washers, in keeping with the new safety regulations. Many of the older Chiltern lines, such as the Hugmee range, were then given plastic noses for a new look. In about 1960, a sleeping bear was introduced, with plastic nose; black, felt, closed eyelids; and a bell in each ear. Washable teddy bears became available in 1964, the year that H.G. Stone & Co. Ltd. became part of the Dunbee-Combex group, makers of vinyl and rubber toys.

EARLY 1960s HUGMEE; MOHAIR

This bear has a moulded plastic, dog-like nose, although some Hugmees were still being produced with the shield-shaped, vertically stitched nose. There is no surviving trademark on this bear, but other, similar bears have been found with Chiltern labels sewn into their side-seams. It would have left the factory with a card swing-tag, like the one on p.109 (bottom left), and a ribbon bow.

Height 68cm (27in)

Fur/stuffing/squeaker: the light golden mohair plush, with specks of dark hair, is commonly used on Chiltern Hugmees; here it is in excellent condition. The teddy bear is soft-stuffed throughout except for wood-wool in the head and around the squeaker.

Pads: the rust-coloured, velveteen, tear-shaped foot-pads are reinforced with thin card, which has become slightly misshapen with wear. There are five claws on the feet (only four remain on the left), sewn across the plush up to the seam.

Ears: the floppy, dog-like ears are sewn into darts down the sides of the head and then caught into the facial seams.

Eyes: the reddish brown, translucent, glass eyes, with black pupils, are sewn into the head.

BEAR PROFILE
At this angle you can see the bear's dog-like ears, which flop to the sides of its head. Despite the modern addition of a plastic nose, it still retains many of the classic Hugmee features, with the long, pointed muzzle, long, curved arms, fat thighs, and shaped, card-reinforced pads.

Claws: the four claws, sewn across the paw-pads, are typical of Chiltern bears from this era.

inner ears lined with clipped, white mohair plush

amber and black, safe, plastic, lock-in eyes

swivel-jointed head; unjointed limbs

clipped, white mohair plush muzzle

mainly silver-tipped, grey mohair plush; white mohair plush on chest and fronts of arms

bear stands in half-seated position

creamy beige, velveteen pads; foot-pads reinforced with card

tops of feet made from separate sections of fabric; no claws

C.1958 MUSICAL BRUIN BEAR

Height: 29cm (11½in)

H.G. Stone produced a similar standing bear in the early 1950s, but this example's realistic, plastic nose dates it to a later period. When wound up by a key at the back of the bear, the musical box plays *Brahms' Lullaby*, and the head moves from side to side.

Printed label

realistic, moulded plastic nose; only vertical stitch remains of original, inverted-Y-shaped mouth

brown, plastic eyes with black pupils and integral plastic shank; sewn in and fastened off at back of head

looped, gold cord across chest represents ring-master costume

artificial-silk plush in range of colours; soft stuffed; unjointed

red-painted, metal tricycle with rubber tyres, handlebars, and pedals

C.1958 BEAR ON A TRICYCLE

Height: 28cm (11in)

This was the first bear designed by Pam Howells, *née* Williams, (*see p.180*) when she joined H.G. Stone & Co. as assistant designer. She based the bear on a character from the Disney cartoon *Dumbo*. The tricycle was created by a colleague, Basil Rogers.

Printed label

amber and black, safe, plastic, lock-in eyes

black, realistic, moulded plastic, safe, lock-in nose

inverted-Y-shaped, double-stitched mouth

fully jointed, short, pointed arms

beige, velveteen pads (fabric favoured for Chiltern bears from 1920s); no claws

short legs with small, tear-shaped feet

EARLY 1960s MUSICAL

Height: 34cm (13½in)

This golden, mohair-plush bear, with its moulded plastic nose, still possesses its original swing-tag. The reverse of the tag reads: "To play a tune just turn my key and listen to the melody." Like the example on p.57, it plays *Brahms' Lullaby*.

Printed card tag

unusual, blue, glass eyes with black pupils, sewn in and knotted at back of head

realistic, black, moulded plastic nose, pushed into muzzle; no washer

mainly silver-tipped, grey mohair plush; white mohair plush on chest, face, and fronts of ears

rounded, pale blue, velveteen pads

C.1958 UNJOINTED; PLASTIC NOSE

Height: 25cm (10in)

Pam Howells (*née* Williams) designed this bear when plastic noses were first introduced. With its unjointed, short, stubby limbs, it exemplified a break with tradition. Similar bears, composed entirely of nylon plush and stuffed with "Fairy Foam" (one-piece foam filling), were made in the early 1960s as part of the Washable Chiltern Toy series.

Steiff: 1950s

NEW NOVELTY BEARS; MODIFIED EARLIER DESIGNS

In the 1950s, Steiff introduced several "new-look" teddies into its programme, though some still followed pre-World War II designs. The Jubilee celebrations of the first Steiff teddy bear in 1953 heralded not only Jackie-Baby but also Nimrod-Bear, dressed in a hunting suit, available in four different colours of felt, and carrying a wooden rifle. Steiff made a new 30cm (12in) Teddy-Baby and used the same head design on its 1950s Teddyli, which had a soft fabric body, dangling, unstuffed arms, and stiff legs. Some had rubber bodies but, due to the perishable nature of this material, few survive intact.

1953 JACKIE-BABY

Jackie-Baby, representing an endearing bear cub, was produced to celebrate the 50th anniversary of the first Steiff teddy bear, and was made until 1955. This particular example was the largest of the three sizes available (18cm/7in; 25cm/10in; and 35cm/14in). The navel and embroidered nose design are features unique to this bear. Steiff produced replicas of Jackie-Baby, also in three sizes, in 1986, 1989, and 1990. The bear has a new-style 1950s Steiff button, with raised, cursive lettering, in the left ear, and a printed label in the side-seam reading "US Zone Germany", only used from 1947–53.

Height: 35cm (14in)

Embossed button

Ears: *the ears are large and rounded.*

Eyes: *the brown, glass eyes on wire shanks are sewn in, wide apart, along the top edge of the muzzle.*

Nose: *the shield-shaped nose is vertically stitched, with central stitches dropped, and a single, pink, horizontal stitch across the upper, central part.*

Arms: *the relatively long arms are straighter than on previous examples, to represent the squat features of a bear cub.*

Feet: *the large feet have beige, felt pads with no claws.*

Navel: *the small, dark area representing the navel is a unique feature of Jackie-Baby.*

BEAR PROFILE
At this angle you can see how Jackie-Baby differs from the traditional, Steiff teddy-bear design: he has a straight back, short, stubby legs with large thighs, and squared-off paws. However, he still retains the distinctive, large, protruding muzzle.

Legs: *the legs are short and stubby with fat thighs and large, ovoid feet.*

dark brown, vertically stitched, shield-shaped nose; central stitches dropped to meet inverted-V-shaped mouth

small, brown, glass eyes with black pupils, sewn in on wire shanks

light brown mohair plush on back, limbs, head, and tail; cream mohair plush on front of body

fully jointed, short limbs

beige, felt pads, in very good condition

originally four claws on each paw

1955 BABY-BEAR

Height: 25cm (10in)

The mohair-covered, metal, U-shaped tail activates the head movement via an internal mechanism similar to that of the Schuco Yes/No bear, although the head and neck are joined in this version. This is the larger of the two sizes available; 3,539 examples were made in all.

Embossed button

typical Steiff, triangular nose, horizontally stitched with border stitching; inverted-Y-shaped mouth in brown thread

black, glass bead eyes, sewn in

fully jointed (Steiff later produced a range of unjointed, miniature bears)

straight arms, slightly wider at shoulders; no pads

legs have fat thighs and clearly defined, large feet; no pads and no claws

attractive, apricot-coloured mohair plush

1950s–70s MINIATURE

Height: 10cm (4in)

The first miniature Steiff teddy bears were produced in 1909, but have changed little over the years. Often it is only the different buttons, labels, and chest-tags that can help to date them. (Schuco miniatures are distinguished by their straight legs and little feet.)

Embossed button

typical Steiff, shield-shaped, dark brown, vertically stitched nose

clipped, light brown, mohair-plush muzzle

open mouth reveals felt palate, painted tongue, and brown painted lips

blond, shaggy mohair plush on dark brown, woven backing, gives two-tone effect

peach-coloured, mohair-plush chest plate

short, fat legs and large feet; peach-coloured, felt pads

1950s ZOTTY

Height: 35cm (14in)

First introduced in 1951, Zotty has remained a firm favourite until the present day. The name is derived from the German word *zottig* (shaggy) referring to its unique fur. Other manufacturers copied the style but only Steiff bears have the peach-coloured chest plates.

Embossed button

brown circles of felt, sewn on with two diagonal stitches in pink thread, to represent closed eyes

shaggy, blond mohair plush on dark brown, woven backing, the typical Zotty fabric

spreadeagled, unjointed limbs

clipped, mohair-plush muzzle, and open mouth with peach-coloured, felt palate

brown, shield-shaped nose like that of Zotty (left)

1950s SLEEPING ZOTTY

Length: 20cm (8in)

Steiff made Zotty in a lying-down position as well as in six sizes, from 17cm (7in) to 50cm (20in), in the standing pose. The sleeping bear is made of the same, shaggy, dark-backed, blond mohair plush, with open mouth and clipped muzzle, but with felt "eyelids".

Embossed button

Schuco: 1949–76

POST-WAR NOVELTIES: CLOCKWORK, FLEXIBLE, TALKING BEARS

Post-war production recommenced at Schreyer and Company's Schuco plant (*see pp.40–43*) around 1949. New, novelty lines included the clockwork Rolly Bear (1954) wearing roller skates, and the Dancing Bear (1956–62) who turned in circles while throwing a ball up and down. When Heinrich

Müller died in 1958, his son, Werner, took over alongside manager, Alexander Girz. In the 1960s, the Bigo Bello series was introduced; this included Parlo, the talking bear, (speaking German, French, or Italian) with a pull-cord mechanism (1963). Schuco was bought by Dunbee-Combex-Marx in 1976.

c.1950 TRICKY

The earlier Yes/No bear (*see pp.42–43*) was reintroduced after World War II as Tricky, and displayed a ribbon bow and plastic medallion that read on the reverse: "Made in US Zone Germany", indicating its pre-1953 production. Tricky was produced in seven sizes, in blond, hazelnut, or reddish brown mohair plush, and with a growler mechanism. Two sizes were available with Swiss musical boxes incorporated, and Tricky pandas were also made.

Height: 33cm (13in)   Plastic medallion

Eyes: *the large, brown, glass eyes, with black pupils, are sewn in.*

Nose: *the black, vertically stitched nose is shield shaped; some late-1950s examples have been found with moulded, plastic noses.*

Fur/stuffing: *the mohair plush is hazelnut coloured; the stuffing is wood-wool throughout. (This size was also available in blond mohair plush.) Four sizes were available with soft, kapok stuffing, and the 14cm (5½in) size had a metal, internal frame.*

Claws: *three black claws are sewn across the plush on each paw and foot.*

Pads: *the beige, felt pads are in perfect condition.*

BEAR PROFILE

Tricky's short tail which, like that of its predecessor (*see p.42*), acts as a lever for operating head movement, is clearly visible. This later bear also has flat, stiffened feet, but the legs are longer and thinner than earlier, often chubby-thighed examples. The unusual, begging arms, with their very broad paws, are typical of the post-war Yes/No bears.

Feet: *the oval feet, wider at the toes and with card-reinforced pads, are a typical Schuco design.*

clear, glass eyes, painted brown on backs; black pupils sewn in

small, slightly cupped ears, centred over facial seams

black, vertically stitched, square nose

open mouth with beige, felt palate; airbrushed tongue

oatmeal-coloured mohair plush; internal squeaker

squared-off paws, with beige, felt pads; four claws across plush

squared-off feet; five claws on right foot, four on left, sewn across plush

flexible, internal wire armature allows limbs to be bent into various positions

1960s BRUMMI; BIGO BELLO SERIES

Height: 23cm (9in)

This is the smallest in a range of open-mouthed, mohair-plush bears advertised as Brummi (from *brummen* – to growl like a bear). A similar design, Urso, was produced in Dralon. Both were part of the Bigo Bello series of fully "poseable" bears.

Printed label

convex, plastic, "googly" eyes

horizontal seam across top of head

open mouth; black, felt lower jaw, with smaller piece of beige felt glued on top

black, triangular, moulded plastic nose

light golden, short mohair plush; white, cotton torso beneath clothes; soft stuffing

red, brushed-nylon shirt tucked into black shorts

square, beige, felt pads on paws

flexible, internal wire armature allows body to be fully "poseable"

long, white socks sewn onto legs

LATE 1960s GERMAN SOCCER PLAYER

Height: 34cm (13½in)

One of a range of bears dressed in the coloured strips of German soccer teams, this bear has lost its black and white plastic boots, and the paper emblem on the shirt has been partly removed. Originally, it would have possessed a triangular, card tag reading "Hegi" – a Schuco range named after Herta Girz, who became a director in the late 1950s.

small, cupped ears sewn just behind horizontal head-seam; hard, internal "mask" structures head shape

large, white and black, plastic, convex, button eyes give wide-eyed look

small, rounded, black, plastic, nose

pale peach brushed-nylon on lower half of face

brown, cotton, smiling mouth

mushroom-coloured mohair plush with soft stuffing; internal wire frame allows body to be bent into various poses

three black claws stitched across plush on hands and feet

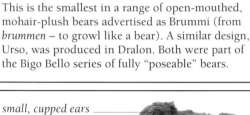

1960s PUZZI; BIGO BELLO SERIES

Height: 23cm (9in)

This unusual little bear was available in one size, although the design was reused in a larger 42cm (16½in) size for one of the Bigo Bello talking bears, described in catalogues as "*Jungbär*". The original triangular, white-edged, red, card tag with the words "Original Schuco Bigo Bello DRGM", and a ribbon bow, has been removed from the chest.

golden mohair plush over internal, metal frame

black, metal, bead eyes with white, painted, metal surrounds

black, metal, bead eyes

red, celluloid tongue

black, metal, bead nose with white, painted, metal mouth

jointed limbs

straight legs with small feet

1954 JANUS; TWO-FACED

Height: 9cm (3½in)

These little bears show the two faces of a unique novelty whose head can be "swapped" using a knob at the base of the torso. They share many characteristics with other miniature bears in Schuco's Piccolo series, which was reproduced, from the 1950s until the 1970s, in a fractionally larger size, and was advertised as "Original Schuco Talisman".

Germany: post-1945

SIMILAR TRADITIONAL STYLES; INTRODUCTION OF TAGGING

Many manufacturers operated in the Neustadt area after World War II (*see pp.30–31*). Some, like the two Hermann factories, had recently arrived from nearby Sonneberg following Russian occupation. Post-war designs did not change much from those of the pre-war period: many firms used similar patterns with narrow bodies, straight legs, small feet, and inset muzzles. By this time, however, several firms had introduced labels to their products to aid identification and recognition. The labels varied in form, and included triangular tags, scalloped, circular tags, chest-buttons, and oblong, metal, foot-tags.

c.1960 ANKER PLÜSCHSPIELWARENFABRIK

Anker was a Munich-based company. In 1954, it bought Artur Hermann's soft-toy company, J. Hermann Nachf. Inh. Artur Hermann (*see pp.94–5*), a firm that had moved from Sonneberg to Munich in 1940. Anker's trademark – an anchor (*Anker*) superimposed on a lion – is printed on a metallic paper tag similar to those used by both Hermann companies after the war. The side with the logo is blue with silver, and the reverse is silver, with the words *"Anker Plüschtiere aus München"* printed in blue. Anker ceased business during the 1970s.

Height: 47cm (18½in)

Printed tag

Ears: *the flat, slightly padded ears are sewn across the facial seams.*

Eyes: *the brown, glass eyes have black pupils.*

Nose/mouth: *the oval, black nose is horizontally stitched; the mouth is a double-stitched, inverted Y shape.*

Muzzle: *the inset, beige, short-pile, mohair plush muzzle is elongated and pointed.*

BEAR PROFILE
In profile, you can see the inset, elongated, pointed muzzle of contrasting short-pile plush, a feature of bears made by Hermann and other German manufacturers. The bear has a straight body with no hump on the back; thin, slightly curved arms; slender, tubular legs; and small feet.

Body seam: *the front, central seam is interrupted by the knot of the chest-tag. The final seam is at the back.*

Fur/stuffing/growler: *the curly, synthetic plush has a shiny appearance; the stuffing is wood-wool; there is a tilt growler.*

Foot-pads: *the circular foot-pads are in good condition, except for insect holes in the right pad.*

Trademark: *the front of the blue and silver, paper chest-tag is printed with an anchor superimposed on a lion.*

amber, glass eyes
with black pupils,
on wire shanks

black, horizontally
stitched, shield-like,
nose; inverted-Y-
shaped, single-
stitched mouth

inset, pointed,
short-pile, beige,
wool-plush muzzle

original green, rayon,
ribbon bow, now faded,
tied around neck

long, curved
arms with
spoon-shaped
paws and
peach-coloured,
felt pads

dark brown-
tipped, beige
mohair plush;
wood-wool
stuffing

straight legs
with little foot
definition

tear-shaped
foot-pads

c.1960 EM TOY AND DOLL CO.

Height: 38cm (15in)

Printed tag

This EM Toy and Doll Co. bear demonstrates the typical Sonneberg/Neustadt design, with its inset muzzle of contrasting plush. The scalloped, metallic, blue and silver swing-tag has a stylized "EM" with "the sign of quality" written in German.

black, safe,
plastic eyes

curly, rose-
tinted, beige
plush; internal
tilt growler

black, horizontally
stitched, triangular,
nose; inverted-Y-
shaped mouth

plastic chest-tag
embossed with
outline of
dressed cat

certificate of
authenticity
tied around
neck

tan, felt foot-
pads; "Kessel"
signature with
limited-edition
number

1985 ALTHANS

Height: 40cm (16in)

Plastic tag

Karl Althans, a Sonneberg teddy-bear company dating from the 1920s, moved to Birkig in the US Zone of Germany after World War II, and formed a new firm, Althans KG, in 1949. The present manager, Günther Kessel, introduced limited-edition bears.

small, flat ears sewn
across facial seams

black,
horizontally
stitched, lozenge-
shaped nose;
inverted-Y-
shaped mouth

brown, plastic eyes
with black pupils,
sewn in on integral
short, round shanks

typical "Grisly"
oversized head

original blue,
rayon bow

beige, felt
paw-pads

red mohair plush
(one of 11 available colours)

feet with
no pads

c.1983 GRISLY SPIELWAREN

Height: 18cm (7in)

GRISLY

Printed tag

Karl Unfrecht founded this company in 1954; his two children took it over after his death in 1980. Pre-1964 bears had inset muzzles and metal chest buttons with a "Grisly" logo. The company's small, coloured bears proved popular exports for the US collectors' market.

inset muzzle of
short-pile, pale
golden mohair plush

slightly cupped ears
sewn over facial seams

black, horizontally
stitched, triangular
nose; inverted-Y-
shaped mouth

brown, glass eyes
with black pupils
on wire shanks

pale peach-coloured,
felt pads; three
black claws
stitched across
plush

beige mohair
plush; wood-
wool stuffing

unusual body
made up of one
front and two
back pieces

c.1959–60 HANS CLEMENS

Height: 40cm (16in)

W-GERMANY

Printed tag

Clemens founded his company in 1949. The first teddy bears were made, with his sister's help, from army blankets. This bear has the triangular, metal chest-tag introduced in 1957. It was replaced by plastic in 1963, but reintroduced in 1968, and it is still used today.

Germany: post-1945

ZOTTY LOOK-ALIKES; SYNTHETIC MATERIALS

Certain German manufacturers borrowed ideas from Steiff's novelty lines of the 1950s, such as the popular Zotty range (see p.111). Both of the Hermann factories (see pp.96–99) and Clemens produced their own Zotty bears, while other firms hinted at the Zotty design by combining shaggy fur and an open mouth with inset muzzle. The traditional teddy remained popular, while incorporating modern materials and safety measures. Cheaper East-Asian imports forced some firms, such as Petz and Eli, to close during the 1970s; others, such as Heunec, assembled some of their bears outside of Germany to cut costs.

1980S BAUMANN & KIENEL

Franz Baumann, the son of Adelheid Hermann (see pp.94–95), and an old friend, Franz Kienel, formed this company in 1951. Its tradename, "Baki", is derived from the two founders' names. Classic designs, such as this example, as well as souvenir Berliner bears, are all traditionally made by hand, as indicated by the embroidered cloth seam-label, at their original factory at Rodach near Coburg. Franz Baumann and his partner's son, Walter, presently manage the company.

Height: 30cm (12in)

Embroidered label

Ears: the inner edges of the ears are caught into the facial seams and sewn down the sides of the head.

Eyes: the large, safe, plastic eyes are brown with black pupils.

Nose/mouth: the black, triangular nose is horizontally stitched; the mouth is an inverted Y shape.

Bow: the original cream-coloured, ribbon bow is tied around the neck.

Trademark: there is a circular, card chest-tag printed with a scalloped edge seal design resembling the Hermann chest-tag.

Fur/stuffing: the fur is short-pile, golden mohair plush; the bear is stuffed throughout with compact soft stuffing.

Pads/claws: the paw-pads are made from beige felt; three black claws are stitched across the plush.

BEAR PROFILE
Notice how this bear follows the traditional design with its protruding muzzle, but with some features reduced: it has a shapeless, narrow body; almost straight limbs of equal length; and the legs have only slight indications of small stubby feet. The embroidered cloth label, sewn into the seam in the lower back, is clearly visible.

Feet: the feet are small and oval.

discoloured, white mohair plush; wood-wool stuffing

inset, short, clipped, white, mohair-plush muzzle

short, plush pads; inner edge ends in Zotty-style point

amber, glass eyes with black pupils

vertically stitched, black nose extends down to open mouth with felt palate and painted tongue

large, oval, cream, plush foot-pads; three large, airbrushed claws

unusual mauve tipping

c.1960 HUGO KOCH
Height: 30cm (12in)

Hugo Koch's logo, seen on the tag, depicts a bear wearing a chef's hat and holding a spoon (*Koch* is German for cook). This bear's design loosely follows Steiff's Zotty (*see p.111*) and the earlier Teddy Baby (*see p.37*) with its shaggy, tipped plush, open mouth, and "begging" paws.

Printed tag

---

amber, plastic, button-like eyes

small, rounded, brown, vertically stitched nose across point of muzzle; no mouth

short, tubular arms with no pads or claws

all-in-one legs and body; small feet allow bear to stand up; no pads or claws

large, narrow, flat ears sewn down sides of head

pointed muzzle, shaved to reveal woven backing and central seam

printed, red trademark on gold paper tag tied with yellow cord around neck

brown, shaggy, synthetic plush; one-piece foam rubber body

1981 KÄTHE KRUSE PUPPEN
Height: 30cm (12in)

Käthe Kruse was renowned for her 1920s–1930s life-like dolls. After World War II, her family firm moved from the East to Donauworth in West Germany. Her daughter, Johanna, introduced teddies to the new pro-duction programme (Modell Hanne Kruse) in 1967.

Printed tag

black, horizontally stitched, narrow, oblong nose; inverted-Y-shaped, single-stitched mouth

brown mohair plush; wood-wool stuffing; internal tilt-growler

large, flat ears, slotted into head

translucent, amber, glass eyes with black pupils

button made of milk glass with indented red symbol

beige, felt paw-pads

body made of single piece of fabric

c.1950s PETZ COMPANY
Height: 56cm (22½in)

This Neustadt-based company made soft toys and traditional teddy bears for German department stores until 1974. Marked with glass chest buttons, those produced just after World War II also bore cloth tags reading "Original Petz US Zone".

Glass button

black, safe, plastic, button eyes

black, horizontally stitched, triangular nose; inverted-V-shaped mouth

red, plastic trademark with gold, embossed lettering

dark brown, felt pads; no claws

cupped ears

traditional protruding muzzle

brown, short-pile mohair plush; soft-stuffed throughout

curved, tapering arms

large feet

1983 ALTHANS
Height: 43cm (17in)

This classic design bear with a humped back and safe, plastic, button eyes carries the "Albico" trademark, used by Althans (*see p.115*) from the early 1950s to the 1980s. "Albico" is derived from the first two letter of Althans, Birkig, and Coburg.

Embossed tag

Switzerland & Austria: post-1945

FIRMS BASED IN ZÜRICH AND GRAZ

S ince the 1920s, Switzerland has exported its famed musical mechanisms to the United States, United Kingdom, and Germany, for use in teddy bears. The Swiss did not generally make teddy bears themselves, although the company MCZ Schweizer Plüschtierchen (meaning little Swiss plush animals) operated after World War II. A number of Austrian teddy-bear manufacturers, including Schwika, Fechter, and Schenker, based in Graz, and SAF in Mittendorf, also existed in the post-war era. The Berg company in Fieberbrunn is currently the largest teddy-bear manufacturer in Austria.

1950s MUTZLI

Early MCZ bears carried metal, chest or ear buttons; the button featured the company logo, a white teddy-bear glove-puppet and the tradename "Mutzli" (Swiss-German for little bear). MCZ probably stands for "Mutzli Company Zürich". This Swiss firm, based in Zürich, also produced bears dressed as little girls, boys, and cooks, as well as floppy, unjointed bears (including one with a rattle in each paw).

Height: 34cm (13½in)   Printed button

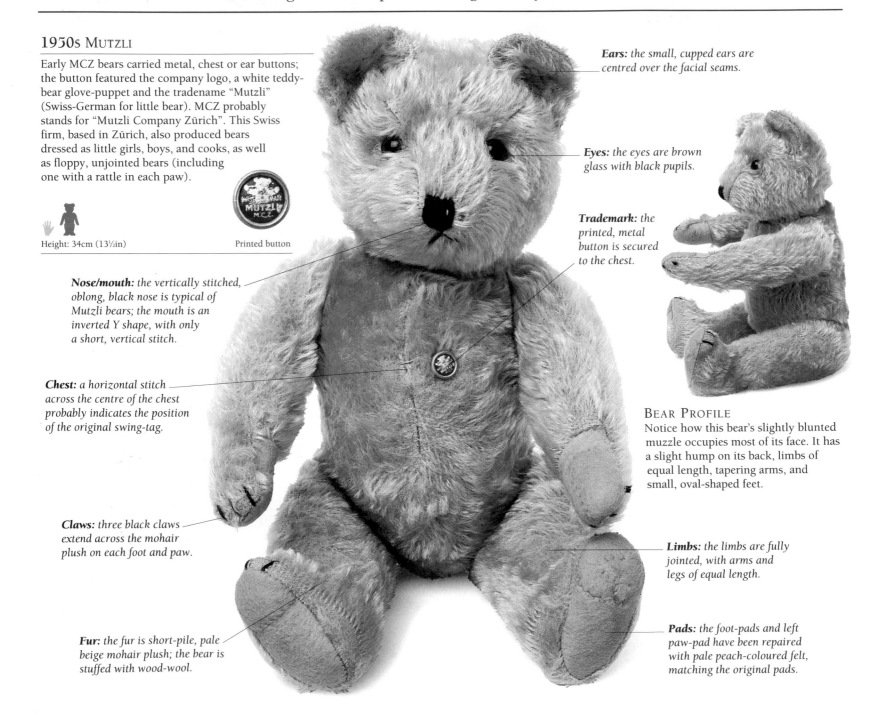

Ears: *the small, cupped ears are centred over the facial seams.*

Eyes: *the eyes are brown glass with black pupils.*

Trademark: *the printed, metal button is secured to the chest.*

Nose/mouth: *the vertically stitched, oblong, black nose is typical of Mutzli bears; the mouth is an inverted Y shape, with only a short, vertical stitch.*

Chest: *a horizontal stitch across the centre of the chest probably indicates the position of the original swing-tag.*

Claws: *three black claws extend across the mohair plush on each foot and paw.*

Fur: *the fur is short-pile, pale beige mohair plush; the bear is stuffed with wood-wool.*

BEAR PROFILE
Notice how this bear's slightly blunted muzzle occupies most of its face. It has a slight hump on its back, limbs of equal length, tapering arms, and small, oval-shaped feet.

Limbs: *the limbs are fully jointed, with arms and legs of equal length.*

Pads: *the foot-pads and left paw-pad have been repaired with pale peach-coloured felt, matching the original pads.*

pale yellow, short-pile, mohair plush; compact, synthetic fibre stuffing

small ears, sewn across facial seams

brown, glass eyes with black pupils

typical expansive forehead with small, flattened muzzle

short, slightly curved arms

dark brown, vertically stitched, round nose; wide, inverted-Y-shaped mouth

short legs

1980s BERG
Height: 14cm (5½in)

Berg made its first bears from army blankets after World War II, and began using plush in 1951. A cloth label with "Berg", and occasionally "Made in Austria", was sewn into the ear or body. *Tiere mit Herz* ("animals with heart") eventually became Berg's trademark. The red metal heart is attached to the chest. Sometimes fabric labels were also used.

large, flat ears

label with brown, embroidered bear motif

reddish orange, glass eyes with black pupils

black, outlined top lip; felt palate with red, felt tongue

black, vertically stitched, shield-shaped nose

shaggy, light golden mohair plush; wood-wool stuffing; tilt-growler

oval feet

beige, felt pads with no claws

1950s–1960s FECHTER
Height: 55cm (22in)

Wilhelm and Berta Fechter started as a small, cottage industry in Graz, Austria, after World War II. They opened a factory in 1948, but ceased business in 1978. This typical Fechter bear came from unsold warehouse stock brought to California in 1983.

Embroidered label

reddish brown, glass eyes with black pupils, sewn-in

inset muzzle of short-pile, beige mohair plush

brown, vertically stitched, shield-shaped nose

peach-coloured, felt palate with red, felt tongue; lips outlined with black paint

light brown mohair plush; wood-wool stuffing

arms curve downwards in Steiff Teddy Baby fashion (see p.37)

narrow ankles and large, slender, oval feet

peach-coloured, felt pads; no claws

1950s–1960s SCHWIKA
Height: 25cm (10in)

Like Fechter, Schwika was based in Graz, Austria, and its bears (distinguished by an embossed, round, metal button attached to the left ear with a red cord) were similar in design to Fechter's bears. The curved, slender wrists are typical of this Zotty-like model.

Embossed button

cupped ears sewn across facial seams

brown, glass eyes with black pupils

black, vertically stitched, square nose; inverted-V-shaped mouth

protruding muzzle

brown mohair plush; soft-stuffed limbs; wood-wool elsewhere

original green, rayon, ribbon

mint condition, beige, felt pads

fully jointed limbs and head

1982 MUTZLI
Height: 33cm (13in)

Only 600 of these Jubilee Bears were made, of which 150 were exported to the US. The card chest-tag, with bear motif, and the basic Mutzli bear design, changed little from the 1950s, although in later years Felpa AG of Aarau, Switzerland produced the bears.

Printed tag

Merrythought: 1940s–60s

CHEEKY DESIGN AND OTHER POST-WAR NOVELTY BEARS

The Cheeky design was so named during the 1956 British Toy Fair because of the bear's wide smile. The "bell in ear" concept was later borrowed by other manufacturers as well as being used again by Merrythought in its Pastel Bear of 1957, a soft-stuffed and unjointed, artificial-silk plush bear.

Merrythought reused the Cheeky design in different plushes and again, in 1962, with an open mouth. From the late 1950s on, the company also produced many soft toys based on television or movie cartoon characters – Sooty, a British TV glove puppet appeared in 1960, and Disney's Winnie the Pooh in 1966.

1966–68 MR. TWISTY CHEEKY

Mr. and Mrs. Twisty Cheeky formed part of a range of comical, dressed, standing toys that was heralded, in 1965, by Mr. and Mrs. Twisty Bear, who could be "twisted" into different positions with the aid of an internal wire frame. Mr. Twisty Cheeky, illustrated here, is the smaller of the two sizes that were manufactured. He wears removable red dungarees with braces, which are fastened at the back with Velcro. His partner, Mrs. Twisty Cheeky, wore a skirt and pinafore.

Height: 28cm (11in)   Printed label

Fur: only the head is made of golden mohair plush.

Eyes: the safe, plastic, orange-coloured eyes have black pupils.

Nose and mouth: the nose is a tall, rectangular shape, vertically stitched in black; two curved stitches form the wide Cheeky smile.

Paws: the white, woven fabric paws have well-defined thumbs.

Collar: the white, felt collar is original; the original ribbon bow-tie is missing.

Dungarees: the red, woven fabric, now very faded, would have been bright red originally. There is a blue patch on the left knee.

Feet: the very large, clown-like feet are made of dark brown, woven fabric.

Muzzle: the typical Cheeky muzzle, made of pale golden velveteen, is a protruding, oval shape.

Body: the body is made from sky-blue woven fabric. The internal wire frame allows the body and limbs to be twisted into various positions.

BEAR PROFILE

From this angle you can see clearly the bear's bulbous head, with large ears positioned low down. The pert muzzle and wide smile are important features of the Cheeky design, as are the pot-belly and the long, flat feet.

unique domed head

large ears with metal bell sewn inside

safe, lock-in, plastic eyes

inset, golden, velveteen muzzle

tightly bound, black, vertically stitched nose at tip of muzzle; wide smile formed by four long stitches

curly, honey-coloured nylon plush

unusual large, circular pads; four claws across seams

brown, felt pads with five claws across seams

c.1960 CHEEKY; NYLON PLUSH

Height: 38cm (15in)

The Cheeky registered design, with its unique domed head and large, flat ears, each containing a bell, first appeared in the 1957 catalogue. It was originally produced in artificial-silk plush or golden mohair plush; nylon plush was also used from 1960.

Printed label

Mohican-style scalp lock of long, silvery grey mohair plush

clear, glass eyes, painted white on back; sewn in on wire shanks

discoloured, white mohair plush on chest and insides of ears; brown elsewhere

beige, velveteen muzzle, of similar design to that of Cheeky

slightly S-shaped arms

oval, beige, felt pads

beige, velveteen feet; beige, felt pads

1949–56 PUNKINHEAD

Height: 42cm (16½in)

Cheeky existed in a different form in Canada, as the mascot for Eaton's department store in Toronto. He became the hero of several storybooks, as well as the leader of the annual Santa Claus parade. A replica Ancestor of Cheeky appeared in 1986.

Printed label

amber, glass eyes with black pupils, sewn in on wire shanks

large, pointed ears with blue, felt linings

bluebird motif added by Donald Campbell, who named all his vehicles "Bluebird"

black, vertically stitched nose

original red, felt coat with pocket; fastened with two white buttons

all-in-one body, arms, and legs; bulbous thighs

blue, felt feet

1956–57 MR WHOPPIT

Height: 23cm (9in)

This bear represents one of three characters from *Robin* comic produced as soft toys in the mid-1950s. He belonged to world land and water speed record-maker, Donald Campbell. The kapok filling allowed the bear to float to the surface of Coniston Water, England, after Donald Campbell's fatal record attempt in 1967. Merrythought made a replica in 1992.

flat, white, plastic eyes; painted, black pupils with white "glints"; eyelashes drawn in above eyes

beige, velveteen, heart-shaped face, with inset muzzle of same material

wide, smiling, W-shaped mouth, drawn in on this factory sample

wide, black, vertically stitched nose, with outer stitches dropped

original pink ribbon bow

round, felt pads, machine-stitched in place

jointed arms and head

shoe-shaped, beige, velveteen feet; brown, felt pads reinforced with card; three claws drawn in

faded, golden mohair plush

1962–63 PETER BEAR

Height: 34cm (13½in)

This very rare, caricatured bear with unjointed legs (the one shown here is a factory sample) was produced briefly, in one size only, and has the same wide smile as Punkinhead and Cheeky. The "googly" eyes give him an endearing expression.

Printed label

Wendy Boston: 1945–76

DEVELOPMENT OF FIRST FULLY WASHABLE TEDDY BEAR

Ken and Wendy Williams (*née* Boston) started their pioneering, soft-toy business in south Wales after World War II and moved to larger premises, at Crickhowell and Abergavenny, in 1948. As Wendy Boston (Crickhowell) Ltd., they invented the safe, screw-locked, plastic eye and then, in 1954, the first washable teddy bear, which revolutionized the soft-toy industry. A decade later, as Wendy Boston Playsafe Toys Ltd., they were producing over a quarter of the UK's total, soft-toy exports. In 1968, they were taken over by Denys Fisher Toys (subsequently Palitoy and General Mills), but the factory closed in 1976.

C.1963 LARGE; NYLON

During the early 1960s, Wendy Boston produced this unjointed, foam-filled bear in 19 sizes – from 23cm (9in) to 1.83m (6ft) – mostly in white, gold, honey, and honey-tipped, brown nylon plush. It was first shown on British television in 1955, being put through a mangle. Hoover awarded the bear a "certificate of wash-ability". The large ears, cut all-in-one with the head, were designed to be pegged to a washing line without strain.

Eyes: *each screw-locked eye has an outer ring of amber-coloured plastic; a black, nylon screw and bolt form the pupil.*

Nose: *the black, tightly bound, nose is vertically stitched.*

Claws: *three black claws across short-pile plush of paw-pads.*

Height: 55cm (22in)   Printed label

WENDY BOSTON
Made in England
Wash in luke-warm suds

Pads: *the short-pile, nylon-plush pads at the end of the stocky legs are oval in shape.*

BEAR PROFILE
This typical Wendy Boston, unjointed bear, made of soft, shaggy nylon plush, inspires a small child's affection, with the slightly curved arms stretching out to demand a hug; the straight, legs have no ankle or foot definition.

Fur/stuffing: *the fur is shaggy, honey-coloured nylon plush; the bear is stuffed throughout with granulated foam-rubber – a material originally prized for its washability and lightness, but which later proved to be a fire hazard, as it gives off toxic fumes when alight.*

amber-coloured, safe, plastic eyes with small, black pupils; attached by screw-on nut at back of eye

black, vertically stitched, rectangular nose with inverted-T-shaped mouth

curved, unjointed arms, projecting outwards

clipped, short-pile mohair plush on muzzle

three claws on pads

slightly discoloured, white mohair plush

printed label sewn into leg seam

short-pile, clipped, mohair-plush pads

c.1955 WHITE MOHAIR
Height: 36cm (14⅛in)

This unjointed bear is one of Wendy Boston's earlier bears made from mohair plush supplied by Norton (Weaving) Ltd. of Yorkshire. In 1987, House of Nisbet produced a replica of a golden, mohair-plush Wendy Boston bear that once belonged to Peter Bull.

Printed label

small, three-part, Wendy Boston patent, safe, plastic eyes

ears cut all-in-one with head

black, vertically stitched, rectangular nose; inverted-Y-shaped mouth

inset, rounded, blunt muzzle of white, short-pile nylon plush

three black claws stitched over paw seams

short-pile, pink, nylon plush; foam-rubber stuffing

legs in permanent sitting position

c.1955 SMALL; NYLON
Height: 24cm (9½in)

One of the smallest Wendy Boston bears of this period, the design was available in white, gold, honey, blue, and pink. The label reads "Wash in lukewarm suds" (some specify "Persil" – a washing-powder whose maker endorsed Wendy Boston bears).

Printed label

three-part, Wendy Boston patent, safe, plastic eyes

golden yellow, nylon-plush head, feet, and paws

inset, rounded, blunt muzzle

small, rounded, yellow, plush paws; no claws

outstretched, pink, brushed-nylon arms

red, fringed trim at neck and waist (later additions)

tartan trousers and red, brushed-nylon top form body; granulated foam-rubber stuffing

pointed, "realistic" feet

1960 DRESSED, ALL-IN-ONE TEDDY
Height: 30cm (12in)

Wendy Boston made dressed soft toys from the early 1950s. Its costume formed the body; the paws and head were of plush. This example wears Royal Stewart tartan, Dutch-style trousers. The red, fringed trim at neck and waist are later additions.

Printed label

dark beige nylon plush

separate, traditional-style ears

small, black, vertically stitched, rectangular nose

white, nylon-plush, inset muzzle

curved, outstretched, unjointed arms

slightly defined feet, unlike completely straight legs of original Wendy Boston bears

white, nylon-plush pads

1972 MUSICAL; NYLON
Height: 33cm (13in)

This bear was produced after the takeover by Denys Fisher Toys. Its safe, plastic eyes are not the typical Wendy Boston, three-part type. The musical box, which plays *The Teddy Bears' Picnic*, is inside the head; a key projects from the back of the head.

Printed label

UK: post-World War II – c. 1970

BRITISH INDUSTRY STRUGGLES; SHEEPSKIN AND TRADITIONAL

Several new companies were established in the UK after World War II. Due to the rationing of traditional mohair at the time, these companies made teddy bears of sheepskin, a material that remained popular until the 1960s. The economic climate in Britain during the 1970s forced the demise of many newly formed traditional teddy-bear manufacturers: Gwentoys Ltd. (established in 1965) was taken over by Dean's in 1972; Acton Toycraft Ltd. (established in 1964) closed in the 1970s; and Real Soft Toys (established in 1969) was later taken over by Lefray Ltd., another post-war firm.

1965–72 GWENTOYS LTD.

The general shape of this teddy bear is reminiscent of the Chiltern Hugmee range manufactured in the late 1950s and early 1960s. It also shares such features as nose design, velveteen pads, and seam-label design and positioning. The similarities are not surprising since Gwentoys Ltd., based in Pontypool, was formed by three former managers of the Chiltern factory, also located in Pontypool, following the latter's takeover by the Dunbee-Combex group. "Gwentoys" is derived from Gwent, the old Welsh name for Monmouthshire (recently renamed Gwent), the county in which Pontypool is situated .

Height: 58cm (23in)　　　Printed label

Nose: *the black, squarish nose, vertically stitched across the junction of the facial seams, is Chiltern-like. The mouth is an inverted Y shape.*

Fur/stuffing/squeaker: *the fur is golden mohair plush, soft-stuffed except for the muzzle, which is stuffed with wood-wool. The bear has a tilt- squeaker.*

Pads: *the beige, velveteen pads are in perfect condition except for a few stains on the right foot. There are no claws.*

Ears: *the large, flat ears are sewn across the facial seams.*

Eyes: *the amber and black, safe, plastic eyes are fixed into the facial seams with washers.*

BEAR PROFILE

This bear's straight head and gently rounded muzzle is evocative of the earlier, flat-faced Hugmees. At this angle, you can see how the bear exemplifies archetypal features of the British 1960s bear with its shorter limbs, small, rounded feet, and lack of claws. The blue on white, printed label is sewn into the side-seam under the left arm.

orange and black, plastic eyes

area around eyes, ears, and mouth trimmed with electric clippers

cinnamon-coloured, dyed sheepskin

straight legs with dark brown, sheepskin pads

only two black knots remain of original, vertically stitched, Tinka-Bell square nose

swivel-jointed, short, curved arms

label sewn into foot-pad seam

1964 PLUMMER, WANDLESS & CO.
Height: 43cm (17in)

This is one of 70,000 sheepskin teddy bears produced annually by this Worthing-based firm during the mid-1960s. It was available in eight sizes and was exported worldwide. The company, which was founded in 1946, was sold in 1972.

Printed label

realistic, black, moulded plastic nose, locked in with washer

original blue, satin ribbon

soft, dense, golden lambskin; musical box plays Brahms' Lullaby

cheap, orange, translucent, plastic eyes on wire shanks; pupils painted black behind

triangular head with upturned muzzle moves from side to side when musical box plays

short, straight arms and legs with small feet

c.1957 LECO TOYS (WEST END) LTD.
Height: 33cm (13in)

This bear was one of a 1957 range of animated musical items produced by Leco Toys, a London company established by Ludwig and Martha Levy. The company moved to larger premises in 1965, but ceased business in the early 1970s.

Printed card swing-tag

large, flat ears sewn into horizontal dart across facial seams

black, vertically stitched, square nose, with inverted-Y-shaped mouth

short, golden mohair plush; cotton "sub" stuffing

black "pupils" are an optical illusion – created by hollow space on integral shank of plastic eye

short arms with chocolate-brown velveteen pads

fat thighs and stubby feet; no claws

MID-1960s LEFRAY LTD.
Height: 40cm (16in)

Throughout the 1960s, Lefray Ltd. (established in 1948) was based in St Albans, Hertfordshire; this bear was probably made shortly before the company's move to Aberbeeg, Gwent, in south Wales, where it is still operating.

Printed label

black, tightly bound, vertically stitched oblong nose with black, felt underlay

soft, cream, Rexine pads, cracked to reveal woven backing; no claws

large, translucent, orange, plastic eyes with black pupils, on wire shanks, sewn into face and knotted at back

curly, white wool and, possibly, synthetic mix plush

large, narrow feet; thick thighs

1960s ACTON TOYCRAFT LTD.
Height: 63cm (25in)

In 1964, J.K. Farnell split into two operations, Acton Toycraft taking over the company's works in Acton, west London, and trading as "Twyford". Several light-coloured Twyford bears have been found with red, felt pads, also used by Farnell.

Printed label

Dean's: c.1960–80

TRADITIONAL AND UNJOINTED BEARS MADE BY SUBSIDIARIES

The 1960s and 1970s was an era of change for Dean's Rag Book Company Ltd. Its main production continued at the factory in Rye, Sussex, which was extended in 1961. The company used the Childsplay Toys trademark until 1965, when Childsplay Ltd. (one of two divisions formed in the 1950s, the other being Merton Toys Ltd.) became Dean's Childsplay Toys Ltd. From that time, the familiar fighting dogs logo was dropped from the label. In 1974, two years after the buyout of Gwentoys, some production moved from Rye to Pontypool in south Wales. The Rye plant eventually closed in 1980.

c.1980 DEAN'S/GWENTOY GROUP

Dean's continued Gwentoy's line of teddy bears after buying out the company in 1972 (see p.124), with the label indicating the use of both the Pontypool and the Rye factories. This branch of the Dean's/Gwentoy Group specialized in the cheaper end of the market, supplying bears wholesale for chainstores and the mail-order trade. Although this bear is traditionally styled with jointed arms and legs, the stiff, unjointed neck denotes a cheaper toy.

Height: 31cm (12⅓in)

MADE IN BRITAIN BY
Dean's/Gwentoy Group

Printed label

Ears: *the cupped ears are positioned towards the back of the head, caught into the facial seams, and sewn down the sides of the head.*

Eyes: *the brown and black, safe, plastic, lock-in eyes are set on the outer edges of the facial seams.*

Nose/mouth: *the black, vertically stitched, shield-shaped nose and inverted-V-shaped, single-stitched mouth are joined by a tiny, vertical stitch.*

Bow: *the red, nylon bow is original.*

BEAR PROFILE

This is a simplified version of the Gwentoys example shown previously (see p.124). The limbs are shorter, however, and the head is less Chiltern-like and more typical of a Dean's design, with the rounded muzzle projecting almost at right angles to the face. The short limbs, small, rounded feet, and lack of claws, are typical features of 1960s British bears.

Fur: *the short-pile, golden mohair plush is in perfect condition; the bear is filled with soft, synthetic wadding.*

Trademark: *the printed, cloth label is sewn into the left side-seam, just above the leg joint.*

Pads: *the pads are made from dark brown, brushed, knitted, synthetic fabric; there are no claws.*

brown, plastic eyes with black pupils and integral shanks, sewn into face

large, flat ears sewn across facial seams

fat shoulders; slightly curved arms with tapering paws and remains of pink claws

replacement wide, black, embroidered, inverted-V-shaped mouth

golden mohair plush; soft stuffing, probably "sub"; wood-wool around internal squeaker

replacement beige, felt pads; original woven fabric beneath

short, fat legs and stumpy feet

C.1960 CHILDSPLAY TOYS

Height: 38cm (15in)

This bear's moulded, soft rubber nose, a feature from the mid-1950s, and usually sewn on, has been glued, perhaps by a repairer. The Childsplay Toys label, sewn inside the right arm joint, was first used in 1956, after Dean's move to Rye in Sussex.

Printed label

all-in-one ears, made from same fabric as heart-shaped head

square, black, vertically stitched nose and inverted-Y-shaped mouth

brown and black, safe, plastic eyes

inset, egg-shaped muzzle with central dart, made from same fabric as pads

rust-coloured, knitted, brushed-nylon pads

straight, stick-like feet

LATE 1960S DEAN'S CHILDSPLAY TOYS

Height: 28cm (11in)

In 1965, Dean's produced an unjointed, Bri-Nylon plush bear in four large sizes. In the 1960s and 70s Dean's increasingly used synthetic fabrics, such as the curly, brown plush and the brushed-nylon pads and muzzle illustrated here.

Printed label

large, cupped ears, cut from two different cloths; set wide apart

large, black, bulbous, safe, plastic, eyes

inset, wool-like, short, synthetic-plush muzzle

square, black nose, vertically stitched and sewn centrally across muzzle seam

triangular, white chest plate

limbs and rounded body cut all-in-one

large, wide feet with three black claws tightly sewn across plush, giving quilted effect

shaggy, golden nylon plush

C.1972 DEAN'S CHILDSPLAY TOYS

Height: 79cm (31in)

This large Super Bear attempts to resemble a real "spectacled" bear, with its paler chest plate and eye markings, instead of following the traditional jointed teddy-bear design. The printed card tag gives instructions to dry clean.

Printed label

black, vertically stitched, shield-shaped nose

brown and black, safe, plastic eyes

double-stitched, inverted-Y-shaped mouth

short, tan mohair plush; soft stuffing, probably synthetic, with wood-wool in muzzle

dark brown, brushed, knitted, synthetic pads; no claws

C.1980 DEAN'S/GWENTOY GROUP

Height: 33cm (13in)

This bear has a small, round bell in its left ear, a feature often used by manufacturers after the appearance of Merrythought's Cheeky (see p.120). Dean's used this label on bears from 1972–82, sewn into the left side-seam, and on other toys until 1986.

Printed label

Steiff: 1960s–90s

NEW TRADITIONAL AND UNJOINTED BEARS; SYNTHETIC FABRICS

S teiff developed a number of designs at this time, notably in the soft-filled, unjointed range of teddies. Zooby of 1964 was an unjointed, standing bear with felt claws, whereas Tapsy was less menacing, with her airbrushed, smiling face and short, sleeveless dress. In 1975,

Steiff revived the ever-popular Zotty with a new Minky Zotty in a mink-like synthetic plush. During this time, manufacturers increasingly used man-made fabrics for the outer skin, and foam-rubber for the filling. They used airbrushing techniques, with non-toxic paints, for defining delicate facial features.

1966–90s ORIGINAL TEDDY

This is the Original Teddy design which was first introduced in 1966. A revised version of the bear was launched in 1992. The design represents a complete change for Steiff, with its inset, heart-shaped muzzle of clipped mohair plush. Although this particular example is made from honey-coloured mohair plush, the design is also available in beige, caramel, and chocolate-brown and, as always, comes in numerous sizes. This bear carries a post-1972 card chest-tag and a post-1982 woven label in the ear, attached by an incised, cursive "button in ear".

Height: 35cm (14in)   Incised button and label

Muzzle: *the unusual, heart-shaped muzzle, made from clipped mohair plush, matches the body plush.*

Nose: *the brown, shield-shaped nose is vertically stitched; the inverted-V-shaped mouth has a rather gruff expression.*

Arms: *the arms are tapered and curve upwards at the paws.*

Chest-tag: *the Steiff card tag is secured to the chest.*

Fur: *the long mohair plush is honey coloured; the stuffing is synthetic.*

Legs: *the legs are shorter than those of the early Steiff bears; the feet are large.*

BEAR PROFILE

In profile, this bear's unusual, heart-shaped, inset muzzle, which protrudes in the traditional manner, is clearly seen. The relatively long arms are slightly curved, like those of the old bears. However, the legs are short and stubby, although the feet are large. Unlike the early Steiffs, the back is almost completely straight.

Pads: *the pads are made from golden Dralon, a brushed, synthetic fabric.*

1980s COSY TEDDY

safe, plastic, lock-in eyes with airbrushed, brown "tear" falling from base of eye

mouth represented by single, airbrushed, brown dot

brown plush body, head, and limbs

part-synthetic plush is 70% acrylic and 30% cotton

"button in ear" with 1980s yellow product label behind

brown, shield-shaped, vertically stitched nose

oatmeal-coloured, plush chest plate and muzzle

card chest-tag with bear's name

light brown plush pads

1980s COSY TEDDY Height: 35cm (14in)

This is a simplified version of a bear that first appeared in Steiff's programme in the 1960s, when it was much more Zotty-like in design. This bear is unjointed, and the mouth is represented by a single, airbrushed, brown dot.

Incised button and label

1967 LULLY

nutmeg-brown plush head, muzzle, and limbs; clipped muzzle

typical, shield-shaped, vertically stitched nose

original blue ribbon

shaggy, honey-gold plush on paws and feet

unjointed bear in standing position

small, silver-coloured button with incised, cursive "Steiff"; typical 1967–77, stiff, yellow, linen tag

felt, open mouth with airbrushed tongue and lips

white, plush chest plate

wool and cotton mix plush; soft-stuffed

1967 LULLY Height: 20cm (8in)

This unjointed baby bear was made in a small size, to be a perfect comforter for a young child. Its name is from the German *einlullen*, meaning to lull a restless infant. Lully is made from several different colours of wool/cotton plush.

Incised button and label

1980 MOLLY-TEDDY

black, soft, plastic, leather-like nose, folded and padded to appear realistic

inverted-Y-shaped mouth, airbrushed in black with single, red dot representing tongue

Steiff "button in ear" and cloth product label

large, black, safe, plastic, button eyes

clipped muzzle and pads

white, plush chest plate

pale, honey-coloured, 70% acrylic and 25% cotton plush

1980 MOLLY-TEDDY Height: 55cm (22in)

This bear's name (*mollig* is German for "cosy" or "plump") describes it well, as it is very soft and floppy, and was designed as the perfect cuddly toy for a small child. Steiff produced a similar Molly-Bear, which lies flat on its stomach.

Incised button and label

1960s DRALON PETSY

brown, plastic eyes with black pupils; sewn in and finished off at back of head

light brown, Dralon plush; wood-wool stuffing in muzzle and head

fully jointed

small button with incised, cursive "Steiff"; stiff, yellow, linen label behind

brown, vertically stitched, oval nose

pale peach, brushed Dralon pads

1960s DRALON PETSY Height: 30cm (12in)

Steiff first introduced the new-style Petsy in 1961. It was made of Dralon (a new, German-invented, synthetic fabric), and its body was filled with foam-rubber. A 1984 Petsy was the first, fully jointed, machine-washable Steiff teddy bear.

Incised button and label

Chad Valley: 1960-78

TRADITIONAL AND UNJOINTED BRITISH BEARS: CHILTERN/CHAD VALLEY TAKEOVER

In 1960, when it celebrated its centenary, Chad Valley was operating seven factories and employing over 1,000 workers. After Chiltern Toys became a subsidiary in 1967, it became the largest manufacturer of soft toys in the UK. The 1970s recession, however, led to the closure of the Wrekin Works at Wellington, leaving Pontypool as the company's only surviving soft-toy plant. In 1978, Chad Valley was taken over by Palitoy, later to be bought by US-owned Kenner Parker. The tradename was bought in 1988 by Woolworths, who introduced a new range of Chad Valley soft toys, made in East Asia.

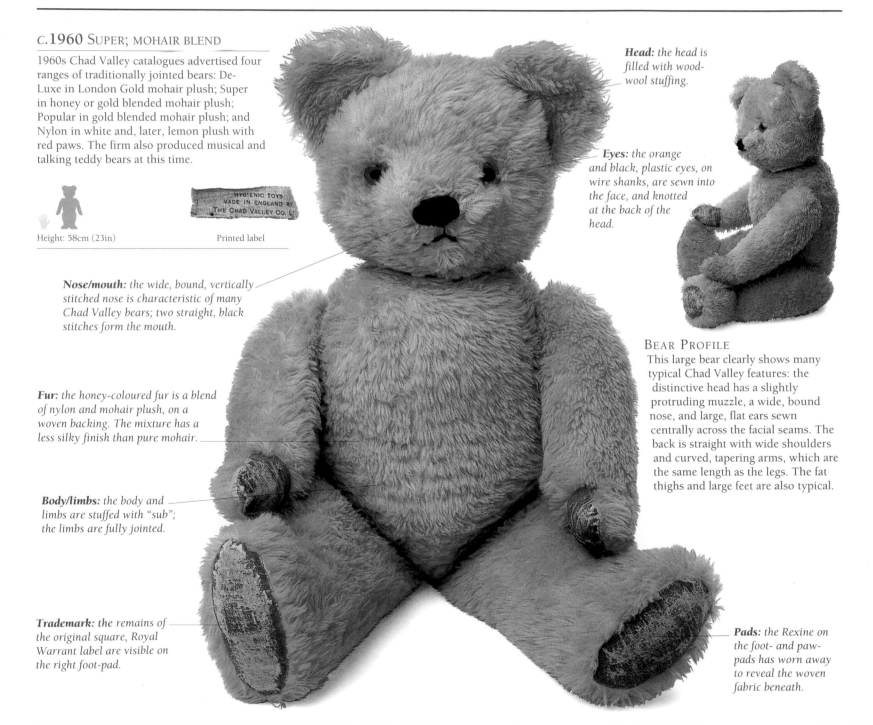

C.1960 SUPER; MOHAIR BLEND

1960s Chad Valley catalogues advertised four ranges of traditionally jointed bears: De-Luxe in London Gold mohair plush; Super in honey or gold blended mohair plush; Popular in gold blended mohair plush; and Nylon in white and, later, lemon plush with red paws. The firm also produced musical and talking teddy bears at this time.

Height: 58cm (23in)

Printed label

HYGIENIC TOYS MADE IN ENGLAND BY THE CHAD VALLEY CO. L

Head: *the head is filled with wood-wool stuffing.*

Eyes: *the orange and black, plastic eyes, on wire shanks, are sewn into the face, and knotted at the back of the head.*

Nose/mouth: *the wide, bound, vertically stitched nose is characteristic of many Chad Valley bears; two straight, black stitches form the mouth.*

Fur: *the honey-coloured fur is a blend of nylon and mohair plush, on a woven backing. The mixture has a less silky finish than pure mohair.*

Body/limbs: *the body and limbs are stuffed with "sub"; the limbs are fully jointed.*

Trademark: *the remains of the original square, Royal Warrant label are visible on the right foot-pad.*

BEAR PROFILE
This large bear clearly shows many typical Chad Valley features: the distinctive head has a slightly protruding muzzle, a wide, bound nose, and large, flat ears sewn centrally across the facial seams. The back is straight with wide shoulders and curved, tapering arms, which are the same length as the legs. The fat thighs and large feet are also typical.

Pads: *the Rexine on the foot- and paw-pads has worn away to reveal the woven fabric beneath.*

reddish brown, safe, plastic eyes with black pupils

moulded, black, safe, plastic nose

original nylon ribbon bow

"honey-pot" attached to paws with Velcro

dark brown, brushed-nylon pads

inner edge of ear folded and sewn into facial seam; rest of ear sewn into dart down side of head

single stitch, inverted-Y-shaped mouth

golden nylon plush on knitted backing

unjointed limbs in permanent, sitting position

c.1967–77 UNJOINTED; NYLON
Height: 25cm (10in)

This unjointed bear, with legs in a permanent sitting position, holds a honey-pot made of soft-stuffed, brushed-nylon fabric, attached to the paws with Velcro. The label in the left side-seam indicates that the bear was made after the Chiltern takeover in 1967.

Printed label

ears sewn across head; inner edge begins at facial seams

inset, shaved, mohair muzzle

golden mohair plush; body filled with soft stuffing, possibly "sub"

unjointed legs in permanent, sitting position

round, bulbous head with high forehead

brown, safe, plastic eyes with black pupils

moulded, black, safe, plastic nose; no mouth

outstretched arms fixed in position

beige, knitted, synthetic pads; no claws

c.1967–77 UNJOINTED; MOHAIR
Height: 39cm (15½in)

Although unjointed like the bear (left), this example is made from good quality, golden mohair plush with random dark strands, as seen in Chiltern's Hugmee bears (see pp.108–09), indicating its Pontypool origins. The label is sewn into the top of the left leg-seam.

Printed label

ears and head made from single piece of fabric; head stuffed with wood-wool

inset, slightly protruding muzzle; inverted-Y-shaped mouth

red, white, and blue artificial-silk plush (back of bear is blue)

pale blue, safe, plastic eyes with black pupils date bear to early 1960s

unusual triangular, black, felt nose

all-in-one body, arms, and legs

EARLY 1960s ARTIFICIAL SILK
Height: 58cm (23in)

This patriotic bear of red, white, and blue artificial-silk plush is unjointed; the body and legs are cut from one piece of fabric. Chad Valley also produced a cheaper range of unjointed, flame-resistant, acrylic plush bears and pandas, under the tradename "Acme".

Printed label

brown, safe, plastic eyes with black pupils

vertically stitched, black nose; single horizontal stitch across top

original orange ribbon bow

high-quality, golden mohair plush; body filled with synthetic waste stuffing; internal red, plastic, concertina-style squeaker

small, pointed, tear-shaped feet with brown, synthetic pads; no claws

1977 JOINTED; MOHAIR
Height: 30cm (12in)

Chad Valley manufactured this classic mohair-plush bear shortly before the takeover by Palitoy; it would have been made at the Pontypool works. It has a slight resemblance to earlier Chad Valley bears, but has lost the typical wide, bound nose.

Printed card-tag

Pedigree: 1960s-80s

WASHABLE, SYNTHETIC MATERIALS; NEW CANTERBURY LABEL

I n the 1960s, Pedigree factories in Northern Ireland and New Zealand were making teddy bears. This period saw an increase in the use of washable, synthetic materials, such as nylon plushes and foam-rubber stuffing. Pedigree later introduced novelties, such as the battery-operated Simon the Walking Bear and a talking Rupert Bear. In 1966, when the Lines Brothers group reorganized into Rovex Tri-ang Ltd., Pedigree – a subsidiary of Lines Brothers – moved all its soft-toy production to Canterbury, England. Dunbee-Combex-Marx took over Lines in 1972. Pedigree ceased business in 1988.

EARLY 1960s NYLON; UNJOINTED

Once pictured in a small girl's arms on the front cover of a 1961 catalogue, this cream-coloured, nylon plush bear with foam-rubber stuffing is fully washable. It is almost identical to the Wendy Boston design (see pp.122–23), with its outstretched arms, all-in-one ears and head, and safe, lock-in, plastic eyes. However, the remains of a Pedigree label sewn into the neck-seam verifies its origins.

Height: 35cm (14in)　　　Printed label

Ears: the ears, cut all-in-one with the rest of the bear, are simple projections of the head.

Eyes: the safe, plastic eyes closely follow the Wendy Boston design; they have a central, opaque, black pupil fused onto a translucent, amber surround.

Nose: this bear's vertically stitched, oblong, black nose has lost a few stitches on the left.

Mouth: the typical Pedigree mouth is a double-stitched, inverted T shape.

BEAR PROFILE
The similarity between this Pedigree bear and the Wendy Boston design is evident in the flattened, rounded muzzle; the ears extending from the large head; the straight back; and in the tubular legs, which are sewn at right angles to the body so that the bear is in a permanent sitting position.

Arms: the unjointed, slightly curved arms project from the sides of the body.

Fur: the slightly shaggy, cream-coloured nylon plush is on a woven backing.

Claws: unusually for Pedigree bears, there are three double-stitched, black claws on each paw.

Legs: the unjointed legs are made from straight tubes of plush; no feet are discernible.

large, bulbous head

large, slightly cupped ears

translucent, pale orange and black, safe, plastic eyes

inset muzzle

vertically stitched, oblong, black nose, with inverted-T-shaped mouth

bright yellow, Bri-Nylon plush on woven backing; foam-rubber stuffing

short, curved outstretched arms sewn onto body

disc-jointed legs

clipped plush pads

1960s Bri-Nylon; semi-jointed

Height: 48cm (19in)

In 1960, "Bri" was registered as a trademark by the British Nylon Spinners Ltd. (part of ICI) of Ponty-pool, Monmouthshire. Pedigree was one of several teddy-bear manufacturers who began using Bri-Nylon products extensively during this decade.

Printed label

translucent orange and black, safe, plastic eyes

large ears with inner edges folded over; sewn into slit in fabric

inset, shaved muzzle

small, vertically stitched, black nose; embroidered, open, smiling mouth

red, felt tongue

shaggy, brown-tipped, beige nylon plush; internal tilt-growler

dark brown, velveteen pads in perfect condition

1960s Shaggy nylon; jointed

Height: 39cm (15½in)

Although similar to the bear (left) with its large, head and muzzle, this example is fully jointed with wood-wool stuffing in the body and a red, felt tongue. Other versions have three-colour, layered glass eyes, and plush muzzles with open mouths.

Printed label

large, narrow ears, sewn flat across facial seams

brown, safe, plastic eyes

black, safe, moulded plastic nose on inset, clipped, nylon plush muzzle

black, inverted-T-shaped, mouth

golden, flame-resistant, nylon plush on knitted backing; internal tilt-growler

jointed legs and arms of equal length

irregularly shaped, oval feet with no claws

dark brown, synthetic velvet pads

1975 Canterbury label

Height: 40cm (16in)

This bear has the new label, designed after Pedigree moved its soft-toy production to Canterbury, England. Ann Wood, designer at the Belfast factory, first introduced the inset muzzle to Pedigree teddy bears in about 1960.

Printed label

white, short-pile nylon plush; soft stuffed throughout

ears made of separate pieces of plush, sewn down sides of head

vertically stitched, square, black nose; inverted-Y-shaped mouth

fused, amber and black, safe, plastic eyes

unjointed, short, straight arms; no pads or claws

straight legs with no feet, pads, or claws

1960s White nylon; unjointed

Height: 34cm (13½in)

This bear follows the style of earlier Pedigree bears (see pp.92–93) with its bulbous head and fused amber and black, safe, plastic eyes. However, it is made of a synthetic plush and is unjointed, with short, stubby limbs projecting out from the body.

Printed label

Merrythought: 1970s–80s

MODERN "M" DESIGN; TRADITIONAL BEARS AND NOVELTIES

During this period, the traditional, golden mohair "M" teddy (*see p.60*) continued to be made, but additional colours were also introduced. Updating of the design began in 1983 with the Aristocrat Bear, was available in seven sizes, with shaved muzzle, and dropped outer stitch nose design.

Merrythought's popular Cheeky design was reintroduced during the 1970s, and was available in both mohair and synthetic plush. In 1972–73, the London Bears, dressed as Guardsman, Policeman, Beefeater, or Highlander, were introduced; the 45cm (18in) Beefeater and Guardsman bears were reinstated in 1985.

1976 SMALL; TRADITIONAL "M" DESIGN

From 1965 until the present, Merrythought has manufactured a series of traditional, jointed teddy bears in "London Gold" mohair plush, available in nine sizes. This is the smallest size, first added to the range in 1975. In the catalogues, its code name was "GM/10" – "G" refers to the colour (gold); "M" to the style; and "10" to the height in inches. This teddy bear is stuffed with kapok, and with woodwool in the muzzle.

Height: 25cm (10in)   Printed label

Ears: *the large, flat ears are centred over the facial seams.*

Eyes: *the amber and black, plastic eyes are of the safe, lock-in type.*

Nose: *the rounded, square nose is vertically stitched in black, with a few horizontal stitches across the top edge – a design introduced in the 1950s.*

Ribbon: *the red ribbon, tied in a bow around the neck, is original.*

Fur: *the mohair plush is a colour known in the trade as "London Gold".*

Arms: *the short, tapering arms end in upward-curving paws with no claws.*

Legs: *the short, stubby legs end in barely distinguishable small feet; the limbs are fully jointed.*

Feet: *the oval feet are irregularly shaped, with no claws.*

BEAR PROFILE
Compare this to the earlier Merrythought bear (*see p.88*), and notice how the design has developed: the muzzle is less protruding; the limbs are shorter and of equal length; the feet are ill-defined; the back is straight.

Pads: *the pads are made of brown, knitted, synthetic fabric.*

large, flat ears, sewn across facial seams

brown and black, safe, plastic eyes

brown, knitted, synthetic pads; no claws

tightly bound, black, vertically stitched nose with two horizontal stitches across top

thin body; fully jointed head and limbs

slightly curved, tapering paws

"London Gold" mohair plush; soft-stuffing; wood-wool in muzzle

irregularly shaped, oval feet

1970s MEDIUM; "M" DESIGN

Height: 40cm (16in)

Nine sizes were available in this design, ranging from 35cm to 101cm (14in to 40in), from 1965 onwards, with the addition of the 25cm (10in) and 30cm (12in) sizes from 1981. A 122cm (48in) model was made from 1971 to 1981, and again in 1984.

Printed label

ears set further down sides of head than on "M" design

brown and black, safe, plastic eyes

inverted-Y-shaped, double-stitched mouth

original cream satin bow

new 1980s design, printed chest-tag with Union Jack

nutmeg-coloured, soft, short-pile, synthetic plush; soft stuffing throughout

beige, soft, short-pile, synthetic plush pads

1986 "AR" DESIGN; PLASTIC NOSE

Height: 44cm (17½in)

The "AR" was a new design of traditional, jointed bear, first introduced for the 1986 catalogue. This example is made from nutmeg-coloured synthetic plush, but the design was produced in various colours, always with a moulded, plastic nose.

Printed label

large, flat ears, sewn across facial seams

large head with flat, rounded muzzle and high forehead

black, vertically stitched nose, with horizontal stitches across top, similar to Chad Valley design

brown and black, safe, plastic eyes

soft, off-white, synthetic plush on woven backing; soft stuffed throughout

arms same length as legs, with slightly curved paws

thin body

stubby feet

orange, velveteen pads

1980s "LM" DESIGN

Height: 45cm (18in)

This "Champagne Luxury Bear", an "M" design in a new plush, was first introduced in 1982; two years later it became available in seven sizes. An earlier 1970s range of bears was made in a similar material, described as "champagne mink plush".

Printed label

large, flat, slightly cupped ears, sewn centrally across facial seams

orange and black, safe, plastic eyes

brown, synthetic plush; wood-wool stuffing in muzzle; soft stuffing elsewhere

black, vertically stitched nose, with few horizontal stitches across top; inverted-Y-shaped, double-stitched mouth

slightly curved arms, same length as legs

fully jointed limbs and head

brown, knitted, brushed-nylon pads

small, stubby feet

1974–75 "NY" DESIGN; SYNTHETIC

Height: 39cm (15½in)

In 1974–75, a series of brown bears was produced in six sizes, from 35cm to 122cm (14in to 48in). This example is very threadbare, with much of the pile worn away. It follows the basic "M" design, with large, rounded head, slim body, and short limbs.

Printed label

Australia & New Zealand: 1970–90s

COMPETITION FROM EAST ASIA; GROWTH OF COLLECTORS' BEARS

In the 1970s, several manufacturers based in Australia (*see pp.80–81*) and New Zealand – for example, Luvme Toys and Pedigree of Auckland – were forced out of business by cheaper East Asian imports. New Australian firms, including Teddy & Friends, Tomfoolery, and C.A.Toys, emerged, designing the bears themselves, but having them assembled in China or Korea. Jakas remained one of the few firms to make all-Australian bears in the 1980s and 1990s. Smaller firms, such as Sheepskin Products Ltd., Harrisons Textiles, and Robin Rive's Robbity Bob, also appeared, some targeting the collectors' market.

1978 JAKAS SOFT TOYS

This unjointed, synthetic, blue bear with its long, floppy legs is a typical 1970s Jakas design, although some of their bears did have stiff legs. Australia's longest-running children's TV programme *Playschool* featured a similar model. Wendy McDonald, the company's owner since 1989, introduced a limited-edition, synthetic, jointed range in 1991 to meet the growing demand from the collectors' market. She marketed a similar mohair-plush range the following year.

Height: 34cm (13½in)

Embroidered label

Eyes: *the small, blue, safe, plastic eyes have black pupils.*

Head/muzzle: *the head is round with a high forehead and flat muzzle.*

Nose/mouth: *the black, shield-shaped nose is vertically stitched; the inverted-T-shaped mouth is single stitched.*

Arms/claws: *the short, straight arms have no paw-pads, but three black, embroidered claws are stitched across the plush.*

Body: *the body, arms, and legs are made from one piece of plush fabric.*

Fur/stuffing: *the fur is blue nylon plush; the bear is stuffed with foam-rubber pieces.*

Label: *the Jakas Toys embroidered label is stitched to the inside of the right leg.*

BEAR PROFILE

Notice how this typical Jakas design resembles the similarly constructed, British Wendy Boston bears (*see pp.122–23*). Its rounded head, flattened muzzle, small, squarish body, stubby arms, and long legs (unstuffed at the point where they project out from the torso) all resemble the British manufacturer's design.

Legs: *the legs are long and straight; the feet are small and rounded with no pads or claws.*

black, safe, plastic eyes

inset muzzle of short-pile plush in contrasting colour

large, dark brown, short-pile plush pads

large ears, sewn to back of head

brown, vertically stitched, square nose

soft, shaggy, synthetic plush; soft, synthetic stuffing

printed, cloth label sewn into right foot seam

1989 HARRISONS TEXTILES

Height: 107cm (42in)

Adam was manufactured by Clive and Precille Harrison at their Auckland-based firm (established 1977), exclusively for the US store, Bear Hunt. They sold Harrisons Textiles in 1989, and resumed trading as Bear with Us in 1992.

Printed label

cupped ears, lined with suede

amber, safe, plastic eyes with black pupils

black, safe, moulded, plastic nose

pure New Zealand lambswool, dyed, clipped, and finished by hand; wood-wool stuffing

straight, stumpy legs; hardly distinguishable feet

circular, suede pads

1986 SHEEPSKIN PRODUCTS

Height: 40cm (16in)

This bear, made of pale, golden-dyed lambswool, is also a nightdress case. Valda McCombe, the designer, founded her Auckland business with husband Peter in 1981. Together, they produce the widest range of sheepskin toys in the world.

Printed label

amber, safe, plastic eyes with black pupils

original peach-coloured, satin, ribbon bow

soft, dyed, golden-brown New Zealand sheepskin; soft-stuffed throughout

short, straight, stumpy legs

nose consists of twisted piece of brown suede

short, straight arms with pointed paws

"Lambskin Products" printed label

1982 MAXWELL HAY

Height: 30cm (12in)

Maxwell Hay founded his family-run, sheepskin firm in 1964 in Mount Albert, a suburb of Auckland. The firm made mainly soft toys, adding teddies from 1976 to 1982. Only materials from New Zealand are used on this unjointed bear.

Printed label

amber, safe, plastic eyes with black pupils

inset, rounded muzzle

unjointed, L-shaped arms, with pointed paws and three black claws

straight legs with small, slightly pointed feet

large, square head with ears positioned at each corner

black, safe, plastic, moulded nose; mouth indicated with black stitches

bright yellow nylon plush; soft stuffed throughout

1970s MALROB CUDDLE TOYS

Height: 32cm (12½in)

This yellow, nylon, plush bear has a satinized label with kangaroo logo secured to the base of its left foot. Malrob Cuddle Toys (established in Brisbane, in 1961), specialized in unjointed synthetic bears. The company ceased operations in 1985.

Printed label

US: 1950s–80s

SAFE, SOFT, AND SYNTHETIC BEARS MADE IN EAST ASIA

I n the late 1950s and early 1960s, several new companies were formed in the United States: R. Dakin & Co. (1955); California Stuffed Toys (1959); Russ Berrie & Co. (1963); and Princess Soft Toys (1965). They set a trend by manufacturing their bears in East Asia where labour costs were much cheaper. Many old-established firms still flourished, such as the Mary Meyer Corporation and Gund, who introduced its innovative Luv-me-Bear in the early 1970s. However, the 1980s saw the demise of Knickerbocker, Character, and Ideal, whose teddy-bear range was discontinued after the takeover by CBS Inc.

EARLY 1960S KNICKERBOCKER TOYS

The spangle-effect, safe, plastic eyes, with lines radiating around the irises, are typical of bears made by the Knickerbocker Toy Co. Inc. during this period. The New York label immediately dates this bear to the early 1960s, because the company had moved to new premises in Middlesex, New Jersey by the latter half of the decade. Knickerbocker also produced a similar, fully-jointed, white plush bear with red, felt paws and three jingle bells down the central body-seam. Their unjointed "floppy" bears of the 1960s and 1970s, including the Kuddles range, possessed inset muzzles like the one shown here.

Height: 35cm (14in)

Printed label

Eyes: *the large, amber, safe, plastic eyes have radiating lines around the irises, a Knickerbocker feature.*

Muzzle: *the muzzle is made from the same honey-coloured velveteen as the pads.*

Nose/mouth: *a vertically stitched, triangular, black nose leads onto a smiling, inverted-Y-shaped mouth.*

Fur/stuffing: *the fur is a slightly curly, golden nylon plush. The bear is stuffed with cotton and "Ico" (a material similar to "sub" or cotton waste).*

Pads: *the pads are made from honey-coloured velveteen. There are no claws.*

BEAR PROFILE

This bear retains a relatively traditional shape with its long, curved arms and protruding muzzle, although its legs are short and stumpy. Notice the "Animals of Distinction" label stitched into the side-seam; prior to the 1950s the label was sewn into the front-seam.

round, bulbous head, with no distinct muzzle

long, narrow ears sewn to sides of head

triangular, engraved, leather swing-tag

brown, safe, plastic eyes

raglan-style seams join arms to body

vertically stitched, triangular, brown, wool nose, with inverted-T-shaped mouth

matching scarf and socks in red and cream wool

short, white, wool pile on knitted, polyester backing

1982 R. DAKIN & CO.

Height: 53cm (21in)

Woolie Bear is also available in golden plush wearing a green and beige scarf and socks. Smaller examples called Wee Woolie Bear were made wearing only a scarf. The legs are in a permanent seated pose, but its head is swivel jointed.

DAKIN

Printed label

ears set wide apart on sides of expansive forehead

bulbous, black, safe, plastic eyes with airbrushed eyelashes

oval, white plush muzzle with black, triangular, air-brushed nose

pale grey, soft acrylic plush; very soft, synthetic stuffing

pale grey, short-pile plush pads

1983 APPLAUSE INC.

Height: 48cm (19in)

Wallace Berrie bought the Applause Company, a division of Knickerbocker Toys, in 1982; the whole business was later renamed Applause Inc. The Avanti line, first introduced by Wallace Berrie, was continued by Applause, in a smaller range of colours and sizes.

Embroidered label

slightly cupped ears set wide apart at back of head

inset, oval muzzle of white acrylic plush; airbrushed nose and mouth

large, black, safe eyes with airbrushed black eyelashes

tan acrylic plush; very soft, synthetic stuffing

light tan, acrylic plush pads

1982 WALLACE BERRIE & CO.

Height: 70cm (28in)

The Avanti range was designed by Riccardo Chiavetta of Jocky srl, Rome. Wallace Berrie acquired the world marketing rights in 1982. Extremely cuddly, the bears are reminiscent of those made by Aux Nations for whom Chiavetta had worked previously.

Embroidered label

embossed, plastic disc

amber and black, safe, plastic eyes

stylized, triangular, black, safe, plastic nose

open, smiling mouth lined with black felt, overlaid with pink, felt tongue

off-white, short-pile, synthetic plush pads (match ear linings)

1986 RUSS BERRIE & CO

Height: 38cm (15in)

Snuggle was produced by Russ Berrie under license from the international company, Lever Bros., who used the bear to advertise a fabric conditioner of the same name. The bear's name varied worldwide according to national variations in the product name.

Snuggle

Woven label

US: late 1970s–80s

MASS MARKET, SPECIAL EDITION, COLLECTORS' BEARS

From the late 1970s, many US teddy-bear firms began to make special editions, sometimes limited to a few thousand, for the burgeoning collectors' market, in addition to their standard ranges of toys. Gund, for example, introduced its Collectors Classics range in 1979, and its annual Gundy limited-edition series from 1983. Bears were made to mark special occasions, such as the anniversary of the firm. In 1988, for example, both California Stuffed Toys and Determined Productions Inc. produced bears representing the first Ideal bear, in celebration of the 85th anniversary of the birth of the teddy bear.

1984 WALLACE BERRIE

Wallace Berrie & Co. produced this Valentine Bear of pure white plush in 1984 as a special collectors' limited edition of 6,000. It is an Avanti bear, characterized by an unjointed, cuddly body, soft acrylic plush, and soft stuffing (*see p.139*), and is identical to other Jockline-designed Avanti bears, except that it wears a bright red, satin ribbon around its neck and has a unique red and white printed label that displays the bear's edition number: 0113.

Height: 40cm (16in)

Printed label

Ears: *the large, slightly cupped ears are set wide apart, with the insides airbrushed.*

Eyes: *the large, rounded, black, safe, plastic eyes have airbrushed "sockets".*

Nose: *as on many Avanti designs, the black, triangular nose is airbrushed, with smudged edges.*

BEAR PROFILE
You can clearly see here the classic rounded profile of an Avanti bear, with features typical of the range: a moderately protruding muzzle, a slight pot-belly, and straight, stubby, unjointed legs and arms. The bear has a large bulbous head, with eyes set low down to produce a deep forehead, and large ears.

Ribbon: *the red, satin, ribbon is tied in a bow around*

Pads: *the rounded pads at the end of the arms and feet are made from the same plush as the rest of the bear, but clipped short.*

Fur/stuffing: *the soft, shaggy fur is pure white, acrylic plush; the bear is stuffed with soft, synthetic, probably polyester, wadding throughout.*

Limbs/feet: *the arms and legs are short and stubby; the feet are large and chubby.*

black, vertically stitched, shield-shaped nose; inverted-T-shaped mouth

large, brown and black, safe, plastic eyes

inset, rounded, blunt muzzle of white, short-pile, synthetic plush

light brown, acrylic plush; soft, nylon fibre stuffing

fabric patch with "The Original Ideal Teddy Bear"

white, synthetic plush pads stencilled with pad markings

1978 IDEAL TOY CORPORATION

Height: 40cm (16in)

This collectors' edition bear was created to celebrate the 75th anniversary of the Ideal Toy Company, which claims to have produced the original teddy in 1903. Although this bear has lost its label, those found on other examples record the registration number, Hollis New York address, assembly in Haiti, and that the bear can be machine-washed and tumble-dried.

round, black, safe, lock-in, plastic eyes

soft, white, acrylic plush; soft, synthetic stuffing

three claws, sewn close together across plush

black, vertically stitched, triangular nose; inverted-Y-shaped mouth

round, bronze-like chest-tag; incised, black lettering

stumpy legs with large feet

white, synthetic, velvet-like pads; reinforced with card

1985 R. DAKIN

Height: 40cm (16in)

Dakin's white, special-edition Bentley Bear celebrated the firm's 30th anniversary. According to company literature, this bear "salutes our entry into the field of collectibles". Dakin later produced a limited-edition Baron Bear with a similar chest-tag.

Embroidered label

large, brown and black, safe, lock-in, plastic eyes

wide bound, vertically stitched, silvery grey nose; inverted-Y-shaped mouth

blue/grey, synthetic, brushed fabric ear lining

metal chest-tag embossed with "California Stuffed Toys 25th Anniversary"

blue/grey, synthetic, brushed fabric pads

1984 CALIFORNIA STUFFED TOYS

Height: 30cm (12in)

Silver Bear is the smaller of two bears celebrating the 25th anniversary of this Los Angeles-based firm and the Year of the Teddy Bear. 25,000 Silver Bears (the firm's first limited edition) were made, with a label carrying the signature of the firm's president.

25th Anniversary **Silver Bear** *Limited Edition 25,000*

Printed label

soft, shaggy, golden acrylic plush

new, brown, crystal eyes

narrow, beige, velveteen pads

fully jointed head and limbs

brown, vertically stitched, rectangular nose

unusual, gold-embossed, leather chest-tag

1988 GUND

Height: 38cm (15in)

Collectors Classics, such as Winston, Dickens, and Golly Golly, heralded Gund's entry into the collectors' market, followed by its 85th anniversary bear in 1983. "1898–1988" is embroidered on a seam label on this 90th Anniversary Commemorative Bear.

Printed tag

UK: 1970s–80s

NEW FIRMS; TRADITIONAL AND UNJOINTED, SYNTHETIC BEARS

D espite the fact that many British firms making traditional-style teddy bears closed down or were taken over in the 1970s, several new soft-toy companies were established and many of these flourished as a result of the craze for teddy-bear collecting. Little Folk began making soft toy animals in 1976, but its first teddy bear, introduced in 1980, became the company's most important product. Alresford Crafts (1970–92) also made soft toy animals originally, but later concentrated on teddies. Big Softies (est. 1978) turned to traditional teddies about 1982, and now focuses on the collectors' market.

1980s GOLDEN BEAR PRODUCTS LTD.

This company, based in Telford, Shropshire, in the same area as the Merrythought factory, was established in 1979 and is now reputed to be the largest soft-toy manufacturer in the UK. It concentrates on making soft and cuddly, often unjointed, teddy bears for the mass market. They all meet British, toy safety standards, with their lock-in eyes and nose, and flame-resistant materials. As well as having a printed fabric label, the bear has a red, rosette-shaped, card swing-tag, with a golden teddy bear in the centre.

Height: 29cm (11½in)   Printed label

Ears: *the ears are lined with short-pile fabric; the backs are made from the same plush as the body.*

Head: *the large, rounded head has a high, slightly projecting forehead.*

Muzzle: *the small, inset, protruding muzzle is made of golden, short-pile, synthetic plush.*

Fur: *the light brown, shaggy, synthetic plush is flame-resistant.*

Arms: *the short, slightly curved arms have pointed paws.*

Pads: *the pads are made of short-pile, synthetic plush.*

Legs: *the legs are short, straight, and stumpy with round pads.*

BEAR PROFILE
At this angle, you can see the bear's large, bulbous head and the contrasting, fabric ears that match the slightly projecting muzzle. The muzzle is sewn, at an angle, down the sides of the head. Notice, too, the large, rounded tail.

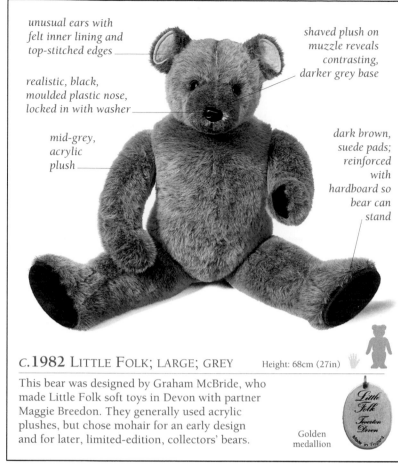

unusual ears with felt inner lining and top-stitched edges

realistic, black, moulded plastic nose, locked in with washer

mid-grey, acrylic plush

shaved plush on muzzle reveals contrasting, darker grey base

dark brown, suede pads; reinforced with hardboard so bear can stand

C.1982 LITTLE FOLK; LARGE; GREY
Height: 68cm (27in)

This bear was designed by Graham McBride, who made Little Folk soft toys in Devon with partner Maggie Breedon. They generally used acrylic plushes, but chose mohair for an early design and for later, limited-edition, collectors' bears.

Golden medallion

large, flat ears, sewn across facial seams

narrow, shield-shaped, vertically stitched, black nose

straight, unjointed limbs; no pads on paws

small feet with white, plush pads

safe, plastic, lock-in eyes

white, plush, inset muzzle

washable, flame-resistant, grey acrylic plush; stuffed with polyester stuffing

original triangular, card chest-tag

C.1982 ALRESFORD CRAFTS LTD.
Height: 53cm (21in)

Although the bear shown is unjointed, this company from Hampshire also produced traditionally jointed, as well as dressed bears, which were exported all over the world. They were designed by Margaret Jones, who founded the business with her husband John.

Printed label

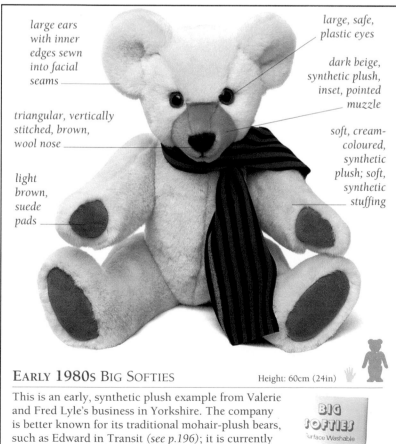

large ears with inner edges sewn into facial seams

triangular, vertically stitched, brown, wool nose

light brown, suede pads

large, safe, plastic eyes

dark beige, synthetic plush, inset, pointed muzzle

soft, cream-coloured, synthetic plush; soft, synthetic stuffing

EARLY 1980s BIG SOFTIES
Height: 60cm (24in)

This is an early, synthetic plush example from Valerie and Fred Lyle's business in Yorkshire. The company is better known for its traditional mohair-plush bears, such as Edward in Transit (see p.196); it is currently introducing limited-edition bears for collectors.

BIG SOFTIES
Surface Washable

Printed label

lock-in, safe, plastic eyes, set wide apart

black, shield-shaped, vertically stitched nose; inverted-Y-shaped mouth

dark brown, short-pile, synthetic pads

large, flat ears sewn across facial seams

large, unjointed head with expansive forehead

small, rounded, inset muzzle

short-pile, golden, nylon-plush fur, with soft, synthetic stuffing throughout

C.1986 MULHOLLAND & BAILIE LTD.
Height: 81cm (32in)

After Pedigree's move to Canterbury in 1971, former manager James Mulholland set up his own business in Belfast, where this bear was made. Similar to later Pedigree designs, its satinized Nylena label is sewn into the left seam at the back of the head.

A Nylena

Printed label

House of Nisbet: 1976–89

PETER BULL-INSPIRED BEARS AND COLLECTORS' BEARS

I n 1975, Jack Wilson acquired Peggy Nisbet Ltd., a company specializing in portrait dolls. He renamed the firm, House of Nisbet Ltd., and introduced its Childhood Classics traditional teddy bears. Peggy Nisbet's daughter, Alison (who later married Jack Wilson) designed the range. The firm was known for its limited-edition character bears. In 1979, Nisbet invited British arctophile Peter Bull to collaborate on the creation of a Bully Bear range. Nisbet reproduced his bear, "Delicatessen", in 1987, using distressed mohair, a material that Jack Wilson helped to invent. Dakin UK bought House of Nisbet in 1989.

1981 BULLY BEAR

This limited-edition bear was the initial result of collaboration between Peter Bull and the House of Nisbet. It became the central character in six books written by Bull, and inspired various other versions of the bear: the smaller Young Bully and Bully Minor; special editions Captain Bully, Harrods Bully and Tribute Bully Bear (made after Bull's death, wearing a replica of his famous sweater); and Woolly Bully in scarf and hat.

Height: 45cm (18in)

Printed label

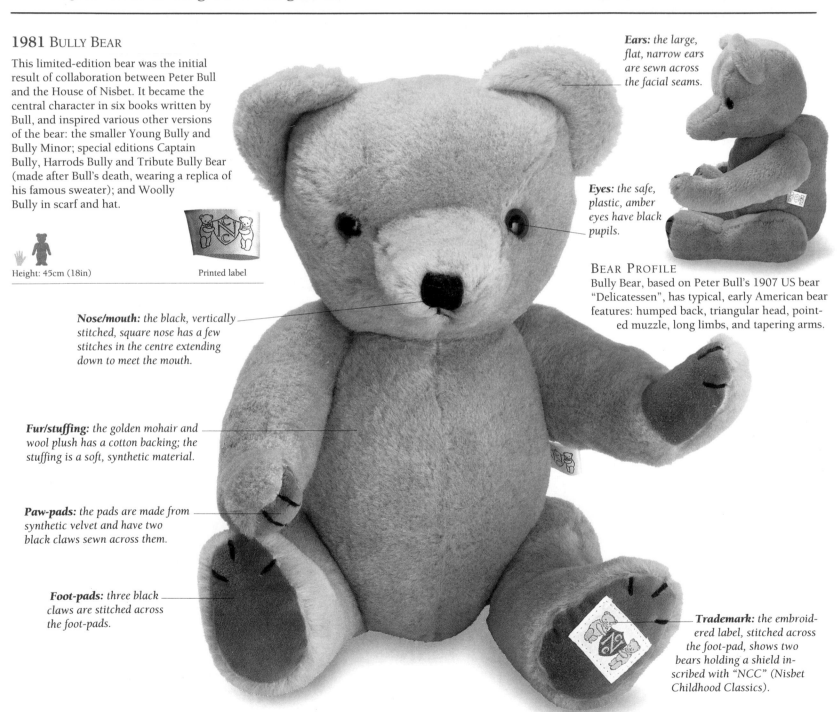

Ears: *the large, flat, narrow ears are sewn across the facial seams.*

Eyes: *the safe, plastic, amber eyes have black pupils.*

BEAR PROFILE

Bully Bear, based on Peter Bull's 1907 US bear "Delicatessen", has typical, early American bear features: humped back, triangular head, pointed muzzle, long limbs, and tapering arms.

Nose/mouth: *the black, vertically stitched, square nose has a few stitches in the centre extending down to meet the mouth.*

Fur/stuffing: *the golden mohair and wool plush has a cotton backing; the stuffing is a soft, synthetic material.*

Paw-pads: *the pads are made from synthetic velvet and have two black claws sewn across them.*

Foot-pads: *three black claws are stitched across the foot-pads.*

Trademark: *the embroidered label, stitched across the foot-pad, shows two bears holding a shield inscribed with "NCC" (Nisbet Childhood Classics).*

large, flat, narrow ears

floppy, yellow and black gingham, peaked cap

black, vertically stitched, shield-shaped nose; inverted-Y-shaped, single-stitched mouth

red-brown, safe, plastic eyes

inset muzzle

brown, synthetic plush; soft, synthetic stuffing

large, yellow bow-tie

dark green, corduroy bag

beige, synthetic velvet pads

1984 ZODIAC BEAR

Height: 35cm (14in)

Peter Bull, a devotee of astrology, and co-owner of London tearooms, "Zodiac: the Astrological Emporium", wrote 12 books in the Zodiac Bear series. Nisbet recreated each of the characters (Tunbridge, shown here, is one) and published the books.

Printed label

distressed, beige mohair plush; soft-stuffed throughout

black, vertically stitched, oblong nose

inverted-Y-shaped mouth

three claws on paws

fully jointed limbs

pale peach-coloured felt pads

four claws stitched across plush

label with limited-editon number

1988 YES/NO bear

Height: 28cm (11in)

This bear, inspired by Fritz Ferschl, forms part of the Nisbet Celebrity Collection, introduced in 1987, to honour bear-makers and arctophiles. Ferschl was a Schuco toolmaker from 1945; he later renovated Schuco toys and wrote a book on the company.

Embroidered label

flat ears sewn across facial seams

black, safe, plastic eyes

black, vertically stitched, oval nose; inverted-Y-shaped mouth

white, leather pads

badge sewn on left side of chest

golden mohair plush

maroon, fine woollen scarf

printed label under left arm, with shield and limited-edition number on reverse

1987 BODY LANGUAGE BEAR

Height: 38cm (15in)

This fully "poseable" bear came in three different plushes, with eyelets on the base of the feet that fit into a metal stand. Jack Wilson's signature appears on a leather strip on the back of the right leg; only 5,000 of these signed bears were made.

Printed label

red and blue fabric rosebud

brown, vertically stitched nose; inverted-Y-shaped mouth

blue and black, safe, plastic eyes

blue, satin bow-tie

red and white, striped jerkin with blue trim

pale blue, synthetic velvet pads

white wool plush

embroidered label on left foot-pad

1987 THE ANYTHING BEAR

Height: 23cm (9in)

This bear was inspired by Rosemary Volpp, and named for her grandson Jess whose wish was to be an "Anything Man", doing anything to make people happy. This Signature Edition series honours other collectors and authors, such as Linda Mullins.

Embroidered label

North American Bear Co: 1979–92

PERSONALITY BEARS, SOME COSTUMED, FOR COLLECTORS

The North American Bear Company was founded by New Yorker, Barbara Isenberg, following the creation of Albert the Running Bear – the hero of three books that Barbara co-wrote. The Very Important Bear series is based on historical, literary, and Hollywood characters; each is given a punning name – hence the phrase "The ones with the puns". Apart from bears such as Oatmeal and Ruggles, most are clothed, including the very popular VanderBear family. The bears are created by plush designers and Barbara Isenberg; and the bears' costumes are designed by Odl and Katya Bauer.

1980–83 AMELIA BEARHART

Inspired by the 1930s American aviator, Amelia Earhart, this was the first bear in the Very Important Bear series, introduced in 1980. It is a second edition, and is dressed in a beige suit; the first version wore a magenta suit. Four new Very Important Bears are produced annually and are later "retired" so that only twelve different styles are available each year. Others in the series include Scarlett O'Beara, Bearb Ruth, Cyrano de Beargerac, Bear Trek: Mr. Spock, and Hans Christian Anbearsen: The Snow Queen.

©1979 ALL RIGHTS RESERVED
NORTH AMERICAN
BEAR CO., INC.
CHICAGO, ILLINOIS
NOT RECOMMENDED FOR
CHILDREN UNDER 3 YRS. OLD

Height: 50cm (20in)

Printed label

Flying helmet: *the soft, leather-like, plastic helmet allows the ears to emerge through openings in the corners.*

Flying goggles: *the turquoise, plastic goggles enclose the small, round, black, safe, plastic eyes.*

Nose: *the rounded, black, plastic nose is a safe, lock-in type.*

Aviator's scarf: *the scarf is made of a cream, silk-like fabric.*

Flying suit: *the beige, cotton suit has a zip fastener down the front, and is elasticated at the waist and ankles.*

Fur/stuffing: *the soft, synthetic, velour fabric is always used for the Very Important Bears series; the bear is filled with mixed, synthetic stuffing.*

BEAR PROFILE
The distinctive, large, protruding, dome-shaped muzzle is similar to that of other examples in the Very Important Bear series, and is constructed from a separate section of the brushed-nylon fur fabric.

black, safe, plastic eyes

horizontally stitched, black, wool nose

Aloysius's own hairbrush

curly, soft, synthetic fur on knitted backing; soft, synthetic stuffing

brown, synthetic, velvet-like pads

fully jointed limbs and head

1991 ALOYSIUS
Height: 53cm (21in)

The North American Bear Company produced the original, unjointed Aloysius in 1984, inspired by the popular TV serial *Brideshead Revisited*. The House of Nisbet also made a replica but since it did not own the copyright it called its bear Delicatessen.

ALOYSIUS® #4011
From Brideshead Revisited
© 1981 NORTH AMERICAN BEAR CO, INC.
Chicago, IL 312/329-0020
All Rights Reserved

Printed label

ears emerge through traditional Dutch head-dress

black, safe, plastic eyes

fully jointed head and limbs

pale golden, soft, acrylic plush

red and green, felt tulip

black, hand-stitched claws

hand-carved, wooden Dutch clogs

1980s MUFFY: DUTCH TREAT
Height: 18cm (7in)

Muffy, the smallest member of the VanderBear family – Alice, Cornelius, Fuzzy, and Fluffy – was introduced in 1984, wearing a white christening gown. She now has an extensive collection of special outfits, including this Dutch costume.

MUFFY® Dutch Treat™ # 4327/4328
MUFFY COLLECTION
Valentine/Easter 1992
Costume by Ddl Bauer
Made in Korea
Not recommended for children under
three years due to small parts & trim.

Printed label

golden, synthetic plush

black, safe, plastic, bead eyes, set close together

large, triangular, black, velour nose

red, knitted, Hug scarf

beige, synthetic pads on large feet

1983 TED MENTEN'S HUG
Height: 70cm (28in)

This bear is based on a cartoon character in the *World According to Hug* by Ted Menten, New York bear artist, writer, and collector. The arms seem to have been put on backwards, but this is how Hug is illustrated. A Junior Hug was also produced.

HUG © ™
FROM "WORLD ACCORDING TO HUG"
ALL RIGHTS RESERVED
© 1983 TED MENTEN

Printed label

ears poke through opening

brown acrylic plush; soft, polyester stuffing

black, safe, plastic eyes

black, embroidered nose

blue, tricot fabric jogging suit with removable trousers

white, fabric trainers with laces

1978–82 ALBERT THE RUNNING BEAR
Height: 48cm (19in)

Adventures of Albert the Running Bear was published by Houghton Mifflin on Good Bear Day (October 27th) 1982. Now retired, Albert was produced in a choice of outfits by the North American Bear Company, which also made smaller version.

RUNNING BEAR ™ ©
NORTH AMERICAN BEAR CO, INC
645 NORTH MICHIGAN AVENUE
CHICAGO, IL 60611
312-943-1055

Printed label

Russ Berrie: Mass-produced Bears

MODERN BEARS FROM EAST ASIAN FACTORIES; SOLD WORLDWIDE

Russ Berrie and Company Inc. manufacture and distribute the world's largest range of "impulse gift" products, including soft toys, mugs, figurines, greetings cards and posters, candles, and dolls. Now a world-wide organization, with sales topping $400,000,000, the company has been a leader in the soft-toy industry since the late 1970s, selling to over 95,000 international retailers in a variety of locations such as shopping-malls, airports, hospitals, and college campuses, and as far apart as Africa, the Middle East, India, Russia, Iceland, Europe, North America, and Australasia.

Russ trademark
On teddy bears, the trademark (above) with its butterfly motif (registered in the 1960s) is often found on a plastic, embossed medallion attached to the ear.

In 1963, Russell Berrie, then a manufacturer's representative and now the president of this world-famous organization, founded a business selling novelty merchandise in Palisades Park, a suburb of New York City. Using a converted garage as a warehouse and his home as an office, he worked each day from 6.00 a.m. to 10.00 p.m. calling on retailers, packing orders, and completing paperwork. Early on, Russell created a character named Fuzzy Wuzzy that proved particularly successful; he later added the Bupkis and Sillisculpts figurines to the range.

A MODERN ORGANIZATION
Through Russell's flexibility, and his total commitment to his customers, the company achieved rapid sales growth and worldwide distribution, and, in 1982, Russ Berrie and Co. was recognized by *INC* business magazine as one of the 500 fastest-growing, privately owned firms in the US. The company went public in March 1984.

Staff at Russ Berrie's headquarters in Oakland, New Jersey are responsible for product research, design, and development; marketing and advertising; finance, accounting, and the budgets; and administrative and

Ready for shipping
The toys are carefully packed and boxed (below) for shipping, with not too many in each container, to prevent squashing.

executive functions. The company's Market Research Department studies trends in the rapidly changing gift industry, working closely with Product Development to maintain an ongoing supply of new products. Each of these is thoroughly market-tested to ensure consumer appeal.

The company is divided into two divisions that together market more than 10,000 seasonal and everyday products: the Gift division markets figurines and troll products, picture-frames, stationery, greetings cards, and mugs; the Plush 'n' Stuff division markets stuffed animals and other "soft" products, including teddy bears, and fabric dolls. There was a third division, Expression Centre, marketing items such as keyrings and pins with printed maxims, but this amalgamated with the Gift division at the beginning of the 1990s.

WORLDWIDE ACTIVITIES
Russ Berrie employs 2,600 people worldwide, including more than 800 sales representatives, executives and managers; and over 350 employees in the offices in Hong Kong, Korea, Taiwan, Thailand, and Indonesia. There are four regional distribution centres throughout the US, as well as a subsidiary company, Amram's, in Canada. Russ Berrie (UK) Ltd., based in Southampton, not only distributes throughout Europe, but also has

New Jersey HQ
Russ Berrie's corporate headquarters at 111 Bauer Drive, Oakland, New Jersey (above), where all the company's worldwide activities are coordinated.

Teddy-bear leprechauns
Ceramic teddy-bear leprechauns (above), made especially for St. Patrick's Day, 1988. Figurines are an important part of Russ Berrie's Gift division.

Equal stuffing
Workers in a Chinese factory (above) weigh wads of polyester fibre to ensure that each teddy is stuffed with the same amount of filling.

Safety check
Each teddy is passed over a metal detector (above) to ensure that no needles have been left in the fabric.

Product Development and Market Research offices, which develop ideas to match European as opposed to American trends. Russ Berrie & Company (Australia) Pty. Ltd. is a wholly owned, Australian business based in Kirrawee, New South Wales. It carries many Russ items, with the addition of koalas and kangaroos designed and manufactured specifically for the Australian market. It is one of the largest manufacturers of such soft toys in Australia. Each distribution centre is staffed by management, sales force, order processing, customer service, and packing departments. Russ is very much a sales-driven company, which lives by the motto: "Nothing happens until the sale is made", and close links are developed between representatives and retailers. Training programmes help to keep Russ sales personnel among the most knowledgeable in their field.

An art and design department exists at the Hong Kong Tri Russ office, which also deals with world export. Staff are employed in other East Asian offices to find suitable factories to manufacture

Russ's soft toys – these are generally either in Korea or China. However, because of increasing expense in recent years, Korea has been replaced by Indonesia as a manufacturing base. The factories can range from small, family businesses to large concerns. Russ's teddy bears are made under the highest quality control. No animal skins or products are used, and all materials are non-allergenic, surface washable, and meet worldwide safety laws.

Luv Pets, Caress, and Yomiko

Russ has produced three special brands of soft toy: Luv Pets, Caress, and Yomiko. Today their most popular line is the Caress product which has come to symbolize the firm because of its excellent quality, softness, cuteness, and reasonable price range. Their most well-known bears Brittany, Benjamin, and Gregory (*see p.170*) are all made from an increasingly popular, synthetic, curly, long-pile plush.

Australian Bears

In February 1993, Russ (Australia) launched two teddy bears – Barton and Deacon – as part of an independent, Australian-made, quality range under the name "Koala Families", which proved instantly popular with the collectors' market. They were unique for Russ, whose bears are usually made in Chinese factories; and unique for Australia, where the majority of commercially made teddy bears are also East Asian imports.

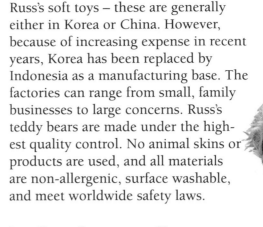

Gregory
Gregory is one of Russ's most popular 1990s teddies (above). Made from curly, long-pile synthetic plush, he is a modification of an original design by US bear artist, Carol-Lynn Rössel Waugh – a new departure for the company, which normally employs its own designers.

The three bears
Three mugs (above) marketed by Russ's Gift division in 1988, and sold in a boxed set.

Final inspection
Each bear is checked (left) to make sure that it is firmly sewn, that the face is satisfactory, and that the product matches the master sample supplied by the company.

Snuggle Bear
This 1986 bear (left) featured in a world-wide promotion for Lever Brothers' fabric conditioner. The name of the bear varied according to the product name in different countries.

Canterbury Bears: 1980-90s

TRADITIONAL COLLECTORS' BEARS BY A BRITISH FAMILY BUSINESS

John Blackburn established Canterbury Bears with his daughter Kerstin in 1980, at their home in Westbere, Kent. His wife Maude and children Mark and Victoria later joined the firm which moved to its present workshop in Littlebourne, a village outside Canterbury, in 1984. Canterbury Bears are fully jointed, and are made of natural or top quality synthetic fabrics; they come in a Classic or Special range, which expands each year. They often have unusual features, such as partially shaved faces or unique claws. The firm introduced special commissions, limited editions, and replicas in the later 1980s.

1989 CLASSIC RANGE

Louise is the largest of seven sizes in Canterbury Bears' Classic range which extends in size from 15cm (6in) to 68cm (27in). The firm also makes a similar, golden mohair-plush model called Gregory. In 1987, the Mayor of Canterbury granted the firm the privilege of using the historic city's Coat of Arms on its labels, as seen on the card tag around this bear's neck.

Height: 69cm (27in)

Ears: the large, flat ears are sewn across the facial seams.

Eyes: the brown, safe, plastic eyes have black pupils.

Nose/mouth: the black, vertically stitched nose is oval; the mouth is an inverted Y shape.

BEAR PROFILE
You can see here the slightly protruding muzzle; the thick, curved arms; the large feet, and the large, flat ears.

Tag: inside the card tag is printed "My name is Louise", along with the Blackburns' signature.

Bow: the pink, satin ribbon bow is original.

Fur/stuffing: the fur is soft, white mohair plush; the bear is stuffed with soft, polyester fibre.

Pads: the clawless pads are made of pale grey suede, a favourite choice of Canterbury Bears.

Legs: the legs are swivel-jointed, as are the arms.

brown, safe, plastic eyes with black pupils

long, rectangular, black, vertically stitched wool nose

distressed, blond, mohair-plush head; soft, polyester fibre stuffing throughout

traditional jabot of nylon lace ruffles

authentic, McKinnon tartan kilt; leather belt with brass buckle

label with Canterbury Coat of Arms

chocolate-brown, suede pads

1990 CLAN BEAR   Height: 45cm (18in)

Canterbury Bears launched its Clan Bear at Easter 1990 in the US, and in June 1990 in the UK. The firm made these bears to special order in one of 700 genuine tartan fabrics, with calf or suede pads, and heads in coloured mohair, wool, or alpaca.

Embroidered label

cupped ears with brown, leather linings; inner edges caught in facial seams

brown, alpaca fur; polyester fibre stuffing

cream-coloured, vertically stitched, square nose

cream claws; three on paws, four on feet

brown, leather pads

John and Maude Blackburn's signature

embroidered label states "Exclusively for Gund"

1991 MADE FOR GUND   Height: 25cm (10in)

Sophie, a brown, alpaca bear is one of 11 special designs that Canterbury Bears produced in 1991 for exclusive distribution by Gund throughout the US and Canada. Canterbury Bears produces a new range of limited-edition bears for Gund annually.

Embroidered label

vertically stitched nose, wider than on most Canterbury bears

small ears set wide apart; suede linings

long, pointed muzzle

exceptionally long, curved arms, with long pads

original brown, satin ribbon

unusual claw configuration, sewn across plush and pads

Blackburns' signature and limited-edition number

light brown, suede pads

1990 10TH ANNIVERSARY BEAR   Height: 65cm (26in)

This mohair bear, launched on 1 April 1990, celebrates the firm's 10th birthday. Its antique, glass eyes and elongated features caricature older bears. Limited to 500, this model belongs to the Blackburn Family Collection of prototypes and "one-off" bears.

Embroidered label

orange and black, safe, plastic eyes

golden, synthetic plush on woven backing; soft, polyester-fibre stuffing

narrow, rectangular, black, vertically stitched nose

Bethnal Green Museum of Childhood logo

card swing-tag with Canterbury Coat of Arms

cream, woven, synthetic pads

***c*.1987 BETHNAL GREEN MUSEUM BEAR**   Height: 28cm (11in)

Since 1985, British shops and museums such as Daks-Simpson, Daihatsu, Liberty's, Laura Ashley, Harrods, the Victoria & Albert Museum and their Bethnal Green Museum of Childhood branch have commissioned Canterbury Bears to produce teddy bears exclusively for them. The Bethnal Green Museum of Childhood sells this particular model in its shop.

Steiff: 1980–92

REPLICAS FOR COLLECTORS; SPECIAL COMMISSIONS

I n 1980, a limited-edition replica of the 1905 Original Teddy was produced to celebrate the centenary of Steiff's earliest soft toy, initiating an annual programme of reproductions of archive samples (often in limited editions). Other trends followed: copies of one-off celebrity bears, such as "Alfonzo" (*see p.19*) and "Happy" (*see p.37*); editions exclusive to certain countries; special collectors' items, such as the Goldilocks and the Three Bears sets; and a miniature historical series. Special commissions, beginning with the 1970s Olympic mascot, Waldi, have also been produced for museums and shops.

1987–88 TEDDY ROSE REPLICA

Steiff originally made 5,000 Teddy Rose bears in 1925–30. In 1987–88 the company issued a limited edition of 10,000 replicas, distributed worldwide. Each bear came in a presentation box with a certificate guaranteeing authenticity. A smaller 25cm (10in) version was produced in a limited edition of 8,000 in 1990, and a 20cm (8in) Record Teddy Rose, part of Steiff's Museum Collection, was introduced in 1992. The white ear-tag, as opposed to a yellow tag, indicates that the bear is one of a limited edition.

Height: 40cm (16in)

Incised button

Trademark: *the white ear-tag, attached with the cursive Steiff button, indicates that this bear is one of a limited edition.*

Nose/mouth: *the nose is a brown, vertically stitched, shield shape; a few central stitches drop to meet the inverted-V-shaped mouth.*

Fur/stuffing/growler: *the fur is pale pink, shaggy mohair plush; the stuffing is wood-wool throughout. This bear has an internal tilt-growler.*

Arms: *the traditional, curved, tapering arms are longer than the legs.*

Pads: *the pads are made from pale pink felt with brown, embroidered claws over the plush.*

BEAR PROFILE
In profile, you can see this bear's distinctive face, imitating the earlier design, with an endearing smile embroidered along the length of the long, slightly upturned, shaved muzzle.

Feet: *the feet are large, narrow, and oval in shape.*

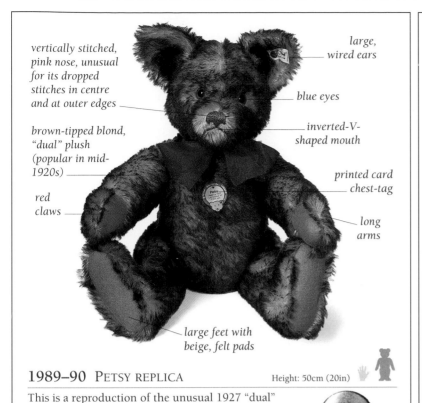

vertically stitched, pink nose, unusual for its dropped stitches in centre and at outer edges

large, wired ears

blue eyes

brown-tipped blond, "dual" plush (popular in mid-1920s)

inverted-V-shaped mouth

printed card chest-tag

red claws

long arms

large feet with beige, felt pads

1989–90 PETSY REPLICA

Height: 50cm (20in)

This is a reproduction of the unusual 1927 "dual" plush mohair bear with blue eyes and large, wired ears (*see p.37*). The white, printed ear-tag indicates that this bear is one of a limited edition; its card chest-tag copies those used on 1928–50 bears.

Incised button

"button in ear" with printed ear-tag

black, safe, plastic eyes, imitating original boot-buttons

black, safe, moulded plastic nose, reproducing the original sealing-wax nose

long, distressed, golden mohair plush

very long, curved arms

printed, card chest-tag

long, narrow, oval-shaped, beige, felt pads

black claws across mohair plush

1991 BÄR 35 PB REPLICA

Height: 50cm (20in)

This limited-edition bear of 6,000 pieces with unique card-disc and string jointing copies the 1904 bear that represented the design between the now lost "55 PB" and the rod-jointed "28 PB" (*see pp.16–17*). It won the TOBY Design Concept of the Year Award in 1991.

Incised button

black, safe, plastic, replica boot-button eyes

"button in ear" with embroidered ear-tag

black, vertically stitched nose, with dropped central and outer stitches

golden wool and cotton plush; soft, polyester stuffing

long, curved arms with spoon-shaped paws

beige, felt pads

1984 MR. CINNAMON BEAR

Height: 40cm (16in)

Based on the 1903 *Bärle* (*see pp.38–39*), this bear represented the central character in the 1907 children's story by US author Sara Tawney Lefferts, which was reprinted in 1984. The story describes how a little girl tries to make her toys accept the new German bear.

Incised button

comical face with open mouth, felt palate, and brown, outlined lips, unique to Dicky

"button in ear" with printed ear-tag

vertically stitched, shield-shaped nose, airbrushed above and below

pale golden, mohair plush with inset muzzle of short-pile mohair plush

outfit of felt lederhosen, checked shirt, and green tie

curved paws, unique to Dicky design, with black claws

flat feet with reinforced soles

1989 DICKY REPLICA

Height: 30cm (12in)

This replica of the 1930 Dicky was specially produced for the New York store, F.A.O. Schwartz, to celebrate the reopening of San Francisco's Golden Gate Bridge in 1989. Many reputable stores, including Harrods and Hamleys, now sell their own "house" Steiff bears.

Incised button

Gebrüder Hermann: 1980s–92

UNJOINTED BEARS; COLLECTORS' SPECIAL EDITIONS AND REPLICAS

F ollowing the retirement of the original three Hermann brothers (*see pp.96–97*), the 1980s saw this company under the management of their daughters (*see p.95*). Although still producing teddy bears for children, the business began to expand into the field of adult collectables. In 1984, Model 63 was produced, replicating the classic first Gebrüder Hermann teddy bear. Other replicas and special limited editions followed, including Bernhard Bear (named after the original founder). Special commissions included three 91cm (36in) bears made for the store P. & E. Rubin, each in a limited edition of ten.

c.1983 UNJOINTED; SYNTHETIC

This unjointed bear, made of soft, shaggy, rust-coloured, synthetic plush on a knitted backing (denoting a lower-quality material), is soft-stuffed throughout with polyester fibre. Designed as a child's toy, it has safe, plastic eyes and a safe, stylized black, plastic nose. Apart from the metallic, green and golden, paper swing-tag, the bear also possesses a printed, green on white, cloth label, which reads: "Hermann Teddy Original", sewn into the right side-seam.

Height: 38cm (15in)

Card swing-tag

Ears: *the slightly cupped ears are set wide apart.*

Eyes: *the large, brown and black, safe, plastic eyes are set into the facial seams.*

BEAR PROFILE
This bear has the distinctive features of the safe teddy of the post-war period: a large, bulbous head, large ears, short arms, straight back, and long legs with large feet.

Nose: *the stylized, black, moulded, plastic, oval nose is locked in with a washer.*

Ribbon: *the red, ribbon bow is original.*

Fur/stuffing: *the shaggy, rust-coloured, synthetic plush has a knitted backing; the bear is stuffed with soft, polyester fibre.*

Pads: *the pads are made from pale golden, brushed, knitted, synthetic fabric.*

Feet: *the large, narrow, oval feet are traditional in shape.*

cupped ears, sewn across facial seams

black, horizontally stitched, oval nose; inverted-Y-shaped mouth

brown and black, plastic eyes, sewn in

inset, clipped mohair-plush muzzle

original ribbon around neck, printed with teddy bears in romper suits

pure golden mohair plush on cotton backing; wood-wool stuffing; internal tilt-growler

three black claws on feet and paws

cream, felt, oblong foot-pads

1991 REPLICA OF SONNEBERG BÄR

Height: 50cm (20in)

One of a limited edition of 4,000, this bear reproduced a 1922 design, produced when Bernhard Hermann's company operated from Sonneberg. The toy horse pictured on the information card refers to Sonneberg's long tradition of making wooden toys.

Embroidered label

unusual pink, vertically stitched, shield-shaped nose, with inverted-Y-shaped mouth

white, safe, plastic eyes with black, cartoon-style pupils

black fur, composed of 53% wool and 47% cotton; wood-wool stuffing; internal tilt-growler

original red ribbon bow around neck

fully jointed limbs and head

1982 FUDDO

Height: 40cm (16in)

This unusual black bear represents American Sally Bowen's story-book character Fuddo. As well as a special, signed, black label, the bear has the usual green, printed, Hermann label sewn into the arm-seam, and a red, plastic seal attached to the chest.

FROM THE BOOK BY
Sally Bowen
©1982

Printed label

brown and black, safe, plastic eyes

ears sewn across facial seams

black, vertically stitched, shield-shaped nose; inverted-Y-shaped mouth

wool plush on cotton backing

inset muzzle with swelling on left-hand side indicating toothache

red, plastic seal attached to chest

Bear With Us label (limited edition No. 76)

large, narrow, oval feet

beige, brushed, synthetic, knitted fabric pads

c.1983 PAYNE, THE TOOTHACHE BEAR

Height: 30cm (12in)

Specially commissioned by the Los Angeles bear store Bear With Us, this limited-edition "Toothache Bear" wears a scarf around his swollen muzzle, and carries a plastic tooth on a chain. In 1992, the Austrian company Berg produced a similar bear.

PAYNE©
THE ORIGINAL
"TOOTHACHE BEAR"®

Printed label

black, vertically stitched, shield-shaped nose

original ribbon bow in colours of German flag

golden, short-pile mohair plush; soft, polyester-fibre stuffing; internal tilt-growler

traditional long, curved arms

cream, felt paw-pads and left foot-pad

three black claws on each paw and foot

1990 GERMAN UNIFICATION BEAR

Height: 43cm (17in)

This limited edition bear, No. 642 of 4,000, was manufactured to celebrate the reunification of East and West Germany on 3 October 1990. The right foot-pad is made up of stripes of black, red, and yellow felt, to represent the German flag.

Embroidered label

Germany: 1980s–90s

TRADITIONAL RANGE INCLUDING LIMITED EDITIONS AND REPLICAS

Since the 1980s, many German firms have been making bears specifically aimed at collectors. These are either traditional (sometimes limited-edition designs) or replicas of their own or other firms' earlier lines. In 1992 Hermann-Spielwaren, for example, introduced a limited-edition replica of a teddy made in 1910 by the old Sonneberg firm, Leven. This commemorated the return of Leven to its rightful owners, Dora-Margot Hermann and her sister, after German reunification. Firms are also making bears to celebrate national and international events, such as Sigikid's 1993 United Europe bear.

1990 HERMANN-SPIELWAREN JUBILEE BEAR

This bear, part of Hermann-Spielwaren's *Jubiläumsbären*, is a reproduction of Max Hermann's 1920s 111 series. It was made to celebrate the firm's 70th anniversary and heralded its entry into the market of collectables. Hermann-Spielwaren introduced a number of limited editions appealing to the European market, such as *Berlin Deutsche Hauptstadt-Bär*, (meaning Berlin German capital city bear), and the US collectors' market with American Cheerleader Bears, for example.

Height: 20cm (8in)   Printed tag

Ears: *the small, narrow, flat ears are sewn across the facial seams.*

Eyes: *the brown, safe, plastic eyes have black pupils.*

Nose/mouth: *the nose is horizontally stitched; the mouth is an inverted Y shape.*

BEAR PROFILE
This bear's traditional features include an elongated, protruding muzzle; long limbs of similar length; curved, tapering arms; and small, defined feet.

Trademark: *the folded, printed label is sewn into the right arm-seam.*

Chest-tag: *the green and gold card tag is attached to the chest with gold-coloured thread.*

Fur/stuffing: *the fur is short, golden mohair plush; the bear is stuffed with wood-wool throughout.*

Limbs: *the curved, tapering arms are the same length as the legs.*

Pads: *the pads are made from a shorter pile plush than that used for the rest of the bear.*

fully jointed head and limbs

large, cupped ears

black, horizontally stitched, shield-shaped nose; inverted-Y-shaped, single-stitched mouth

brown, glass eyes with black pupils

dark brown-tipped beige mohair plush; wood-wool stuffing

"Old German Teddy Bear" and limited-edition number

tapering arms with spoon-shaped paws

oval, beige, felt pads

1991 HERMANN-SPIELWAREN; REPLICA   Height: 39cm (15½in)

Hermann-Spielwaren produced two replicas of Old German Teddy Bear, a design featured in the 1929 Max Hermann Sonneberg factory catalogue. The replicas of bear 115 (*above*) and bear 113 (golden mohair) were both sold as limited editions of 3,000.

Printed label

translucent, amber, glass eyes with black pupils

ears with beige, felt linings

round, black, vertically stitched nose; inverted-Y-shaped mouth

"Certificate of Authenticity"

beige, felt pads; three black, stitched claws

short-pile, golden mohair plush

small, narrow, oval-shaped feet

1992 SIGIKID; MIRO COLLECTION   Height: 20cm (8in)

In 1992, Sigikid introduced replicas of Hamiro designs, a Czech firm confiscated by the Communist government. "Made in CSFR" on the label indicates that this bear was made at the new Miro factory, established by the original founder's son.

Embroidered label

fully jointed head and limbs

amber and black, safe, plastic eyes

black, vertically stitched, shield-shaped nose; inverted-Y-shaped mouth

apricot-coloured, synthetic plush on knitted backing; soft-stuffed; internal tilt growler

printed, mauve chest-tag with Clemens logo

1980s CLEMENS; TRADITIONAL   Height: 50cm (20in)

During the 1980s, Clemens produced a range of traditional, jointed bears in a variety of plushes, including miniatures and dressed models. The firm introduced a Collectors' Range in 1992, with a camel-coloured woollen bear, to celebrate their 40th anniversary.

Printed label

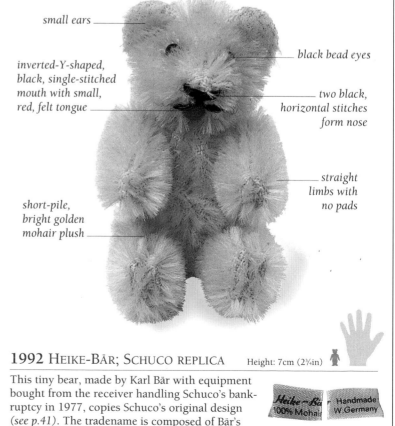

small ears

black bead eyes

inverted-Y-shaped, black, single-stitched mouth with small, red, felt tongue

two black, horizontal stitches form nose

straight limbs with no pads

short-pile, bright golden mohair plush

1992 HEIKE-BÄR; SCHUCO REPLICA   Height: 7cm (2¾in)

This tiny bear, made by Karl Bär with equipment bought from the receiver handling Schuco's bankruptcy in 1977, copies Schuco's original design (*see p.41*). The tradename is composed of Bär's wife's name, Heike, and their surname, Bär.

Printed label

Ireland: 1938–79

SUBSIDIZED TOY INDUSTRY AND TRADITIONAL STYLE BEARS

Irish manufacturers, such as Philip Sher's Hibernian Novelty Company in Dublin, had been making soft toys since the World War I period. In 1938, an Irish government department, the *Gaeltacht* Services Division (the Board of *Gaeltarra Eireann* from 1957), established a subsidized toy industry, operating three factories. (*Gaeltarra Eireann* means "Irish produce".) The toys were marketed from Dublin until 1969, when the head offices moved to County Galway. Because Ireland remained neutral during World War II, exports of Irish soft toys rose dramatically at this time to meet overseas demand.

1964 "REPUBLIC OF IRELAND" LABEL

This traditional, disc-jointed bear was made by Tara Toys, the soft-toy section of the Irish Government-funded toy industry, at their Elly Bay factory in County Mayo. In 1969, production was transferred to Crolly, County Donegal, under a new company called Soltoys Ltd., which eventually ceased business in 1979. Traditional bears like this are typical, but they also produced novelties such as Freddie the Laughing Bear and the musical bear, Tara the Tuneful Teddy.

Height: 50cm (20in)

Embroidered label

Eyes: *the amber, glass eyes with black pupils are sewn into the face on wire shanks.*

Nose/mouth: *the vertically stitched, black nose is shield-shaped; the mouth is a double-stitched, inverted Y shape.*

Fur/growler: *the pale golden mohair plush has faded from orange-yellow and is slightly worn in places. The bear has a tilt-growler.*

Pads: *the pads are made from chocolate-brown felt.*

Feet: *the oval feet have no claws.*

Label: *the original embroidered label is sewn into the foot-pad seam.*

BEAR PROFILE

In profile this bear demonstrates clearly several typical features of the post-World War II Irish teddy: its pointed, protruding muzzle, high forehead, and large, flat ears. The curved arms are the same length as the legs, and taper to a sharp point at the paws. The feet are distinctively rounded and stubby.

unjointed head

brown, glass eyes with black pupils

glued-on, triangular, black nose

double-stitched, inverted-Y-shaped, black mouth

golden mohair plush

short, slightly curved arms

two printed, card chest-tags

straight legs and small feet with oval pads

red, embroidered foot-label

brown, suedette pads with no claws

1960s TARA TOYS; FELT NOSE
Height: 30cm (12in)

This bear possesses its original foot label and two printed, card swing-tags. The reverse of the triangular tag reads, "Hi! Little Girl...Ho! Little Boy/ I want to be your Plushy Toy!/I'd like to have you hold me tight/And go to bed with you each night!"

Embroidered label

MADE IN REPUBLIC OF IRELAND

wide, shallow ears, sewn across facial seams

high forehead with horizontal seam across top of head

amber, glass eyes with black pupils, sewn into face on wire shanks

horizontally stitched, shield-shaped, black nose with inverted-Y-shaped mouth

golden mohair plush; soft-stuffing in limbs; wood-wool and soft stuffing elsewhere

short, curved, pointed arms

short, stubby legs with fat feet

red, embroidered foot label

rust-red, felt pads

1938–49 "MADE IN EIRE" LABEL
Height: 40cm (16in)

From 1937 until 1949, when Ireland left the British Commonwealth and became a Republic, the country was known as Éire (the Gaelic word for Ireland, used in their 1937 constitution). Labels with this wording therefore date a bear to the 1938–49 period.

Embroidered label

MADE IN ÉIRE

large ears sewn across facial seams

vertically stitched, triangular, black nose with single, long stitch extending from each top corner

amber and black, plastic eyes sewn into head on wire shanks

dark golden mohair plush; wood-wool stuffing in head; wood-wool and kapok mix elsewhere

tapering arms

replacement corduroy pads, originally Rexine

small, stumpy feet

c.1957 TARA TOYS; UNIQUE NOSE
Height: 56cm (22½in)

Although unmarked, this bear's shape, and particularly its unique nose design, resembles that of bears seen in trade journal advertisements for the *Gaeltarra Eireann*. Bears were designed for the *Gaeltacht* by former Sonneberg toy designer, Hans Weberpals, from 1950 until 1965, when he left to start his own factory, Celtic Toys, in County Cork.

flat ears, sewn across facial seams

small, pale orange, glass eyes with black pupils

inset, rounded muzzle with T-shaped seam extending across nose and down chin

worn, horizontally stitched, triangular, black nose; black, embroidered mouth almost worn away

short, tapering arms with unusual pointed paws

stubby feet with brown, felt pads

white cotton plush; stuffed with wood-wool; internal squeaker

c.1947 ERRIS TOYS; COTTON PLUSH
Height: 33cm (13in)

Teddy bears made at Elly Bay bore the "Erris Toys" trademark until c.1953, then changed to "Tara Toys". This rare Gaelic label *"Bréagáin Iorruis; Déantús Na Gaeltachta"* means "Erris Toys; Made in the *Gaeltacht*". The cotton plush is typical of the era.

BRÉAGÁIN IORRUIS DÉANTÚS NA GAELTACHTA

Embroidered label

Merrythought: 1982–92

COLLECTOR BEARS; REPLICAS AND SPECIAL COMMISSIONS

In 1982, Merrythought introduced a range of limited-edition teddies for import into the US by Tide-Rider Inc. of Baldwin, New York – a partnership that continues today. Novelties included a green/blue, traditional-style teddy bear and the 1984 Seasonal Bear series, in which each bear represented either Spring, Summer, Autumn, or Winter. In 1992, Merrythought introduced Mr and Miss Mischief, depicting naughty "children". By 1986–87, replicas of Punkinhead and the Magnet bear were in production followed, in 1992, by replicas of Mr Whoppit, Bingie, and *Titanic* survivor Gatti.

1983 EDWARDIAN BEAR

This bear's name refers to its "antique-look" design, with a long muzzle and limbs and humped back, emulating bears of the Edwardian period of British history (1901–10). As indicated on the printed label sewn into the left side-seam, this particular example is No. 493 of a limited edition of 1000. It was the second design in the Tide-Rider collectors' series; the first was the golden mohair-plush Anniversary Bear, with slightly rounder features and a black, embroidered nose.

Height: 50cm (20in)

Printed label

Fur: the pure mohair plush is described as "Old Gold", possibly because it resembles the colour of old teddies.

Claws: four brown, webbed claws are embroidered across each felt pad.

Label: the label, with wording used since the late 1950s, is machine-stitched onto the foot-pad.

Swing-tag: this printed, card tag guarantees that the pile is made from pure mohair, and illustrates its source – an angora goat.

Nose: with its wide shape, vertical stitching, and dropped, central stitch meeting a wide, inverted-Y-shaped mouth, the nose is modelled on those of pre-World War I Steiff and Bing bears.

Muzzle: the elongated muzzle has been shaved down to bristly stubble, revealing the woven cloth backing beneath.

BEAR PROFILE

In profile, you can clearly see this bear's humped back and extremely long, curved arms – features that were typical of teddy bears at the beginning of the century, before Merrythought's foundation.

Pads: the beige, felt pads are spoon-shaped on the paws and slightly pointed on the large, narrow feet.

horizontally stitched, rectangular nose; slightly smiling, inverted-Y-shaped mouth

black, plastic, replica boot-button eyes

protruding, shaved muzzle

original floral ribbon

slim torso, narrowing at chest

pointed, shaved, mohair-plush paws

finest mohair and silk plush; soft-stuffed body and limbs; wood-wool head

two black, diagonal stitches, forming V-shaped claws, on each pad

1992 TOUCH OF SILK   Height: 45cm (18in)

Shown in the International Collectors' Catalogue in 1992, this bear's unusual arms and pads depart from the traditional style. It was designed by Jacqueline Revitt, Merrythought's design director since the 1970s, and carries the 1990s wishbone label.

Embroidered label

brown and black, safe, plastic eyes

shaved muzzle stuffed with wood-wool

black, vertically stitched nose, with dropped outer stitches

green, Harrods ribbon

short, golden mohair plush; soft, polyester stuffing

dark brown pads of soft synthetic, Dralon-type fabric

green label with gold lettering, exclusive to Harrods

four black, webbed claws on paws; three straight claws on feet

1986 HARRODS BEAR   Height: 30cm (12in)

During the 1980s, Merrythought produced various bears, such as this one, for Harrods – the large, London department store. These included a standing bear dressed in the green, Harrods' commissionaire's livery. The green and gold label is exclusive to Harrods.

Embroidered label

large, black, safe, plastic eyes, resembling boot-buttons

black, vertically stitched nose with dropped outer stitches

mauve-tipped, beige mohair plush on beige woven backing; soft, polyester stuffing

original mauve, satin ribbon around neck

printed foot label with 1957–80s wording

beige, synthetic fabric pads

1990 LAVENDER; MAGNET REPLICA   Height: 19cm (7½in)

This reproduction of the 1930s Magnet design is made from mauve-tipped, beige, "dual" mohair plush, and is impregnated with lavender perfume. It is one of several scented bears produced by Merrythought. Others included Rose Petal and Peach Blossom.

Printed label

beige-tipped, mushroom-coloured mohair plush; soft, polyester stuffing

swivel-jointed head; bear in permanently seated position

black, shield-shaped nose

inset muzzle of darker plush, stuffed with wood-wool

red ribbon around neck and on right arm

hand-made accordion with poker-work decoration and mother-of-pearl keys

short, dark, plush pads, with airbrushed paws and feet

1992 BIRTHDAY BEAR   Height: 39cm (15½in)

Since 1984, Karin Heller, a German doll designer, has sold a range of teddy bears, manufactured by Merrythought, in Germany. This bear is one of four, 500-piece, limited-edition bears produced in 1992, dressed by Karin in clothes suited to the German market.

Printed label

Dean's: 1980s–90s

COLLECTORS' SERIES; PLAINTALK TAKEOVER; NEW LABEL DESIGN

I n 1981, Dean's launched into collectables with a limited-edition series of three bears inspired by Norman Rockwell illustrations. Aiming at the US market, the company also made a nightshirt-clad Porridge Bear, based on a 1909 illustration by Jessie Willcox Smith. In 1983, Dean's produced a limited-edition, 80th anniversary bear, and in 1984, it collaborated with Donna Harrison and Dottie Ayers of the Baltimore shop, The Calico Teddy, to make Teddy B and Teddy G to their design. In 1986, Dean's was taken over by the toy and gift importers Plaintalk, forming The Dean's Company (1903) Ltd.

1987 TRADITIONAL DESIGN

This traditional, fully jointed teddy bear was originally marketed with a printed calico drawstring bag. The bear has a red on white embroidered label in the left side-seam, designed after the takeover by Plaintalk in 1986. Rationalization forced the firm into voluntary liquidation, but the newly appointed director, Neil Miller, bought out the firm and commenced trading as a new company on 7 March 1988.

Height: 48cm (19in)

Embroidered label

Ears: the small, flat ears are sewn into the vertical seams down the sides of the head.

Eyes: the safe, plastic eyes are amber-coloured with black pupils.

Mouth: the wide, smiling mouth curves upwards.

Nose: the black, shield-shaped nose is vertically stitched.

Bow: the red, ribbon bow is original.

Fur/stuffing: the fur is "London Gold" mohair plush on a woven, woollen backing; the bear is stuffed with polyurethane foam granules.

Arms: the arms are the same length as the legs, and end in curved, tapering paws.

Feet: the feet are large and rounded, and have brown, synthetic-velvet pads.

BEAR PROFILE

In profile, you can see the smiling mouth embroidered onto the inset, blunt, protruding muzzle. The large, rounded head is made up of four pieces of plush; the ears are set into the side-seams. The bear has short arms, unusual squared-off shoulders, and small, tapering paws.

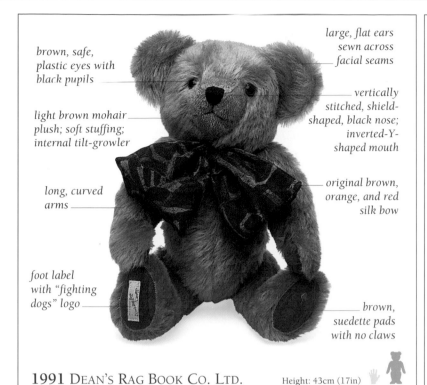

brown, safe, plastic eyes with black pupils

light brown mohair plush; soft stuffing; internal tilt-growler

long, curved arms

foot label with "fighting dogs" logo

large, flat ears sewn across facial seams

vertically stitched, shield-shaped, black nose; inverted-Y-shaped mouth

original brown, orange, and red silk bow

brown, suedette pads with no claws

1991 DEAN'S RAG BOOK CO. LTD.
Height: 43cm (17in)

The old Dean's Rag Book Co. name was dropped during the Plaintalk takeover, but Neil Miller purchased the trading rights and logo in 1990. In 1991, the company launched a new range of limited-edition bears, using the old "fighting dogs" logo.

Printed label

reddish brown, safe, plastic eyes with black pupils

realistic, black, safe, moulded plastic nose

original red, nylon, ribbon bow

curved, tapering arms

small, tapering feet

black, inverted-T-shaped, smiling mouth

golden mohair plush; soft-stuffed except for wood-wool in head; internal tilt-growler

dark brown, brushed-nylon pads

C.1984 DEAN'S CHILDSPLAY TOYS
Height: 40cm (16in)

From 1982 to 1986, Dean's employed a new green embroidered label (retaining the name Dean's Childsplay Toys), for use only on teddy bears. The label, which was sewn into a side-seam, was used on bears in both the general and the collectors' ranges.

Deans Childsplay Toys
PONTYPOOL · GWENT · U.K.

Embroidered label

black, safe, plastic, button eyes

original red, velvet bow-tie

brown, Dralon pads; three black claws across mohair plush

vertically stitched, shield-shaped, black nose; inverted-T-shaped mouth

champagne-coloured, "distressed" mohair plush; wood-wool stuffing in head; foam stuffing elsewhere

foot label with "fighting dogs" logo

1991 LIMITED-EDITION REPLICA
Height: 43cm (17in)

Dean's launched a series of replicas in 1991; this bear is based on a 1940s design by sales manager, Jack Crane, father of the present sales director, Michael Crane. The label reads "Made in Great Britain"; pre-1956 labels read "Made in England".

Printed label

bulbous head with high forehead and central seam

large, round, black, safe, plastic eyes

golden woollen plush, made in Britain, as indicated on card chest-tag

stubby feet; no pads or claws

large, slightly cupped ears

vertically stitched, narrow, rectangular, black nose with inverted-Y-shaped mouth

original red ribbon

thick, curved arms; no pads or claws

BRITISH WOOL

1985 NORMAN ROCKWELL SERIES III
Height: 30cm (12in)

The last in a limited-edition series, based on Rockwell bears featured on *Saturday Evening Post* front covers, this bear is based on one in his painting "Election Day" (1948). 1,000 bears were made with Republican ribbons; another 1,000 with Democratic ribbons.

Deans Childsplay Toys
PONTYPOOL · GWENT · U.K.

Embroidered label

France: post-1945

NEW COMPANIES PRODUCING CUDDLY, UNJOINTED BEARS

S ome French companies founded before World War II, such as Pintel and A.L.F.A. (producing popular, dressed teddy bears from 1936), continued after 1945, but using synthetic materials. Several new companies were also established during the 1950s and 1960s, such as Anima (1947), Boulgom (1954), and Nounours (1963). They all used the new, foam-rubber filling that revolutionized the soft-toy industry. Though some manufacturers failed during the 1970s and 1980s, several were bought by Nounours who, by the 1990s, was responsible for 80 per cent of all French soft-toy exports.

c.1980s BOULGOM

M. Frenay founded Boulgom at Oullins in 1954. In 1964, the company moved to Chaponost, near Lyon, where the factory is still situated. Boulgom was one of the first soft-toy manufacturers to produce washable bears with foam-rubber stuffing. The company expanded considerably during the 1970s, buying Anima in 1972, but went bankrupt in 1990. It is now part of the well-known French manufacturing group, Alain Thirion, along with the other toy manufacturers, Joustra and Vulli.

Height: 23cm (9in)   Printed label

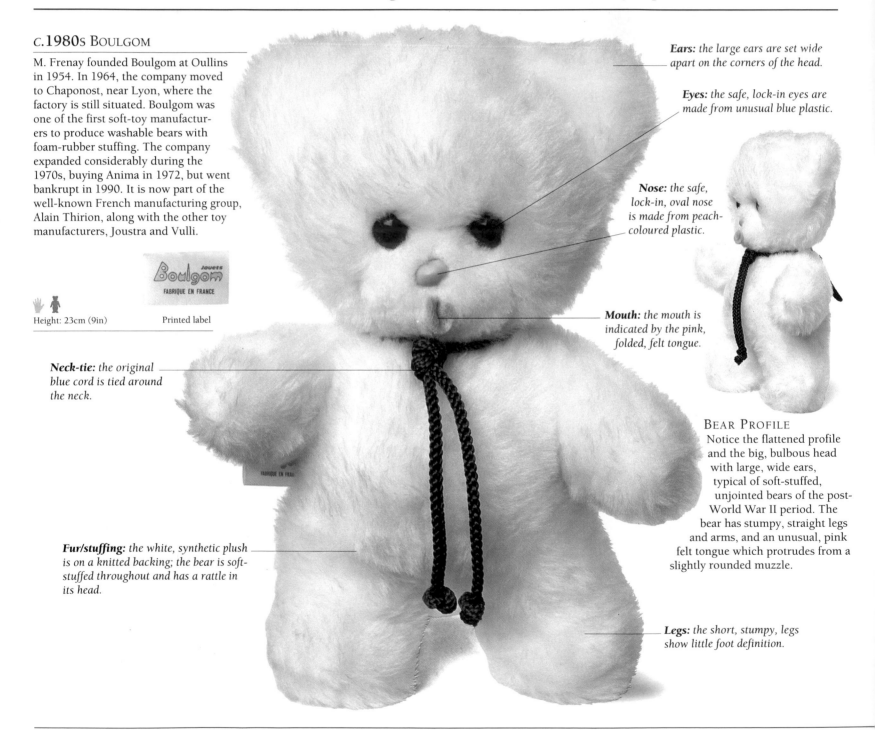

Ears: the large ears are set wide apart on the corners of the head.

Eyes: the safe, lock-in eyes are made from unusual blue plastic.

Nose: the safe, lock-in, oval nose is made from peach-coloured plastic.

Mouth: the mouth is indicated by the pink, folded, felt tongue.

Neck-tie: the original blue cord is tied around the neck.

Fur/stuffing: the white, synthetic plush is on a knitted backing; the bear is soft-stuffed throughout and has a rattle in its head.

BEAR PROFILE
Notice the flattened profile and the big, bulbous head with large, wide ears, typical of soft-stuffed, unjointed bears of the post-World War II period. The bear has stumpy, straight legs and arms, and an unusual, pink felt tongue which protrudes from a slightly rounded muzzle.

Legs: the short, stumpy, legs show little foot definition.

*black, safe,
plastic eyes*

*muzzle seams
form mouth*

*black, leather-
like, vinyl nose*

*short,
unjointed
arms*

*brown, shaggy,
synthetic plush;
soft-stuffed
throughout*

1980s NOUNOURS

Height: 71cm (28in)

"Nounours", a colloquial French term for "teddy",
is derived from *un ours* (a bear). Jacky Dubois
established the firm in 1963, which eventually
became the Brittany-based Nounours Group, with
factories in France, Italy, Tunisia, and Mauritius.

Printed label

*large, flat ears
set wide apart*

*black, safe, locked-
in, plastic eyes*

*hard, padded,
suede nose*

*printed card
chest-tag with
French flag,
paw-print, and
Anima's logo*

*shaggy,
honey-
coloured
plush; soft-
stuffed*

c.1983 LES CRÉATIONS ANIMA

Height: 45cm (18in)

Suzanne Vangelder established Anima in Paris in
1947 and, in 1972, after becoming a subsidiary of
Boulgom, it moved to Chaponost. Gund bought
the firm in 1992. Special sewing machines, used
in the fur-coat trade, are used on their teddy bears.

Printed tag

*shorter pile,
plush muzzle*

*brown and black,
safe, glass eyes*

*realistic black,
leather nose*

*folded leather strip
creates realistic
mouth*

*embroidered,
label sewn to
top of left hip*

*long, dark brown
nylon plush;
soft-stuffed
throughout*

c.1988 AUX NATIONS

Height: 55cm (22in)

Inspired by Annaud's film *The Bear*, Frédérique
Quentin designed Kodiak Bear for Aux Nations.
(Another French company produced the official
licenced product.) Established in the 1960s,
Aux Nations became part of Nounours in 1975.

Embroidered label

*large, round,
brown, safe,
plastic eyes*

inset muzzle

*safe, oval, velvet-
covered nose*

*circular, printed
card tag attached
to right paw*

*synthetic
fabric shirt*

*leather badge
printed with
name "Léon"*

*light brown,
synthetic, short-
pile plush on
woven backing;
soft, polyester-
fibre stuffing*

*large feet;
no claws*

c.1980 AJENA

Height: 39cm (15½in)

This bear, named Léon, was bought in the large Paris store Printemps
about 1980. In 1989, Ajena, a company based in Le Lude, near Tours,
was bought by Nounours, who retained the tradename. The firm now
produces a cheaper quality Ajena range that is distributed to French
supermarkets and made at Nounours' factories in Tunisia and Mauritius.

Europe: 1930s–80s

EASTERN EUROPE; MEDITERRANEAN; SCANDINAVIA; BENELUX

From the interwar years until its nationalization in 1948, Czechoslovakia had a thriving teddy-bear industry. In 1938, Hamiro was the second largest European soft-toy manufacturer and, from 1925 until 1948, Wilhelmine Walter made Kersa bears at Lobositz, then in Bohemia. Poland also was a major exporter of teddy bears from the 1950s. Lenci introduced teddies to Italy in 1931 (Three Bears, with open mouths and bibs); GZB made similar examples, and Trudi and Jocky have produced bears in more recent years. A few teddies originate from Spain, such as G. Fali's Osito, a *c.*1959 googly-eyed baby bear.

*c.*1960 POLAND

Although unmarked, this bear shares many characteristics with the few existing bears that still retain their "Made in Poland" paper labels – the latter either stuck to the foot-pad or in the form of a swing-tag. Dating from the 1950s to the 1960s, these bears were produced with traditional embroidered facial features as well as with leather noses and felt tongues as seen here. The most popular colour was golden, but white, grey, and brown examples were also made in a range of sizes.

Height: 38cm (15in)

Ears: *the flat, narrow ears are sewn across the facial seams.*

Eyes: *the clear, glass eyes, painted amber on the backs, are sewn in on wire shanks.*

Mouth: *only part of the original semi-circular, red, felt tongue remains.*

Nose: *the nose consists of a narrow piece of brown leather, with the ends curled under tightly to form the "nostrils"; it is secured to the end of the muzzle with fuse wire.*

Fur/stuffing: *the short, curly, golden cotton plush is typical of Polish bears. The bear is solidly stuffed with wood-wool – another typical feature.*

Limbs: *the limbs are fully jointed, with thin, plywood discs connected by metal rods across the body at the shoulders and thighs; this is a cheap method of jointing that makes the arms or legs move back and forth simultaneously.*

BEAR PROFILE
From the side you can see the solid shape of this bear. The wide head, with its very square muzzle and thick neck, is set on a body that is deeper than it is wide; the short, curved arms end in tapering paws, and the slightly longer legs, with "drumstick" thighs, narrow at the ankles and end in rounded, stubby feet.

Pads: *the pads, typical of those of Polish bears, are made from the reverse of the plush, revealing the pale yellow (now discoloured and stained) woven fabric. The lack of claws is also typical.*

large, triangular head with all-in-one ears

smooth, triangular, safe, moulded plastic nose; no mouth

inset, pointed muzzle

short, stubby, unjointed arms; no pads or claws

"Certificate of Origin No. 998089"

large, brown and black, safe, plastic eyes

original chain around neck, to mimic dancing bears of Europe

soft synthetic plush

short, unjointed legs with large, rounded feet, slightly splayed out from body

1980s LENCI
Height: 40cm (16in)

This soft-stuffed, unjointed, wide-hipped bear is typical of the Italian firm Lenci's modern work. World-famous for its 1920s dolls with moulded felt heads, Lenci's tradename is derived from the Latin motto: "To Play Is Our Constant Work".

Embroidered label

large, natural lambskin ears

amber and black, plastic eyes, sewn in

narrow, shield-shaped, dark brown, vertically stitched nose; mouth represented by two horizontal stitches beneath nose

original red, satin ribbon around neck

dyed, golden-brown lambskin; soft, Styrofoam stuffing

brown, suede pads on feet and paws; no claws

fully jointed limbs and head

large, oval feet

1980s AB MERIMEX
Height: 43cm (17in)

This lambskin and suede bear is typical of Ab Merimex, the most well-known Swedish teddy-bear manufacturer, founded after World War II by refugee Emil Grünfelt. Originally based in Mälmo, the company has since moved production to Portugal.

Card swing-tag

large, flat ears sewn across corners of head

large head, with flattened muzzle

safe, black, moulded plastic, realistic nose with nostrils; no mouth

unjointed arms and legs; no pads; no feet

amber and black, safe, plastic eyes

narrow, red ribbon around neck

shaggy, cream-coloured, synthetic plush; soft stuffing

c.1973 FLUFFIES
Height: 43cm (17in)

This is a typical example of the synthetic, unjointed, 1970s bears made by this Belgian company. According to the Benelux Association of Toy Manufacturers, there are no longer any teddy-bear manufacturers in either Belgium or the Netherlands.

Embroidered label

small, flat ears sewn on sides of head; lined with contrasting white, rayon plush

small, bulbous, dark turquoise-green, plastic eyes with black pupils, glued in place

short, stumpy, fully jointed legs and arms; no pads or claws; slight foot definition

large, rounded head with centre seam

black, moulded plastic nose, glued to end of muzzle

original yellow ribbon bow

silky, beige rayon plush on knitted backing; soft stuffed

1960s POLAND
Height: 33cm (13in)

The printed tag indicates that this bear was made at the Bajka Toymaking Co-operative Works in Lublin, south-east of Warsaw. "Bajka" means "fairy-tale" or "story", the logo being a blonde girl. In the mid-1960s, 15 toy-making co-operatives existed in Poland.

Printed paper tag

Worldwide Expansion: post-1945

EXPORT AND HOME-MARKET TRADE BY ISRAEL, CANADA, CHINA & SOUTH AFRICA

After World War II, teddy-bear manufacture was no longer restricted to Europe and the US. Many countries, including China, Israel, and Brazil, began making cheap-quality bears largely for the export market to the UK, US, and Australia. Canada, too, established several soft-toy companies during the 1950s, such as Ganz Brothers and Mighty Star Ltd. who, by the 1990s, also produced a range of collectors' bears to meet the demand at home and abroad. In South Africa, teddy bears are manufactured primarily for the home market, such as those produced by Prima Toys' Durban-based factory.

1980 TOYLAND

Israeli-produced teddy bears have been exported to various countries, including the United Kingdom, the United States, and Australia, since the 1960s. Some, like this shaggy, brown and beige Toyland bear, give the manufacturer's name, as well as the sitting poodle logo, on the label which is sewn into the left side-seam; others simply have "Made in Israel". Toyland Ltd. is a division of Caesarea, whose headquarters are based in Glenoit, Indiana.

Height: 40cm (16in)   Printed label

Ears: *two large pieces of contrasting plush, sewn centrally across the facial seams, make up the ears.*

Eyes: *the brown, safe, plastic eyes have black pupils.*

Nose: *the safe, stylized nose is made from black, moulded plastic.*

Muzzle: *the inset, protruding muzzle is made from two pieces of pale golden, synthetic, velvet-like fabric.*

Bow: *the original red, ribbon bow is tied around the neck.*

Arms: *the curved arms end in tapering paws.*

Fur/stuffing: *the fur is shaggy, brown and beige, synthetic plush with contrasting beige plush on the muzzle and pads; the stuffing is shredded polyurethane.*

BEAR PROFILE

In profile, you can see this bear's unusually constructed, protruding, two-piece, inset muzzle, as well as the large, two-piece ears sewn down the sides of the head. The slightly curved arms are shorter than the legs, which have clearly defined ankles; the feet are small and rounded.

Legs: *the legs are short and drumstick-shaped; the feet are small.*

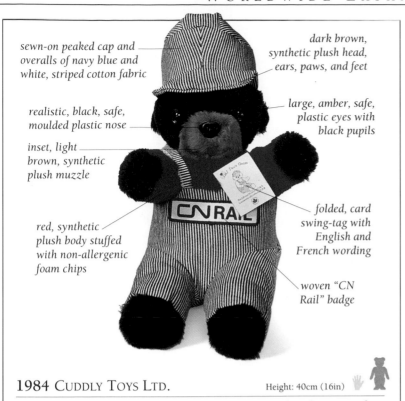

sewn-on peaked cap and overalls of navy blue and white, striped cotton fabric

dark brown, synthetic plush head, ears, paws, and feet

realistic, black, safe, moulded plastic nose

large, amber, safe, plastic eyes with black pupils

inset, light brown, synthetic plush muzzle

folded, card swing-tag with English and French wording

red, synthetic plush body stuffed with non-allergenic foam chips

woven "CN Rail" badge

1984 CUDDLY TOYS LTD.

Height: 40cm (16in)

Oscar (the nickname for railway engineers in Montreal) is the mascot for the Canadian National Railways and was designed by Dalyce Feir of Mara's Stuffed Animals for their associated firm Cuddly Toys Ltd., which specializes in the distribution of corporation mascots. All their bears are designed and produced in Canada with Canadian raw materials.

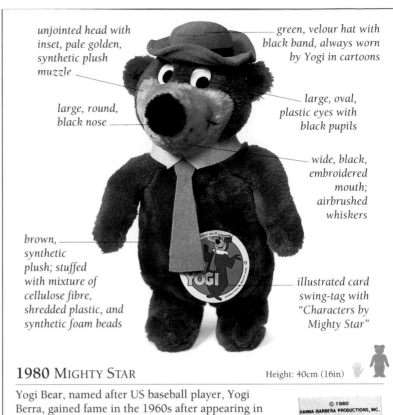

unjointed head with inset, pale golden, synthetic plush muzzle

green, velour hat with black band, always worn by Yogi in cartoons

large, round, black nose

large, oval, plastic eyes with black pupils

wide, black, embroidered mouth; airbrushed whiskers

brown, synthetic plush; stuffed with mixture of cellulose fibre, shredded plastic, and synthetic foam beads

illustrated card swing-tag with "Characters by Mighty Star"

1980 MIGHTY STAR

Height: 40cm (16in)

Yogi Bear, named after US baseball player, Yogi Berra, gained fame in the 1960s after appearing in US television programmes by Hanna Barbera. He featured in a film in 1964, and has inspired many children's toys, including this Canadian-made bear.

© 1980 HANNA-BARBERA PRODUCTIONS, INC. BY/PAR MIGHTY STAR

Printed label

brown and black, safe, plastic eyes

large, cupped ears sewn from facial seams down sides and towards back of head

dark brown, square, synthetic fabric nose; black, inverted-Y-shaped, single-stitched mouth

short-pile, golden synthetic plush on woven backing; soft stuffed

dark brown, synthetic fabric pads with three black, stitched claws

foil rosette with "SDF Shanghai Dolls Factory"

1980s SHANGHAI DOLLS FACTORY

Height: 38cm (15in)

Teddy bears have changed little since they were first exported from mainland China after World War II, although safe, plastic eyes have replaced glass eyes. The Shanghai Dolls Factory is one of China's main teddy-bear manufacturers.

Printed tag

large, cupped ears with inner edges caught into facial seams

modacrylic, high pile, knitted fabric; polyester-fibre stuffing

black, triangular, moulded nose; black, double-stitched mouth

short, stumpy legs; pads of dark brown plush

tag with intructions, "Cool gentle wash in machine; brush when dry"

cloth label sewn into leg-seam

1992 BUNJY TOYS

Height: 25cm (10in)

Honey Bear (*above*) was made by South African firm Bunjy Toys, founded by Eve Mayhew in 1980. The firm moved to larger premises in Estcourt, Natal, in 1982, to meet growing demand. Their soft-toys are made from imported and South African materials.

BUNJY TOYS C.C. ESTCOURT MADE IN SOUTH AFRICA A Bunjy TOY

Embroidered label

Mass-market Collectables: 1980s-90s

MASS-PRODUCED, ARTIST-DESIGNED BEARS FOR COLLECTORS

The growth of arctophily prompted an alliance of bear artists and manufacturers to produce mass-market, limited-edition collectables. The US company Applause heralded this approach by introducing Robert Raikes' bears to its range in 1985. From 1987, the House of Nisbet in Britain reproduced the designs of well-known US artists, including Carol-Lynn Rössel Waugh, Beverly Port, Ted Menten, Dee Hockenberry, and April Whitcomb. By 1990, other companies in the UK, US, and Germany had followed suit. Limited editions could number as many as 10,000 when produced by major manufacturers.

1991 CAROL-LYNN RÖSSEL WAUGH

Carol-Lynn Rössel Waugh designed Gregory, named after her brother, for the New York company Effanbee in 1989. The company was later bought by Russ Berrie, who first introduced Gregory in 1991 along with Eureka, designed by US bear artist Linda Spiegel Lohre. The original Gregory was 35cm (14in) high and jointed; the manufacturers later developed this smaller, unjointed design.

Height: 23cm (9in)   Embroidered label

Eyes: the black, safe, plastic eyes resemble boot-buttons.

Muzzle: the plush on the protruding muzzle is clipped.

Nose/mouth: the square, brown nose is vertically stitched; the mouth is an inverted Y shape.

Bow: the maroon, satin, ribbon bow is original.

Arms: the elongated arms are the same length as the legs, and have spoon-shaped paws.

Fur: the fur is shaggy, curly, golden synthetic plush; the stuffing is a soft, polyester fiberfill.

Feet/pads: the oval feet have brown, synthetic, velvet-like fabric pads and no claws.

BEAR PROFILE

It is difficult to distinguish the arms, legs, and body, or the positioning of the ears on the sides of the head, on this shaggy bear. However, you can see the protruding muzzle, and the short, stubby tail. Notice that the arms are as long as the legs.

brown plastic eyes; pupil formed by hole drilled into wood behind

light brown acrylic plush

hand-carved face

mouth described as "pouty face"

carved, button-like nose

sailor's jacket with brass buttons

fully jointed limbs and body

carved feet with defined toes

1986 ROBERT RAIKES
Height: 45cm (18in)

Robert Raikes, a professional wood sculptor during the 1970s, began carving dolls, and then, in 1982, teddy bears; these were known as "Woody Bears" and later "Raikes Originals". He signed a contract with the US company Applause, which has been producing his bears since 1985. This sailor bear, Christopher, has unique carved wooden head and paws.

horizontally stitched, oval nose and inverted-Y-shaped mouth

black, safe, plastic eyes, resembling boot-buttons

golden mohair plush; stuffed with plastic pellets and polyester fiberfill

long, tapering arms with upward curving paws

fully jointed body and limbs

long, slightly bent legs

red, plastic chest-tag

1992 JOYCE ANN HAUGHEY
Height: 38cm (15in)

During the 1980s, Werner Hermann and his niece Traudel Mischner, designed Gebrüder Hermann's bears. Then, in 1992, Hermann introduced bears designed by US bear artists Joyce Ann Haughey and Jenny Krantz for the collector's market. Robin Hood (above), one of a limited edition of 2,000, was nominated for a TOBY award in 1992.

charcoal-grey acrylic plush; polyester fiberfill stuffing

large, flat ears lined with blue suede

square, black, vertically stitched nose; inverted-Y-shaped mouth

original spectacles

blue, suede pads; three black claws stitched over plush

limited-edition number on right foot-pad

fully jointed limbs

large, oval feet

1990 CATHIE HANNA
Height: 50cm (20in)

Ohio-based artist, Cathie Hanna, designed this Grandmother Brompton bear and her grand-daughter Abbey (a white bear); she also wrote a story about Abbey, whose photograph is in Grandmother Brompton's silver locket. Canterbury Bears (see pp.150–51), whose work is normally designed by John and Maude Blackburn, manufactured these bears.

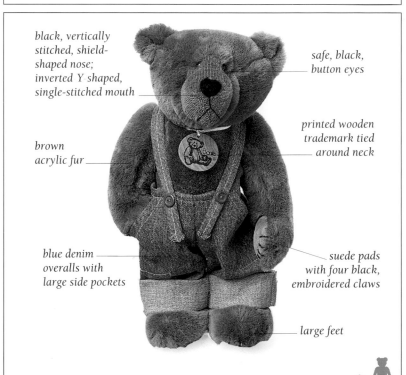

black, vertically stitched, shield-shaped nose; inverted Y shaped, single-stitched mouth

safe, black, button eyes

printed wooden trademark tied around neck

brown acrylic fur

blue denim overalls with large side pockets

suede pads with four black, embroidered claws

large feet

1990 BONITA WARRINGTON
Height: 35cm (14in)

Bonita began to make bears in 1983, inspired by a reproduction, antique teddy bear. She later successfully exhibited her work at the San Jose convention, and turned to full-time bear-making at her California home. C. Owen, shown here, came in three sizes in a limited edition of 5,000, and was one of her first designs produced by Applause.

Bear Artists

INDIVIDUAL CREATIONS FROM AROUND THE WORLD

Bear artistry has spread throughout the world since it began on the West Coast of the US in the early 1970s. Many other countries are now renowned for the work of their bear artists, including the UK, Germany, France, the Netherlands, New Zealand, Australia, and Canada. It is not possible to include an example of the work of every bear artist, as there are now hundreds worldwide, but a selection of work, covering a range of nationalities and design trends, is illustrated on the following pages.

A bear artist is someone who both designs and handmakes a bear, thereby producing an original work. Some artists are helped by family and friends, and a few, with the growing demand for their work, have enlarged their businesses and employed cutters, machinists, or stuffers. The artist, however, generally hand-finishes each bear, giving the final personal touches. Arctophiles often question whether this can be counted as true artistry; it is perhaps comparable to great painters of the past who have had the help of artisans to mix colours and transfer designs to canvas. Bear artists usually produce limited editions in small numbers, up to 25; those with extra workers make more. The value and unique character of each bear is ensured by limiting the numbers produced.

Bear artists frequently use decorative printed or embroidered labels as trademarks. The artist's signature and the edition number often appear on the label or the foot-pad, while some individualized symbols appear on other parts of the body. Some bear artists sell their bears from home; others market them in specialist shops or at conventions. Several bear artists even design bears for production by major manufacturers on a much larger scale *(see pp.170–71)*.

brown synthetic plush

black, replica boot-button eyes

silver-painted medallion with embossed standing bear

black, horizontally stitched, triangular nose

cream, felt paw-pads; four embroidered claws

blue, synthetic plush body with musical box inside

c.1980s BEVERLY PORT — Height: 40cm (16in)

Beverly Port, from Retsil, Washington State, is considered to be the first recorded, professional bear artist. Originally a porcelain doll-maker, Port turned to teddy bears in 1974. She has won many awards for her innovative work, some of which has been exhibited in art galleries. Her children, Kimberlee and John Paul, are also bear artists.

antique, black, boot-button eyes

three-piece head with shaved, pointed muzzle

black, horizontally stitched, narrow, oval nose; small, inverted-T-shaped mouth

golden mohair plush; polyester fiberfill stuffing

beige, ultrasuede pads

pear-shaped torso

c.1988 STEVE SCHUTT — Height: 35cm (14in)

Steve, an art teacher from Clarion, Iowa, has been involved in puppetry for 17 years. He began making bears for the collectors' market in 1980, and later became a bear artist under the tradename "Bear-'s'-ence". Steve has won prestigious awards for his work; Tyler and Pawpet are shown here. Since 1983, his assistant Barbara Smith has cut and sewn for him.

black, horizontally stitched, triangular nose; inverted-T-shaped mouth

black claws stitched across plush

black, replica boot-button eyes

red velour plush

gold-coloured, metal heart fixed onto plush

spoon-shaped, black velour pads

traditional large feet and narrow ankles

1984 K. AND H. CALVIN   Height: 45cm (18in)

Karin Calvin first made bears with friends in 1979, then formed a partnership with Howard in 1982. Their Ballard Baines Bear Company takes its name from a bear Karin bought. They made this bear for the 1984 Great Western Teddy Bear Show.

BALLARD BAINES Bear Company (c) Bellevue, Wash.

Printed label

bonnet decorated with rosebuds and ribbon

replica boot-button eyes

pink, woollen plush

black, horizontally stitched, triangular nose; inverted-T-shaped mouth

salmon-pink cotton dress with white polka dots

felt cub

cream, felt pads

broderie Anglaise apron

1983 LINDSAY PURPUS   Height: 33cm (13in)

Cheryl Lindsay and Joanne Purpus of California, created Purpusly Prairie (above); she is dressed in early nineteenth-century, American pioneer clothing, with a wide-brimmed bonnet, and carries a bear cub made of felt.

Lindsay Purpus

Printed label

black, boot-button eyes with single, diagonally embroidered eyebrow

brown, vertically stitched, shield-shaped nose with inverted-Y-shaped, single-stitched mouth

shaggy, cinnamon-coloured mohair plush

chocolate-brown, velvet pads

four dark brown, embroidered claws

painted, white ceramic heart pendant

1989 C-L. RÖSSEL WAUGH   Height: 38cm (15in)

Carol-Lynn Rössel Waugh, of Winthrop, Maine, the creator of PJs (above), was one of the first US bear artists and writers on the subject of bear artistry. She began making porcelain and latex teddies in 1975, and mohair bears from 1985 onwards.

Handwritten label

black, blown-glass eyes

black, vertically stitched, triangular nose; inverted-Y-shaped mouth

shaved, pointed muzzle

medium grey, German mohair plush; polyester fiberfill stuffing

curved paws with grey, felt paw-pads

long, fully jointed legs; large feet

1983 CHESTER FREEMAN   Height: 25cm (10in)

This bear artist, a former chaplain, began making teddy bears in 1982. In 1983, he formed Baskets and Bears, a mail-order firm, with basket-maker John McGuire. They work in an 1820 Federal row house in Geneva, New York State.

A HAND-MADE ORIGINAL ©1983 by Chester Freeman

Printed label

brown, vertically stitched, shield-shaped nose

collarless shirt with vertical stripes

cameo brooch with bear's head

denim overalls and dark jacket

three-pronged pitchfork

thumb indicated on paws

polka-dot apron with rick-rack braid

beige mohair plush

four brown claws stitched to each paw and foot

1990 BARBARA CONLEY
Height: 48cm (19in)

At a teddy-bear convention in Clarion, Iowa, in 1990, bear artists were asked for their interpretation of Grant Wood's "American Gothic" painting, which depicts an elderly couple in front of their mid-western home. The winning entry, by Barbara Conley, of San Jose, California, was exact in detail, down to the wife's brooch and the husband's spectacles.

toy rifle with wooden stock, metal barrel, cork "bullet", and leather sling

eyes set inside shaved area of face

hunter's fringed, soft leather shirt

fake, racoon-skin hat

large, rounded, shaved muzzle

1985 BARBARA SIXBY
Height: 48cm (19in)

This Californian bear artist recreated the 18th-century, American frontiersman Daniel Boone in 1985. Boone, a skilful hunter, reputedly wore a fringed, hunting shirt that reached down to his knees. Only two of these bears were made.

ZÜCKER BEARS
SAN RAMON, CA.
©

Printed label

hand-made, mohair-yarn curls

baked, moulded, black nose

lollipop refers to famous Shirley Temple song, On the Good Ship Lollipop

black, embroidered mouth with broad smile

beige, synthetic plush; kapok stuffing

red, polka-dot cotton dress with pleated ruff

1983 BEV MILLER LANDSTRA
Height: 20cm (8in)

This artist from Veneta, Oregon, first made teddies for her son in 1963. As well as Shirley Teddy, shown here, Bev is renowned for her sets of personality bears from 1983, including Stan and Ollie, The Marx Bears, and T.R. Bear.

HANDCRAFTED ORIGINAL BY BEV MILLER
Shirley Teddy
© COPYRIGHT 1983 ALL RIGHTS RESERVED

Printed label

wide-brimmed, straw hat

plastic, replica, boot-button eyes

large, flat ears sewn to sides of head

head tilts to one side with endearing expression

black, embroidered nose and mouth

grey plush

small, wooden catapult protruding from left pocket

baggy, blue, denim overalls

1984 DORIS KING
Height: 33cm (13in)

This bear pays homage to American literary hero, Huckleberry Finn, and is described by the artist as "a picture of innocence". Second in The Pre Loved Ted series, he is dressed in denim overalls and straw hat. The bear was created in 1984, as a limited edition of 75, only a year after Doris, from Sacramento, California, made her first teddy bear.

head opens to reveal lipstick

bright, cerise-pink, synthetic, velvet-like fabric

cotton lace ruff and pink ribbon around neck

black, embroidered, triangular nose with smiling mouth beneath

pink, felt pads with four tiny, black claws

black, bead eyes

jointed arms and legs

1984 SARA PHILLIPS   Height: 2.5cm (1in)

These tiny bears, made in 1984, conceal a perfume bottle and compact respectively; they emulate the intriguing designs of similar, miniature bears made by Schuco in the 1920s and 30s. Sara, from Westminster, Maryland, began making copies of miniature antique bears in 1981 for a tiny teddy-bear shop she was opening. She also creates her own designs.

tiny, black, horzontally stitched, oval nose

inset, slightly protruding, cream, felt face; eyes sewn in near seam

wide, smiling mouth in style of Steiff's Dicky

fully jointed limbs and head

short-pile, good quality, golden mohair plush

cream, felt feet, with four long, black claws

1988 E. FUJITA-GAMBLE   Height: 7.5cm (3in)

Elaine is a physical education teacher in Washington State, but she has been making teddy bears, particularly miniatures, in her spare time since 1979, and selling them at shows in the US. A keen teddy-bear collector, Elaine likes to base her creations on antique bears: this tiny bear is a replica of Steiff's 1930 Dicky. Her husband pins and cuts out the pieces.

red ribbon bow

small, black, bead eyes

fully jointed head and limbs

red, felt jacket and pill-box hat trimmed with gold braid

black, embroidered claws

light brown plush

large, narrow feet

c.1984 SUSAN L. KRUSE   Height:15cm (6in)

Baby Bear Hop, created in 1984, copies Bing and Schuco Bell Hop teddies from the 1920s. This Californian bear artist taught herself with Margaret Hutching's *Teddy Bears and How to Make Them* when expecting her first child.

Printed card tag

golden mohair plush

shaved muzzle

horizontally-stitched, black, rectangular nose

inverted-Y-shaped, smiling mouth

baggy, knitted cardigan

large, narrow, spoon-like paws

light gold, synthetic fabric pads

large, oval feet

1985 D. & T. MICHAUD   Height: 45cm (18in)

The Professor is a replica of an antique US bear, from Doris and Terry Michaud's Carrousel Museum Collection. Their first commercially manufactured bear appeared in 1980; they produce both reproductions and original designs.

CARROUSEL
505 W. Broad st.
Chesaning, Mi. 48616

Printed label

fully jointed head
and limbs

shaggy,
purple-maroon
plush; internal
tilt-growler

suede pads
painted to
represent
paws

maroon,
vertically
stitched, wide,
rectangular nose

traditional
long limbs

curved,
spoon-shaped
paws

large feet

1983 LORETTA BOTTA Height: 63cm (25in)

This 1983 "one-of-a-kind" bear, adorned with plastic imitation grapes, is called Vino: Wine Country Bear. Loretta Botta, of San Francisco, was one of the first bear artists to operate in the US, under the name Botta Bears. She ceased business in 1992.

Handwritten label

fully jointed
head and limbs

hand-
embroidered,
flannel blanket
comforter,
with pink,
ribbon bow

beige
alpaca plush

black, glass bead
eyes with tears
embroidered in
clear thread
under each eye

brown,
horizontally
stitched,
oblong nose

embroidered
flower
trademark

ultrasuede
pads

c.1990 LYNN LUMLEY Height: 11cm (4½in)

Born in 1921, Lynn Lumley of Carson City, Nevada, started bear-making in 1983 despite crippling arthritis, and produces her work in three small sizes: 11cm (4½in), 14cm (5½in), and 16cm (6½in). Her trademark is an embroidered flower on the left foot. She makes 250–350, limited-edition bears a year, under the label "Grandma Lynn's Teddy Bears".

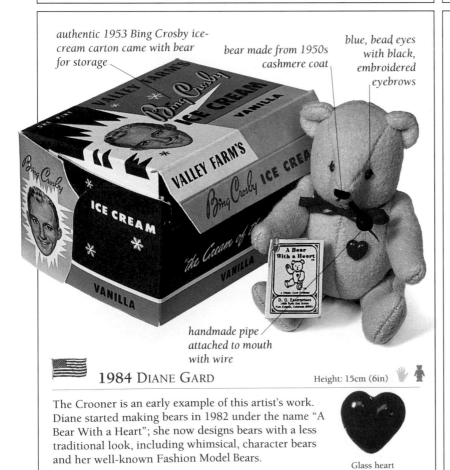

authentic 1953 Bing Crosby ice-
cream carton came with bear
for storage

bear made from 1950s
cashmere coat

blue, bead eyes
with black,
embroidered
eyebrows

handmade pipe
attached to mouth
with wire

1984 DIANE GARD Height: 15cm (6in)

The Crooner is an early example of this artist's work. Diane started making bears in 1982 under the name "A Bear With a Heart"; she now designs bears with a less traditional look, including whimsical, character bears and her well-known Fashion Model Bears.

Glass heart

unusual oval, black
nose with dropped
stitches on outside
and down centre

removable jacket
with brass
buttons

leather,
hobnailed boots

black, replica
boot-button eyes

white, cotton
shirt

short-pile, grey
mohair plush

c.1985 G. AND M. NETT Height: 45cm (18in)

Bears by Nett is a partnership between Gary, who began bear-making in 1983 after losing his job, and his mother Margaret, a professional seamstress. They produce detailed, historical US figures, like this Civil War Union Artillery Sergeant.

Embroidered logo

white, synthetic plush hat with pink-lined rabbit-ears

black, horizontally stitched, oval nose; inverted-Y-shaped mouth

safe, plastic eyes

pink, satin, ribbon bow

pads made of imitation upholstery velvet

three black claws

golden synthetic plush

1984 LINDA SPIEGEL LOHRE

Height: 18cm (7in)

Wee Bunny Basil is disguised as a rabbit, with his long-eared hat and pompom tail, a popular conceit amongst bear artists. Linda, from Fountain Valley, California, established Bearly There in her garage in 1980, and now employs several staff and outworkers.

BEARLY THE[
FOUNTAIN VAL[
DESIGNED BY L[

Embroidered label

nightcap with small pompom

shaggy, distressed, golden mohair

glass eyes

brown, vertically stitched nose; inverted-T-shaped mouth

long arms with spoon-shaped paws

button-down nightshirt

ultrasuede pads

long legs and large feet

1987 SERIETA HARRELL

Height: 35cm (14in)

Serieta Harrell of San Diego, California, worked as a chief designer before turning to bear-making. She has won awards for her distinctive, Sersha Collectibles creations. This 1987 Beddy-Bye-Bear has a belly-button made from gathered mohair.

Serieta ♥ 1988

Handwritten label

brown, glass eyes with white, suede eyelids

rhinestone earrings and choker

pink, horizontally stitched, shield-shaped nose; pink, inverted-Y-shaped mouth

short-pile, white mohair plush; compact, polyester-fibre stuffing

S-shaped arms

long gloves

full length, pink, silk-like evening gown and matching head bow

1988 TED MENTEN

Height: 58cm (23in)

Ted Menten, a New York bear artist, made this unique bear for *Teddy's Bearzaar*, a parody of fashion magazine *Harper's Bazaar*. Ted Menten also wrote *The Teddy Bear Lovers Catalogue* (1984) and created the comic strip *The World According to Hug*.

TED MENTEN ©1988

Handwritten label

black, glass eyes

wire antennae

black, vertically stitched, triangular nose; inverted-Y-shaped mouth

muzzle shaved on top

organza wings edged with gold-coloured thread

fully jointed limbs and head

ultrasuede pads with black claws

*c.***1990** GINGER T. BRAME

Height: 21cm (8½in)

Ginger T. Brame, from Raleigh, North Carolina, hand-makes her bears with imported fur; each carries a bell around the neck. Bumblebear, in three sizes, is made of black and gold mohair. Brame's tradename, The Piece Parade, reflects the fact that her bears start out in pieces.

The Piece Parade
Ginger T. Brame

Printed label

brown, lead-crystal eyes with black pupils

dark brown mohair plush

suede nose with needle-sculpted nostrils

green, knitted balaclava with holes for ears

printed lapel badge reads: "Some people have one of those days. I have one of those lives."

brown, suede pads

elasticated trousers

miniature metal frying pan and fish-slice

1988 JOANNE MITCHELL — Height: 65cm (26in)

Joanne, from Houston, Texas, became a bear artist in 1984 after collecting teddy bears for years. Rusty the Bagman, pictured here, is dressed as a "hobo" with his worldly goods, including a teddy bear, in his pocket. He represents the spirit of a friend of Joanne's, a Marine, who died in action. Joanne's Paws for Peace bear won a TOBY award in 1990.

curly, shaggy, golden mohair plush; stuffed with polyester fibrefill throughout

polyester-stuffed head and limbs

black, shield-shaped nose; inverted-Y-shaped mouth

amber and black, glass eyes

pale golden, felt pads; four black claws stitched across plush

jointed, long, curved arms

jointed, long legs with narrow ankles

very large, slender, feet

1988 CINDY MARTIN — Height: 88cm (35in)

Cindy from Fresno, California, made her first bear in 1982, inspired by antique teddies. Her bears range from miniatures to those over 122 cm(48in) high. Sailor Bear, with distinct, elongated limbs and neck, is typical of her larger creations.

Handwritten label

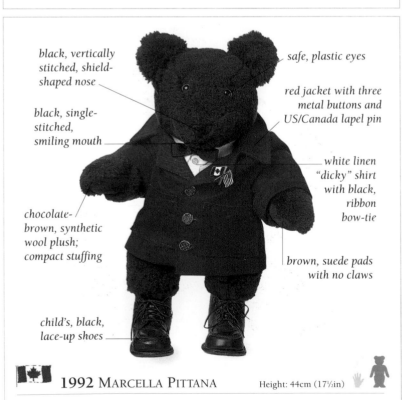

black, vertically stitched, shield-shaped nose

black, single-stitched, smiling mouth

safe, plastic eyes

red jacket with three metal buttons and US/Canada lapel pin

chocolate-brown, synthetic wool plush; compact stuffing

white linen "dicky" shirt with black, ribbon bow-tie

brown, suede pads with no claws

child's, black, lace-up shoes

1992 MARCELLA PITTANA — Height: 44cm (17½in)

Vagabond Teddy is the central character in a series of story colouring books, created by this retired, Niagara College French teacher. The books, published since 1986, were the first of their kind to appear in Canada. Marcella Pittana has a large collection of teddy bears at her Port Colborne, Ontario home and runs bear-making workshops in Canada and the US.

amber and black glass eyes

red, woven jacket with three brass buttons and stand-up collar

black, vertically stitched oval nose; inverted-Y-shaped, mouth

Canadian national flag on pole

pointed muzzle

curved arms with chamois leather pads; no claws

straight legs with large feet

extra dense, golden mohair plush; polyester fiberfill stuffing; internal tilt growler

1992 TRUDY TENEYCKE — Height: 45cm (18in)

Trudy Teneycke, from Regina, Saskatchewan, has been a bear artist since 1987 and has won several awards. Sergeant Sam Brown is one of a limited-edition of 150; he wears an approved Royal Canadian Mounted Police uniform and holds the national flag.

Printed tag

brown, vertically stitched
nose and inverted-Y-
shaped mouth

slightly cupped ears,
set on sides of head

pointed muzzle,
clipped between
nose and mouth

brown glass eyes
with black pupils

S-shaped arms
bent at elbows
and wrists

large, oval feet
with dark brown,
leather pads

four
brown,
stitched
claws

light brown
mohair plush

🇨🇦 **1989 JOAN RANKIN**

Height: 33cm (13in)

Joan, a retired art teacher from Moose Jaw,
Saskatchewan, began making bears in 1988. She
created Baxter Brown Bear in 1989, and has
written and illustrated stories about him, soon
to be published and sold with replicas of Baxter.

Printed label

large, rounded
ears, set wide
apart

brown and black,
safe, plastic eyes

black, vertically
stitched, circular,
nose; inverted-Y-
shaped mouth

speckled
synthetic plush;
soft stuffed;
internal tilt
growler

long, curved,
tapering arms

narrow
ankles and
large feet

orange,
synthetic,
velvet-like
fabric pads
with no claws

🇬🇧 **1990 SUSAN RIXON**

Height: 45cm (18in)

Susan Rixon and husband David from Berkshire have
made bears since 1979 under the label Nonsuch Soft
Toys. This bear, named after British archaeologist Sir
Mortimer Wheeler, was created to celebrate the
centenary of the excavation of Silchester, Berkshire.

Nonsuch
Mortimer
Bear ©
Limited Edition
of 200 only

Printed label

pink-brown, safe,
plastic eyes with
black pupils

vertically stitched,
square nose;
inverted-Y-
shaped, double-
stitched mouth

shaved muzzle

original bow

short-pile, cinnamon
mohair plush;
internal tilt
growler

fully
jointed
limbs

long arms;
brown,
suedette
pads with
five claws

long legs
and large feet

🇬🇧 **1990 BEDFORD BEARS**

Height: 35cm (14in)

Bedford Bears makes mohair collectors' bears and a
modacrylic plush range, all designed by Eddie Owen
in Dunton, Bedfordshire. This limited-edition bear,
made for the firm's 10th anniversary, is sold
from their stall in Covent Garden, London.

Embroidered label

brown, safe, plastic
eyes with black pupils

synthetic plush on
acrylic backing; soft,
polyester stuffing;
internal tilt
growler

black, hand-embroidered
nose and mouth

suedette pads; four
black claws stitched
across each pad

leather
school
bag

cotton
poplin
shirt

grey
school
trousers

🇬🇧 **1987 SUE QUINN**

Height: 38cm (15in)

Sue, who has made soft toys since the 1960s, founded Dormouse Designs
in 1978, in an old drapery in Renfrewshire, Scotland. She introduced
teddies to her range in 1982, and began making limited editions in 1986.
In 1987, inspired by her son going to school, she created Bramble School-
days and, in 1983, Sue was acclaimed British Toymaker of the Year.

felt cap with badge

muzzle, front of ears, and above eyes shaved to appear worn

blue, felt blazer with schoolboy treasures in pocket

blond, distressed mohair; wood-wool stuffing in muzzle; soft stuffing elsewhere

black, plastic, replica boot-button eyes

black, wool, vertically stitched nose; inverted-V-shaped mouth

white shirt; blue and yellow striped tie

brown, leather pads

1991 STACEY LEE TERRY   Height: 33cm (13in)

Stacey, a full-time bear artist since 1987, who lives in Winslow, Bucks., produced this teddy in 1991. It is based on Theo, a schoolboy bear character drawn by British teddy-bear illustrator Prue Theobald, and was produced in a limited edition of 250.

Embroidered label

black, plastic, replica boot-button eyes

original, red, printed cravat

narrow, beige, velvet-like pads; three black claws across plush and pad

black, vertically stitched nose

elongated, very slender muzzle

alpaca plush, popular in 1930s

1987 BRIAN BEACOCK   Height: 40cm (16in)

Brian Beacock, bear artist, collector, and restorer, designed this caricature of the classic old teddy bear for Joan Bland of Asquiths (the first exclusive teddy-bear shop in the UK) in 1987. It was produced by Big Softies (see p.143) in three colours and sizes. Although this is a manufactured sample, Brian's artistry is well known on both sides of the Atlantic.

safe, plastic, replica boot-button eyes

brown, vertically stitched nose with dropped centre and outer stitches; inverted-Y-shaped mouth

shaggy, golden mohair plush

long legs with large feet

hat trimmed with fabric roses

protruding, shaved muzzle

cotton lace collar

brown, velvet pads; four, webbed claws on paws and feet

1991 PAM HOWELLS   Height: 43cm (17in)

Pam was a designer at Chiltern's factory in Pontypool from 1957–67, but she has been making her own soft toys since 1972. This mother bear is part of a tableau called Feeding the Ducks, made in 1991.

Embroidered label

wide, rectangular, vertically stitched nose; long muzzle

Welsh woven fabric bow-tie

very long arms with curved, spoon-shaped paws

large, narrow feet

black, safe, plastic, replica boot-button eyes

carved, wooden, Welsh love-spoon

distressed golden mohair plush

beige, felt pads

1991 SUE SCHOEN   Height: 34cm (13½in)

Dewi hails from the workshop of Sue Schoen, whose Welsh business name "Bocs Teganau" means "toy box". Sue has been making bears since 1986, producing standard and limited-edition ranges, many with Welsh names.

Printed label

1985 NAOMI LAIGHT

elongated muzzle

small, folded ears, lying flat at back of head

black, vertically stitched, oval nose

flat, black, plastic eyes, resembling flat, metal studs of early British bears

long, tapering arms with curved paws

original scarf around neck

four, black claws on paws and feet

light brown, suede pads

narrow ankles with large, slender feet

1985 NAOMI LAIGHT Height: 33cm (13in)

This bear was made for a Save the Children charity auction in 1985 using a khaki, chenille-like, short plush. Naomi has been making limited-edition, collectors' teddy bears from her home since the early 1980s.

A Naomi Laight COLLECTORS BEAR

Embroidered label

1992 A. & W. MULLANEY

clipped mohair plush on muzzle

black, glass, boot-button eyes

vertically stitched, rectangular nose; inverted-Y-shaped mouth

long, curly, grey-gold mohair plush; stuffed with compact wood-wool throughout

arms much longer than legs, with upward-curving paws

beige, felt pads; four claws on paws and feet

fully jointed

1992 A. & W. MULLANEY Height: 60cm (24in)

Alistair was made in 1992 by Alan and Wendy Mullaney from their home in the Scottish Highlands. They started designing and making bears in 1989, and their original range consisted of six sizes and three colours. They produce eight bears in a week.

Atlantic Bears

Printed label

1991 LIZ CARLESS

German black, blown-glass eyes

blue, satin ribbon tied around head

shaved, protruding muzzle

long limbs with internal, American Loc-Line system, allowing range of poses

black, vertically stitched, triangular nose

polka-dot, synthetic dress

typical American toddler's black, plastic shoes

1991 LIZ CARLESS Height: 63cm (25in)

Named after her creator, Elizabeth Anne was a special commission for the Cotswold Teddy Bear Museum in 1991. Liz used to live in both Florida and London, hence her business name Transatlantic Teddies. She has been making bears since 1987.

An Original Design *Lillibet TRANSATLANTIC TEDDIES*

Printed label

1991 ROMSEY BEAR CO.

black, vertically stitched, triangular nose

black, safe, plastic, replica boot-button eyes

original, blue ribbon bow

mohair dyed red in Nottingham, especially for Romsey Bears

traditional body shape with curved arms

big feet with maroon pads; name machine-embroidered on right pad

"1991" and limited edition number "19" embroidered on left pad

1991 ROMSEY BEAR CO. Height: 40cm (16in)

Li.Bear.A.Ted is the second of three, limited-edition bears produced in 1990, 1991, and 1992 to commemorate the liberation of the Channel Islands in 1945. The company is named after Romsey, Hampshire, where the bears are made.

ROMSEY BEAR CO. COLLECTORS BEARS SO51 7RF

Embroidered label

distressed, shaggy mohair plush; soft, polyester stuffing

black, boot-button eyes, handmade by artist

vertically stitched, oblong nose; inverted-V-shaped mouth

darned patch on left foot gives worn appearance

long, curved arms

beige, felt pads

oval feet with four brown, stitched claws

1992 MADDIE JANES   Height: 32cm (12½in)

Cobweb, one of a limited edition of 12, is the work of Maddie Janes from Shropshire, England, who began making teddies in 1991. The bear's body is filled with polyurethane pellets to give a sagging, "antique" feel. The handwritten label displays the bear artist's name.

Handwritten label

small, black, bead eyes

short, golden mohair plush on head, hands, and lower legs; soft-stuffed throughout

navy blue, felt hat

beige, suede pads with three black claws

horizontally stitched nose; inverted-Y-shaped mouth

green, felt lower body and thighs

1992 DEBORAH CANHAM   Height: 6cm (2½in)

This Devon-based artist designs and makes tiny, jointed bears. Her largest bear is 7cm (3in). Punch and Judy, the dressed character bears illustrated here, are special, limited editions based on a traditional French Punch and Judy design. In 1992 Deborah was voted Bear Artist of the Year by S.M.A.L.L. (Society for Miniature Arctophiles Loving and Learning).

brown, vertically stitched nose; inverted-Y-shaped mouth

shaggy, pink mohair plush

slightly clipped, white, mohair plush muzzle

sewn-in, black, bead eyes

lace ruff with satin rosebud

fully jointed limbs and body

lilac, leather pads

1991 CATHERINE M. WHILE   Height: 9cm (3½in)

Catherine M. While produced her first tiny bear in 1989 from her home in Chesterfield, Derbyshire, England, inspired by a newly acquired, limited-edition Raikes bear. She made Hyacinth (*above*) in 1991. Her mother helps to cut and hand-sew the bears, her father helping to stuff them. The creations are sold under the label, Chasing Rainbows.

black, embroidered eyes

black, horizontally stitched nose; inverted-V-shaped mouth

hand-knitted, Fair Isle sweater

very soft, short-pile, golden, bonded fabric; kapok stuffing

long, curved arms

golden, synthetic-velvet pads

fully jointed limbs and head

long legs and large feet

1991 ANITA OLIVER   Height: 6cm (2½in)

Boris Bear, one of a limited editon of 200, came in a hand-marbled paper box. He is a typical example from Anita Oliver, one of the earliest British miniature-bear artists. She made her first small teddy in 1980, after a career in graphic design and publishing, though making soft toys and dolls was her hobby. Her bears are sold in Europe and the United States.

black, safe,
plastic eyes

black, oblong
nose; inverted-Y-
shaped mouth

brown, felt
pads with
three black
claws stitched
across plush

distressed golden
mohair plush;
polyester stuffing
throughout

pointed, clipped muzzle
stuffed with wood-wool

hand-knitted,
red scarf

long, fully
jointed, limbs

1992 IRENE MOORE

Height: 35cm (14in)

Oscar, one of a limited edition of 25, is the
creation of the first bear artist to emerge from
Northern Ireland. Irene Moore began making
traditional bears in 1991, and named her business,
Pinecroft Bears, after her County Down home.

NECROFT BEARS"
ditional Teddy Bears
in Newtownards, Co. Down.
BT23 3RJ/149

Printed label

safe, black,
replica boot-
button eyes

golden, distressed
mohair; stuffed with
soft, polyester
fiberfill

black, vertically
stitched, shield-
shaped nose; inverted-
Y-shaped mouth

long, curved
arms

narrow
ankles and
large feet

brown, velveteen pads
with four black claws

1991 JOAN HANNA

Height: 34cm (13½in)

Joan, from County Cork, is believed to be the first
bear artist from the Republic of Ireland. She made
soft toys in her teens, and formed Craft-T-Bears in
1990. Joan works alone, with some family help at
busy times. Tufty is one of her traditional range.

Craf
Made in C
NOT FOR U

Printed label

shaved, pointed
muzzle

four stitches
form W-shaped
mouth

fully jointed
limbs

paws
curved at
right angles
to arms; no
pads

low-set ears

small, amber, glass
eyes with black pupils

velour nose

cinnamon-
coloured
synthetic
plush

straight legs
with beige, felt
pads reinforced
with card

1992 JONETTE STABBERT

Height: 28cm (11in)

Honey Bear was made by the first Dutch bear artist,
US-born Jonette Stabbert. With a background in art
and design, she was one of the world's leading cloth
doll artists until she turned to bear-making in about
1983, with the tradename "Poppette Bears".

Poppette Bears
AMSTERDAM

Embroidered label

black bead eyes
over red felt

wide, inverted-Y-
shaped, double-
stitched mouth

long, curved
arms

beige,
felt pads

slightly cupped ears

nose stitched in
thick, black thread

distressed, black
mohair plush;
soft stuffing

fully
jointed
limbs
and
head

narrow ankles
and large feet

1991 JANE HUMME

Height: 13cm (5in)

Jane Humme, from Bodegraven in the Netherlands,
began making traditional bears in 1989. This tiny
reproduction of a 1912 Steiff black bear is the only
replica Jane has made. Too small for a label, Jane
embroidered her initials in red under its arm.

HANDMADE BY
Jane Hu

Embroidered label

1992 MARCELLE GOFFIN

clear, glass eyes with black pupils and hand-painted backs

ears lined with 1940s red, silk-velvet; sewn across facial seams

pale gold, medium-pile mohair plush; wood-wool stuffing

red, embroidered, Y-shaped nose

fully jointed limbs

long, slightly curved arms and tapering paws

leather tag with inscription "Les Ours de Marcelle"

large, oval feet with red, silk-velvet pads

1992 MARCELLE GOFFIN Height: 34cm (13½in)

Rouen-based Marcelle Goffin specializes in copies of old French bears. Tintin is a 1990s replica of a 1940s teddy that was originally made from woollen blanket fabric. Marcelle has formed a club "Teddy's Patch" with fellow artist, Marylou Jouet.

Embroidered label

1991 ALINE COUSIN

sewn-in, antique, black, boot-buttons eyes

wide head stuffed with wood-wool

inverted-T-shaped, single-stitched mouth

semi-circular nose hand-embroidered in black thread

short-pile, cotton and rayon plush; stuffed with kapok

three long, black, stitched claws

dark beige, felt pads

long, slender feet

slim legs; narrow ankles

1991 ALINE COUSIN Height: 26cm (10½in)

Aline Cousin has made limited-edition, collector bears from Noisy le Grand, outside Paris, since December 1990. She uses old and new mohair, cotton, wool, and rayon plush fabrics, and favours traditional designs, such Napoleon, shown here.

Embroidered label

1992 MARYLOU JOUET

black, vertically stitched, oval nose

flat ears sewn across facial seams

pointed muzzle

antique, black, boot-button eyes

patchwork of printed cotton fabrics; wood-wool stuffing

inverted-Y-shaped, double-stitched mouth

printed, card label

curved, tapering arms

three black claws

large thighs, narrow ankles, and large, oval feet

1992 MARYLOU JOUET Height: 28cm (11in)

This special Christmas bear, called Patchnours, is made from 150 pieces of American fabric. Marylou Jouet (her surname means toy in French), from Rennes, Brittany, is a member of the Paris Patchwork Association. She has been teaching quilting since 1984. She also makes traditional mohair-plush bears, dressed and in miniature.

1988 DAWN NICHOLL

black, plastic button eyes

large, flat ears

black, triangular nose; inverted-T-shaped mouth

hand-made, woollen felt; wool stuffing

felt bag contains card with bear's details

short, stumpy, bulbous legs

1988 DAWN NICHOLL Height: 30cm (12in)

Dawn Nicholl, from Whangarei, North Island, New Zealand, has experimented with art forms to produce her distinctively designed bears, made of hand-made, pure New Zealand wool felt. She made Mr. Oz E. Bound for the 1988 Australian World Expo.

Embroidered label

1991 J. AND M. WALTON

small, black, safe, plastic eyes

small, slightly cupped ears set on sides of head

black, vertically stitched, shield-shaped nose

inverted-V-shaped mouth

printed swing-tag

long, curved arms extend beyond legs; spoon-shaped paws

beige, suede pads with no claws

large, oval feet

short-pile mohair plush; stuffed with cotton fibre waste

1991 J. AND M. WALTON   Height: 34cm (13½in)

Halifax was designed by the Waltons of Upper Hutt, New Zealand. Part-time bear artists since 1989, Judy is also a registered nurse, and her husband Michael is a dentist. They are members of the Antipodean Bear Makers Co-op and the British Toymakers' Guild.

Printed label

1992 JANIS HARRIS

amber and black, translucent, glass eyes; white opaque glass beneath

oblong, black nose with inverted-Y-shaped mouth

cinnamon-coloured mohair plush; soft-stuffed

black and gold, heart-shaped card; black ribbon with brass bell

slightly curved arms

brown, leather pads

long, oval feet; no claws

1992 JANIS HARRIS   Height: 35cm (14in)

Originally a doll-maker, Janis Harris has also made limited-edition and one-off bears from her home in Auckland since 1985. Baby Bobby has unusual glass "googly" eyes but follows the traditional design preferred by this award-winning artist.

ALMOST SOUTH POLE BEARS
MADE IN NEW ZEALAND BY JANIS HARRIS

Embroidered label

1992 FRANCES McLEARY

brimmed hat

head of long-pile, grey mohair on golden plush base

large, flat ears, sewn to sides of head

black, safe, plastic, button eyes

black, vertically stitched, triangular nose

double-stitched, inverted-Y-shaped mouth

striped, button-down shirt with stand-up collar and cuffs

golden synthetic plush fur; Dacron polyester stuffing

pale beige, suede paw-pads

baggy, tweed trousers with elasticated waist

black, leather-like boots

1992 FRANCES McLEARY   Height: 53cm (21in)

Frances McLeary created the gardener Garmonsway as part of her Colonial Character collection, with the help of her husband, Bill, at their farm "Braid-wood", Frankton, on the North Island. Frances holds several New Zealand bear-making awards.

A Braidwood Bear

Printed tag

1992 ALLIE AND NIGEL HANTON

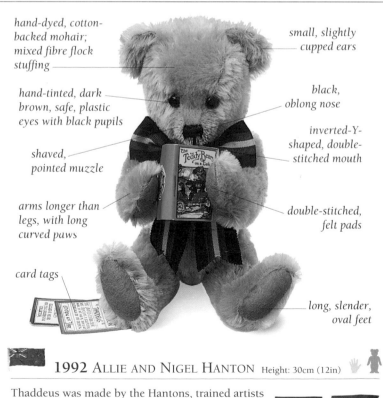

hand-dyed, cotton-backed mohair; mixed fibre flock stuffing

small, slightly cupped ears

hand-tinted, dark brown, safe, plastic eyes with black pupils

black, oblong nose

shaved, pointed muzzle

inverted-Y-shaped, double-stitched mouth

arms longer than legs, with long curved paws

double-stitched, felt pads

card tags

long, slender, oval feet

1992 ALLIE AND NIGEL HANTON   Height: 30cm (12in)

Thaddeus was made by the Hantons, trained artists and teachers who turned to bear-making in 1989. Each limited-edition bear is made to order at their Wellington home studio, and based on traditional designs from the Edwardian era (1901–10).

Printed label

safe, plastic eyes

felt, bushman's hat

leather waistcoat

suede thong around neck

golden, synthetic plush; Dacron stuffing; internal growler

leather belt

cream, suede pads

plastic knife

denim jeans

toy, rubber crocodile

1989 PAT LOVELOCK

Height: 45cm (18in)

This 1989 Crocodile Dunbear was inspired by actor Paul Hogan's character "Crocodile Dundee" in the film of the same name. From Rosebud, Victoria, Pat Lovelock has been a bear artist since 1984 and has won awards in Australia for her Pat L. Original Bears.

An Original by Pat L.

Printed label

black, horizontally stitched, shield-shaped nose; inverted-T-shaped, smiling mouth

artist's, red, felt beret

unusual red and black, glass eyes

large, red, ribbon bow around neck

grey, felt pads on feet

wooden palette with real paint brush

grey, synthetic plush

1985 MARJORY FAINGES

Height: 28cm (11in)

Rembearandt, dressed as an artist, is an early example of Marjory Fainges' work. Most of her bears are now limited editions, sold under the trade-name "Miffi", which is derived from her initials. From Everton Park, Queensland, Marjory is well known throughout Australia and the US as an artist, restorer, collector, teacher of bear-making, and author.

brown and black, safe, plastic eyes

wide-brimmed, straw hat

beige, synthetic plush; polyester stuffing

black, shield-shaped nose; inverted-T-shaped mouth

long, curved arms with elongated, spoon-shaped paws

beige, felt pads

long legs with narrow ankles and slender, oval feet

striped dungarees printed with bears

1987 GERRY WARLOW

Height: 40cm (16in)

Gerry first made bears in 1983, and Edgar is an early example of her work; her more recent bears are made of mohair plush. Gerry works from her home in Rosewood, Queensland, Australia, under the name Gerry's Teddy and Craft Designs.

Gerry's

Printed label

German, golden mohair plush

German, black, glass eyes

brown, vertically stitched, narrow, rectangular nose; inverted-Y-shaped mouth

original blue and maroon, satin bow

long, curved arms

light brown, suede pads; three brown claws stitched across plush

relatively large feet; narrow ankles

1992 JENNIFER LAING

Height: 20cm (8in)

This Sydney artist has made traditional bears since 1990, following her appointment as manager of *The Teddy Bear Shop* in Neutral Bay, New South Wales. Jennifer's bears are all hand-stitched. She is a member of the Antipodean Bear Makers's Co-op.

Totally Bear

Printed tag

German, white, string mohair (unbrushed and undyed)

black, glass eyes

black, horizontally stitched, triangular nose; inverted-Y-shaped, single-stitched mouth

pointed, shaved muzzle

traditional, elongated arms with curved, spoon-shaped paws

large, slender, oval feet; narrow ankles

beige, suede pads

1991 JENNY ROUND   Height: 43cm (17in)

Jenny Round, of Round-A-Bout Bears, won Best Bear Artist Award for Ben (*above*) at the 1991 Australian Doll and Teddy Fair. She began making bears, including their joints, in 1988. She lives in New South Wales, Australia, and has a collection of 400 bears.

Printed label

brown and black, safe, plastic eyes

felt, bushman's hat with corks and gum leaves

"swag" (rolled-up bushman's bed)

"swagman's" red, open-necked shirt and tweed waistcoat

brown, synthetic plush

beige, leather paw-pads

wide legs; foot-pads reinforced with wood

hessian "tucker bag" (food bag)

1990 BOB WHITE   Height: 45cm (18in)

A Fine Art teacher at Tasmania's Latrobe High School, Bob White decided to make his first bear when he could not find an Australian-made example in a teddy-bear shop. His bears, made under the tradename Bob's Bears, are always masculine characters.

Printed logo

sewn-in, black, bead eyes

sewn-on, soft, black, oilcloth nose; black, embroidered, inverted-Y-shaped mouth

straight arms

four black, embroidered claws

golden, short-pile velveteen

beige, suedette pads

jointed limbs

wide, flat body with final side seam

1992 MARY KELLY   Height: 26cm (10½in)

Bear-making has been Mary Kelly's hobby for years, but she only began to sell her bears commercially after opening Bear Basics in Simon's Town in 1991 – the first teddy-bear shop in South Africa. Aided by her daughter Samantha, Mary makes her bears mainly in velveteen and upholstery fabrics, as traditional plushes are expensive and not readily available.

sewn-in, brown and black, plastic eyes

black, leather nose

smiling mouth made with two, black stitches

black, leather pads

unjointed body

leather tag with "wa me" ("why me")

1990 BOTSWANA MADE   Height: 25cm (10in)

Bears like "Wa Me", shown above, are made by a woman on a farm in a Botswana village. Local women help with the decorated boxes that imitate wooden animal transit crates. The bear is crocheted in 100% wool; special loops incorporated in the stitching give the impression of shaggy, mohair plush, while the plain stitches on the muzzle create a shaved appearance.

Teddy-bear muff
Teddy muffs have always been popular; this German example (*right*) has a squeaker.

Silver nurseryware
Late 19th and early 20th century cutlery (*above and left*) decorated with bears.

Tea for two
Mother bear's skirt (*above*) is a tea-cosy; the baby is jointed.

Teddy philately
Teddies depicted on postage stamps from around the world (*left*).

First friend
Studio portraits featuring teddies are attractive to collect. This 1913 photograph (*left*) was taken in Hackney, east London.

Feeding-bottle cover
This 1940s–50s feeding bottle, with its ingenious cover (*below*), was also available in pink plush.

On the shelf
This collection of childhood teddies (*left*) was gathered from members of the design and editorial team who worked on this book.

ARCTOPHILY: BEAR COLLECTING

BY THE MID-1980S, teddy-bear collecting had achieved a relatively serious status as a hobby; it had also acquired a commonly accepted name, "arctophily", to describe it – the word is derived from the Greek *arctos* (bear) and *philos* (love).

The beauty of teddy-bear collecting is that it can be approached on different levels, according to individual circumstances, making it a pastime for both children and adults, of varying means. You can concentrate on antique bears, bear artists' bears, modern limited editions, or cheap, secondhand teddies. Or you can collect just anything that features teddy bears, which, again, can vary from expensive silver or china, to cheaper items, such as biscuit wrappers, postage stamps, or badges. Arctophily in its true sense, therefore, can encompass anything that is bear-related. As a collector, you can widen your boundaries to include, for example, polar bears, pandas, or even objects relating to Teddy Roosevelt, who gave teddies their name. The choice is yours.

As well as looking at the historical development of bear collecting as a hobby, this practical chapter discusses what being an arctophile entails, suggests possible types of collections and their various sources, as well as indicating how and where you can learn more about this extraordinarily fascinating and internationally popular subject.

Arctophily: Bear Collecting

A COMPREHENSIVE SURVEY OF THE HOBBY

Adults as well as children have long accepted teddy bears as mascots. Until recently, however, collecting teddy bears was a relatively unknown pastime. The English actor Peter Bull (1912–84), who is recognized as the catalyst behind the arctophily movement, not only encouraged the collecting of teddy bears as an acceptable hobby, but also introduced his philosophy of "bear awareness" in the late 1960s. Recognition of the hobby did not come of age, however, until the resurgence of teddy-bear mania in the 1980s. In 1981, Sue Arnold, in an article in the UK's *Observer* colour magazine, described Peter Bull as an "ursophile" (*urso* is Latin for bear). By the mid-1980s, the words "arctophile", "arctophilia", and "arctophily" had become accepted terminology amongst collectors of teddy bears.

Father of arctophily
Peter Bull (above) *with Bully Bear, the first bear he produced with House of Nisbet.*

TEDDY AMBASSADOR

When Peter Bull was sixteen, his mother gave away his childhood teddy, causing him great anguish. In the late 1960s, he realized that others experienced similar trauma, and he resolved to investigate the subject further. During an appearance on the American NBC chat-show *Today*, he asked the audience for interesting teddy-bear stories and, within a week, he had received over 2,000 letters. His research culminated in the publication of

House of Nisbet bear
This giant bear (left) *is wearing Peter Bull's own sweater, which features some of his favourite sayings. The 1984 Tribute Bully wears a replica sweater.*

Bear with Me (Hutchinson) in 1969. Already the author of several autobiographical books, this work marked the beginning of a career as an international ambassador for the teddy bear. He attended rallies and conventions in the United Kingdom and the United States, and collaborated with the House of Nisbet (*see pp.144–45*) on a range of limited-edition bears. His now-celebrated teddy "Aloysius" fuelled the teddy-bear renaissance of the early 1980s when he featured in the British television adaptation of Evelyn Waugh's novel *Brideshead Revisited*, later inspiring replicas by the House of Nisbet and the North American Bear Company (*see p.147*).

Peter Bull's book *A Hug of Teddy Bears* was published in 1984, the year of his death. His collection of around 250 teddy bears was bequeathed to the London Toy and Model Museum, where most of them are still displayed. However, some of the teddies were sold, including "Aloysius", who now resides at the Californian home of Paul and Rosemary Volpp.

CARING BEARS

Collecting teddy bears is now a worldwide hobby with universal appeal. For some, it is not just a pleasure, but an investment like any other form of antique collecting. For most, however, teddies provide companionship. Their suitability for dressing up and investing with personalities, and their endearing facial expressions, has often led to teddies becoming honorary family members. As Peter Bull pointed out, there is a strong emotional attachment between a human

"Hug" of bears
A collection of teddy bears is often described as a "hug". An old suitcase provides a perfect platform for this group of Gebrüder Hermann bears (above).

and his or her teddy, which, from childhood days, has been his or her earliest and closest confidante.

GOOD BEARS OF THE WORLD
Inspired by such sentiments, Jim Ownby, an American, thought up the idea of "Good Bears of the World", an organization dedicated to distributing bears to sick or traumatized children, and to the elderly and infirm. Chartered in Berne, Switzerland in 1973, the organization celebrates "Good Bear Day" on 27th October, in honour of Theodore Roosevelt's birthday. Members can join individually or as "dens" – groups who raise funds to make or buy bears to give to hospitals, police departments, nursing homes, and other suitable institutions. The late Colonel Bob Henderson of Edinburgh, Scotland, introduced Good Bears of the World to the United Kingdom. There are now "dens" worldwide.

THERAPEUTIC BEARS
For several years, American police departments have used teddy bears to help children talk through traumatic experiences, and this procedure is now practised in other countries. Some hospital doctors perform "operations" on teddy bears to help to minimize pre-surgery fears

Injured bears
The bear on crutches, by Softouch Inc. (above), and Port Wine by E. Kay Peck (below), are examples of teddies designed to help children cope with disabilities.

Bear lover
Nick Bisbikis Jr. (right) and his wife Cassie have accumulated around 700 old and new collector bears since the early 1980s at their California home. Nick Bisbikis also sells Gebrüder Hermann bears, as well as Fechter bears (seen here).

among young patients. Special bears have also been made to help children overcome difficult circumstances. Muffin Enterprises' Sir Koff-a-Lot, for example, was created by two cardiovascular surgeons as a therapeutic aid for patients recovering from open-heart, thoracic, and abdominal surgery.

Teddy bears have been developed for use in schools for the deaf: Honey the Signing Bear (invented by Pat Yockey of California-based Quiet Bears) allows for hands to be slipped through the unstuffed arms as an aid for teachers of sign language. Teddies with "heart-beats" have been made to lull fretful infants to sleep. Bears frequently symbolize children's charities, often becoming fund-raisers themselves – in the United Kingdom, Pudsey represents the BBC's annual "Children in Need" campaign, and, in Australia, Bandaged Bear can be adopted to raise money for the Royal Alexandra Hospital for Children in Campertown, New South Wales.

Fundraisers
Teddy-bear dealer and writer Linda Mullins (above) organizes conventions in San Diego, California, the proceeds of which go to a local home for abused children. The gift of an early Steiff from her husband Wally in 1974 launched Linda on the road to arctophily.

Past histories
"Fritz" (above), an early Steiff, was hidden under the floor of a British Nissen hut by his original owner, a German POW.

A COLLECTING STRATEGY

When launching into serious arctophily, you will have to adopt a strategy tailored to your individual circumstances, considering funds and space available, as well as personal taste. You may decide to concentrate on antique teddy bears, the term "antique" in this case referring to teddies manufactured before World War I. Teddies made in the 1920s and 1930s are now reaching higher prices in the sales rooms, however, and even 1950s and 1960s bears are becoming sought-after. Alternatively, you may choose to collect by manufacturer, by country, or by specializing in a particular design.

TEDDIES PAST AND PRESENT

Within the wider area of antique teddy-bears, it may be interesting to collect bears with colourful pasts, such as those belonging to famous people, or acting as sporting mascots. However, this can also prove to be costly; "Alfonzo", an early Steiff bear made of unusual red mohair and wearing a cossack outfit, said to have been made by the nanny of its Russian princess owner (*see p.19*), was sold at Christie's for a record price of £12,100.

Some arctophiles specialize in limited editions produced by modern manufacturers or by bear artists, of whom there are many around the world. You may decide to concentrate on the work of one particular artist, or buy simply because

the "face fits"; or you might prefer to be guided by colour, collecting white teddy bears exclusively, for instance.

INTERNATIONAL BEARS

You can also collect bears from around the world, or those designed as souvenirs – for example, the many Berliner bears (a bear is part of Berlin's coat-of-arms), with crown and sash, usually reading "Greetings from Berlin". Of the thousands produced by firms in the Neustadt region of Germany, most of these Berliner bears are unmarked. Some major names, such as Steiff and Schuco, also produce this type of bear. Another interesting souvenir is one sold at Yellowstone Park during the late 1930s – a small bear whose tag bears a poem beginning: "I'm just a loving, hugging bear...."

MINIATURE COLLECTION

If space is likely to pose a problem, focus your attention on miniature examples, either those made by past masters of the miniscule, such as Steiff or Schuco (*see pp.40–41*), or concentrate on the work of the many modern bear artists (*see pp.172–87*) who are producing smaller and smaller bears, all perfectly formed and traditionally jointed.

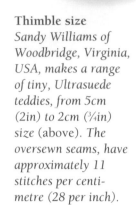

Thimble size
Sandy Williams of Woodbridge, Virginia, USA, makes a range of tiny, Ultrasuede teddies, from 5cm (2in) to 2cm (⅗in) size (above). The oversewn seams, have approximately 11 stitches per centimetre (28 per inch).

"Sergeant Culver"
A c.1914 American bear, "Sergeant Culver" (below, left) was the mascot for Culver Military Academy, in Logansport, Indiana.

Working bears
Harmles (below, left), a Steiff, was the pre-1914 sports mascot for the US boys' school, Kimbal Union Academy. Another Steiff (below, right) saw active duty with the London Fire Brigade during the Blitz in World War II.

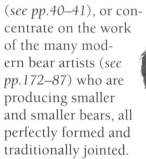

KEEPING RECORDS

Once the hobby of arctophily has become a serious occupation, it is as well to consider practicalities such as cataloguing, numbering systems, and photographic records. Some form of checklist or pictorial record is useful for easy reference when you are researching or sending information to other collectors, valuers, or appraisers. You can make up your own system, using lined, index cards, a simple exercise book, or by filing individually completed sheets for each bear in a ring binder. You can also store this type of information on a computer.

Whatever method or degree of sophistication you employ for your records, you must make sure that the information listed is consistent for each bear. In the case of an old, antique bear, for example, this should include: name, manufacturer, date of manufacture, exact label details, and any background history regarding provenance; purchase date, place, and price paid; plus basic information on height and materials used for fur, stuffing, eyes, pads, etc. You should also note whether the clothing is original, as well as whether the bear has a growler or squeaker in working order or otherwise.

Also describe any repairs in detail. It is useful to keep all associated ephemera such as card-tags, original photographs, and receipts with the documentation. If you have a large collection, number each bear, giving the same number to its corresponding record sheet. Numbering can be written on card, paper, or cloth tags, and tied to the bear or to its clothes.

It is advisable to take photographs of your bears not just for insurance and valuation purposes, but also to provide a useful aid when you are studying or showing off your collection. Take both front and side views of the bears, as it is useful, from the

evaluator's point of view, to see the shape and size of the bear's muzzle or hump. Where possible, include written details, such as the type of stuffing or the method of attaching the eyes, as this will not be shown on a photograph.

Satisfactory documentation is essential for insurance purposes and collectors should ensure that their teddy bears are adequately covered by their household contents policies. You may discover that you can claim only the original cost of a bear, and not the present market value, so it may be advisable to arrange further cover, scheduling each article separately, with their agreed value alongside. You must retain all documentation on the bear's original price, and at the same time keep abreast of current pricing trends.

Survivor
This early Bing (above), *now at England's Ribchester Museum of Childhood, is a "good luck" charm that survived the 1912 RMS Titanic disaster – unlike its unfortunate owner, Gaspare Gatti, the First Class Catering Manager.*

Cheeky collection
This group of Merrythought Cheeky teddy bears (right) *includes the Cotswold Teddy Bear Museum's 1992 Bedtime Bertie* (top), *based on the earlier 1977 Bedtime Cheeky, but with the addition of a miniature hot-water bottle.*

Zotty bears
Collectors may try to acquire each size of a particular popular design, such as these various versions of Steiff's Zotty (above).

TEDDY-BEAR VALUATION

You can form a rough idea of the value of your collection from the various teddy-bear and soft-toy price guides that have been published since the 1980s. These are regularly updated and give values in US dollars, pounds sterling, and Deutschmarks. Reputable teddy-bear dealers or international auction houses such as Sotheby's, Christie's, and Phillips, with specialist departments staffed by experts who deal with teddy-bear enquiries, can also give advice on the value of a bear.

Record-breaker
Bunny Campione, who introduced teddy-bear sales to Sotheby's, holding Lot 19, the c.1926 Steiff (above) sold for the record sum of £55,000 on 19 September 1989.

Frannie Bear
The limited-edition bear (below) was created to celebrate the opening of the Teddy Bear Museum in Naples, Florida.

FACTORS TO CONSIDER

I am often asked what makes a teddy bear valuable? Of course, many childhood bears are of great sentimental value and are therefore priceless. However, if you are interested in financial gain, there are several, often closely related, criteria to take into account regarding antique bears. Bears made by those manufacturers considered to be world leaders in the soft-toy industry – for example, Steiff, Bing, and Schuco – hold greater value than others, and if a bear's button, label, or card-tag trademark is still attached, this will also instantly raise the price. Age is obviously important, too: pre-World War I bears are generally considered to be the most valuable, although 1920s–30s British bears are now increasing in price. Other factors such as rarity of design, colour, and past history can sometimes affect the value. The condition of the bear plays an important part, too: severe wear and tear, or obvious repairs, will lower the price. A 1904, 75cm (30in), white Steiff was sold for £5,280 at Sotheby's in Chester, England in 1986. Its early date, rare colour and size, and its mint condition (it had never been played with by its original owner), all contributed to the then record price.

The expression on these old teddies also helps to increase their value. The record-breaking price of £55,000 paid in 1989 for "Happy" far outstripped the £3,520 raised a year later by a similar "dual" plush Steiff with large, bulbous, glass eyes. This was due not just to the fact that prices vary, depending on who is bidding, but also because of the sweet, enigmatic expression on "Happy's" face.

Teddies at auction
Christie's (above), fine art auctioneers since 1766, was the first auction house to hold a teddy-bears-only sale. It was held on 13 December 1985 at the South Kensington branch in London.

British fine-art auctioneers Christie's, Sotheby's, and Phillips, held their first teddy-bear sales in the mid-1980s. Prices soared in a short space of time, attributed to the increasing interest in arctophily, and influenced perhaps by popular antique-appraisal shows on television. Sales are now held several times a year and collectors can subscribe to their catalogues, which are useful guides for new collectors. Attending previews and sales also provide good lessons.

Antique teddy bears can also be purchased from specialist dealers, many of whom have emerged since the early 1980s. In the United Kingdom, these include Pam Hebbs in London and Ian

Exclusively bears
In 1984, Joan Bland opened the first exclusive teddy-bear shop in the United Kingdom, in Windsor, Berkshire (above).

Archie
Designed by bear artist, Brian Beacock, Archie (above) is made exclusively for Asquiths Teddy Bear Shop.

The Calico Teddy
Donna Harrison and Dottie Ayers make exclusive bears for their shop (label, above).

Pout in Oxfordshire. In the United States, Barbara and Bob Lauver in Annville, Pennsylvania; Barbara Baldwin of Sparks, Maryland; and New York's The Rare Bear shop all sell antique teddy bears.

SHOWS AND CONVENTIONS
Some dealers, particularly in the US, organize conventions where a variety of teddy bears, from antique bears to the work of bear artists, can be purchased. Dealers Dottie Ayers and Donna Harrison organize an annual show in Baltimore, Maryland, and Linda Mullins arranges shows in San Diego, California. Numerous teddy-bear shows are now held throughout the United States, the dates of which are advertised in specialist magazines. Collectors can buy special limited-edition bears unique to a particular convention – for example, those produced by manufacturers and artists for the annual show at Disney World, Florida. The United Kingdom has followed suit, the main annual event being *Hugglets* British Teddy Bear Festival held in London on August Bank

Holiday Monday. In Australia there is Jacki Brooks' October Sydney show, which was first introduced in 1989; New Zealand held its first teddy-bear convention in Tauranga in 1992.

TEDDY-BEAR SHOPS
Shops exclusively selling teddy bears and related items have developed as demand grew. Bear in Mind Inc., of Concord, Massachusetts, was established in 1978 by Fran Lewis and a friend. They also publish a quarterly newsletter *The Arctophile* for collectors of new bears. In the United Kingdom, Asquiths was the first of this type of shop, a trend which has spread to nearly every major town.

In Australia, the first exclusive teddy-bear shop, *Teddy & Friends*, opened in Neutral Bay, New South Wales, in the early 1980s. Today, a number of stores called *The Teddy Bear Shop* can be found, in most major Australian cities. Such shops sell teddy bears aimed at the collector – limited editions and replicas, and sometimes bear artists' bears, as well as designs particular to that shop. Exclusive teddy-bear shops are now to be found worldwide, in Canada, New Zealand, South Africa, Northern Ireland, Jersey, and Hawaii. In the United States, collector bears are even sold on television shopping channels. Remember, though, that teddy bears do not have to be bought new: jumble sales, charity and junk shops, or car boot sales are sources to consider, and, if you are lucky, they can turn up a few interesting finds.

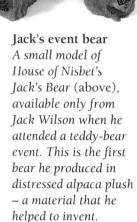

Jack's event bear
A small model of House of Nisbet's Jack's Bear (above), available only from Jack Wilson when he attended a teddy-bear event. This is the first bear he produced in distressed alpaca plush – a material that he helped to invent.

Limited editions
The three teddy bears (below) were all made as limited editions, exclusively for certain shops. Steiff made "Klein Archie" (left) and Merrythought created a special bear (right) for the 25th anniversary of Vermont's Enchanted Doll House. Sapphire (centre) was produced for the US store The Bear Tree by Canterbury Bears Ltd.

BOOKS FOR COLLECTORS
As a serious arctophile, it is important to build up a comprehensive library of books on teddy bears. The seminal works by US collectors Patricia Schoonmaker (*The Collector's History of the Teddy Bear*), Linda Mullins (*Teddy Bears: Past and Present; Volumes 1 and 2*), and Margaret Fox Mandel's series of identification guides are invaluable. Although many of the early works, for example by the Bialoskys, Ted Menten, Carol-Lynn Rössel Waugh, and the Volpps – are American, do not forget the sterling work of British authors Phillipa and Peter Waring whose *In Praise of Teddy Bears* first published in 1980, was followed by a number of teddy-bear books, notably by Pam Hebbs, Sue Pearson – and my own titles, including *The Ultimate Teddy Bear Book*.

In Australia, Romy Roeder and Jacki Brooks lead the field in teddy-bear publications. A rising number of arctophiles in other countries are also now writing books: for example Geneviève and Gérard Picot in France; Christina Björk in Sweden; and Erika Casparek-Türkkan in Germany.

Old toy-trade journals are useful sources of information about the history of teddy-bear manufacture; in England, *The Toy Trader* and *Games and Toys* can be viewed at the British Library's Colindale branch in north London. In the United States, the equivalent journal is *Playthings*, first introduced in 1903. Old manufacturers' catalogues are useful for identification purposes, but only a few companies – notably Merrythought and Steiff – maintain archives.

Gyles' Bear
The Nisbet bear (above) is named after Gyles Brandreth – arctophile, founder of the Teddy Bear Museum, in Stratford-upon-Avon, British Member of Parliament, TV personality, and a man renowned for his personally designed sweaters.

Helen Sieverling
A California-based collector (right) and feature writer for the magazine Teddy Bear and Friends, *Helen Sieverling holds an early Steiff and Gebrüder Hermann's limited-edition bear, produced to commemorate her work for US publishers Hobby House Press.*

Edward in Transit
This pure mohair-plush bear (above) by Big Softies (see p.143) comes in a cardboard box with "air" holes.

All-in-one ears
Some early Bings have ears cut all-in-one with the head (below) – useful to know when identifying unmarked antique bears.

IDENTIFICATION KNOW-HOW
You cannot expect to find out everything by reading books, however. Try to do as much background research as possible by going to auctions and conventions, by talking to experts, and by actually handling old bears. Learn to tell the difference between mohair and artificial-silk plush, and between kapok and wood-wool stuffing (the latter is heavier and "crackles" under your fingers). Get to recognize the tell-tale signs that indicate a bear's age or origins – examine the body shape, including the length of the limbs, the muzzle, and the presence or otherwise of a hump; identify the materials used for fur, eyes, pads, and stuffing. Familiarize yourself with the particular characteristics of certain manufacturers – for example, the stitching employed on early Bing noses – and learn to spot replacement eyes. You must also be

ID parade
Notice the subtle difference between an early Steiff (above left) and a Schuco (above right) miniature. The latter has a thinner, straighter body and limbs, a more pointed muzzle, and smaller feet.

aware that there are now fake antique bears on the market, sometimes with the addition of fraudulent trademarks.

TEDDY-BEAR MUSEUMS

Museums are another source of bear facts. Teddy bears can usually be found in the various museums of childhood and toy museums around the world. However, the first museum devoted entirely to teddy bears was opened in Berlin in 1986, to hold Florentine Wagner's collection of around 2,000 bears. This was followed by Judy Sparrow's Bear Museum at Petersfield, Hampshire, England. Other museums soon opened in the UK: Gyles Brandreth's collection at Stratford-upon-Avon (1988); the Cotswold Teddy Bear

Californian collector
Mrs. Sydney Charles (above) holds her childhood Knicker-bocker, "Frederic Pooh Robinson III" and an early American bear.

Florida museum
George B. Black Jr., son of founder Frannie Hayes, is director of the Teddy Bear Muse-um of Naples, Florida (above). Purpose-built, it is surrounded by specially commis-sioned bear sculptures and attractive pine woodland.

Museum at Broadway (1991); and Teddy Melrose in Scotland (1992). Dealer Ian Pout displays his collection of bears in a separate room off his shop Teddy Bears of Witney in Oxfordshire. The first teddy bear museum in the United States opened in December 1990, in Naples, Florida, based on Frannie Hayes' collection of around 1,800 bears. The curator is also building up an archive of information on bear manufacturers and artists. Doris and

Terry Michaud's museum collection of around 200 old bears can be viewed as part of their shop at Chesaning, Michigan; opening times vary, so make enquiries before a visit.

LIMITED EDITIONS

During the 1980s, a new form of collectable, the limited edition, was intro-duced by manufacturers and bear artists to meet the demand for special bears. Numbers to choose from are increasing constantly as manufacturers produce replicas of past models. On these bears, the limited-edition number is usually printed on a label sewn into the bear, sometimes with a printed, director's signature, and there is usually an authentication certificate. Smaller companies and bear artists generally hand-write their edition number, perhaps on a foot-pad or on a sewn-in label. Collectors can also get their bears signed at conventions or shops, further increasing the bear's value. Limited editions and replicas are fast becoming a high investment market, with retired VIBs *(see pp.146–47)*, Raikes Bears *(see p.171)*, and Steiff replicas *(see pp.152–53)* being sold as arctophiles continually strive to upgrade their collection. Collecting limited-edition bears is not necessarily a cheaper hobby than collecting antique teddy bears.

"Happy" inspirations
Steiff introduced a limited edition replica (top) of the record-breaking "Happy" in 1990, followed by a smaller size the next year. In addition, House of Nisbet pro-duced Happy Inspired (above), part of their Way We Were series.

Reproducing "Happy"
Jorg Jünginger (below), Steiff's chief designer, archivist, and grand-nephew of Margarete Steiff, measuring "Happy" for the replica. No original patterns of "Happy" exist in Steiff's archives.

BEAR MEMORABILIA

Few arctophiles can resist the temptation to include teddy-related items in their collection. Indeed, this off-shoot of the hobby can become a consuming passion in itself. Various useful books, for example Dee Hockenberry's reference and price guide *Bear Memorabilia*, have been written about this aspect of teddy-bear collecting.

Advertisements in the US trade journal *Playthings*, and in women's magazines from around 1907, show that the love of teddies is not a modern phenomenon; during the earlier craze, children's coats were made of mohair plush with brass buttons embossed with teddy bears; muffs, purses, and bags in the shape of teddies were also popular, as were infants' robes, crib covers, and pillow tops, all decorated with teddy-bear designs.

All kinds of teddy-bear containers can be found. In the catalogue section, I have already illustrated teddy-bear hot-water bottles (*p.23*), perfume and compact cases (*pp.40–41*), and nightdress-case bears (*p.91*) in traditional plush.

Sweet containers, dating from *c.1910* were also made, one example consisting of a traditional teddy bear with a lift-off head revealing a card tube inside the neck. Other container bears include American-made, cast-iron money boxes, lithographed biscuit tins, and vinyl toothbrush holders.

SILVERWARE

Before World War I, a number of sterling silver teddy teething rings and rattles were made; the latter often had mother-of-pearl handles, and the silver, cast teddies had small bells attached to their feet or sides. These originated mainly from England, and were notably the work of Birmingham silversmiths, renowned for their production of small silver objects. The serious collector should have access to a book of hallmarks to help establish exact dates and provenances.

Other small silver items made during this period include boot-button hooks, charms, hat-pins, thimbles, pin-cushions, menu-holders, napkin-rings, egg-cups, letter-openers, and sand-shakers. Silver spoons, with the handles, and sometimes the bowls, decorated with embossed teddy bears, or realistic bears engaged in various activities (*see p.200*) are particularly popular among collectors. Examples also exist on which whole cast bears form the ends of the handles. Many have English hallmarks though several, originally designed as souvenirs, hail from the US, Switzerland, or Russia, some dating from the nineteenth century.

Brass, bronze, or pewter writing accessories, such as inkwells, pen-wipers, letter-openers, and paper weights, were also produced in the shape of, or decorated with teddy bears, and are believed usually to be of German origin.

CARVED, WOODEN ARTEFACTS

Various carved, wooden bear items – from large, bulky pieces of furniture, such as hat-stands and seats, to more delicate smoking and writing accessories, bottle-stoppers, brush-holders, and nut-crackers – are also highly collectable. Dating from the late nineteenth century to about 1914, they are often referred to as "Black Forest", since that area of Germany is traditionally renowned for its carved wooden objects. However, many also originate from either Switzerland or Russia. Reproduction bear furniture was also made by such firms as Bartholomew & Company during the 1980s.

TEA SETS AND CHINAWARE

China nurseryware and children's tea sets printed with teddy-bear images are much prized by arctophiles

Mohair-plush coat
Following the 1907 teddy craze, children's coats were produced in mohair plush, and fastened with brass buttons embossed with bears. The coat (above) is a fine example of cinnamon mohair plush.

1920s sweet box
The bear-shaped lid of moulded card (above), covered in golden velveteen, has black bead eyes glued on.

Studio portrait
Photographs of children with their teddy bears, such as the "Little Lord Fauntleroy" example (above) from c.1905, are highly collectable, and are charming when framed.

Teething-ring rattle
This hollow, silver-plated, teddy-bear rattle with a bone teething-ring attached (below), was made in England c.1910.

Badges and buttons
Some arctophiles collect any bear-related items, such as the Roosevelt badges, advertising lapel pin, and brass, child's coat buttons (above).

– especially those with a teddy bears' picnic theme. The Three Bears motif was popular even before the teddy was invented and can be found on pre-1903 babies' plates. Many items, sadly, are unmarked, but some have been found to come from Stoke-on-Trent, the home of English pottery, while others were made in Germany or Japan. Other popular ceramic items include bisque (unglazed porcelain) bears or figurines of children holding teddy bears, as well as jugs, honeypots, salt and pepper sets, and toothpick holders made to resemble teddy bears.

TEDDY ROOSEVELT COLLECTION

Some arctophiles collect items relating to Teddy Roosevelt: books written by the statesman or about him; campaign items *(see p.200)*; commemorative pins, medals *(left)*, china and moulded glass plates. Various versions of "Teddy and the Bear" – small, cheaply made, china toothpick-holders showing a bear and the President crouched down beside a tree-stump – are now highly collectable. A 53-piece set of carved, wooden figures, including the President, entitled "Teddy's Adventures in Africa" by the US doll manufacturers Schoenhut is much sought-after. Dating from 1909, it is an expensive set, especially if complete. Some arctophiles also collect Clifford K. Berryman cartoons, either in newspapers or originals, although the latter are expensive. Roosevelt devotees can visit Harvard College Library, where some memorabilia is housed, or his birthplace in New York City, which is now a museum.

TEDDY STORYBOOKS

Arctophiles often start collecting teddy-bear storybooks, of which there are thousands. Some of the early examples, such as Frederick L. Cavally's *Mother Goose's Teddy Bear*, published by the Bobbs Merrill Company of Indianapolis in 1907, are rare. You could specialize, for example, in versions of *The Three Bears* or famous bear character books such as Pooh, Rupert dressed in checked trousers and scarf, and Paddington from "deepest, darkest Peru". First-edition Pooh books (published by E.P. Dutton in the United States and by Methuen in the United Kingdom) are highly collectable. For those with healthy bank balances, original Shepard drawings occasionally turn up at auction. Other printed Pooh ephemera includes early 1930s board-games, produced by Parker Bros. in the US, or the English Teddy Toy Company.

Rupert annuals illustrated by Alfred Bestall, first published in 1936, are fiercely collected; other Rupert memorabilia includes the rare 1920s Dutch *Bruintje Beer* (Brown Bear) postcard series. Paddington items are numerous.

It may also be fun to include in a collection books and other printed ephemera produced in a variety of foreign languages. After 1906, the Roosevelt Bears, based on stories by Seymour Eaton appeared printed on a variety of items, including postcard sets, china plates and jugs, and toys.

Handkerchief sachet
Well-known for her cloth dolls and mascots, Norah Wellings designed this bear sachet (above) in the 1930s at her factory in Wellington, Shropshire, England.

Sporting bear
The motif (below) was very popular from c.1910 to the 1930s, and can be found on many pieces of china, of varying quality, originating from England, Czechoslovakia, Germany, and Japan.

Teddy postcard
Teddies often feature on stationery (above).

Silverware
The early 20th-century silver mug and spoon (above) *are embossed with an attractive teddy-bear design.*

POSTCARDS AND OTHER EPHEMERA

Collecting teddy-bear postcards is a popular branch of arcto-phily, which has many themes. You might choose to concentrate on cards celebrating Christmas and Easter; souvenirs; photo-graphs; or humorous cards, such as the renowned "Mary and her Little Bear Behind" series.

Paper teddy-bear "dolls" date back to around 1907, and are still

Steiff tableau
Collectors prize early Steiff postcards (above), *always with the "Knopf im Ohr" trademark.*

made today, along with reproductions of some early examples. Paper scraps (printed, embossed, shaped pictures that were collected, particularly during the Victorian and Edwardian periods, in scrap albums) have been produced over the years, featuring bears or teddies, and are now sought-after by arctophiles. Stamps and photographs are another interesting area for collection, as is teddy-bear ephemera such as booklets, magazine or newspaper cuttings, metal lapel pins, jars, boxes advertising all kinds of products such as Teddy Bear Bread and Bear Brand Hosiery; or the various consumer offers, such as the 1926 printed, cloth, cut-out "Three Bears" series made for Kelloggs.

Warming plate
A child's c.1920 china warming-plate with metal base (above).

Given that 400 songs were registered between 1907 and 1911 with titles including the words "teddy" or "teddy bear", there are plenty of music scores to collect – many with attractive covers. There are also recorded songs, such as *The Teddy Bear's Picnic*.

MODERN TRENDS

Do not feel you have to specialize in antique bear memorabilia. Plenty of contemporary teddy-bear items are available, from clothing and jewellery, to paintings and ornaments. A growing number of illustrators around the world are producing paintings or drawings of teddy bears, either in book form, or for adorning the walls. Prue Theobalds and Jane Hissey in the United Kingdom, and Rosalie Upton in Australia are three such contemporary artists.

Figurines are increasingly popular: "The Cherished Teddies Collection" by Hamilton Gifts Ltd. of California (limited editions based on illustrations by artist Priscilla Hillman), or Peter and Frances Fagan's "Colour Box Miniature Teddy Bears", introduced in 1988, and based on real teddies in their collection in Lauder, Berwickshire, Scotland. The latter now boasts a thriving Collectors' Club.

Few areas are untouched by teddy-bear mania: there are teddy car alarms, and teddy telephones; and even a computer which, with a few accessories, can be turned into a teddy-bear shape.

TEDDY MAGAZINES

Arctophily is a sociable hobby; collectors worldwide are linked by a variety of magazines and clubs. "Good Bears of the World" (*see p.191*) issues a quarterly jour-nal, *Bear Tracks*, from its base in Ohio, with news updates on "dens" around the world, and forthcoming con-ventions, as well as articles and letters.

In the United States, magazines such as *Teddy Bear and Friends*, *The Teddy Trib-une*, and *The Teddy Bear Review*, which

Vote-catcher
Worn on the lapel by Roosevelt supporters during the 1904 Presidential election campaign, this 7.5cm (3in) bear with paper paws and sealing-wax nose (above) *is now much sought-after.*

Billy the Buccaneer
The limited-edition bear (above) *was made especially for the Robert Raikes Collectors' Club convention.*

were introduced during the 1980s, are essential reading for dedicated arctophiles. In the United Kingdom, Glenn and Irene Jackman, who originally produced teddy-bear kits as well as a bear-making manual under the name *Hugglets*, went on to publish the *UK Teddy Bear Guide* in 1988, a booklet listing essential contacts, including bear artists, manufacturers, material suppliers, shops, and museums. In 1990 they published *The Teddy Bear Magazine*. In the same year, another British magazine, *The Teddy Bear Times*, was launched; this is also distributed in Canada and the United States.

For Antipodean readers, the *Australian Doll Digest* was first published in 1985 by Jacki Brooks. This incorporated a section called "Bear Facts", which went on to become a separate magazine, *Bear Facts Review*, in 1991. In the Netherlands, where arctophily is a growing passion, the magazine *Beer Bericht* (Bear News) was launched in Amsterdam.

CLUB NETWORK

The number of clubs is growing throughout the world, not only of the Good Bears of the World variety, but also the type run by specialist teddy-bear shops, in order to inform arctophiles of what products are currently available.

Manufacturers, such as Steiff and Canterbury Bears, have their own clubs. In the United States, Robert Raikes (*see p.171*) runs a collectors' club from his home in Mount Shasta, California; he organizes an annual convention where he signs collectors' bears.

There are also clubs organized by collectors who wish to meet regularly and exchange news and ideas, although most also engage in philanthropic activities. In the United States, many have been inspired by the work of the Californian-based B.E.A.R. (Bear Enthusiasts' All 'Round Collectors Club Inc.), founded in 1983.

In the United Kingdom, *Hugglets* officially launched the British Teddy Bear Association in 1991, issuing their regular newsletter *Bearings* to keep members informed of new bears and shops, as well as linking clubs and individual collectors.

Clubs are forming in other parts of Europe, including the *Berenfanclub* in the Netherlands and *Club Francais de L'Ours Ancien*, and Teddy's Patch: *Le Club des Amis de l'Ours*, in France.

Collectors and organized groups of bear lovers also exist in Canada, Australia, New Zealand, and South Africa, and there is now an International League of Teddy Bear Clubs that attempts to unite all the clubs. It looks as if the hobby of arctophily is definitely here to stay.

Bear press
Teddy-bear collectors' magazines are now published in Europe, the US, and Australia, including: (below, left) Beer Bericht (Bear News) launched in Amsterdam in 1991, and (below, right) Hugglets Teddy Bear Magazine launched in Brighton, UK in 1990.

Convention bear
The bear (above) was created as a limited edition of one by Doris and Terry Michaud, for auction at the 1983 Teddy Tribune convention.

Club/magazine bears
Jamie (below, left) was made in 1988 by Irene Jackman of Hugglets, a bear-making business turned publisher. The bear (below, centre) was issued in the UK by Teddy Bear Times. The second Good Bears of the World bear (below, right) was made by Dakin.

1930s J.K. Farnell collectable
The worn teddy (*right*), with make-shift trouser-button eyes, could be more suitably restored using glass eyes from the same period.

1930s Victim of childhood
The wood-wool stuffing in the limbs of this bald and blind old bear (*right*) has turned to powder and settled in the paws and feet, leaving the tops of the arms and legs empty.

Replacement plush
Look for plush from old soft toys or clothing to patch a teddy or to make replacement parts.

Traditional joints
Use new card discs, washers, and pins to replace old joints.

Split seams
Repair split seams with strong cotton thread, in an appropriate colour.

1930s Swiss musical boxes
These typical Swiss musical boxes no longer work, but it is possible to buy modern, Japanese replacements.

Threadbare bear
This ailing 1930s bear needs a complete over-haul, including a surface wash, fumigation, extra stuffing and a new ear.

Wash-day disaster
Card disc-joints will not survive submersion in water.

1950s Mohair bear
Attractive outfits protect worn areas or disguise imperfections; detached pads and lost stuffing should be replaced.

Early Steiff bear
Despite fur loss, pad damage, and potential loss of stuffing, this bear still has its original, boot-button eyes.

Metal joint pins
Cotter pins and nails, used to secure disc joints, can suffer from rust or metal fatigue.

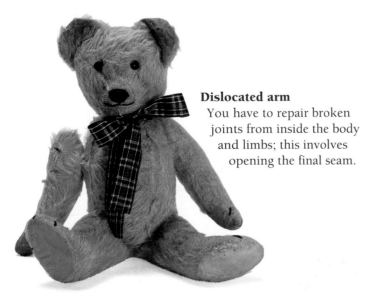

Dislocated arm
You have to repair broken joints from inside the body and limbs; this involves opening the final seam.

BEAR CARE AND REPAIR

TEDDY BEARS ARE MADE from a variety of fabrics and stuffings and, like all textiles, they are affected by a number of potentially destructive factors. Dust, light, humidity, and pests, as well as children and dogs, can cause damage to your precious teddy bear.

Many teddy-bear hygiene products are now on the market: moth-repellents, shampoo, dust covers, and even vanity sets. However, basic care procedures, as discussed on the following pages, are simple, using readily available household products.

The development of arctophily has led to the emergence of the professional teddy-bear restorer; teddy-bear "clinics" and "trauma centres" – once a minor offshoot of the dolls' hospital – are now a burgeoning, worldwide phenomenon. For major repairs, only entrust your valuable teddy bear to a recommended, reputable restorer who is skilled in sewing and understands the construction and history of the teddy bear. Avoid using glue in repair-work; the superficial effect may seem satisfactory, but glue is fundamentally detrimental.

With patience, a steady hand, and an understanding of teddy-bear construction, you can do many minor repairs on your teddy bear at home; the clearly illustrated, step-by-step instructions on the following pages will help you in the task.

Restoring Traditional-style Bears

DISMANTLING AND REASSEMBLY; REPAIR AND RENOVATION

Traditional-style teddy bears are those most likely to need restoration and repair, and you must carry out such work carefully and sensitively if the original charm and character of the bear is to be preserved. This is especially true of valuable old bears, which may be best entrusted to a professional repairer. The step-by-step overhaul of an old teddy bear shown on the following pages illustrates how traditional-style bears are constructed, which will give you the confidence to dismantle a bear that needs repairing. Washing the fabric of an old bear by immersion in water is not generally recommended, but it is necessary to dismantle a traditionally made bear in the way shown if you want to repair or replace joints, or to add extra stuffing.

Bear to be restored
This 1930s Merrythought bear, with its button trademark still intact, is showing signs of advanced deterioration: the left ear is loose; the original eyes are lost; the body is sagging; and the original pads have been covered in inappropriate fabric.

head droops due to loss of stuffing around neck joint

unravelled threads on nose and mouth

mohair plush discoloured, stained, and badly worn

worn, circular area on chest indicates presence of squeaker

body sags due to disintegration and loss of stuffing

original pads covered by inappropriate fabric

DISMANTLE

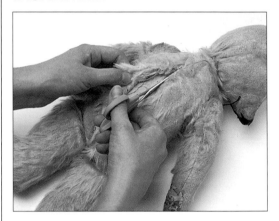

1 **Unpick main seam.** With sharp scissors, carefully cut a few stitches on the main seam (the final seam, usually at the back of the body, hand-sewn after the bear is stuffed); gently unpick the hand-sewn stitches.

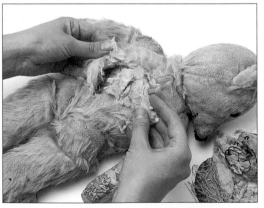

2 **Unstuff body.** Remove stuffing and reserve for re-use. Gently feel for the voice box, which may be in pieces; remove for later renovation. This bear is filled with kapok; wood-wool around the oval squeaker prevents kapok clogging the reed.

BUGBEARS!
Teddies suffer from the effects of light, dust, damp, and pests. Before repairing, look out for signs of insect life, such as larvae casings. If you find any bugs, seal the bear in a plastic bag with flea powder or moth balls, and leave overnight.

Professional bear-repairer's toolbox
Basic equipment – thread, needles, scissors, pliers – is easy to obtain. Joints, eyes, cotter pins, and washers, as well as plush and felt, are available from specialist handicraft shops.

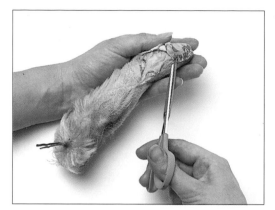

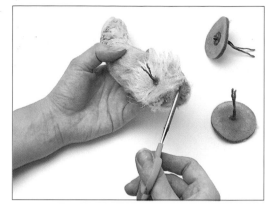

3 **Detach limbs.** Holding arm joint inside body casing, straighten curled prongs of cotter pin with pliers; slide disc over pin; remove arm. Repeat for other limbs. The head has already been removed in this way.

4 **Unpick replacement pads.** With sharp scissors, carefully unpick stitches attaching replacement fabric, to reveal original pads beneath. Take care not to destroy any remnants of the original manufacturer's label.

5 **Remove limb joints.** Unpick final, hand-sewn seam around the top of the limb. Pull back opening to remove card disc-joint and straightened cotter pin. Repeat process for remaining limbs.

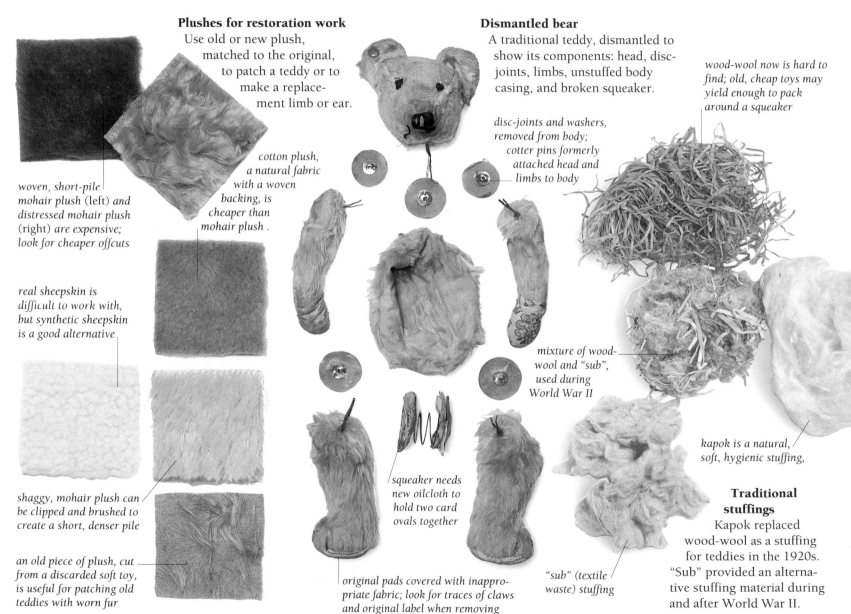

Plushes for restoration work
Use old or new plush, matched to the original, to patch a teddy or to make a replacement limb or ear.

Dismantled bear
A traditional teddy, dismantled to show its components: head, disc-joints, limbs, unstuffed body casing, and broken squeaker.

wood-wool now is hard to find; old, cheap toys may yield enough to pack around a squeaker

disc-joints and washers, removed from body; cotter pins formerly attached head and limbs to body

cotton plush, a natural fabric with a woven backing, is cheaper than mohair plush .

woven, short-pile mohair plush (left) and distressed mohair plush (right) are expensive; look for cheaper offcuts

real sheepskin is difficult to work with, but synthetic sheepskin is a good alternative

mixture of wood-wool and "sub", used during World War II

shaggy, mohair plush can be clipped and brushed to create a short, denser pile

an old piece of plush, cut from a discarded soft toy, is useful for patching old teddies with worn fur

squeaker needs new oilcloth to hold two card ovals together

original pads covered with inappropriate fabric; look for traces of claws and original label when removing

"sub" (textile waste) stuffing

kapok is a natural, soft, hygienic stuffing,

Traditional stuffings
Kapok replaced wood-wool as a stuffing for teddies in the 1920s. "Sub" provided an alternative stuffing material during and after World War II.

WASH AND DRY

You should never immerse old, jointed teddies in water: metal parts, such as cotter pins and washers, will rust, and mould will develop if you do not dry the bear properly. Some materials, including kapok and artificial silk, react badly to water, causing staining. I have removed the joints and stuffing from this bear, leaving only the mohair-plush casings to be washed. Take care, as the delicate fibres could disintegrate further during washing.

white, cotton towel is absorbent and avoids colour bleeding

use hair dryer, on coolest temperature and lowest speed, held 30cm (12in) away from fabric, to hasten drying process

when dry, fluff up pile with nylon comb

soft-bristled brush

use soft toothbrush on stubborn stains

a washing-up bowl is ideal for washing teddy-bear fabric

dissolved in water, baby shampoo makes a gentle lather for washing delicate old fabrics

Wash mohair plush
Squeeze gently in a solution of mild shampoo and warm water; rinse well; fabric conditioner in last rinse removes odours and softens fabric.

Drying
Gently squeeze out excess water; towel-dry; leave in airing cupboard or blow dry.

MEND THE PAW-PADS

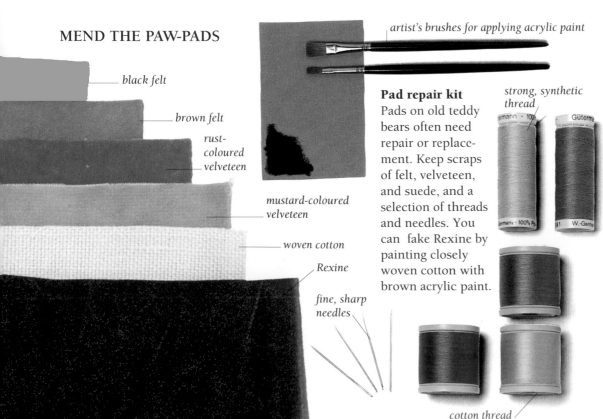

black felt

brown felt

rust-coloured velveteen

mustard-coloured velveteen

woven cotton

Rexine

fine, sharp needles

artist's brushes for applying acrylic paint

Pad repair kit
Pads on old teddy bears often need repair or replacement. Keep scraps of felt, velveteen, and suede, and a selection of threads and needles. You can fake Rexine by painting closely woven cotton with brown acrylic paint.

strong, synthetic thread

cotton thread

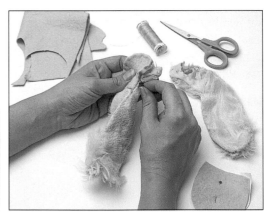

6 **Replace pads.** Match new material to original pads. Here, I used cream felt, but bears of a similar age may require velveteen or woven-cotton pads. Make a paper template, slightly larger than the pad, and cut new pads from the felt. Fold under excess felt, matching the pad size, and tack in place, over the original pads. With synthetic thread and fine needle, oversew pads into place with tiny stitches. Repeat for second paw and feet.

FIX THE HEAD

wood-wool stuffing for muzzle

kapok stuffing

wooden knitting needle useful for pushing stuffing firmly into position

7 **Restuff head.** Insert a little wood-wool into the muzzle and fill the rest of the head with kapok. Reuse original stuffing material if it is in good condition. Pack stuffing firmly, but do not overstuff.

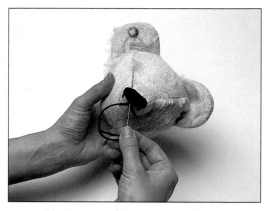

10 **Stitch nose and mouth.** Remove remnants of old features, noting stitch pattern. Restitch with black embroidery thread, following previous needle holes.

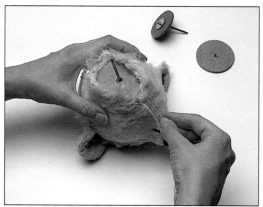

8 **Fit neck joint.** Place new disc, with washer and cotter pin (or reuse old ones if sound) inside neck opening, with pin pointing upwards. With needle and strong thread, tack around opening, near top edge.

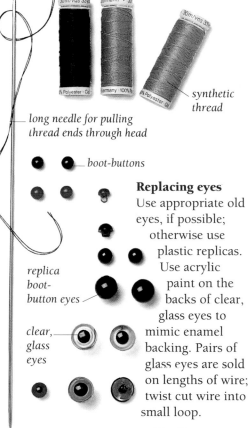

synthetic thread

long needle for pulling thread ends through head

boot-buttons

Replacing eyes
Use appropriate old eyes, if possible; otherwise use plastic replicas. Use acrylic paint on the backs of clear, glass eyes to mimic enamel backing. Pairs of glass eyes are sold on lengths of wire; twist cut wire into small loop.

replica boot-button eyes

clear, glass eyes

glass eyes with wire cut and twisted into loops

pairs of glass eyes attached by wire

glass eyes

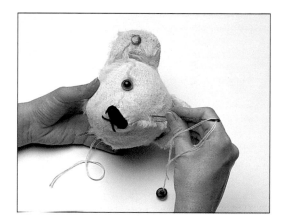

11 **Insert new eyes.** Select appropriate new eyes, in this case glass eyes on wire shanks. Fasten strong, doubled thread to wire shank; with long needle, position eye and bring thread out through back of head.

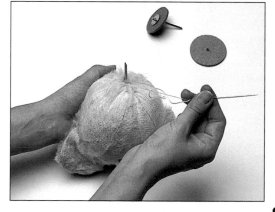

9 **Close neck opening.** Grasping head securely in palm of hand, pull tacking thread tightly so that fabric gathers tightly around cotter pin. Finish off, bringing needle out at back or side of head.

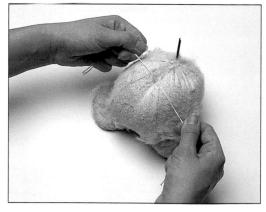

12 **Fasten off eyes.** Firmly pull loose threads from eyes outwards at back of head. Fasten off threads securely, tying together with several knots; cut off excess thread, or sew back into head.

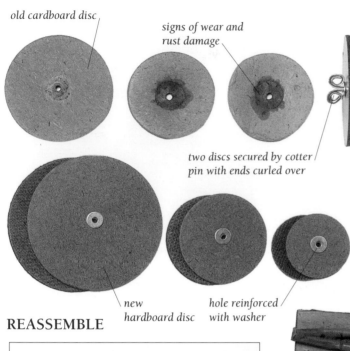

old cardboard disc

signs of wear and rust damage

two discs secured by cotter pin with ends curled over

cotter pin

pin curled in "crown" design

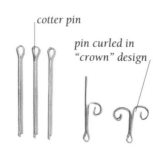

outer reed

pins hold fabric while glue sets

REASSEMBLE

new hardboard disc

hole reinforced with washer

Replacing disc joints

To repair disintegrated joints, you need new card or hardboard discs of appropriate sizes, metal washers, and cotter pins. To secure a disc in place, curl the ends of the cotter pin over with pliers, in a design known as the "crown".

Renovated card squeaker

The deteriorated oilcloth on the bellows was replaced with a new strip of fabric, glued in place between the two card ovals, and secured with pins until the glue had set.

lead-weighted, wooden tilt-growlers

card squeakers

13 **Check for split seams.** Seams may split or fray during washing of delicate, old fabric. Check when dry and repair if necessary with matching thread.

15 **Fix head to body.** Insert pin from head joint through top of body casing, with right sides together. Slide second disc and washer over pin; curl ends of pin over.

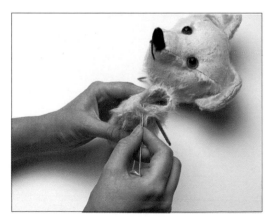

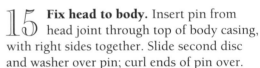

bisque-weighted tilt-growlers

Voice boxes

Early tilt-growlers (*top*) disintegrate with age, often losing their original tubular containers. Card squeakers (*centre*) fall apart: the spring comes adrift, the outer reeds are damaged, or the bellows develops a leak. Bisque-weighted tilt-growlers (*bottom*) may no longer slide inside their containers.

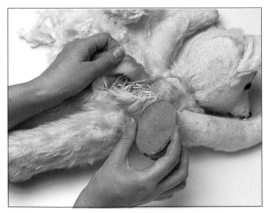

14 **Finish off limb.** After stuffing with kapok, place one disc inside top of limb; insert pin through disc and original hole in fabric. Hand-sew final seam, using ladder stitch (*opposite*). Repeat for each limb.

16 **Replace squeaker.** Insert squeaker, with reed at front, in centre front of body; surround with wood-wool. Fill rest of cavity with kapok; reuse old material if intact. Avoid over- or under-stuffing.

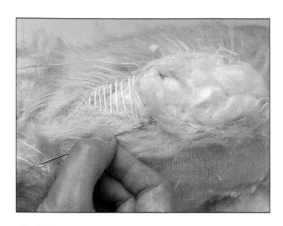

17 **Ladder-stitch final seam.** Use ladder-stitch to close final seams on limbs and body; pull thread tight to finish off.

18 **Stitch claws.** With thread matched to originals, stitch claws, following original or classic design – in this case, the Merrythought, webbed-claw design.

Claw materials
Embroidery silk is ideal for replacing missing claws. Match colour of originals or, if none remains, use appropriate colour.

embroidery silks

Renovated bear
Clean, upright, and with new facial features and paws, this bear has been restored to something of his former glory. The restorer should, of course, renovate with caution and sensitivity, to avoid destroying a much-loved teddy's unique charm.

head firmly stuffed

webbed claw design on paws

three black claws on each foot

new, cream felt pads

original plush very worn, revealing woven backing

SPLIT EAR TECHNIQUE

1 **Remove ear.** One ear is often missing from teddies with ears sewn across the head, and not caught into seams. Carefully remove the remaining ear. Unpick the seam and gently ease the two flat ear pieces apart.

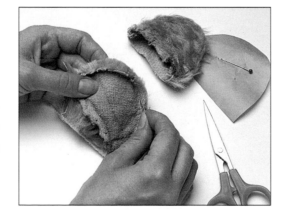

2 **Make new ear.** Using original ear as a template, cut two new ear pieces from matching plush. With right sides facing, place one old ear piece against a new piece; back-stitch together. Repeat for other ear.

3 **Sew ears onto head.** Turn the two new ears right sides out; carefully pin into position, centring across facial seams, with original plush to the front. Oversew in place, with tiny stitches, along the front and back.

Caring for Modern Bears

WASHING AND GROOMING UNJOINTED, SYNTHETIC BEARS

The introduction, in 1955, of the unjointed, machine-washable teddy bear revolutionized the soft-toy industry. Made from synthetic fur and filling, and with safe, plastic eyes, the new teddy could be washed and dried, and quickly re-united with its young owner. However, not all synthetic bears are fully immers-able: foam-rubber-filled bears are happy to be bathed, but some other man-made materials react badly to water. Pay close attention to washing instructions on seam labels, particularly when these indicate "surface washable only". On these pages we illustrate the components of a modern teddy bear, and show you how to keep it in optimum condition, including the recommendation that hand-washing and natural drying methods will prolong teddy's life.

Synthetic bear
This nylon-plush bear, stuffed with granulated foam rubber, shows signs of wear: the pile is grubby, matted, and worn, revealing the knitted backing. Use synth-etic thread to repair seams.

worn plush revealing knitted backing, indicates a cheaper quality bear

washer locks in plastic nose

Moulded, plastic noses
Modern, moulded plastic noses come in realistic and stylized designs; a metal washer pushed over the shank holds the nose in position.

integral shank

plastic joint

Plastic joints
Available in different sizes, each joint consists of a disc with integral shank, a second disc, and a smaller washer.

two plastic discs and washer

strong, polyester thread

modern, plastic eye

teeth of metal washer locks eye in place

 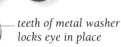

safe, replica, boot-button eye

SAFE EYES

Manufacturers introduced safe eyes during the 1950s and they quickly became a requirement under toy-safety laws. Teddy bears today undergo rigorous testing to ensure that eyes are irremovable. If you plan to give your old teddy to a child as a toy, replace the original sewn-in eyes with safe, lock-in replacements.

Modern, plastic eyes
Available in a variety of sizes and colours, the eyes are locked securely in place with a washer.

metal washer

Inserting a safe, lock-in, plastic eye
Insert shank through fabric; push toothed washer over shank to secure eye in place. To insert new eye in teddy, first remove stuffing from head to allow access to back of fabric.

WASH A SYNTHETIC TEDDY

1 Wash bear. Immerse the bear in a bowl of warm water with a little baby shampoo added, and gently scrub the stained areas with a stiff, natural-bristled brush.

2 Dry outside. Place the bear in a muslin bag pegged to the clothesline. Do not hang the bear on the line by its ear.

3 Groom bear. When completely dry, brush bear firmly with a teasel brush; the fine, wire "bristles" will separate and fluff-up the matted fibres of the plush.

Pad fabrics

After World War II, synthetic materials, such as Ultrasuede and Dralon, replaced cotton and velveteen as the most commonly used pad fabrics. Unjointed, synthetic teddy bears often have pads made from contrasting plush.

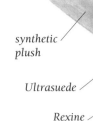

synthetic plush

Ultrasuede

Rexine

woven cotton fabric

velveteen

felt

Modern voice boxes

Modern tilt growlers and squeakers are usually made of plastic. Most modern musical boxes are made in Japan.

flat, plastic squeaker

tilt growler in plastic container

musical box

tilt growler

plastic, concertina squeakers

synthetic plush fabric

Synthetic fabrics

Nylon (first commercially produced in 1938), and other synthetic materials such as Orlon, Dralon, Acrilan, and Courtelle, have all been woven into plush for teddy bears. Cheaper synthetic plushes have a knitted backing.

Dralon

synthetic plush on knitted backing

Post-World War II stuffing

Foam-rubber became popular because it was light and washable; waste from synthetic fabric mills was used in a similar way to "sub" (*see p.205*); polyester wadding is now widely used.

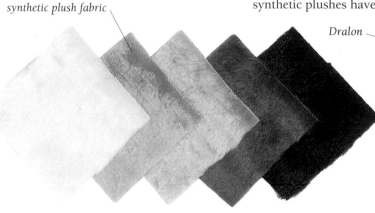

polyester wadding

foam-rubber and polystyrene pellet mix

granulated foam-rubber

wood-wool

low-grade synthetic waste

Preventive Care and Grooming

DEBUGGING, VACUUMING, SURFACE-CLEANING, AND PATCHING

The teddy-bear lover must consider the many hazards, including direct sunlight and dust, that can damage his collection. Teddy-bear fur attracts the larvae of the carpet beetle and the clothes moth, which feed on natural woollen fibres. New pinpricks in the felt pads can indicate that furniture beetle larvae are attacking the wood-wool stuffing. Even animal fleas will thrive in long pile.

Systematic checks, regular dusting, and prompt action are vital if such infestations are to be prevented. But cleaning must be done with caution: chemical dry-cleaning should never be considered, for example, and no traditional, jointed bear should ever be immersed in water. Only surface-washing is advisable for mohair, and must be followed by thorough drying. A bran bath is a useful method of drawing grease from bear fur.

1 Check for bugs. You must regularly check your bears, particularly old ones, for bugs. Systematically part the pile, looking for signs of infestation; pay particular attention to ear and joint crevices. If you find any bugs, treat with the appropriate insecticide.

Larva in plush
Papery casings indicate the presence of carpet beetle larvae. Immediately fumigate the bear and check entire collection.

carpet beetle larva

Fumigation
Place an infested teddy overnight in a sealed, plastic bag with moth-balls or flea-powder. Treat all newly acquired, old teddies likewise.

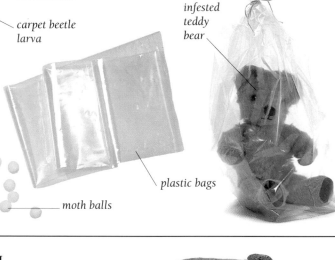

infested teddy bear

plastic bags

moth balls

2 Vacuum fur. Bears collect dust, which ultimately damages the fur as well as detracts from the appearance. Clean regularly with a vacuum-cleaner; if using a powerful, full-size cleaner, cover the end of the nozzle with fine gauze for a gentler suction.

A FAMILY HEIRLOOM
"Jessica" is a very special bear; her bald, sagging, well-patched body represents many childhood memories for the author – including the games of doctors and nurses during which "Jessica" was the willing patient, as the lovingly stitched "operation wound" testifies. "Jessica" is an example of a bear whose priceless charm would be destroyed by restoration. This is also true of bears like the Blitz survivor (p.192) with his scorched feet or the well-worn Aloyius (p.190), who would lose not only their unique appeal but also their value, if signs of their colourful pasts were eradicated.

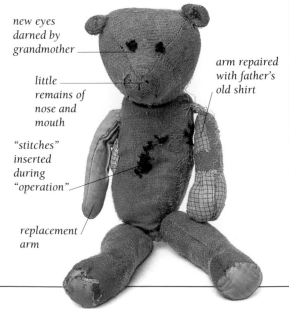

new eyes darned by grandmother

little remains of nose and mouth

"stitches" inserted during "operation"

replacement arm

arm repaired with father's old shirt

HOW TO PATCH

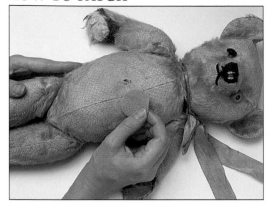

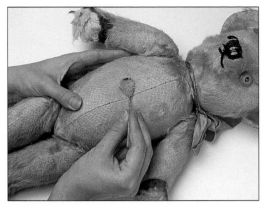

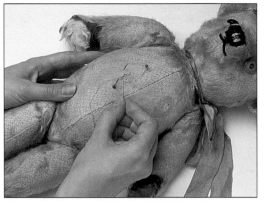

1 **Match fabric.** Choose plush to match colour and pile. For a bald bear, reverse plush, with woven backing uppermost. Cut the patch a little larger than the hole.

2 **Fit patch.** Fold the patch around a darning-needle, and push it into the hole. Flatten and manoeuvre gently into position, with the weave matching.

3 **Stitch patch in place.** Pin the patch securely in position. Oversew the edges of the hole to the new patch. Finish off and lose the end of the thread inside the body.

GIVE A BRAN BATH

1 **Rub in bran.** Fill a clean, plastic bag with bran (available from health-food or pet shops). Place the teddy bear in the bag and rub the bran liberally into the fur.

2 **Brush out.** When you have drenched the teddy with bran, brush it out with a stiff, natural-bristled brush. Use a damp cotton bud to wipe any dust from the eyes.

SURFACE WASH AND DRY

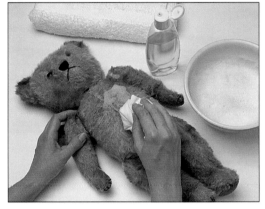

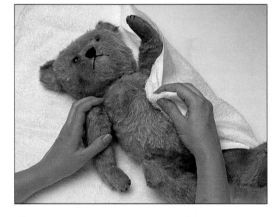

1 **Surface wash.** Fill a bowl with warm water and mild shampoo; whisk to create a lather. Dab lather onto the fur with a wad of cotton; wipe over the surface of the fur.

2 **Towel dry.** Rinse the surface with clean water; pat bear dry with a white towel. Leave to dry naturally, avoiding sunlight.

Blow-dry
If you are in a hurry, use a hair dryer, but be careful. Set it to the coolest temperature and the slowest speed, and hold it at least 30cm (12in) away from the bear.

3 **Groom.** When dry, use a metal comb or a natural-bristled brush to fluff up the pile. Brush downwards for a smooth effect, or upwards to give the plush more volume.

Display and Storage

SHOWING OFF AND PRESERVING YOUR COLLECTION

Teddy bears must be treated with care and respect if they are to survive, so do consider their security and well-being when planning a display. Fragile old teddies, in particular, will deteriorate rapidly if constantly handled and exposed to dust, direct sunlight, and insects. Glass display cases, such as nineteenth-century glass domes or – for large collections – wall cabinets with glass doors, are ideal for showing off and protecting your teddy bears. You will need to check them regularly for insects, though. Remember that dressing bears can help to protect them from the damaging effects of dust and sunlight.

Effects of sunlight

These old bears demonstrate the damage that is caused by excessive sunlight. The 1920s musical bear (right) was originally bright green, but only traces of the colour are now visible in joint crevices. The 1930s Bingie Guardsman (right, centre) is now a dirty grey except for a patch on his head, where the original, bright cinnamon colour has been protected by the bear's hat.

green mohair visible at edges of neck joint

original colour seen when hat is removed

faded patches on red felt jacket

Protection
An elderly, balding Steiff is protected by his "Little Lord Fauntleroy" suit, which also helps to hide any imperfections.

Bear display
A display of teddy bears and related memorabilia (above) arranged on shelves at the Volpps' home. An antique tricycle supports a large Steiff bear.

BOXED BEAR

When your collection has outgrown all available display space, you may need to pack and store some teddy bears. Plastic bags are not recommended, except for short periods, as moisture can build up inside, encouraging mould. Calico bags, clean brown paper tied with string, or cardboard boxes in which the teddy bear is first wrapped in white, acid-free, tissue paper are ideal (a shoe-box is perfect for a small bear). Add mothballs, anti-moth, drawer lining-paper, cedar-wood shavings, or cloves in order to help prevent insect damage. Store the teddy bear away from damp, dust, and extremes of temperature.

THE
TEDDY BEAR
DIRECTORY

THE INTRODUCTION to this Encyclopedia (*pp.8–13*) gives an overall survey of the history of the teddy bear; the teddy's development is examined more closely in The Catalogue (*pp.14–187*), and the practicalities of collecting are reviewed in the chapters on Arctophily: Bear Collecting (*pp.188–201*) and Bear Care and Repair (*pp.202–215*). Here, the Teddy Bear Directory consolidates essential reference information in the Teddy Bear Time Chart, Factory Histories, Useful Addresses, and Glossary, which arctophiles, both amateur and professional, will find invaluable.

The Time Chart plots the history of the teddy bear, setting it chronologically against the world events that so influenced its evolution; while the Factory Histories give concise accounts of each of the main teddy-bear manufacturers. An exhaustive list of Useful Addresses gathered from around the world, provides you with information that will help you develop this absorbing hobby: addresses of museums, specialist shops, clubs, and magazines, all devoted to the teddy bear. Delve into this Directory and you will discover the extent to which arctophily has developed and gained inter-national stature in the world of serious collecting.

Teddy Bear Time Chart

A CONCISE HISTORY OF THE TEDDY BEAR

Bears are known to have figured in western culture as far back as Neanderthal man's bear-worshipping rituals, and have also featured widely in stories and legends. In Greek mythology, Zeus's lover, Callisto, was transformed into a she-bear by jealous queen Hera, while another bear, "Mishka", has been part of Russian folklore since the twelfth century. "Bruin", a popular name for bears, was first used in Caxton's 1481 translation of *Reynard the Fox*. Bears have been hunted for their fur and for use in home remedies, as well as being captured and trained to dance or to take part in the "sport" of bear-baiting.

Children's playthings often reflect life, and so it was natural that bears should feature widely as the toy industry developed in the nineteenth century. They did so in the work of German toy-makers, and in the creations of the Russian co-operatives which, from the 1890s, produced small, carved, wooden bears in Bogorodskoye. The French firms Roullet et Décamps and Martin, based in Paris, made many ingenious mechanical tin and fur bears during this period. Bears at this time were usually depicted on all-fours or standing up on their back legs, unlike today's seated teddy.

NURSERY BEARS
Though wild bears no longer roamed the British Isles by the late nineteenth century, bears were known to British children, familiar with the performing bears that came to Britain from mainland Europe (an 1890s photograph shows a muzzled bear with its trainers in a London school playground). The original *Three Bears* story was first written down in 1831, and the soft-toy makers W.J. Terry and J.K. Farnell (later major teddy-bear manufacturers) were established by 1890 and 1897.

Bears have always played a key part in North American heritage and by the late nineteenth century, they were appearing in children's stories. The standard version of *The Three Bears*, featuring Goldilocks, was published in 1888. In the 1890s, Joel Chandler Harris's *Uncle Remus* books with the Br'er Bear character appeared. Patterns for soft toys, including bears, were also regularly seen in women's magazines.

SOFT-TOY INDUSTRIES
Until the outbreak of World War I in 1914, Germany was the toy-making capital of the world. Particular regions specialized in certains products; for example, tin toys were made in Nuremberg, and doll and wooden toy manufacture was centred around Sonneberg. By the late nineteenth century, several major toy manufacturers were established. Margarete Steiff *(see pp.38–39)* had added soft toys to her felt-clothing business by 1880 and bears became part of her range in 1892; these were later developed by her nephew Richard Steiff.

Reinhold Schulte opened a mohair-weaving factory in Duisberg in 1901 to supply soft-toy manufacturers with plush; mills in northern England provided the mohair for the plush.

PRESIDENTIAL INFLUENCE
Although many children's nurseries were already equipped with toys modelled on the wild bear, it was the 26th President of the United States, Theodore ("Teddy") Roosevelt (born 27 October 1858) who precipitated a movement in which bears became a model for the world's favourite toy, and one of the most endearing phenomena of the twentieth century.

WORLD WAR I

1902–03 | 1904–05 | 1906–07 | 1908–09 | 1910–14 | 1915–20

1902–03

1902
12 November: Theodore Roosevelt leaves for Smedes, Mississippi, for four-day hunt; he fails to bag a bear.

16 November: Clifford J. Berryman's cartoon in the *Washington Post* shows Roosevelt refusing to shoot a bear cub (the cartoon title "Drawing the Line" refers to Roosevelt's attempt to settle a boundary dispute between Louisiana and Mississippi, the main reason for his visit to the southern states).

Inspired by Clifford J. Berryman cartoon, Russian emigrés Morris and Rose Michtom make "Teddy's Bear" to sell in their Brooklyn stationery and novelty store.

1903
February: Steiff sends shipment of soft toys to Paul Steiff in New York, including *Bär 55 PB*; it is not successful.

March: *Bär 55PB* shown at Leipzig Toy Fair; Hermann Berg of New York wholesalers Geo. Borgfeldt & Co. orders 3,000.

July: Steiff registers jointed bear pattern. Richard Steiff continues to experiment with methods of jointing.

August: Henry Samuel Dean establishes Dean's Rag Book Co. in London.

Morris Michtom establishes Ideal Novelty & Toy Co., becoming first US teddy-bear manufacturer, with backing of wholesalers Butler Bros.

1903–08: Steiff factory expands three times in period known by the company as the "Bärenjahre".

1904–05

1904
February: last entry of *Bär 55 PB* on Steiff's price list.

March: Steiff registers new improved *Bär 35 PB*, with string jointing. Franz Steiff conceives "button in ear" trademark; blank buttons introduced.

November: Steiff introduces elephant button.

December: Steiff patents improved, double-wired, jointed design; "button in ear" trademark registered in US.

By end of year, Steiff introduces rod-jointed *Bär 28 PB* to range; total of 12,000 bears produced during year.

1905
February: Steiff registers *Bär 35 PAB*, first disc-jointed, now standard, teddy-bear design.

May: Steiff's "button in ear" trademark officially confirmed.

June: Steiff patents rod-jointed bear *Bär 28 PB*.

August: *Bär 35 PAB* first features in Steiff's price list as "Bärle", with elephant button.

1905–06: Seymour Eaton's Roosevelt Bears poems first copyrighted, appearing in US newspapers, and, from 1906, appear in series of books; soon followed by dressed bears made by Steiff and US manufacturers, Kahn & Mossbacher and D.W. Shoyer & Co.

1905–09: US President Theodore Roosevelt's second term of office coincides with height of teddy-bear craze.

1906–07

1906
May: US toy trade journal *Playthings* first uses term "Teddy's Bear".

July: Steiff becomes private limited company.

October: term "Teddy Bear" first used in *Playthings*.

November: Charles Sackman and Martha Borchardt file individual patents for teddy-bear designs in New York.

1906–07: many short-lived manufacturers set up in US, producing teddy bears; often using imported German mohair and growlers – eg. Aetna, Bruin, Hecla, Columbia, Miller, Harman. As competition grows, Steiff and other manufacturers create novelty bears.

1907
February: term "teddy bears" first used in Seymour Eaton's poem *The Roosevelt Bears Abroad*, published in *The Sunday Oregonian*, Portland.

Mr. Cinnamon Bear by Sara Tourney Lefferts published in US.

Steiff produces 975,000 bears – the company's still unbeaten record.

US composer, John W. Bratton writes *The Teddy Bear's Picnic*.

The Teddy Bears, first moving picture featuring teddy bears, made by US Thomas A. Edison Co.

First teddy comic strip, *Little Johnny and the Teddy Bears*, appears in *Judge* magazine.

1907–11: 400 songs registered with "teddy" or "teddy bear" in title.

1908–09

1908
US businessman asks Karl Hofmann company in Neustadt area of Germany to produce teddies for US market, launching Neustadt teddy-bear industry.

German exporters Eisenmann suggests to English firm J.K. Farnell that it makes its own teddy bears, launching British industry.

Tilt-growler first mentioned in Steiff's catalogues; glass eyes first used by Steiff for British market.

William Taft elected US President: various mascots created to rival teddy bear – eg. Billy Possum (Steiff and US manufacturers); Billiken (Horsmann in US).

Dean's Rag Book & Co. produces teddy bear as part of printed, cloth Knockabout Toys series, and teddy-bear rag book.

First lawsuits between Steiff and German companies such as Wilhelm Strunz and Gebrüder Bing over "button in ear" trademark.

1909
9 May: Margarete Steiff dies, aged 61.

Teddy Bright Eyes published, one of first British teddy-bear stories.

Steiff introduces golden mohair to previous range of light brown, dark brown, and white bears.

1909–12: Heinrich Schreyer works for Nuremberg firm, Gebrüder Bing.

1910–14

1910–13: Steiff appoints agents and opens warehouses in New York, Sydney, and in several European countries.

1912
Steiff introduces special black bear for British market with boot-button eyes over orange felt.

Heinrich Müller and Henrich Schreyer establish Schreyer & Co. in Nuremberg.

Steiff introduces red, white, and blue Dolly-Bär for US election.

1913
October: first Hermann bear produced by Artur, Adelheid, and Max Hermann in Neufang, near Sonneberg.

Steiff introduces Record Teddy on wheeled chassis, later copied by British manufacturers – eg. British United Toy Manufacturing Co.

1914–15: soft-toy industries established in Great Britain as German imports are banned.

East London Federation Toy Factory founded by Sylvia Pankhurst; Wm. H. Jones establishes soft-toy firm as unable to get work as agent for German doll manufacturers; Teddy Toy Company founded by B.C. Hope and Abe Simmonds; Harwin & Co. founded, assisted by former Steiff sales agent.

1914–18: World War I disrupts production in Germany as men called up for military service; factories used for war work – Steiff factory makes armaments and aeroplane parts; borders closed preventing export; Margarete Steiff Frères, Paris agents, closed.

1915–20

1915–16: Dean's and Chad Valley produce first jointed, mohair teddies.

British firms make patriotic bears: eg. Dean's The Bear of Russia, Germany's Crusher; Harwin's Ally Bear.

1919
Thiennot, one of first French manufacturers, established.

Josef Eisenmann dies, leaving Chiltern Toy Works to Leon Rees.

Bobby Bear appears in *Daily Herald*, first comic-strip bear in British newspaper.

1919–21: Steiff produces bears from reconstituted nettle plant because of shortage of plush.

1920
February: London's Teddy Toy Company patents "Softanlite" kapok stuffing; copied by other UK firms during early 1920s: Terry's "Ahsolite"; Chad Valley's "Aerolite" bears.

November: Mary Tourtel's Rupert Bear first introduced in UK newspaper *Daily Express*.

Chad Valley moves soft-toy production from Birmingham to Wellington, Shropshire.

Harry Stone and Leon Rees establish H.G. Stone, to produce Chiltern soft toys.

Thiennot wins bronze medal for teddy design at Lépine competition.

1920s–30s: ban on toy imports from Germany and imposition of import duty lead UK firms to supply UK and foreign markets: eg. Chad Valley, J.K. Farnell, H.G. Stone, Merrythought, and Dean's.

	WORLD WAR II	

1921–29

1921
J.K. Farnell registered as private limited company; Alpha Works built, and tradename "Alpha" used.

A.A. Milne's wife buys bear (possibly Alpha) from Harrods for son Christopher Robin's first birthday.

Steiff introduces glass eyes and kapok stuffing; Hugo Steiff introduces conveyor-belt system.

Schreyer & Co. registers trademark "Schuco" and patents Yes/No bears.

First Rupert Bear merchandise produced.

1923
First Chiltern Hugmee bears advertised.

1925–28: "Dual" plush mohair popular; novelties such as Gebrüder Süssenguth's open mouth/rolling-eyed Peter; Gross & Schild's talking Bruno; and Swiss squeeze-type musical bears introduced.

1926
October: Winnie the Pooh published by Methuen.

Teddies wearing pierrots' hats and ruffs (Steiff's Clown-bear; Chad Valley's Tubby Bear) become popular.

1929
Wall Street crash and economic depression leads to production of low-quality teddy bears such as US "stick" bears.

Artificial-silk-plush bears such as J.K. Farnell's Silkalite bear (March) and Chiltern's Silky Teddy (July) first advertised.

J.K. Farnell opens showrooms in New York and Paris.

1930–37

1930
Steiff launches unique and influential Teddy Baby and Dicky designs.

Merrythought Ltd. established in Iron-bridge, Shropshire.

Mary Plain by Gwynaed Rae published (character later produced as soft toy by J.K. Farnell).

Lyrics added to *The Teddy Bears' Picnic* by Jimmy Kennedy in UK.

1930–35: Winnie the Pooh toys and games made in UK by Chad Valley and Teddy Toy Co; in US by Parker Brothers and F.W. Woolnough.

1930s: novelty teddies become popular – eg. Schuco's miniatures; nightdress cases and other sachets by UK firms.

1933
Hitler comes to power; rise of National Socialist Party affects German toy industry: Ernst and Hugo Steiff removed from office because of Jewish sympathies. Adolf Kahn, a Jew, leaves Schuco for England.

1935
US patent application filed for nylon, invented by W.H. Carothers.

1937
British Lines Bros., then largest toy manufacturer in world, launches Pedigree Soft Toys.

Coronation of British monarch George VI, following Edward VIII's abdication, inspires production of patriotic red, white, and blue bears.

Chicago Zoo receives first giant panda in West, launching panda-bear industry.

1938–44

1938
Chad Valley awarded Royal Warrant, by appointment to HM The Queen Elizabeth (consort of George VI).

First commercial use of US invention, nylon.

1939
Outbreak of World War II forces many European soft-toy factories to close or turn to war work.

Late 1930s–50s: teddy bears in all-in-one clothes popular, saving on plush.

1940–45: raw materials in short supply, resulting in reduced output and economy measures, such as use of alternative fabrics; new designs with shorter limbs and muzzles; unjointed necks.

Magazines publish knitting patterns for bears, using unravelled wool.

Teddy-bear firms turn to essential war-work; eg. Dean's makes life-jackets; Chad Valley makes children's clothing; Merry-thought produces military uniform accessories. In Germany, Steiff makes munitions and Schuco telephone equipment.

Some factories, including Schuco and J.K. Farnell suffer air-raid damage.

1941
Polyester invented by J.R. Whinfield and J.T. Dickson in UK.

1944
Smokey the Bear becomes symbol of US Forest Fire Prevention Campaign.

1945–50

1945
World War II ends. Germany partitioned into four military zones.

1945–51: post-war rationing results in few toys being available.

Cottage industries in Germany, Austria, and UK make teddies from any available materials; sheepskin remains alternative to mohair. "Sub" (textile waste) provides alternative to kapok stuffing.

Nylon and rayon plush commonly used for teddies from post-war period.

1947–48: companies once based in Sonneberg now in Soviet-occupied zone of Germany. Fearing communist regime, many move to US zone, forming new companies. Additional "Made in US Zone" labels sewn on bears.

1948
Wendy Boston patents first screw-in safe eye.

1950–53: first commercial use of synthetic fibres, such as Terylene, Dacron, Orlon, Dralon, and Acrilan.

1950s: rise of Japan as industrial empire; influx of Japanese clockwork, and later battery-operated, bears forces demise of German companies that previously led mechanical tin-toy market.

1950s–60s: synthetic plush and stuffing (eg. Polyester) becomes popular for teddy bears.

1951–57

1951
Steiff introduces innovative Zotty design.

1952
Introduction of vinyl muzzles, particularly by US manufacturers, such as Gund and Ideal.

British glove-puppet Sooty first appears on TV; Chad Valley gains exclusive rights to produce Sooty toy.

1953
Germany divided into Democratic and Federal Republics; "US Zone" labels change to "Made in the Federal Republic of Germany".

Coronation of Queen Elizabeth II prompts production of patriotic bears. Wording on Chad Valley's Royal Warrant label changes from "Queen Elizabeth" to "Queen Mother".

First Smokey Bear produced by Ideal for US Forest Fire Prevention Campaign.

Toffee (BBC Radio *Listen with Mother* story character) produced by Chad Valley.

1954
Wendy Boston test-markets first fully washable, nylon plush, safe-eyed, foam-rubber-stuffed teddy bear in UK.

1955
Wendy Boston's bear launched on BBC TV with demonstration of its washability. Boulgom in France launches similar bear. Other manufacturers follow suit.

1957
Merrythought introduces Cheeky with bell in ear; other British manufacturers copy this feature.

1958–63

1958
Michael Bond's *A Bear called Paddington* first published in UK.

British Standards Institution (B.S.I.) proposes test methods for flammability of soft-toy fabrics.

1959
Wendy Boston introduces new safety eye with nylon screw and bolt. Safe, vinyl noses begin to be used.

1960
Trademark "Bri-Nylon" registered by British Nylon Spinners; Bri-Nylon teddies produced by Dean's and Pedigree.

J.K. Farnell & Co. produces its version of Toffee (BBC Radio *Listen with Mother* character).

Early 1960s: Yogi Bear first features on TV shows, produced in US by Hanna Barbera.

Australian TV character Humphrey B. Bear first produced as soft toy by L.J. Sterne of Melbourne.

Winnie the Pooh cartoon character created by Walt Disney Studios inspires new Pooh merchandise.

First talking teddies, with miniature records activated by pull-cords.

1961
B.S.I. issues first toy standard on flammability of pile fabrics.

Hoover awards Wendy Boston bears Certificate of Washability.

1962
Teddy Edward by Patrick and Molly Mathews published in UK.

1963
Teddy Bear comic launched in UK.

1964–72

1964
Margaret Hutchings publishes *Teddy Bears and How to Make Them.*

Theodore Roosevelt's grandson presents early Ideal teddy bear to Smithsonian Institute, Washington, D.C.

c.1965
All-in-one foam bodies introduced.

1967
Mr. Whoppit, Donald Campbell's Merrythought teddy-bear mascot, survives Campbell's fatal attempt to beat world water-speed record on Coniston Water, England.

1968
B.S.I. recommends that rayon materials used for soft toys be treated with flame-resistant solution, and that eyes be attached in such a way that they cannot be gripped by fingernails or teeth.

1969
Peter Bull's *Bear with Me* published.

Early 1970s: US doll artists begin to produce teddy bears as art objects.

1970s: many leading soft-toy firms, especially old-established UK firms, go out of business as a result of recession and drop in birth-rate. Many firms move production to East Asia to cut costs.

1971
US-invented, synthetic Ultrasuede first used; becomes popular for teddy-bear pads and miniature teddies.

1972
Paddington Bear first produced as soft toy in UK by Gabrielle Designs.

1973–80

1973
Good Bears of the World launched in Switzerland, by James T. Ownby.

1974
Beverly Port shows first artist bear in Reno, Nevada, at International Dollmakers Convention.

1975
Eden Toys gains world rights to manufacture Paddington Bear.

Carol-Lynn Rössel Waugh in Maine makes fully jointed, porcelain artist bears with moulded-on clothing.

1978
Bear in Mind mail-order company established in Concord, Massachusetts.

1979
International Year of the Child marked by teddy-bear events, including one in UK hosted by Marquis of Bath; similar rallies in Australia and New Zealand follow.

Collectors' bears and limited editions popular; Gund launches Collectors' Classics series.

B.S.I. updates toy safety standards on eyes, noses, and flammability.

1980
Steiff introduces first replicas; North American Bear Company launches VIB range; Dakin produces Mishka bear, mascot of Moscow Olympic Games.

The Teddy Bear Catalogue: Prices, Care & Repair, Lore, by Peggy and Alan Bialosky, published in US.

In Praise of Teddy Bears by Philippa and Peter Waring published in UK.

1981–84

1981
Peter Bull's teddy bear "Delicatessen" changes name by deed poll to "Aloysius" after starring in *Brideshead Revisited.*

House of Nisbet launches Bully Bear range.

The Collector's History of the Teddy Bear, by Patricia Schoonmaker, published in US.

Term "bear artist" first coined in US *Doll Reader* article. Bear artistry grows in US and UK.

1982
Merrythought introduces special-edition collector bears.

1983
October: Bunny Campione introduces teddy bears to Sotheby's collectors' auctions.

Teddy Bear and Friends magazine for teddy-bear collectors launched in US by Hobby House Press.

Bear Enthusiasts All Round Collectors Club Inc. (B.E.A.R.) launched in California.

1984
Peter Bull dies, aged 72.

Joan Bland opens Asquiths in Windsor, Berkshire, first exclusive UK teddy-bear shop.

Teddy Bear Artists: Romance of Making and Collecting Bears by Carol-Lynn Rössel Waugh published in US.

Steiff produces Petsy, its first fully washable, soft-stuffed, fully jointed teddy bear.

Gebrüder Hermann introduces special-edition collector bears.

1985–88

1985
May: First teddy bear (Steiff *c.*1905–10) to fetch over £1,000 at Sotheby's, London.

December: Christie's of London holds first teddy-bears-only sale.

Dakin produces Mike Young's Super Ted character after success of cartoon series on US TV.

1985 designated International Year of the Teddy Bear by Good Bears of the World.

American Teddy Bear Artists Guild founded by Rowbear Lohman.

1986
World's first teddy-bear museum opens in Berlin.

Launch of *Teddy Bear Review* in US.

Teddy Bears Past and Present: Vol. I by Linda Mullins, published in US.

House of Nisbet's Jack Wilson invents process for "distressing" mohair.

1987
Golden Teddy Awards launched by *Teddy Bear Review.*

Big Softies produces Tough Ted, Simon Bond's storybook character.

1988
Teddyberendag, first teddy-bear event in the Netherlands, held at Amsterdam's Artis Zoo.

"Loc-Line" articulation introduced to bear artistry in US by Jeff Trager of Beaver Valley.

Gyles Brandreth's Teddy Bear Museum opens at Stratford-upon-Avon.

1989–90

1989
"Happy", a *c.*1926 Steiff bear, enters *Guinness Book of Records* after fetching record-breaking £55,000 at Sotheby's.

Reunification of Germany allows Hermann family to return to Sonneberg to research family history.

Australia's major teddy-bear show first held in Sydney.

Button in Ear, official Steiff history by Jürgen and Marianne Cieslik, published.

B.S.I. updates safety standards regarding soft toys; British Toy and Hobby Manufacturers Association introduces Lion Mark indicating toys manufactured to UK safety standards.

1990
East European firms, formerly confiscated by communists, handed back to descendents of original owners. Replicas of old patterns reproduced, eg. Leven by Hermann-Spielwaren; Hamiro by Sigikid.

UK Hugglets *Teddy Bear Magazine* and Ashdown Publishing's *Teddy Bear Times* launched.

Mary Holden of Only Natural produces Bill Bear, first teddy in UK for the chemically sensitive, with "EVE" environmental safety symbol.

Growing numbers of European bear artists, especially in Germany, France, and Holland.

Teddy Bear and Friends introduces TOBY awards.

CE mark introduced in UK to indicate toys meet EEC safety standards.

1991–93

1991
Teddy-bear museums open in US and UK. First bear-artist festival held in the Netherlands.

Dorling Kindersley publishes *The Ultimate Teddy Bear Book,* No.1 best-seller in UK.

Dean's launches limited-edition replica range.

Jakas introduces limited-edition range and replica of Playschool's "Big Ted".

British Teddy Bear Association launched.

Bear Facts Review launched in Australia, and *Beer Bericht* in the Netherlands.

1992
Steiff Collectors' Club formed, with special limited-editions for members only.

Limited-edition Columbus Bear by Hermann-Spielwaren celebrates 500th anniversary of founding of America.

Hermann-Spielwaren produces Europa Bear.

First New Zealand bear show held in Tauranga.

Berg launches 500 piece limited-edition replica 1952 teddy.

Clemens produces "40 Jahre Clemens-Bären".

Merrythought reproduces "Gatti" to mark 80th anniversary of Titanic disaster.

1992–93: Thiennot launches 100 piece limited-edition 1920 replica teddy.

1993
Sigikid's United Europe bear marks founding of common market.

Factory Histories

A DIRECTORY OF TEDDY-BEAR MANUFACTURERS, PAST AND PRESENT

The factory histories on the following pages were compiled from a wide variety of sources and include, in alphabetical order, all the main teddy-bear manufacturers, past and present, the majority of which feature in this encyclopedia. Each entry includes, wherever possible, the date of found-ation and closure, as well as a brief outline of import-ant events in the history of the factory. Where the company is still in operation, their current address is given at the end of the entry. In some cases, firms have been cross-referenced by their tradename when the latter is more well known than the company name.

Acton Toycraft Ltd. (*see also J.K. Farnell & Co. Ltd.*)
1964 1 October, registered as new private company No. 821,432; directors W.E. Hunt and F.W. Hase. Part of J.K. Farnell, it leases former Farnell factory, the Alpha Works in Uxbridge Road, Acton, west London, after Farnell's move to Hastings. Factory, adjacent to Twyford Avenue, west London, renamed Twyford Works.
Mid-1970s Ceases operations.
Trademark: "A Twyford Product".

Aetna Toy Animal Co.
*c.*1906 Manufactures teddy bears in New York (adver-tisements describe Aetna bear as "formerly the Keystone Bear"). Wholesalers, George Borgfeldt & Co. sole selling agents. Later becomes Aetna Doll and Toy Co.
1919 E.I. Horsmann Co. of New York buys firm
Trademark: "Aetna" in oval outline, on right foot.

Ajena
1965 Founded by Bernard Meffray in Luché-Pringé.
1989 Nounours group buys company. Produces lower quality range to distribute to chainstores; bears made at Nounours factories in Tunisia and Mauritius.
Luché-Pringé, BP 9, 72800, Le Lude, France.

Albico (*see Althans KG*)

A.L.F.A. (Article de Luxe Fabrication Artisanale)
1930s Founded in Paris.
1936 Company produces first teddy bear – unjointed, dressed as little boy or girl, with all-in-one clothes.
Post-1945 Creates first jointed teddy bears.
1960s Dressed bear design, in synthetic fabrics.
*c.*1970s Ceases business.
Trademark: "ALFA" printed on left sole.

Alresford Crafts Ltd.
1970 Established by John and Margaret Jones at The Town Mill, Alresford, Hampshire, England. Margaret Jones designs soft toys; originally includes only one teddy but, due to demand, bears become main product.
1980s At height of success, employs 100 staff, exporting world-wide, with US warehouse.
1991 John Jones dies.
1992 Margaret Jones continues business until year end.

Althans KG
1920s Althans family begins making teddy bears in Sonneberg, Thüringia, Germany.
1945 Soviets occupy area. Karl Althans escapes from Soviet zone to village of Birkig eight kilometres (five miles) away in US zone; marries Else Kessel and becomes farmer; works on in-laws' farm.
1949 Karl and Else Althans form part-time teddy-bear business in farmhouse, cycling with rucksacks of bears

to sell at markets in nearby towns of Neustadt, Coburg, and Lichtenfels. Gradually convert farmhouse to teddy-bear-making. Later firm employs over 100 workers in two factories. Has showroom above old pig-pens.
Early 1950s Tradename: "Albico" (derived from Althans Birkig Coburg).
Early 1980s Tradename: "Althans/Quality you can feel".
Mid-1980s Company introduces limited-edition collectors' teddy bears.
1988 Introduces "Althans Club" trademark for separate range of products manufactured in East Asia under Althans' design and quality control.
1990s Karl Althans' brother-in-law Günther Kessel now manages this family-owned business, and signs feet of limited-edition teddy bears
Horber Straße 4, 8632 Neustadt-Birkig, Germany.

Les Créations Anima
1947 Established in Paris by Suzanne Vangelder.
1972 Company is sold to M. Frenay of Boulgom; head office moves to Chaponost, near Lyon.
1990 The Alain Thirion group buys Boulgom, including the Anima range.
1992 American company Gund buys Anima.
1993 Anima moves to new premises in St Genis Laval.
Parc des Aqueducs, Chemin Favier, 69230 St Genis Laval, France.

Anker Plüschspielwarenfabrik GmbH
*c.*1953 Founded in München-Pasing (part of Munich) by Herr Bäumler, designer of plush animals.
1954 Firm buys soft-toy company belonging to Artur Hermann (son of Johann Hermann), known as J. Hermann Nachf. Inf. Artur Hermann, also located in München-Pasing. Based at Karl-Hromadnik-Straße 3.
Early 1960s Makes plush glove-puppets and animals, including popular donkey Mufti, and range of traditional mohair and Dralon teddy bears; standing bears with chains through noses; open mouth Zotty-like bears; and comical short-legged bear with large paws called Drolly.
1976 Unsuccessful collaboration with Hegi (part of Schuco in Nuremberg).
1977 Ceases business.
Trademark: an anchor superimposed on a lion.

Applause Inc.
1981 Wallace Berrie sells his firm, Wallace Berrie & Co., to Larry Elins and Harris Toibb.
1982 Acquires Applause Company from Knickerbocker Toys; gains marketing rights to Italian Jockline's Avanti line of soft toys.
1985 Introduces teddy bears designed by Robert Raikes.
1986 Changes name to Applause, becoming one of largest manufacturers in the gift industry, producing ceramic items, greetings cards, and other novelty items.

1988 Good Company division of Applause produces Robert Raikes bears.
1989 The Applause and Good Company divisions merge to become Applause Inc.
1991 Introduces bears designed by Bonita Warrington.
6101 Variel Avenue, PO Box 4183, Woodland Hills, California, 91365-4183 USA.
(see also Wallace Berrie & Co.; Knickerbocker Toy Co. Inc.)

Aux Nations
1964/65 Founded by Marc Fremont.
1975 Jacky Dubois of Nounours buys company.
1976 Awarded Oscar of Good Taste (French annual prize for toys) for Aux Nations collection.
Today soft toys are designed at Nounours headquarters in France, but made in Schio, near Venice, Italy.
c/o Nounours 35210 Chatillon en Vendelais, France.

Baki (*see Baumann & Kienel KG*)

Barton Waugh Pty. Ltd.
Post-World War II Established, operating from 7 Con-nells Point Road, Hurstville (a Sydney suburb), New South Wales; produces a range of fully jointed, mohair, kapok-filled bears with leatherette paws, distinct pointed feet, and triangular noses, in various sizes.
Late 1960s Ceases business.

Baumann & Kienel KG
1946 Franz Baumann, son of Hermann Baumann and Adelheid Hermann (daughter of Johann Hermann, and maker along with brothers Artur and Max of first Hermann bear), founds small arts and crafts toy company, Kunstgewerbliches Spielzeug in Flensburg.
1951 Franz founds plush toy company, Baumann & Kienel oHG (later Baumann & Kienel KG) with old friend Franz Kienel in little town of Rodach, near Coburg. Company managed today by Franz Baumann and Walter Kienel (son of original founder).
Trademark: "Baki" formed from **Ba**umann and **Ki**enel.
Coburger Straße 53, 8634, Rodach bei Coburg, Germany.

Bear With Us (*see Harrisons Textiles*)

Berg Spielwaren Tiere mit Herz GmbH
1946 Broschek family makes teddy bears from old army blankets, with army uniform buttons for eyes, and small boxes of pebbles for voices; works from Tyrolean farm-house in Fieberbrunn, Austria; trades under name Berger, the grandmother's maiden name, later shortened to Berg.
1951–52 Business expands when woven plush and glass eyes become available; "Berg" printed on cloth ear-tag becomes trademark.
1957 Trademarks become little red heart sewn into

chest and "Tiere mit Herz" ("Animals with Heart").
1966 New factory is built at Admont, in the Steiemark for assembly; toys are sent to Fieberbrunn factory for final inspection and distribution.
1992 Introduces replica limited editions.
A-6391 Fieberbrunn, Tyrol, Austria.

Berlex Toys Pty.
c.1930s Established in Melbourne, Australia.
c.1971 Based at 311 Boundary Road, Melbourne.
1970s Ceases business.
Trademark: "Berlex Melbourne" and "Made in Australia".

Russ Berrie & Co. Inc.
1963 Russ Berrie establishes business to sell novelty merchandise, including figurines, from converted garage in Palisades Park, New Jersey, USA.
Late 1970s Becomes a leader in soft-toy industry.
1984 Registered as public limited company with divisions, Gift, Plush 'N' Stuff, Expression Centre. Later reduced to first two. Headquarters in Oakland, New Jersey with distribution centres throughout world; soft toys manufactured in Korea, China, and Indonesia.
1993 First Russ teddy made in Australia under tradename "Koala Families".
111 Bauer Drive, Oakland, NJ 07436, USA.

Wallace Berrie & Co.
1964 Wallace Berrie, brother of Russ Berrie (*see Russ Berrie & Co. Inc.*) founds small firm; manufactures drugstore novelty items; slow, steady growth in first decade.
Mid-1970s Gains worldwide rights to Smurfs, creating sales phenomenon. Sells over $1 billion in retail merchandise and becomes one of leaders in licensing industry.
Late 1970s Main lines are plush toys.
1981 Firm is bought by Larry Elins and Harris Toibb.
1982 Acquires Applause Company from Knickerbocker Toys, picking up more classic licenses including Disney; gains worldwide marketing rights for Italian-designed Avanti line of soft toys.
1986 Changes name to Applause (*see Applause Inc.*).

Big Softies
1978 Family business established by Valerie and Fred Lyle, makes life-size, realistic animals, hence tradename.
1982 Firm starts making teddy bears, inspired by thesis on teddy bears' history by one of Fred's college students; teddy bears are now a major part of Big Softies' range – known as Good Companions. Also makes commissioned bears for British shops and department stores as well as collectors' limited editions.
The Old Mill House, Skipton Road, Ilkley, West Yorkshire, LS29 9RN, England.

Gebrüder Bing
1863 Company founded by brothers Ignaz and Adolph Bing in Nuremberg, to sell toys and kitchenware; later establishes own factory manufacturing tin toys – known as Nürnberger Spielwaren Fabrik Gebrüder Bing (Bing Brothers' Nuremberg Toy Factory) in Karolinestraße. Becomes renowned for mechanical trains, boats, and cars.
1880s Company has 100 employees and 120 outworkers.
1890 Establishes factory at Grünhain, Saxony.
1895 Becomes public limited company and name changes to Nürnberger Metall und Lackierwarenfabrik vorm, Bing AG (Nuremberg Metal and Enamelware Works). Adolph Bing leaves company and Ignaz Bing becomes chairman.
1908 Employees number 3,000. Catalogue proclaims Bing the "Greatest Toy Factory in the World".
1909 Legal battle with Steiff over "button in ear" trademark.
1911–15 Lawsuit with Steiff over somersaultng bear.
1909–12 Heinrich Müller (*see Schreyer & Co.*) joins firm.
c.1911 Bings Ltd., sole agents in Britain (part of

Eisenmann & Co. Ltd.) operate from 25 Ropemaker Street, east London; John Bing, sole representative in US, operated from 381 Fourth Avenue, New York.
1917 Agents Concentra markets Bing's complete line under various brand names.
World War I Reduces production.
1918 Ignaz Bing dies.
1919 Agents, L. Rees & Co. form in London to distribute Bing toys in Britain and Commonwealth.
1919 Ignaz Bing's son Stephen takes over as director general and name changes to Bing Werke (Bing Works).
1927 Stephen leaves firm after disagreement with board.
1932 Firm goes into receivership and departments are sold off, for example, to rival Nuremberg toy company, Karl Bub.

Les Créations Blanchet
1953 Current President Director General, Madame Blanchet, creates first teddy bear – girl bear cub in a felt dress, in Argenton-sur-Creuse in central France. Adds boy bear cub in felt pants and cotton shirt later.
1954 These two bears, made of rayon or mohair plush with wood-wool stuffing, blown glass eyes, and card disc or rod jointing, become first in range of animals marketed by Monsieur Blanchet and distributed at toy specialists and general stores.
1956 Moves to larger site in Chabenet Le Pont Chretien.
1962 Madame Blanchet joins forces with son, Michel, the present Director General, and firm becomes Ets O. Blanchet et Fils "Créations Blanchet", launching period of expansion, producing variety of soft toy animals.
1965 Trademark: a red heart with *Les Jouets qui ont un Coeur* ("The toys which have a heart").
1987 S.A. added to status.
1993 Teddy bears still central to range with new limited edition replicas of original bear cubs for collectors.
Chabenet, BP 6, 36800, Le Pont-Chretien, France.

Wendy Boston Playsafe Toys Ltd.
1941 Wendy Boston leaves London home for Crickhowell, south Wales, to avoid Blitz; makes soft toys out of pieces of unrationed material as hobby.
1945 Husband Ken Williams, returns from RAF, staying in Wales to start soft-toy business; Wendy Boston (Crickhowell) Ltd. established in small shop with staff of three.
1947 Staff increases to 16.
1948 Factory opens at Queen Street, Abergavenny, Monmouthshire, and Castle Road, Crickhowell, Brecon, with staff of 30. Firm uses mohair from Norton (Weaving) Ltd. of Yorkshire. Invents and patents safe, lock-in eyes, originally using rust-proof nuts and screws.
1952 Increases capital.
1954 Fully washable, nylon-covered, foam-filled teddy bear test-marketed.
1955 Washable bear is launched on BBC TV. Fire destroys main Abergavenny factory; moves into large warehouse at 79 Queen Street. Introduces printed velvet toys.
1959 Moulded nylon introduced for eye screws and nuts; washability demonstrated at Milan Toy Fair using washing-machine with wringer.
1960 Name changes to Wendy Boston Playsafe Toys Ltd.
1962 New factory opens at Hengoed, Glamorgan; employee numbers rise to 100.
1964 Firm achieves over 25% of Great Britain's soft-toy exports, exporting mainly to Sweden, Belgium, Holland, Italy, and Australia; also exporting to US and Rhodesia.
1968 Denys Fisher Toys (Spirograph inventor) buys firm.
1976 Production ceases.
1987 Replica of Peter Bull's gold mohair-plush Wendy Boston bear produced by House of Nisbet in two sizes.

Boulgom
1954 Company founded by M. Frenay in Oullins, France; first French soft-toy manufacturer to produce

washable teddy bears stuffed with foam-rubber.
1964 Moves to Chaponost, near Lyon.
1972 Buys French soft-toy company Anima.
1990 Becomes bankrupt; Alain Thirion group, which includes toy manufacturers, Joustra and Vulli, buys firm.
Rue des Gileres, BP 91 74150 Rumilly, France.

Britannia Toy Company Ltd.
1914–15 Established, as Britannia Toy Works, by Mark Robin (originally Mark Robin & Co.). Based at 9–11 Worship Street, east London for wholesale and export.
Late 1920s Operates as private limited company at 23 Stamford Hill, north London.
Late 1930s Moves to Alliance Works, Windus Road.
Post-World War II Ceases business.

British United Toy Manufacturing Co. Ltd.
1894 Founded as James S. Renvoize Ltd., principally manufacturing lead toy soldiers.
c.1911 Name changes to British United Toy Manufacturing Co. Ltd. adding teddy bears and other soft toys.
1916 After different locations in north London, moves to Union Works, Carysfort Road, Stoke Newington.
1914 Ban on German toys fuels expansion. Firm claims to be "original and only British makers" of coaster toys (copying Steiff's Record Teddy of previous year); opens north London office and showroom at 114 Fore Street.
1920s Claims to be first to introduce artificial silk to British soft-toy industry; featherweight kapok-stuffed soft-toy range introduced.
1929 Registers trademark "Omega", used since World War I, as No. 494,205.
c.1928 Following death of founder, company managed by H. Stanley Renvoize, until his death in 1952.
Post-World War II Products restricted to supplying wholesalers and export.
Early 1980s Ceases business.

Bruin Manufacturing Co.
1907 First advertised in US trade journal *Playthings*. Based at 497 Broome Street, New York City with trademark "B.M.C." The Strobel & Wilken Co. of 591 Broadway and Frank W. Owens, 714 Broadway, are the selling agents. Manufactures range of soft-toy animals including teddy bears with imported German voices, as well as bear outfits and accessories.

Bunjy Toys
1980 Eve Mayhew starts making teddy bears as hobby; originally based in workrooms in small house in Mooi River, Natal, South Africa, with eight workers. Moves within months to small factory with 16 employees.
1982 Expansion results in relocation to larger factory in nearby Estcourt, where Bunjy Toys now employs 50 people. Produces range of bears for home market; exports pure wool examples to US.
1991 Eve Mayhew retires; sells factory to George Allison. Only South African factory making soft toys for game parks, including Kruger National Park.
210 Albert Street, Estcourt, Natal 3310, South Africa.

California Stuffed Toys
1959 Established in Los Angeles.
Early 1980s Produces character bears (Winnie the Pooh; Br'er Bear; Radar's Teddy from M.A.S.H.) and limited editions for collectors.
1984 Celebrates 25th anniversary with two limited-edition bears, signed by president Nat L. Gorman; manufactured in Korea.
1986 Trades under division name "Caltoys".
c.1989 Ceases business.

Canterbury Bears Ltd.
1980s Established by John Blackburn (member of Society of Industrial Artists and Designers) with

daughter Kerstin (now Managing Director) at family home in Westbere, Kent, England following commission for traditional, fully jointed teddy bear previous year. Later, wife Maude (now chairman), son Mark, and daughter Victoria assist.
1981 Firm first exhibits products at London's Earls Court Toy Fair.
1982 Awarded British Design Council approval. Establishes worldwide export trade.
1983 Wins first prize at First Great Western Teddy Bear Show and convention in San Jose, California.
1984 Moves to Littlebourne, near Canterbury, Kent.
1987 Mayor of Canterbury allows company to use city's ancient Coat of Arms on labels and corporate identity.
1990 Celebrates 10th anniversary. Produces 50,000 bears annually; exports 25%; agents in Australia and Holland.
1991 Gund becomes exclusive distributor in US and in Canada; Canterbury Bears Collector's Society founded. *The Old Coach House, Court Hill, Littlebourne, Canterbury CT3 1TY, England.*

🏭 The Chad Valley Co. Ltd.
*c.*1820 Anthony Bunn Johnson founds printing and book-binding works in Lichfield Street, Birmingham, England.
1860 Johnson's sons, Joseph and Alfred, found stationery firm Messrs. Johnson Bros. in George Street, Birmingham.
1889 Joseph's son Alfred J. Johnson enters business.
1897 Joseph and son move to new factory in neighbouring village of Harborne, trading as private limited company, Johnson Bros. (Harborne) Ltd. Factory is known as Chad Valley Works, named after Chad stream nearby. Firm registers Chad Valley trademark; prints cardboard games to add to range of stationers' sundries.
1904 Joseph Johnson dies; Alfred Johnson becomes chairman and managing director, assisted by E. Dent, brothers Arthur and Harry, and brother-in-law William Riley.
Pre-World War I Simple toys added each year; range increases during war due to ban on German imports.
1915–16 Firm makes first soft toys, including teddy bear.
1916 Alfred Johnson patents soft-toy stuffing machine.
1919 Acquires Harborne Village Institute to house printing works.
1920 Opens Wrekin Toy Works, Wellington, Shropshire for soft toys; firm renamed The Chad Valley Co. Ltd.
1923 Registers "Aerolite" trademark for kapok-stuffed soft toys and dolls (used until 1926). Extends Wellington factory; buys Messrs. Isaacs & Company, Birmingham, makers of bouncing, stuffed "Isa" toys.
1928 Builds new factory at Harborne works.
1931 Buys Peacock & Co. Ltd., London, makers of wooden, kindergarten toys.
1932 Expands Harborne works.
1938 Company is granted Royal Warrant of Appointment "Toymakers to Her Majesty the Queen".
World War II Drastically cuts toy and game production; carries out government contracts for war effort; makes children's clothes at Wrekin Works.
1946 Buys A.S. Cartwright Ltd., Birmingham, makers of aluminium hollowware. Acquires Waterloo Works, Wellington for manufacture of new range of rubber toys.
1950 Becomes public limited company.
1951 Buys Hall & Lane Ltd., Birmingham, maker of metal toys.
1954 Buys Robert Bros. (Gloucester) Ltd., maker of Glevum toys and games.
1958 Buys Acme Stopper & Box Co. Ltd., Birmingham, maker of metal toys.
1960 Celebrates centenary.
1967 Acquires H.G. Stone & Co. Ltd.; some soft-toy production moves to Chiltern's Pontypool factory.
1973–75 Restructuring of company; all but two factories close; all soft-toys are produced at Pontypool.
1978 Taken over by Leicester-based toy firm, Palitoy (later bought by US company Kenner Parker).
1988 Chainstore, Woolworths, acquires Chad Valley tradename; new range is made in East Asia.

🏭 Character Novelty Company Inc.
1932 Founded by New Yorkers Caesar Mangiapani and Jack Levy, at 14 South Main Street, Norwalk, Connecticut; Mangiapani designs and Levy operates sales; within few years moves to nearby 50–52 Day Street.
Post-1945 Business expands producing wide range of soft-toy animals; showroom in New York.
*c.*1960 Jack Levy retires, and later dies.
1983 Mangiapani dies; business ceases.
Trademark: printed cloth ear-tag.

🏭 Chiltern (*see H.G. Stone & Co. Ltd.*)

🏭 Hans Clemens GmbH
Pre-World War II Hans Clemens owns factory and wholesale shoe business in Alsace, France; loses this during war.
1948 Moves to Kirchardt/Baden and opens shop in Mannheim, Germany, selling glass, china, and gifts. Teddy bears not readily available, but with help from sister, begins making them from old, woollen, German army blankets. Later takes on more employees to meet demand.
Today Peter Clemens, son of original founder, runs firm; products include limited-edition teddy bears. *Waldstraße 34-36, D-6926 Kirchardt/Heilbronn, Germany.*

🏭 Columbia Teddy Bear Manufacturers
*c.*1907 Based at 145–49 Center Street, New York City. Produces range of teddy bears made of imported German plush and voices, including Laughing Teddy Bear. Name derives from Christopher Columbus.

🏭 Commonwealth Toy & Novelty Co. Inc.
1934–35 Founded by current president, Steve Greenfield's grandfather in New York.
1937 Produces Feed Me teddy for National Biscuit Company to advertise animal crackers. Still produces novelty bears including one with back zipper revealing red/white heart-shaped bag. *27 West 23rd Street, New York, NY 10010 USA.*

🏭 Cuddly Toys Ltd.
1984 Founded in Alberta, Canada, specializing in distribution of mascots for large corporations. All products designed and manufactured in Canada, using Canadian raw materials; world-wide distribution. *PO Box 3790, Spruce Grove, Alberta, T7X 3B1 Canada.*

🏭 Dakin Inc.
1955 Family business importing expensive, hand-crafted shotguns from Italy and Spain, founded by Richard Y. Dakin in San Francisco.
1957 Son, Roger B. Dakin, joins firm; product diversification including bicycles, sailing skiffs, wooden products, and toys; shipment of battery-operated trains from Japan includes six velveteen, stuffed animals used as packing. Roger orders small number, which are an instant success; toys later designed at Dakin's US headquarters, as Dream Pets, officially launching company into soft-toy business.
1961 Harold A. Nizaman joins as assistant to president.
1963 Sports goods division phased out.
1964 Acquires Dardenelle Company of Lindsay, California, manufacturers of infants' plush toys, where all domestic manufacturing is now handled.
Mid-1960s Has factories in Japan, Hong Kong, Mexico.
1966 Tragic plane crash, in Baja, California, kills Mr. and Mrs. Richard Dakin, Mr. and Mrs. Roger Dakin, and four of their five children. Nizaman appointed president and chief executive officer and other Dakin family members join board of directors along with Norman P. Canright (previously vice-president for sales and advertising).
1970 Sales expands to 35 countries; production is transferred from Japan to Korea.
1987 R. Dakin & Company becomes Dakin Inc.
1989 Acquires House of Nisbet, managed by David Potter, Managing Director for Dakin Europe/UK.
1990s Dakin Inc. has sales to over 80 countries; many international production and distribution centres with over 10,000 production workers throughout world. Company operates six marketing divisions: Gift (for gift and department stores); Fun Farm (for chain stores); Special Markets (mascots and premiums); Baby Things (infant toys and accessories); School Sales (fund-raising merchandise); Dolls (collectors' market). *PO Box 7746, San Francisco, California, 94120, USA.*

🏭 Dean's Rag Book Co. Ltd.
1903 Founded on 5 August by Henry Samuel Dean to launch his rag book for children who "wear their food and eat their clothes", at Gough Square, 160a Fleet Street, east London (site of Dean & Son, established publishing house), with Harry E. Bryant managing binding department. Artist, Stanley Berkeley designs trademark depicting two dogs fighting over rag book.
1905 Introduces Knockabout toy sheets.
1908 Introduces Knockabout teddy bear and Teddy Bear Rag Book.
1912 Binding department and registered offices move to larger premises at 2–14 Newington Butts, Elephant & Castle, south-east London. Richard Ellett joins firm as company secretary, later becoming chief designer.
1915 Markets first catalogued teddy bears under Kuddlemee brand name for The British Novelty Works, a subsidiary company.
1916 Fire destroys early productions (although duplicate copies held elsewhere).
1922 Huge sign with logo is erected over works entrance. First teddy bears with Dean's logo. Registers tradename "A1 Toys" and patents "Evripoze" joints.
1924 New showroom opens at Debrett House, 29 King Street, Covent Garden, London.
1933 New showroom opens at 6 La Belle Sauvage, Ludgate Hill, east London.
1936 Building begins on factory, on site of Lord Nelson's farm, 61 High Path, Merton, south-west London.
1940 Reduces toy production; manufactures Mae Wests and bren-gun covers.
1949 Produces first post-war catalogue.
1952 Sylvia Willgoss joins firm as Richard Ellett's assistant. Company splits with marketing agents Dean & Son, operating own sales organization, hiring travelling salesmen nationwide, including Jack Crane (Dean & Son's representative since 1920) as northern representative (exhibiting products in mobile showroom pulled by Rolls Royce). London showroom moves to factory premises; introduces soft toys made solely to supply wholesalers by subsidiary, Merton Toys Ltd., with bulldog trademark.
1953 Michael Crane joins firm; joins forces with Projects (Coventry) Ltd., makers of plastic and nursery toys.
1955 Sells Merton factory.
1956 Moves to 18 Tower Street, Rye, Sussex. Subsidiary Childsplay Ltd. forms to manufacture soft toys for retail and export trade. Sylvia Willgoss becomes chief designer
1957 Richard Ellett dies.
1959 Marmet Ltd. (pram manufacturers) becomes major shareholder.

1960 New sales policy: production and dispatch continue at Rye, sales office transfers to offices of parent company Marmet (Sales) Ltd., Letchworth, Hertfordshire.
1961 Rye factory expands; new production unit established in Wimbledon (for Merton Toys).
1965 Name changes to Dean's Childsplay Toys Ltd.
1971 H.E. Bryant dies 21 October; Jack Crane dies 18 December.
1972 Company buys Gwentoys Ltd., makers of soft toys for wholesale trade, becoming Dean's/Gwentoy Group.
1974 Some production moves to Gwentoys' Pontypool factory.
1980 Rye factory closes; all production is in Pontypool.
1983 Celebrates 80th birthday; issues anniversary bear.
1986 Toy and gift importer, Plaintalk, takes over firm, funded by substantial shareholders Fine Art International plc. Becomes The Dean's Company (1903) Ltd.
1987 Neil Miller, now Managing Director, joins firm.
1988 Firm goes into voluntary liquidation; Miller buys Wendley Ltd. to achieve management buy-out and buys trading rights to Dean's name and logo; commences trading on 7 March (with wife Barbara as finance director and Michael Crane, sales director). Officially named Wendley Ltd., trading as The Dean's Company (1903).
1990 December, purchases original company Dean's Rag Book Company Ltd.
1991 New range of collectors' bears launched, including replicas of old patterns, using original Dean's Rag Book Company trademark.
1993 Centenary year; anniversary catalogue issued.
The Dean's Company (1903), Pontypool, Gwent NP4 6YY, Wales.

Ealontoys Ltd.
1914 Originally called the East London Federation Toy Factory, founded at 45 Norman Road, Bow, east London by suffragette Sylvia Pankhurst. Firm makes a variety of soft toys and dolls designed by artists from Chelsea Polytechnic including Hilda E. Jefferies.
*c.*1921 Name changes to the East London Toy Factory.
1924 Teddy bears first mentioned in advertisements, produced in 11 sizes in best quality plush.
1926 Tradename Ealontoys registered No. 464,617, with illustration of seated, shaggy dog beneath and "Made in England"; soon after becomes private limited company.
1935 Moves to 74–78 Bingfield Street, Kings Cross, London.
1948 Name changes to Ealontoys Ltd.
1950 Advertisement bills firm "The Teddy Bear People".
Early 1950s Ceases business.

Eisenmann & Co. Ltd.
1881 German fancy goods and toy exporters founded by brothers Josef and Gabriel Eisenmann; Josef deals with British trade at 45 Whitecross Street, London, and Gabriel with German in Fürth, Bavaria.
*c.*1900 Leon Rees moves to England from Germany. He is naturalized, and becomes Josef's business partner.
1908 Rees marries Josef Eisenmann's daughter Maude. First company to introduce teddy bear to Britain; said to have encouraged J.K. Farnell to manufacture teddy bear. Chiltern Works, the firm's Chesham-based toy factory, is in operation.
1912 Produces large number of fabric dolls with porcelain heads for *London Evening News*.
1913 Leon Rees registers patent for eyes for dolls, toy animals, and puppets from 46 Basinghall Street, London.
1918 Gabriel Eisenmann dies.
1919 Josef Eisenmann dies leaving Chiltern Works to son-in-law Leon Rees (see *H.G. Stone & Co.*). Company continues under Josef Eisenmann's nephew, Paul Ellison.
1931 Registers "Bobby the Bear" trademark for toy bears from 25 Ropemaker Street, London.
Post-1945 Become agents for British United Toy Manu

facturing Co., sometimes trading under "Einco".
(see also British United Toy Manufacturing Co.)

Eli Doll and Toy Company
1894 Company founded in Wildenhaib, village near Neustadt, Germany, by Ernst Liebermann, to manufacture bisque dolls and later plush animals.
1925 Franz Liebermann, founder's son, registers trademark "Eli", derived from father's name.
1950s Still manufacturing teddy bears, with triangular chest-tag on cord.

Emil Toys
*c.*1930s Established in Australia, continuing to make teddy bears and soft toys.
*c.*1955 based at 246 Hoddle Street, Abbotsford, Victoria.
1970s Ceases business.
Trademark: "Emil Toys" with bear sitting on base of "E", holding onto upward stroke.

Erle Teddy Bear Company
Post-World War II Established in Neustadt, Germany. Firm's name derives from founder, **Er**ich **Le**istner, well-known lecturer and author of teddy-bear and doll books.
1970s Ceases business.

F.A.D.A.P.
1920 Fabrique Artistique d'Animaux en Peluche (Artistically Made Plush Animals) founded at Divonne-les-Bains, France, small town near Swiss border, with offices in Paris. Celebrated illustrator Benjamin Rabier designs first teddy bears of golden mohair with boot-button eyes, bat-shaped nose, and four claws.
Trademark: embossed metal button over printed card-tag in left ear.
*c.*1925 Other colours introduced, such as red, white, and blue; claws reduced to three; some bears jointed externally with wire. Certain luxury models made with glass eyes and felt pads with four claws.
1930s Firm introduces artificial silk (rayon) plush.
World War II Flannelette bears with button eyes made due to shortage of traditional materials.
1950s Mohair and rayon plush used again. In collaboration with US Ideal Toy Corporation, firm creates new range of bears with soft, moulded vinyl head, mask, or muzzle, using new process called "slush moulding".
1970s Ceases business.

J.K. Farnell & Co. Ltd.
1840 Small family business established by City of London silk merchant, John Kirby Farnell, in Notting Hill, London, to make pen-wipers, pin-cushions, and tea-cosies.
1897 Following founder's death, family moves to Acton, leasing eighteenth-century house, "The Elms", where soft-toy firm is established and run by John Farnell's children, Henry Kirby and Agnes Farnell. Initially uses rabbit skins.
1908 Said to have first produced teddy bears.
1921 Registered as private limited company with £10,000 capital. Firm builds new factory, Alpha Works, next to "The Elms". Employs more staff, including H.C. Janisch, sales manager throughout 1920s (joins Merrythought in 1930). Agnes Farnell designs toys with Sybil Kemp.
1925 "Alpha" (used since early 1920s) officially registered as trademark.
1926 T.B. Wright joins firm as sales representative.
1927 Firm introduces Anima wheeled toys, including a bear. Extends factory space.
1928 Agnes Farnell dies 25 January. Permanent City showroom opens at 19 New Union Street, east London.
1929 Joins forces with Louis Wolf & Co. Inc. for distribution throughout US and Canada with showroom at 215–19 Fourth Avenue, New York. Managing director

A.E. Brett-Rose makes tour of US and Canada. Société Anonyme J.K. Farnell formed at 80 Rue du Faubourg St. Denis, Paris, to sell products throughout France. Silkalite artificial-silk plush bears are introduced.
1931 Introduction of cheap Unicorn soft toys, including Cuddle Bear. G.E. Beer becomes director until 1935.
1932 J.K. Farnell and toy manufacturers, William Bailey (Birmingham) Ltd., managed by Percy V. Goodwin, join forces using one sales team.
1934 Fire destroys entire factory and stocks.
1935 New one-storey, brick, 2,137 square metres (23,000 sq. ft) factory opens, large enough to employ 300 workers. Alpha and Teddy series of bears are reintroduced. Many new lines including Che-Kee (lambswool); Alpac (alpaca) and Joy Day dolls. Moved to larger showrooms at 1 New Union Street, east London.
1937 New wing added due to increased business, particularly new patriotic lines for coronation of George VI.
1940 Factory destroyed by Blitz but later rebuilt.
1944 Henry Kirby Farnell dies.
1950s Trademark redesigned. New City showroom at Condor House, 13–14 St Paul's Churchyard, east London.
1959 Firm establishes production unit with 100 employees at 39 George Street, Hastings, Sussex, later extended to become Olympia Works. 95% of teddy bears produced here are for export. Acton is used for home market. Head office transfers to Hastings.
1960 Registered "Mother Goose" trademark for washable nylon soft-toy range.
1964 All production moves to Hastings. Subsidiary company, Acton Toycraft Ltd., takes over lease of Alpha Works, renamed Twyford Works.
1968 Farnell bought by finance company.
(see also Acton Toycraft Ltd.)

Fechter Co.
1946 William Fechter and wife Berta Bohn (German teddy-bear seamstress in Neustadt during 1930s) start up teddy-bear cottage industry in Graz, south-eastern Austria, originally using US-made towels.
1948 Firm moves into factory at Theodor Körner Straße 49; employs over 20 workers, uses German-made mohair.
1950 First exhibits at Vienna Toy Fair, resulting in wider recognition and continuing expansion; supplies over 200 European dealers.
1963 Buys large, glass factory at Altenmarkt 2 in Wies, south of Graz.
1973 Berta Bohn dies.
1978 Business discontinues.
1984 Antique dealer, Lisl Swinehart, of Davis, California, buys warehouse stock of Fechter soft toys in Austria, importing them to US, where firm was previously unknown.
1985 Wilhelm Fechter dies.

Felpa AG *(see MCZ)*

Gaeltarra Eireann
1938 Irish government department, *Gaeltacht* Services Division, subsidizes new industry making toys and small utility goods, to create jobs in rural areas. Operates in three factories: Elly Bay, County Mayo (soft toys); Spiddal, County Galway (lead toys); Crolly, County Donegal (dolls). Head Office at Oriel House, Westland Row, Dublin, with sole sales agent, William Girvan.
1949 Ireland is declared a Republic and labels change.
1950 Hans Weberpals (studied at College of Applied Arts, Nuremberg; designer at Sonneberg toy factory before World War II) comes to Ireland and joins toy division of *Gaeltacht* Services as Production Manager and Designer.
*c.*1953 Erris Toys tradename, used by Elly Bay soft-toy factory, changes to Tara Toys.

1958 Board of *Gaeltarra Eireann* takes over administration of rural industries from *Gaeltacht* Services Division; reorganization removes management from civil servants (taken over by civilians), and encourages profit-making.
1965 Foam-rubber stuffing introduced. Hans Weberpals leaves *Gaeltarra Eireann* to set up own factory, Celtic Toys, at Millstreet, County Cork with partner. Retires and goes into voluntary liquidation in 1975, but in 1978 reopens factory, assisted by Tom Burke. Present range includes cheap teddy bears, trademark: Clara Toys.
1969 *Gaeltarra Eireann* head offices transfer to Furbo, County Galway. Elly Bay factory closes and production transfers to Crolly, County Donegal, under new company, Soltoys Ltd.
1979 Soltoys Ltd. ceases business.
1980 *Udaras na Gaeltachta* (meaning "body that runs the Irish-speaking area of Ireland") forms to take over from *Gaeltarra Eireann*.

Ganz Bros. Toys
1950 Founded by brothers, Sam and Jack Ganz; manufactures, imports, and distributes variety of gift items, including soft toys. Now the largest teddy-bear manufacturer in Canada; range includes collectors' bears and licenced bears such as Rupert. Sam Ganz is chairman of the board; his son Howard is the current president.
One Pearce Road, Woodbridge, Ontario L4L 3T2, Canada.

Trudi Giocattoli spa
1948 Current President Trudi Mueller marries Antonio Patriarca and settles in Tarcento, village near Venice.
1949 Trudi makes first teddy bear on the occasion of son's birth, and founds family soft-toy business to produce a wide range of plush animals.
1990s Now employs five designers; firm exports throughout Europe and the US. Limited-edition collector bears added to range.
Trademark: circular card chest-tag "Original Trudi Hand Made".
Via Angelo Angeli 120, 33017, Tarcento (Udine), Italy.

Golden Bear Products Ltd.
1979 Established; now reputedly largest soft-toy manufacturer in UK.
*c.***1988** Takes over rights to Tough Ted from Big Softies.
Rookery Road, Wrockwardine Wood, Telford, Shropshire TF2 9DW, England.

Grisly Spielwaren GmbH & Co. KG
1954 Founded by Karl Theodor Unfrecht in family home in village of Kirchheimbolanden, near Mainz, Germany.
1964 Metal button trademark, showing needle and thread superimposed upon grizzly (German: *grisly*) bear on all-fours, replaced by paper tag with same logo.
1980 Karl dies; son Hans-Georg and daughter Hannelore Wirth take over company.
PO Box 1127, Beethovenstraße 1, 67284, Kirchheimbolanden/Rheinphalz, Germany.

Gund Inc.
1898 Gund Manufacturing Company founded in Norwalk, Connecticut, by German immigrant Adolph Gund to make belts, necklaces, novelties, and soft toys.
Early 1900s Moves to new premises in New York City.
1906 Adds teddy bears in four sizes to range.
1909 Jacob Swedlin, Russian immigrant, joins business as janitor, but after training in cutting, pattern-making, and design becomes Adolph Gund's personal assistant.
1925 Gund retires and sells business and all patents to Jacob Swedlin; Swedlin's three brothers later join him, the company becomes J. Swedlin Inc., although still

retains the Gund tradename.
1927 Manufactures mechanical jumping animals of coloured velveteen under trademark "Gee Line".
1948 Expansion after World War II helped by gaining exclusive rights to produce stuffed-animal versions of Walt Disney and, later, King Features and Hanna Barbera cartoon characters.
New trademark with rabbit faced "G".
1956 Factory moves to Brooklyn.
1973 Firm moves to Edison, New Jersey; showroom remains at 200 Fifth Avenue Toy Center, New York City.
1976 Jacob Swedlin dies.
1979 Introduces Collectors Classics range, targeting adults and collectors.
1988 Firm moves to new, larger headquarters in Edison.
1992 Becomes distributor of Canterbury Bears in US and Canada; buys French company Anima. Remains privately owned, in the hands of Jacob Swedlin's daughter Rita (secretary-treasurer and director of design), her husband Herbert Raiffe (president), and their son Bruce (vice president; director of marketing). Teddies now made in Korea.
One Runyons Lane, Edison, NJ 08817, USA.

Gwentoys Ltd.
1965 Founded by three former managers – A. Thwaites, Jack Jacobs, and R.G. Green – from old Chiltern/Stone/ Combex factory in Pontypool, south Wales. Named after Gwent, old Welsh name for Monmouthshire, county where firm is located. Offices and factory of 557 square metres (6,000 square feet) situated at Forge Road, Pontypool.
1968 Builds larger premises Pontypool Industrial Estate.
1971 Extends premises.
1972 Becomes part of Dean's Group, specializing in soft toys for supplying wholesalers and mail-order trade.
(see also Dean's Rag Book Co. Ltd.)

Hamiro
1910 Karel Pospísil establishes foundry near Rokycany, in what was Bohemia; makes lead figures and tin soldiers.
1919 Wife Miluse designs textile rabbit to boost low sales after World War I. Founds soft-toy company at old forge and employs 12 people; exhibits at European trade fairs – exports 60% of products overseas.
1930 Moves to new, larger factory in Rokycany.
1932 "Hamiro" trademark registered (*Hammerwerk* or forge; *Miluse*, Czech nickname for Emilie; Rokycany).
1936–38 An international business with 500 employees; second largest plush-toy manufacturer in Europe.
World War II Produces war materials: military uniforms and underwear.
1948 Company is confiscated by Czechoslovakian communist government; low quality stuffed animals continue to be made in factory but under government ownership. Karel and Miluse's son, Libor, hides firm's archive in attic.
1990 Libor Pospísil sees exhibition of German company H. Scharrer & Koch GmbH's products *(see entry)* in Prague; collaborates and establishes new Miro firm at Hamiro's old factory in Rokycany.
1992 Creates series of 1920s–30s replicas.

Harman Manufacturing Company
1907 Produces teddy bears in nine sizes from 8 West 13th Street, New York City. All have imported German voices. Includes Teddy Bear Shopper, its back containing a gold-coloured, metal-framed, silk-lined pocket with leather handles; and teddy doll.

Harrisons Textiles
1977 Founded by Clive and Precille Harrison at 143 Church Street, Otahuhu, Auckland, New Zealand to make teddy bears. Later goes into partnership with Australian company, and becomes known as

Harrisons Gifts.
1990 Sells share to US firm Milton Bradley (later Hasbro). Australian company operates from Gymea, New South Wales, with Harrisons label, but bears are made in Korea.
Trademark: printed cloth label; red heart superimposed with "Harrisons" in black script.
1992 Clive and Precille Harrison establish new teddy-bear business, Bear With Us; bears designed by Clive.
41 Budgen Street, Mt Roskill, Auckland, New Zealand.

Harwin & Co. Ltd.
1914 Established by G.W. Harwin at Eagle Works, 52 Blackstock Road, Finsbury Park, north London, to produce needlework and Dot's series of felt dolls, caricatures, and teddy bears, designed by his daughter, Dorothy Harwin. Sales manager Fred Taylor had previously worked for Steiff's British agent, Herbert E. Hughes. Notable teddies are Ally Bears in World War I allied uniforms, and Eyes Right with googly eyes in Highland dress; also reputedly making first mascots to cross Atlantic, accompanying Alcock and Brown on momentous 1919 flight.
Registered trademark: although not used on permanent label, includes intertwined letters DOTS inside double circle with words "British Made".
*c.***1930** Ceases business.

Maxwell Hay & Co. Ltd.
1964 Founded by Maxwell Hay in Auckland, New Zealand; sheepskin manufacturers making mainly soft toys, hand-dyed in the early days.
1976 Introduces teddy-bear range.
1982 Ceased production of teddy bears, but continues to make soft toys. Following Maxwell's death, his wife Nancy and their son run the business.
5/22A Willcott Street, Mt Albert, Auckland, New Zealand.

Hegi (Herta Girz & Co.) *(see Schreyer & Company)*

Heike-Bär
1985 Karl Bär, from long line of Neustadt teddy-bear makers, who had previously made Berliner bears, begins to produce replica Schuco miniature teddy-bears using patterns, tools, and equipment bought from Schuco's receiver in 1977. Trades under wife's name: "Heike-Bär".
Glashüttenweg 2, 8632, Neustadt/Coburg, Orsteil Fürth a. Berg, Germany.

Helvetic Company
1928 Cited in trade journal *Toy World* as holding exclusive rights to manufacture teddy bears with squeeze-type musical boxes. Name suggests Swiss origins, but possibly US company using imported mechanisms. In operation for short period during 1920s.

Artur Hermann
1913 Artur Hermann founds teddy-bear firm with sister Adelheid and brother Max at Neufang home, operating under father's name, Johann Hermann Spielwarenfabrik.
Post-World War I Artur Hermann moves to Sonneberg to establish own company, trading under the name Artur Hermann Plüsch-Spielwaren-Fabrik.
Late 1920s Changes name to J. Hermann Nachf. Inf. Artur Hermann.
1940 Company moves to Lackerbauerstraße 1–3, Munich.
1954 Sells to Anker plush toy firm in Munich; Artur Hermann founds Munich toy shop Teddy: Haus des Kindes.

Gebrüder Hermann KG
Post-World War I Bernhard Hermann and wife Ida Jäger move from Neufang home (where he had helped

in father Johann's toy factory, following apprenticeship in trade and business in Meiningen) to Sonneberg to found small firm trading under "Be–Ha". Makes mohair-plush teddy bears. Lower-quality examples are made by piece-workers.

1930s Bernhard and Ida's four sons, Hellmut, Artur, Werner, and Horst, help in family business.

1937 Youngest son Horst dies.

World War II Three brothers go into military service.

1948 Production starts to transfer to factory in Hirschaid, near Bamberg, Bavaria (part of the American zone); company reforms as Gebrüder Hermann KG, with the three brothers as business partners.

1952–53 Entire family and factory relocates to the West. Trademark: "Hermann Teddy Original" introduced.

1959 Bernhard Hermann dies; management passes to Artur; production and design to Werner; direction of operations to Hellmut.

1980 Hellmut retires.

1984 Firm produces first limited-edition collectors' bears.

1985 Hellmut dies; Artur and Werner continue to manage firm briefly. From the mid 1980s, Isabella Reiter, Marion Mehling, Margit Drolshagen, and Traudi Mischner (designer), daughters of the three brothers, manage the firm.

1990 Artur dies.

1992 Three bears are produced, designed by US bear artists Jenny Krantz and Joyce Ann Haughey.
Amlingstadter Straße 9, Postfach 1207, D-8606, Hirschaid, Germany.

Hermann-Spielwaren GmbH

1913 Max Hermann leaves school to help in family teddy-bear business, Johann Hermann Spielwarenfabrik, run by brother Artur and sister Adelheid at father's house in Neufang, near Sonneberg, Germany.

1920 Max founds business at Neufang family home.

1923 Moves to Sonneberg, to Wilhemstraße 17, and again within first month to larger premises at Kirchstraße 4, and later to Karlstraße 23. Trades as Max Hermann, Sonneberg, using trademark "Maheso" with bear and dog logo.

c.1930 Moves to Friedrichstraße 7a.

1933 May–October, exhibits set of dressed bears at special toy exhibition in Sonneberg.

1939–45 Reduces production.

1947 Produces first teddy bears in peacetime and exhibits at Leipzig fair; son Rolf-Gerhard joins firm, forming Max Hermann & Sohn, Sonneberg.

1949 Subsidiary company, Hermann & Co. KG, formed in Coburg, 20km (12 1/2 miles) from Sonneberg in US zone.

1951 Rolf marries Dora-Margot (Dorle) Engel, daughter of joint owner of Sonneberg toy company H. Josef Leven.

1953 February 22, family escapes to West across border at Berlin and relocates entire company in Coburg.

1955 Max dies; Rolf Hermann leads business with wife Dora-Margot responsible for design.

1968 Introduces present swing-tag.

1979 Becomes private limited company Hermann-Spielwaren GmbH.

1990 Celebrates 70th anniversary with introduction of limited editions. Reunification of Germany enables family to return to Sonneberg to research archives; Rolf's daughter and co-director Dr. Ursula Hermann compiles history of firm; Leven company (owned by communists since 1945) is officially handed back to descendent, Dora-Margot Hermann; replicas of old Leven designs made.

1992 Dora–Margot Hermann dies.
Im Grund 9–11, D–8630 Coburg-Cortendorf, Germany.

Hermann & Co. KG (see Hermann-Spielwaren GmbH)

Heunec Plusch Spielwaren Fabrik KG

1891 Hugo Heubach founds company in Sonneberg, as distributor of toys and Christmas tree decorations.

c.1945 firm moves to Neustadt/Coburg area of West Germany and changes name to Heunec (derived from Heubach/Neustadt/Coburg).

1972 becomes manufacturer of plush toys, with only two employees; expansion of buildings and staff follows. Company now employs over 1,000 workers in its three factories in Switzerland, Mauritius, and China, with administration and design department in Neustadt/Coburg, and is one of the top ten European soft-toy manufacturers. Around 1,000 items in range, particularly licensed items for TV, films, mascots for sporting events and companies, as well as range of teddy bears.
Am Moos 11, Mörikestraße 2+6, Neustadt/Coburg, Germany.

Ideal Novelty and Toy Company

1902–03 Russian emigrés, Morris Michtom and wife Rose, produce hand-made Teddy's Bears, inspired by Clifford T. Berryman *Washington Post* cartoon, for sale at their novelty and stationery store on Thompson Avenue, Brooklyn, New York. Large scale production and firm is established after wholesalers, Butler Brothers, purchase stock and support Michtom's credit with plush-producing mills.

1907 Moves to larger premises in Brownsville section, 311–317 Christopher Avenue, Brooklyn.

1912 Abraham Katz joins company as co-chairman.

1923 Michtoms' son Benjamin joins firm as co-chairman.

1938 Michtom dies and Benjamin takes over leadership.

1941 Lionel A .Weintraub joins company.

1953 Licensed to produce first "Smokey Bear" (second and third versions follow).

1962 Lionel A. Weintraub becomes president.

1968 Becomes publicly owned firm, The Ideal Toy Corporation, based in Hollis, New York, with new large factory in Newark, New Jersey and production and distribution in Japan, UK, Germany, Canada, Australia, and New Zealand; employs 4,000 people worldwide.

1978 Celebrates 75th anniversary with special issue bear.

1982 Grandson of founder, Mark Michtom sells company to CBS Toys with President Boyd Browne.

1984 Produces collectors' porcelain replica of first Ideal bear, but bears generally removed from production. Hasbro acquires some assets.

Invicta Toys Ltd.

1935 Founded by G.E. Beer and T.B. Wright (former J.K. Farnell director and sales representative, respectively), at Sunbeam Road, Park Royal Road, north-west London. Soft toys designed by Beer include teddy bears Teddy, Grizzlie, and Sammy.
Early 1950s Ceases business.

Jakas Soft Toys

1954 Founded by English couple, Joe and Marion Stanford, at Altona, a seaside suburb of Melbourne, Australia.

1956 Company is registered and moves to Blackburn, Victoria. "Jakas" derived from first and second names of Stanford family members.

c.1962 Produces Big Ted who appears on Australia's longest-running children's programme *Playschool*.

1984 Company is sold, and undergoes two further shortlived ownerships.

1989 Wendy McDonald, present owner, buys company.

1991 Moves to existing site; merges with Koala Mate, makers of fine quality soft-toy Australiania; introduces limited-edition range.
Unit 1, 85 Lewis Road, Wantirna South, Victoria 3152, Australia.

Jocky srl

Post-World War II Founded in Rome. Produces Jockyline soft toys, including Avanti series designed by Riccardo Chiavetta.

1982 World rights bought by Applause (see *Applause Inc*).
Viale Pola 25, 00198, Rome, Italy.

W.H. Jones

1914 William Henry Jones, a German doll manufacturers' agent since early 1900s, establishes soft-toy firm at 48 Red Cross Street, east London, with six workers.

1915 Moves to large, four-floored, modern factory with large basement at 11 Charterhouse Buildings, with 14 power-driven sewing-machines and 46 workers. Opens another factory of similar size a few months later in south-east London at 60–61 Parish Lane, Penge.

c.1925 Moves to 8–10 Great Arthur Street, east London. Introduces Hugyu (kapok) and Shagylox (shaggy mohair) series of soft toys.

1928 Introduces wheeled soft toys, including bear.

1935 Registered as private limited company, W. H. Jones (Toys) Ltd.

1937 Goes into voluntary liquidation.

Joy-Toys Pty. Ltd.

1920s Reputedly Australia's first commercial teddy-bear manufacturer, established by Mr. and Mrs. Gerald Kirby in South Yarra, Victoria; financial backing from Melbourne business friends including Daryl Lindsay.

1930 Moves to larger premises.

1935 Maurice Court joins company.

1937 Court takes over; restructures firm after Kirbys' move to London, where they found G.L. Kirby Ltd.

Late 1930s Business expands, acquiring franchise for Walt Disney characters; produces set of promotional Three Bears for leading Australian manufacturers of oatmeal products, Jas. F. McKenzie Pty. Ltd. Opens another factory in Whangarei, New Zealand.

1966 Cyclops, owned by British Lines Brothers since 1950s, buys Joy-Toys. Operates from 70 Stephenson Street, Richmond, Victoria 3121.

1971 Ceases business following collapse of Lines Brothers; UK-owned Tube Investments purchases firm soon after.

1976 Maurice Court and Toltoys, a toy manufacturer, buy Sydney soft-toy company Sandman Pty. Ltd.

1979 Maurice Court sells his shares to Toltoys.

1980 Sandman Pty. Ltd. closes but Court is able to buy Joy-Toys equipment and tradename for Toltoys.

Jungle Toys

1914 Established by young girl, Miss E.M. Daniels, who worked for six months for various toymakers before setting up on own with two workers at 82 Richmond Road, Earls Court, London.

1919 Factory runs on co-operative system, employing 13–15 assistants; exports worldwide, including Australia.

1928 Registered design The Bingo Bear – a koala bear. Later includes teddy bears in range. Production continues until c.1950.

Kersa (see W. Walters KG)

G.L. Kirby Ltd.

1938 Established by Gerald L. Kirby (founder of Joy-Toys) at 1–3 Golden Lane, east London to produce dolls and soft toys including Australian native animals, and range of kapok-filled teddy bears called Sun Bears, made of finest plush in range of colours – green, white, sky, pink, ruby, scarlet, gold, peach, canary, lemon, cream, dark brown.
No longer in business.
Trademark: round card swing-tag with "Kirby Toys".

Knickerbocker Toy Company Inc.

1850 Established in Albany, New York State to produce toys such as lithographed alphabet blocks.

1920s Introduces teddy bears and other soft toys.

1930s–50s Becomes incorporated company.
*c.*1968 Moves to Middlesex, New Jersey; licensed to produce "Smokey Bear" until 1977.
1982 Wallace Berrie buys firm's Applause gift division.
1980s Ceases business.

Hugo Koch
Post-World War II Probably established by Hugo Koch.
Early 1950s Based at Bahnhofstraße 233, Pressath. Trademark: bear dressed as cook (German *Koch*) with spoon.
1970s Based in nearby Eschenbach/Opf at Pressather Straße18; son also works for firm.
1990 Ceases business.

Käthe Kruse Puppen GmbH
1911 Käthe Kruse establishes company making unique cloth dolls with sculpted faces of painted, pressed muslin (range later includes famous life-sized, weighted *Träumerchen* used by nursery nurses and midwives).
1912 Family moves to Bad Kösen, founding workshop under Käthe Kruse's personal management.
1947 Sons, Michael and Max Kruse, move to West German city of Donauwörth, north-west of Munich, and open dollmaking workshop.
1950 Käthe Kruse leaves East Germany to join sons.
1952–53 Käthe Kruse withdraws from active manage-ment. Michael Kruse emigrates to South Africa, replaced by son-in-law Heinz Adler (married to daughter Hanne) as technical manager; Max Kruse is general manager.
1956 Käthe Kruse retires; her daughter Hanne takes over as designer; products now marked "Modell Hanne Kruse".
1958 Company is incorporated under name Käthe Kruse GmbH. 70% sold to Schildkröt (doll manufacturers); Max keeps 30% then sells his shares to Hanne and Heinz.
1967 Hanne introduces plush and terry-cloth animals, including teddy bears.
1976 Heinz and Hanne Kruse buy back Schildkröt's shares to own company outright.
1990 Hanne Kruse retires; Stephen and Andrea Christenson and family of Prince Albrecht zu Castell-Castell buy firm.
1993 Tag redesigned; red with "Modell Hanne Kruse" and description.
Alte Augsburger Straße 9, 86609, Donauwörth, Germany.
US office: 22 Westover Road, Troy, NY 12180.

Leco Toys (West End) Ltd.
*c.*1950 Husband and wife team Ludwig and Martha Levy start to make soft toys in small back room of house.
1955 March 8, registered as private limited company, based at 361 Edgware Road, in London's West End. Develops successful business specializing in lambskin novelty toys, including nightdress cases and animated musical items for worldwide export. Moves to 186 Campden Hill Road, Kensington.
1965 Moves to modern, one-storey factory twice size of previous premises, in Lyon Road Industrial Estate, Bletchley, Buckinghamshire.
1971 Last mention in trade directories.

Lefray Toys Ltd.
1948 Established as Lefray Ltd., originally based at 52 Golborne Road, west London.
*c.*1958 Moves to 14b South Hill Park, north-west London.
1960 Relocates to a new factory of over 929 square metres (10,000 square feet), enabling modern methods of manufacture and greatly increased production, at 56 Victoria Street, St. Albans, Hertfordshire.
1969 Transfers to Wales where company is still based.
1980s Takes over Real Soft Toys.
*c.*1990 Obtains licence to produce Rupert Bear. Today

Lefray has separate Real Soft Toy range and specializes in custom-made promotional items.
Glandwr Industrial Estate, Aberbeeg, Abertillery, Gwent NP3 2XF, Wales.

Lenci srl
1919 Founded Turin, Italy. Receives worldwide recognition for pressed-felt-headed dolls, many sculpted by well-known Italian artists.
Registered trademark: *Ludus Est Nobis Constanter Industria* (Latin: "To Play Is Our Constant Work") encircles child's spinning top
1922 Trademark shortened to "Lenci".
1931 First traditional teddy bears appear in catalogue. Present-day teddy bears are unjointed, children's toys.
Via San Marino 56 bis 10137 Turin, Italy.

H. Josef Leven
1891 Hubert Josef Leven and Theodor Sprenger found Leven & Sprenger in Sonneberg, Germany, to make toys mainly for export but also for German customers.
1910 Known as H. Josef Leven; manufactures teddy bears.
1912 Employs 10 office and 150 factory workers; one of largest toy firms in Sonneberg. Exports toys worldwide.
1923 Fred Engel (joined firm in 1904 as apprentice) becomes partner and president of company. Later buys remaining shares, becoming joint owner of firm with daughters Hildegard and Dora-Margot.
Post-World War II The company is gradually expropriated from Engel family by communist government.
1951 Dora-Margot Engel marries Rolf-Gerhard Hermann (*see Hermann-Spielwaren GmbH*).
1972 Becomes wholly state-owned.
1990 Communist regime collapses; company buildings and titles officially handed back to Engel daughters.
1992 Hermann-Spielwaren introduces Leven replicas.

Lindee Toys
1944 Established in Australia.
1969 Wins "Toy of the Year".
*c.*1960s Based at 23–25 Daking Street, Parramatta North, New South Wales 2151.
1976 Ceases business.
Trademark: "Lindee Toys", inside outline of seated fawn and "Made in Australia".

Little Folk
1976 Founded by Graham McBride and Maggie Breedon in Devon, England to manufacture soft toy animals. Based at 700-year-old mill employing eight full time staff and 13–14 outworkers.
1980 Produces first teddy bear. Mainly uses top quality acrylic plush, although today the firm produces some limited-edition mohair bears for the collectors' market. At its height, exports worldwide, 70% going to US.
1991 Maggie Breedon dies.
1992 Firm becomes division of Possible Dreams Europe when Graham McBride forms partnership with directors of US company, Possible Dreams Ltd. of Foxboro, Massachusetts. Now also imports figurines. Produces bears for Wendy Phillips of Lakeland Bears.
3 Blackdown Park, Willand, Devon, EX15 2QH, England.

The London Toy Company
1915 Importer of Japanese lacquer and antimony ware establishes soft-toy company at Three Crowns Court, 11 Jewry Street, Aldgate, east London. Specializes in soft toys of plush, felt, and velvet, including teddy bears, for wholesale and export throughout the 1920s.

Luvme Toy Manufacturing Co.
1939 In operation in Auckland, New Zealand, making soft-bodied dolls with hard heads (import control introduced in 1938 resulted in establishment of home-based industries including toy manufacture).

1950s Makes soft toys, including teddy bears, often with Rexine paws and printed black on white cloth label reading "Luvme/Made in NZ".
1970–80s Ceases business.

Malrob Cuddle Toys
1961 Established in Brisbane, Queensland, Australia, to make unjointed bears from synthetic fabrics.
1985 Ceases operation.
Trademark: "Malrob Cuddle Toys; Made in Australia".

Max Hermann Sonneberg (*see Hermann-Spielwaren GmbH*)

Max Hermann & Sohn Sonneberg (*see Hermann-Spielwaren GmbH*)

MCZ
1950s Established in Zürich, Switzerland, using tradename "Mutzli". Company later known as Felpa AG Spielwarenexport, based in Aarau, with tradename "Felpa".
*c.*1990s Ceases business.

AB Merimex
*c.*1947 Founded in Sweden by refugee Emil Grünfelt, to make white, yellow, and brown sheepskin bears. Originally based in Mälmo, St. Göransgatan 12, 21618; production moves to Portugal where bears are still made
Tradename: "Amica".

Merrythought Ltd.
1919 W.G. Holmes and G.H. Laxton open spinning-mill in Oakworth, near Keighley, Yorkshire, England.
1920s Holmes and Laxton buy Dyson Hall & Co. Ltd. of Huddersfield, a mohair-plush-weaving factory.
1930 Merrythought Ltd. founded and trademark registered; leases temporary premises from Coalbrookdale Company. Hires C.J. Rendle from Chad Valley as production director; H.C. Janisch from J.K. Farnell as sales director for London showroom at 113 Holborn; and 20 workers to make soft toys.
1931 Rents larger factory space from Coalbrookdale Company. Leases two-storey building nearby (the Grand Hall) for staff social area. Produces first catalogue, with designs by Florence Atwood, designer from Chad Valley.
1932 Installs electric motors for sewing-machines. Employs more staff.
1935 Factory expands, reputed to be largest soft-toy factory in England.
1939 Produces first panda bear including special commission from London Zoo for stand-in at filming sessions.
World War II British Admiralty and Ministry of Aircraft take over factory for map-making and storage. Moves to temporary premises in Wellington.
1940–43 Company turns to war work, making textile items for armed forces and hospitals.
1946 Toy production reinstated but flooding of River Severn destroys pre-war samples and supplies.
1949 C.J. Rendle dies. Florence Atwood dies. B.T. Holmes (son of founder, W.G. Holmes) joins company.
1952 Hires Jimmy Matthews of Dean & Son Ltd. as sales agent.
1953 Designer Jean Barber, joins company (until 1965).
1955 US compressed-air stuffing machine introduced.
1956 Company buys factory premises from Coalbrookdale Company.
1967 Designer Jackie Harper joins firm (until 1969).
1970 Designer Jacqueline Revitt joins company (leaves 1977, but rejoins 1983).
1972 Oliver Holmes (son of B.T. Holmes, and grandson of W.G. Holmes) joins company.
1982 Collaborates with Tide-Rider Inc., Baldwin,

New York, to export new collectors' range to US.
1986 Publication of John Axe's company history *The Magic of Merrythought* by Hobby House Press, followed by production of first replica Magnet bear.
1988 Merrythought's shop and museum opened.
1990 Produces special, Diamond Jubilee teddy bear to celebrate 60th anniversary.
Dale End, Ironbridge, Telford, Shropshire TF8 7NJ, England.

Mary Meyer Corporation
1933 Established by Mary Meyer.
1993 Mary Meyer's son, Walter, is presently chairman of the board, and grandson, Kevin, is President and Chief Executive Officer. Offers range of collector bears, including Grandma's Bear and 60th anniversary bears. Company sells to over 15,000 retail stores.
Route 30, PO Box 275, Townsend, Vermont, 05353–0275, USA.

Mighty Star Ltd.
1959 Established in Montreal, Canada. Lines include 24K range of teddy bears, licensed characters, as well as collectors' limited editions, created by their designer, Laval Bourque. Products assembled in factories in Korea or China, then returned to Canada for stuffing, finishing, and distribution.
2250 Boulevard de Maisonneuve Est., Montreal, Quebec, H2K 2E5, Canada.

Mulholland & Bailie Ltd.
1971 James Mulholland, former manager of Pedigree's Belfast works (*see Pedigree Soft Toys Ltd.*), sets up own business with colleague, in part of Castlereagh Road, Belfast factory, to produce soft and chassis toys, under brand name "Nylena". Now retired; son runs firm.
407–09 Castlereagh Road, Belfast, Northern Ireland.

Mutzli (*see MCZ*)

House of Nisbet Ltd.
1953 Peggy Nisbet founds Peggy Nisbet Ltd; makes collector portrait dolls at her home in Weston-super-Mare, England. Later moves to larger premises.
1975 Canadian Jack Wilson becomes executive chairman. Employed by Canadian investment company, which (through UK subsidiary) acquires control of Peggy Nisbet Ltd. from Evans & Owens (Drapers) Ltd.
1976 Changes name to House of Nisbet Ltd; introduces first teddy-bear range designed by Peggy Nisbet's daughter, Alison, later Jack Wilson's wife. Based at Dunster Park, Winscombe, Avon BS25 1AG, England.
1979 Initiation of association with Peter Bull, resulting in Bully series of bears and storybooks.
1983 Reprints Peter Bull's popular *The Teddy Bear Book* as limited edition of 10,000.
1984 Publishes collectors' limited edition of Peter Bull and Pauline McMillan's *The Zodiac Bears*.
1986 Celebrates 10th anniversary of House of Nisbet with two limited-edition bears.
1987 Produces replica of Peter Bull's 1907 Delicatessen (Aloysius) to celebrate bear's 80th birthday. Invents process for distressing mohair, using a 1904 velvet-crushing machine, with Norton (Weaving) Ltd.
1989 May 4, Dakin acquires share capital and David Potter, Dakin's Europe/UK managing director, becomes Nisbet's managing director with Jack Wilson as director and honorary chairman. Jack Wilson and family now live in Florida at Calusa Lakes in Sarasota County.
Dakin Inc., PO Box 7746, San Francisco, CA 94120, USA.

North American Bear Co. Inc.
Mid-1970s New Yorker Barbara Isenberg starts company producing uniquely designed, high-quality bears.
1978 Asks fashion designer friend Odl Bauer to make bear out of old sweatshirt, which eventually evolves into Albert the Running Bear. Brother Paul Levy becomes business partner.
1979 First VIBs (Very Important Bears) appear; clothing first made in New York City toy factory and later in Massachusetts dolls' clothes factory. Parts of bears cut out in New York and sewn in Haiti, then returned to US for machine-stuffing. To further reduce costs, some production transfers completely to East Asia.
1982 Barbara goes to Korea to investigate two potential factories. *Adventures of Albert the Running Bear* by Barbara Isenberg and Susan Wolf, illustrated by Dick Gachenbach, is published by Houghton Mifflin.
1983 VanderBear family introduced.
1984 Muffy VanderBear, company's most well-known bear, introduced. Firm's design studio is in Manhattan.
Main office: 401 N Wabash, Suite 500, Chicago, Illinois, 60611, USA.

Nounours
1963 Jacky Dubois founds family business in Brittany, northern France.
1975 Nounours buys Aux Nations; becomes top of range.
1989 Buys Ajena, producing cheaper quality range to sell to chainstores. Nounours is based in a large natural park setting; some of Nounours range made there, others at Djerba factory in Tunisia and Curepipe factory on Mauritius. The Nounours group is responsible for 80% of French soft-toy exports; also produces baby accessories.
Le Roche Bidaine, 35210 Chatillon en Vendelais, France.

Parker Toys
1950s Soft toy and doll manufacturer established in Australia. Based at 390a Lygon Street, Brunswick, Victoria.
1970s Ceases business.

Peacock & Co. Ltd.
1853 Established as Peacock & Sons, London, makers of wooden kindergarten toys and games (dissected maps, puzzles, alphabet blocks, cubes, etc.).
1904 Listed as William Peacock & Co., 3 Adelaide Terrace, Dane Street, north London. Later becomes Peacock Bros., a partnership between Albert Frank and William Edward Peacock.
1918 July 29, dissolves by mutual consent when Albert is called up for military service; William Peacock registers firm as Peacock & Co. Ltd., operating from both Adelaide Terrace and 2 Prebend Street after World War I.
1931 Chad Valley purchases Peacock & Co. Ltd., moves to modern factory at 175–79 St. John Street, Clerkenwell, east London, and incorporates wooden toys into programme, while manufacturing new range of teddy bears with Peacock label at Chad Valley factory.
1939 Last mention in London trade directory, listed as A. & A. Peacock Ltd., First Avenue House, High Holborn, London.

Pedigree Soft Toys Ltd.
Mid-nineteenth century G. & J. Lines Ltd. established in London by two brothers, George and Joseph Lines, to make wooden toys and baby carriages.
1919 Joseph Lines's three sons, William, Arthur, and Walter, establish Lines Bros. Ltd. in London's Old Kent Road.
1924 Firm moves into new purpose-built factory on 11 hectares (27 acres) in Morden Road, Merton, south-west London. "Tri-ang Toys" registered as trademark, with triangular symbol representing three brothers. Produces mainly large wooden and metal toys (cars, bicycles, prams, nursery furniture, rocking horses), but reported to be also producing fur, felt, and plush toys.
*c.*1931 "Pedigree" registered as trademark for prams.

1937 First catalogue produced by Pedigree Soft Toys Ltd., offering "Pedigree Pets" (soft toys) and "Pedigree Dolls"; operates from Merton Tri-ang Works.
1946 Lines buys Australian-owned Joy-Toys Ltd. factory at Whangarei, North Island, New Zealand, and founds Lines Bros. (NZ) Ltd., later building large factory in Auckland suburb of Tamaki where manufactures "Made in NZ" Pedigree soft toys. Builds factory at 407–09 Castlereagh Road, Belfast (opened October by Countess Granville, wife of Governor of Northern Ireland and sister of HM the Queen Mother) for production of "Made in Ireland" Pedigree soft and chassis toys.
1950 Lines merges activities of subsidiaries, International Model Aircraft Ltd. (plastic division) and Pedigree Soft Toys, the former making and marketing both products.
1951 Lines buys Rovex Plastics Ltd., of Richmond, Surrey, building new factory for them in Margate, Kent; acquires 50% interest in Australia's Cyclops Company, forming Cyclops and Lines Bros. (Aust.) Ltd. Lines' factories in Australia and South Africa do not produce soft toys.
1955 Buys remaining 50% of Australia's Cyclops Company; all UK soft-toy production moves to Belfast.
1966 Lines-owned Cyclops buys Joy-Toys Ltd. in Victoria, Australia. Reorganization of Lines Bros. Group companies results in formation of Rovex Tri-ang Ltd. Belfast factory eventually closes and UK soft-toy production transfers to Canterbury, England.
1971 Rovex Tri-ang Ltd. collapses.
1972 Taken over by Dunbee-Combex-Marx.
1988 Canterbury factory closes; Pedigree ceases business.

Petz Company
1948 Company founded in Neustadt; name of firm derived from German colloquial word for bear. Makers of traditional mohair bears with glass button trademark until 1974, exporting to both US and rest of Europe.

M. Pintel Fils & Cie.
*c.*1918 Established in Paris to make soft toy animals, caricatures, dolls, and teddy bears in range of quality, length of pile, and size, as well as tumbling example.
*c.*1924 Firm exports to UK where exhibits at showrooms of Messrs. Ellis & Amiet, 2 Finsbury Square, London. Boot-button eyes used until 1930s when replaced with glass, with uniquely coloured, painted backs. Pre-World War II bears have very elongated, slender bodies with humped backs and felt pads. Later known as Pintel & Frères.
World War II One of brothers dies in prison; design of bears subsequently changes.
1950s Bears have very short bodies and relatively long legs; plastic noses introduced; firm also produces mechanical bears such as those on bikes or with hula-hoops.
1960s Pintel continues to use kapok and wood-wool stuffing, refusing to produce fully washable bears like those introduced by Boulgom; business declines and eventually ceases.
Trademark: Embossed brass-plated chest-button with embracing bears and "PF France".

Plummer, Wandless & Co Ltd.
1946 April 1, sheepskin soft-toy business established in West Worthing, Sussex, England, by John Plummer and Dudley Wandless with staff of one. Expands greatly over next decade.
1955 Forms subsidiary company to distribute baby linen and nursery accessories.
1957 March 29, registered as private limited company.
1958 Takes over London-based W.H. Kendal Ltd., manufacturers of children's playsuits, tents, and wigwams. Builds new factory at Station Road, East

Preston, Sussex to bring all concerns under one roof. Teddy bear – most popular item – is sold to major stores and exported overseas, particularly to Canada.
1972 Business sold to one of their agents. Tradename "Tinka-Bell", after fairy in J.M.Barrie's *Peter Pan*.

Prima Toys Pty. Ltd. *(see Speciality Manufacturers)*

Real Soft Toys
1969 Founded by R.M. Francis and son N.J. Francis, formerly of Radio Electronic Engineering where they first produced soft toys. Based at Unit 7, Sandown Road Industrial Estate, Watford, Hertfordshire, England. Range includes teddy bears made of real mink fur.
1980s Taken over by Lefray Toys *(see Lefray Toys Ltd.)*

Robbity Bob Ltd.
1972 Established by Robin Rive of Auckland, New Zealand, designing and manufacturing soft-toy collectables
1989 Introduces antique-style, hand-made teddy bears under label "Countrylife New Zealand", including limited editions; largest bear manufacturer in New Zealand. *58 Elizabeth Knox Place, Auckland 6, New Zealand.*

SAF
Post-World War II Manufacturer of teddy bears based in or near Mittendorf, Austria.
No longer in business.

H. Scharrer & Koch GmbH
1856 Trading and export company for beads and toys founded at Friedrichstraße 7, Bayreuth, Germany, by Nuremberg merchant Heinrich Scharrer. Later establishes branch offices in Venice and Gablonz (Bohemia). Scharrer's father-in-law, Christian Koch, owner of Bayreuth's Hotel Sonne joins company soon after foundation.
1872 Bruno Müller from Coburg (Scharrer's son-in-law) appointed managing director.
1900 Theodor Köhler joins as apprentice, later rounding off his commercial training during eight years in England.
1912 Köhler buys company from Müller (continues to manage company until 1930s, exporting exclusively beads; dies aged 87 in 1969).
1968 Grandchildren Sigrid and Josef Gottstein take over, introducing aesthetically pleasing wooden and soft toys for babies; new tradename: "Sigikid" derived from Mrs. Gottstein's first name and English word "kid".
1972 New factory opens at nearby village of Mistelbach for production of ladies', children's, and babies' clothing.
1977 Plush animals introduced to toy range, with independent production line developed at Fürth im Wald, for worldwide export.
1984 Vinyl dolls introduced.
1986 Wooden marionettes introduced.
1989–92 First artist doll collections introduced in vinyl, porcelain, and felt.
1991 Collectors' limited-edition plush animals first introduced; all plush animals in recyclable cotton bags.
1992 Firm first enters replica market with Miro Collection, helping to re-establish Czech firm *(see Hamiro)*. *Am Wolfsgarten 8, 8581 Mistelbach, Germany.*

Schenker
1952 Established by Martin Schenker at Glockenspielplatz 6, A-8010 Graz, Austria, to produce principally sheepskin soft toys.
1975 Company sold to Michael Rosen; operates from same premises until 1982 when ceases business.

Schreyer & Company
1912 November 16, founded by Heinrich Müller, former Gebrüder Bing employee, and Heinrich Schreyer,

former furniture salesman at Rohnstraße 10, Nuremberg, Germany.
1913 First advertisement appears for "Tipp-Tapp-Tiere" wheeled animals, including bear. Moves to Celtisstraße17.
1914–18 Factory closes for duration of World War I; both partners are drafted into military service.
1918 Schreyer leaves business and Müller takes on new partner, wholesaler Adolf Kahn.
1919 Firm moves to Singerstraße 26.
1921 "Schuco" abbreviation of company name, adopted as official trademark.
1929 Firm moves to larger, four-storey premises at Fürther Straße 28–32.
1936 Following Hitler's rise to power in 1933, Adolf Kahn, a Jew, leaves company.
1939 Kahn and wife move to England.
1940 Join son Eric Kahn in US.
World War II Müller recruits Alexander Girz as manager of factory which operates as war plant, making telephone equipment; bombed several times.
1946–49 Operates at quarter capacity making household hardware and toys on small scale.
1947 Adolf Kahn and son Eric establish Schuco Toy Co. Inc. in US with import rights to all Schuco products for US and Canada.
1958 June 3, Müller dies and only son Werner takes over business along with manager Alexander Girz.
1960s–70s Firm sells toys produced by division, Herta Girz & Co. with trademark "Hegi" (Mrs. Herta Girz directs production), which operates within Schuco premises at Fürther Straße 32.
1976 Collaboration between Hegi and Munich-based Anker *(see Anker Plüschspielwarenfabrik GmbH)*, their toys sold by Schuco *(see Schuco)*. Company under management of Klaus Albrecht.
Company is sold to leading toy manufacturers, Dunbee-Combex-Marx as unable to compete with Japanese toy industry.
Schuco trademark is sold to Georg Adam Mangold GmbH & Co. KG, Large Straße 69–75, 8510 Fürth/Bayern, Germany, which it uses for replica model cars. Replica Schuco miniature bears made by Heike-Bär *(see Heike-Bär)*.

Schuco *(see Schreyer & Company)*

Schwika
Post-World War II Manufacturer of teddy bears based at Graz, Austria. No longer in business.

Shanghai Dolls Factory
Post-World War II Manufacturer making teddy bears on mainland China, bearing printed, paper rosette label with trademark "SDF". Teddy bears also exist wearing card tags that read "Shanghai Toys Factory" and give address 159 Puan Road, Shanghai.

Sheepskin Products Ltd.
1981 Founded by Peter and Valda McCombe in Auckland, New Zealand. Company produces widest range of sheepskin toys in world. All products are designed by Valda and each one is hand-clipped and finished. *66c Barrys Point Road, Takapuna, Auckand, New Zealand.*

Sigikid *(see H. Scharrer & Koch GmbH)*

The South Wales Toy Manufacturing Co. Ltd.
1915 Established at 49 Salisbury Road, Cardiff, Wales, to make teddy bears, soft toys, printed calico dolls, and cloth balls for supplying wholesalers and export only. Employs French lady cutter with 11 years' experience in soft-toy-making, Mr. Gigot as manager, and Mr. Joseph Layfield as sales agent.

Trademark: "Madingland".
Ceases business during inter-war period.

Speciality Manufacturers
1951 Australian George Weir (originally soft-toy manufacturer Bunky Doo, Hurstville South, Sydney) establishes small factory, Ark Toys, at Escombe, Natal, South Africa; produces range of golden mohair jointed bears and black and white pandas, using imported mohair (from Nortons, UK), local wood-wool, imported Ceylon kapok, masonite joints with split pins, imported German glass eyes, voice-boxes, and squeakers. Moves to larger site as demand for teddies grows, but increased costs in raw materials and competition from East Asian imports forces firm to concentrate on economy range in rayon and nylon.
1970 Sold business; becomes division of Prima Toys Pty. Ltd., large toy company based in Cape Town. George
Weir remains managing director; son is later appointed a director. Teddy bears continue to be made at Pinetown, outside Durban. Cloth label has both "Prima Toys" and "Ark Toys" trademarks and "Speelgoede". *39 Richmond Road, Pinetown, 3600/PO Box 10307, Ashwood, 3605, Republic of South Africa.*

Margarete Steiff GmbH
1877 Margarete Steiff opens Felt Mail Order company to make felt underskirts and children's clothes in hometown, Giengen, Germany.
1880 Introduces animal toys to range after success of little felt elephant pin-cushion she had adapted from magazine pattern.
1889 Moves to larger premises in Muehlstraße.
1893 March 3, registers business as the Felt Toy Co.
1897 Nephew Richard Steiff joins company to develop range of soft toy animals.
1902–05 Experiments with jointed bear design culminate in Bär 35 PAB (registered 12 February 1905).
1905 May 13 "button in ear" trademark registered.
1902–08 Factory expands three times to meet enormous demand for teddy bears: this time of high productivity and expansion is called the *Bärenjahre* (Bear Years).
1906 Re-registered as Margarete Steiff GmbH, private limited liability company with Margarete Steiff's nephews, Paul, Richard, and Franz-Josef as managing directors.
World War I All three brothers enlist, and factory is used for making war supplies.
c.1920 Conveyor-belt system is introduced.
1930s New managerial staff, hand-picked by Nazi regime, replaces some Steiff family members.
1943 Factory makes munitions for war effort.
1950 Full production and trade resume after lifting of war-time restrictions.
1953 Celebrates 50th anniversary of Steiff teddy bear.
1958 Celebrates 100th anniversary of Theodore (Teddy) Roosevelt's birth.
1965 Subsidiary branch, the Steiff Toy Company founded in Grieskirchen, Austria, to establish better export facilities.
1980 Produces first replica, heralding new successful era of expansion throughout 1980s. Opens museum and publishes an account of company's history, *Button In Ear* by Jürgen and Marianne Cieslik.
1992 Celebrates 90 years of Steiff teddy bear, and begins Steiff Collectors Club on 1 April. *Alleenstraße 2, D-7928, Giengen/Brenz, Germany.*

H.G. Stone & Co. Ltd.
1919 Leon Rees inherits Chiltern Toy Works on death of his father-in-law and business partner, Josef Eisenmann of Eisenmann & Co. *(see Eisenmann & Co. Ltd.)*; leaves company to lease large building at 12 New

Union Street, east London, forming L. Rees & Co., wholesaler of fancy goods, houseware, and toys, and distributor of Bing products (and later Chiltern Toys) in Britain and Commonwealth.
1920 Collaborates with Harry Stone, formerly of J.K. Farnell and forms H.G. Stone & Company, to manufacture soft toys at Chiltern Toy Works, Chesham, Buckinghamshire, moves from Bellingdon Road to larger premises at Waterside. Leon Rees responsible for marketing and sales, Harry Stone for design and manufacture.
1921 Opens second factory – Grove Works – at Grove Road, Tottenham, north London.
1923 "Chiltern Toys" tradename first appears in trade journals (registered 1924), and "Hugmee" teddy-bear range introduced.
1925 Takes over production of "Panurge Pets" of Edinburgh, large soft toys modelled from life by artist Ann Cameron Banks of Paris Salon des Humoristes.
1929 Firm builds new factory, Chiltern Works, Bernard Road, South Tottenham; all production transfers here from old Tottenham factory. Introduces "Silky Teddy", firm's first artificial silk plush bear.
1932 December 31, registered as private limited company.
1934 November 20, Harry Stone dies.
1940 Toy-making ceases at Chesham factory, but some toys made throughout war at London headquarters.
1945 Soft toys made at Amersham Works, Chesham, another Rees-owned wooden-toy factory.
1946 February, training school established at new factory in process of being built on five-acre site near Pontypool, Monmouthshire in Wales.
1947 New factory in operation; managed by Mr. Thwaites. London offices moved to 31–35 Wilson St., east London.
1957 Pamela Williams joins as assistant designer to Madeleine Biggs; takes over as chief designer when Madeleine is in South Africa for four to five years.
1960 Amersham Toy Works, Chesham, closes.
1963 July 23, Leon Rees dies.
1964 Both Rees and Chiltern companies taken over by Dunbee-Combex group. Chiltern Fairy Foam (one-piece, plastic, foam filling) introduced.
1967 Becomes subsidiary of Chad Valley (see The Chad Valley Co. Ltd.), resulting in Chiltern/Chad Valley label.

Strauss Manufacturing Co. Inc.
1907 Described as "the Toy King", based at 395 Broadway, Dept 1, New York City. Manufactures toys, games, and musical novelties; produces novelty teddy bears during height of US teddy-bear craze.

Gebrüder Süssenguth
1894 Founded by the Süssenguth brothers in Neustadt, Bavaria, to make dolls' bodies and composition heads for German doll industry.
c.1925 Company manufactures unique but then unpopular "Peter" bear, introducing doll-making techniques to traditional teddy-bear design.

Tara Toys (see Gaeltarra Eireann)

Teddy & Friends: The Bear Essentials
Unique Australian firm that manufactures as well as wholesales and retails its teddy bears.
Firm developed from single retail store in Neutral Bay, New South Wales in early 1980s. Bears are designed by Carole Williams, and manufactured principally in Korea.
Section 3, 57 Hereford Street, Glebe, NSW 2037 Australia.

The Teddy Toy Company
1914 Established by Beresford Charles Hope and Abraham Simmonds at 45 Golden Lane and 78 Fann

Street, east London. Claims to be largest manufacturer of teddy bears in Britain during World War I.
1920 February, firm patents "Softanlite" kapok-stuffed teddy bears, first of kind in Britain. Uses circular printed card-tag: "Original 'Softanlite' Toys British Made" with letters "TT Co." intertwined.
1930 Produces Winnie the Pooh range of soft toys and board game.
Mid-1930s Moves to Nicholls Buildings, Playhouse Yard, east London; Abraham Simmonds assisted by son Harry, who later takes over management.
1937 Transfers to purpose-built factory at Oxlow Lane, Dagenham, Essex.
1939 Moves to Duke Street, Fenton, Stoke-on-Trent, Staffordshire, to avoid Blitz; produces war materials.
1943 Becomes private limited company.
1945 Becomes known as T.T. Industries Ltd.
1951 Firm goes into voluntary liquidation.

W.J. Terry
1890 William J. Terry claimed to have first established soft-toy business in Stoke Newington, north London.
1909 "Skin merchant and soft-fur-toy manufacturer", opens large, new factory at 25 Middleton Road, Hackney, making name through "Terry'er" soft toy dog, based on King Edward VII's dog, Caesar. "Terry'er" and dog with tag reading "I am Caesar" later registered as trademark.
1913 Operates from Welbury Works, 96 & 96a Lavender Grove, Hackney.
Introduces "Billy Owlett" to "challenge the supremacy of the teddy bear".
1915 Extends premises, taking adjoining building.
c.1919 Produces teddy bears with webbed claws.
1921 "Ahsolight" trademark, indicating kapok first used.
1924 February 3, William Terry dies; son Frederick B. Terry continues business with sales agent J. Hopkins, working from London showrooms, 93 Aldersgate Street. Ceases business by World War II.

Thiennot
1919 Founded in converted barn in Piney, near Troyes in the Champagne region of France by Émile Thiennot. Uses "Le Jouet Champenois" tradename; works for local wholesalers at first, later hiring his own representatives.
1920 Wins a bronze medal for a teddy-bear design in famous Lépine competition run by the Association of French small manufacturers and inventors.
1949 André, youngest son of Emile and Georgette Thiennot, joins firm as an apprentice for 3 years.
1957 Tradename "Le Jouet Champenois" replaced by "Création Tieno".
1959 André Thiennot takes over the management; firm subsequently expands during the 1960s.
1978 Current economic crisis results in selling off Jeux Mercier and Bondrôle enterprises. Launches TV campaign for "Sleepy" small bears with sleeping eyes.
1989 "Petitou" plush toys for babies, including pyjama cases, and "Coati" exotic animal range launched for 70th anniversary. Standard "Tieno" range continues.
1992-93 Produces 1920 replica "Emile"; limited edition of 25, in four sizes. André Thiennot is current President Director General; his son Rémy is Production Director.
BP 6, rue du Stade, 10220 Piney, France.

Tinka-Bell (see Plummer, Wandless & Co. Ltd.)

Twyford (see Acton Toycraft Ltd.)

Verna Toys
1941 Established by Eve Barnett as home-based doll-making concern; moves to large shop in Bay Street, Brighton, Victoria, Australia.
1948 Arthur Eaton buys company, introducing tradename "Verna" and teddy bears to range.
Mid-1980s Ceases business.

W. Walter KG
1925 Founded by Wilhelmine Walter in Lobositz (which was then in Bohemia) about 48 kilometres (30 miles) north of Prague. Wilhelmine originally made teddy bears and other soft toys and puppets for her daughters.
1948 Moves company to Mindelheim, Germany, producing teddy bears, cats, dwarfs, and Easter hares.
Until c.1956 Bears have metal tags with "Kersa" on base of feet.
c.1960 Teddy production ceases; company concentrates on producing range of cloth and wooden puppets. Founder's grandson, Walter Schubert, now manages firm.
Trademark: "Kersa" derived from "Künstlerisch Erzeugte Spielsachen" (meaning "artistically produced playthings").
Ifenstraße 7, D-8948 Mindelheim, Germany.

Norah Wellings
1927 Previously designer of soft toys for Chad Valley, established own business at Victoria Toy Works, Wellington, Shropshire, England.
Trademark: "Norah Wellings Productions" with little girl in large bonnet printed on card swing-tag, as well as permanent embroidered labels.
1929 Moves into new premises, King Street Hall, Wellington, formerly Baptist chapel and latterly local Freemasons' temple. Soon employs around 150 workers.
1935 London showrooms operate at 19 Regent Arcade House, 254 Regent Street, W1; Mr. A. Ferriday becomes sales manager.
1959 Death of Norah Welling's brother, her business partner, prompts winding-up of business the following year.

The Wholesale Toy Company
1914 Soft-toy and doll manufacturers established at 52a Blackstock Road, Finsbury Park, north London, as a result of ban on German goods during World War I.
1916 Firm introduces Hercules series of wheeled animals, including bears in five sizes.
Trademark: "Hercules Brand" with Hercules holding scroll with "W.T. Co. Toys".
1921 Patents Blinka rolling eyes for teddy bears and soft-toy animals.
Ceases business by World War II.

Worthing Toy Factory Ltd.
Post-World War I Established business at Broadwater Road (later Station Road Works), Worthing, Sussex, England.
Trademark: Humpty Dumpty Toys (Humpty Dumpty figure smoking long pipe).
Ceases business by World War II.

The Zoo Toy Company
c.1920 Joseph Burman, merchant previously dealing in South African goods, establishes London firm at 32–36 Whitecross Street, east London, specializing in novelty fur, felt, and plush mascots including teddy bears, but also importing other toys and games.
1926 In partnership with A J Burman.
1929 Although used previously, trademark "Fondle Toy: in every way they're safe for play" is now registered.
1931 Becomes limited company, with directors F. Burman and K.C. Groombridge (managing director since 1920s).
World War II Based at 9–11 London Lane, east London; reduces production to supply export and registered customers only.
1950s Still in production.
No longer in business.

Useful Addresses

TEDDY-BEAR MUSEUMS, SHOPS, CLUBS, AND MAGAZINES

The following international list of useful addresses includes those of specialist teddy-bear stores, museums, clubs, and magazines. The addresses are arranged by country, and each address is preceded by one of three symbols, which indicates whether it is that of a specialist teddy-bear shop 💲, a teddy-bear museum 🏛, or a teddy-bear club/magazine 🐻. At the end of the main country-by-country list, a separate section gives the addresses of major teddy-bear manufacturers throughout the world that are still in business. All addresses included on these pages were correct at the time of publication.

AUSTRALIA

💲 **Bronte's Teddy Bears & Country Wares**
137–41 Victoria Street
W. Melbourne
Victoria 3003

💲 **Dolls & Bears in the Attic**
129 High Street
Kew
Victoria 3101

💲 **Enchanted Bears**
76 Mount Eliza Way
Mount Eliza
Victoria 3930

💲 **Numbat Books**
PO Box 50
Frankston
Victoria 3199

💲 **Quaint Collectibles**
PO Bag 503
Moss Vale
NSW 2577

💲 **Second Childhood**
Shop 11
Claremont Court
Guydri Street
Claremont
WA 6010

💲 **The Teddy Bear Shop**
Shop 6
434 Hay Street
Subiaco
WA 6008

💲 **The Teddy Bear Shop**
28 Regent Arcade
Adelaide
SA 5000

💲 **The Teddy Bear Shop**
Shop 9, Double Bay Plaza
19–27 Cross Street
Double Bay
NSW 2028

💲 **The Teddy Bear Shop**
Shop DF12
Level One, Canberra Centre
City Walk
Canberra
ACT 2600

💲 **The Teddy Bear Shop**
145 Collins Street
Hobart
Tasmania 7000

💲 **The Teddy Bear Shop**
Shop 2
162 Military Road
Neutral Bay
NSW 2089

💲 **Teddy & Friends**
Shop 124a, Chatswood Chase
Chatswood
NSW 2067

💲 **The Twig**
4 Piccadilly Arcade
Perth
WA 6000

🐻 **Bear Facts Review**
PO Box 503
Moss Vale
NSW 2577

🐻 **In Teddies We Trust**
PO Box 297
Rosebery
NSW 2018

AUSTRIA

🏛 **Spielzeugmuseum**
Bürgerspitalgasse 2
A-5020 Salzburg

BELGIUM

🏛 **Musée du Jouet**
Rue de l'Association
2400 Brussels

🏛 **Speelgoed Museum**
Nekkerspoel 21
2800 Mechelen

CANADA

💲 **Banff Bears**
2nd Floor, Banff Avenue Mall
Banff
Alberta T0L 0C0

💲 **Bears Galore**
396 Academy Road
Winnipeg
Manitoba R3N 0B8

💲 **Fascination Dolls & Teddies**
24 Queen Street East
Cambridge
Ontario N3C 2A6

💲 **The Historic Martin House Dolls and Bears**
46 Centre Street
Thornhill
Ontario L4J 1E9

💲 **The Teddy Bear Garden Limited**
557 Mount Pleasant Road
Toronto
Ontario M4S 2M5

💲 **Teddy Bear Magic**
138 Mill Street
Georgetown
Ontario L7G 2C1

💲 **The Teddy Bear's Picnic**
205–2205 Oak Bay Avenue
Victoria
British Columbia V8R 1G4

💲 **Teddies To Go**
1783 Hamilton Street
Regina
Saskatchewan S4P 2B4

💲 **Treasures and Toys**
10436 82nd Avenue
Edmonton
Alberta T6E 2A2

🐻 **BC T-Bear**
7576 Humphries Crescent
Burnaby
British Columbia V3N 3E9

🐻 **Bearly Ours Teddy Bear Club**
18 Welsford Gardens
313 Don Mills
Ontario M3A 2P5

🐻 **Good Bears of the World**
PO Box 69548
Station K
Vancouver
British Columbia V5K 4W7

Good Bears of the World
PO Box 982
Elora
Ontario N0B 1S0

The Peterborough Teddies
1333 Sandalwood Drive
Peterborough
Ontario K9K 1Y1

Teddy Bear Collectors Association of Alberta
PO Box 3056
Sherwood Park
Alberta T8A 2A6

Teddy Bear Tymes
7 Whiteoak Drive
St. Catharines
Ontario L2M 3B3

Vancouver Island Club Ted
6441 Rodolph Road
Victoria
British Columbia V8Z 5W3

Victorian Harvester: Dolls and Teddy Bears
438 Draycott Street
Coquitlam
British Columbia V3K 5K2

FRANCE

Club Français de l'Ours
70 Rue du Docteur Sureau
93160 Noisy Le Grand

Teddy's Patch, Le Club des Amis de l'Ours
34 Rue Lieu de Santé
76000 Rouen

GERMANY

Teddybären und Plüsch
Dossenheimer Landstrasse 64
6900 Heidelberg

Berni Brumm's Teddymuseum
Hauptstrasse 98
8751 Leidersbach

Deutsches Puppen – und Barenmuseum "Loreley"
Sonnegasse 8
5401 St. Goar

Spielzeugmuseum in Alten Rathaustrum
Sammlung Ivan Steiger
Marienplatz 15
8000 München 2

Margarete Steiff Museum
Alleenstrasse 2
Postfach 1560
D-7928 Giengen (Brenz)

THE NETHERLANDS

Käthe Kruse Poppenmuseum
Binnenhaven 25
1781 BK Den Helder

Speelgoedmuseum
Sint Vincentiusstraat 86
4901 GL Oosterhout

Beer Bericht/Berenfanclub
Prinzengracht 1089
1017 JH Amsterdam

NEW ZEALAND

Bear Essentials
648 Dominion Road
Balmoral
Auckland

Bears on Broadway
272 Broadway
Newmarket
Auckland

Mr. Bear's Gift Factory
Shop 28, Queen's Arcade
Queen Street
Auckland

Not Just Bears
137 Victoria Street
Christchurch

Teddy's Toy Box
565 Colombo Street
Christchurch

Bears Unlimited
PO Box 96120
Balmoral
Auckland

Teddy Bear Express Club
PO Box 31195
Ham
Christchurch

The Wellington Teddy Bear Club
34 Park Avenue
Waikanae 6454

SOUTH AFRICA

Bear Basics
The Railway Station
Simon's Town 7995

Bear Collection
Box 13091
Northmead
Benoni 1510

SWITZERLAND

Spielzeugmuseum
Baselstrasse 34
CH-4125 Richen

UNITED KINGDOM

Asquiths Teddy Bear Shop
10 George V Place
Thames Avenue
Windsor
Berkshire SL4 1QP
(branches also in Henley-on-Thames and Eton)

Bears & Friends
32 Meeting House Lane
Brighton
East Sussex BN1 1HB

Bears-on-the-Wold
11 Talbot Court
Sheep Street
Stow-on-the-Wold
Gloucestershire GL54 1AA

Bramwell Brown's Hug Shop
21–23 Church Road
Holywood
Co. Down BT18 9BU

Collector Teddy Bears
24 Journeaux Street
St. Helier
Jersey C.I.

Dolly Land
862–64 Green Lanes
Winchmore Hill
London N21 2RS

Margaret and Gerry Grey's Teddy Bear Shop
The Old Bakery Gallery
38 Cambridge Street
Wellingborough
Northamptonshire NN8 1DW

Growlies of Glasgow
11 Springfield Woods
Ravenscourt Park
Johnstone
Strathclyde PA5 8JR

Heather's Teddys
World Famous Arcade
177 Portobello Road
London W11 2DY

Pam Hebbs
No. 5 The Annexe
Camden Passage
Islington
London N1 8EU

Lakeland Bears
2 Crag Brow
Bowness-on-Windermere
Cumbria LA23 3BX

Merrythought Ltd.
Dale End
Ironbridge
Telford
Shropshire TF8 7NJ

Paddington & Friends
1 Abbey Street
Bath
Avon BA1 1NN

Sue Pearson Antique Dolls & Teddy Bears
13½ Prince Albert Street
The Lanes
Brighton
East Sussex BN1 1HE

Pooh Corner
High Street
Hartfield
East Sussex TN7 4AE

Recollect Studios
The Old School
London Road
Sayers Common
West Sussex BN6 9HX

**Teddy Bears
of Witney**
99 High Street
Witney
Oxfordshire OX8 6LY

The Bear Museum
38 Dragon Street
Petersfield
Hampshire GU31 4JJ

**Bethnal Green Museum
of Childhood**
Cambridge Heath Road
London E2 9PA

**The Cotswold
Teddy Bear Museum**
76 High Street
Broadway
Worcester WR12 7AJ

**The London Toy &
Model Museum**
21–23 Craven Hill
London W2 3EN

Museum of Childhood
42 High Street
Edinburgh
Lothian EH1 1TG

Pollock's Toy Museum
1 Scala Street
London W1P 1LT

**Ribchester Museum
of Childhood**
Church Street
Ribchester
Lancashire PR3 3YE

Sooty's World
Windmill Manor
Leeds Road
Shipley
West Yorkshire BD18 1BP

The Teddy Bear Museum
19 Greenhill Street
Stratford-upon-Avon
Warwickshire CV37 6LF

Teddy Melrose
The High Street
Melrose
Roxburghshire TD6 9PA

**Toy & Teddy
Bear Museum**
373 Clifton Drive North
St. Annes
Lytham St. Annes
Lancashire FY8 2PA

The Wareham Bears
18 Church Street
Wareham
Dorset BH20 4NF

Bear Friends
Mount Windsor
Farnahoe
Innishannon
Co. Cork
Republic of Ireland

**Colour Box
Collectors' Club**
High Tweed Mill
King Street
Galashiels
Selkirkshire TD1 1PX

**Good Bears
of the World (UK)**
256 St. Margaret's Road
Twickenham
Middlesex TW1 1PR

**Hugglets Teddy Bear
Magazine/British Teddy Bear
Association**
PO Box 290
Brighton
East Sussex BN2 1DR

Midland Good Bears
40 Fairfax Road
Sutton Coldfield
West Midlands B75 7JX

Paddington's Action Club
Action Research
Vincent House
North Parade
Horsham
West Sussex RH12 2DA

Steiff Collectors Club (UK)
c/o Ingram Public Relations
69–71 High Street
Epsom
Surrey KT19 8DH

Teddy Bear Times
Shelley House
104 High Street
Steyning
West Sussex BN44 3RD

UNITED STATES

The Bear Care Co.
Suite 957-F, 505 S. Beverly Drive
Beverly Hills
CA 90212

The Bear-ee Patch
Suite 107
2461 San Diego Avenue
San Diego
CA 92110

Bear in Mind
53 Bradford Street
Concord
MA 01742

Bears N Things
14191 Bacon Road
Albion
NY 14411

Bears N Wares
312 Bridge Street
New Cumberland
PA 17070

The Calico Teddy
22 E. 24th Street
Baltimore
MD 21218

The Cross-eyed Bear
PO Box 630061
Miami
FL 33163

Cynthia's Country Store
11496 Pierson Road #C–1
West Palm Beach
FL 33414

Dreamland Toys
Suite G, 555 West Lambert
Brea
CA 92621

Edinburgh Imports Inc.
PO Box 722
Woodland Hills
CA 91365-0722

Grin & Bear It
20 W. Chicago Avenue
Naperville
IL 60540

**Harper
General Store**
RD 2
PO Box 512
Annville
PA 17003

Now & Then
20 Powder Horn Road
Ardsley
NY 10502

The Rare Bear
21 Mill Hill Road
Woodstock
NY 12498

**Tailor Maid Togs
for Teddy Bears**
4037 161st St. SE
Bellevue
WA 98006

The Toy Store
Franklin Park Mall
5001 Monroe Street
Toledo
OH 43623

**Aunt Len's Doll
and Toy Museum**
6 Hamilton Terrace
New York
NY 10031

**The Carrousel Shop
and Museum**
505 W. Broad Street
Chesaning
MI 48616

**Children's Museum
of Indianapolis**
PO Box 3000
Indianapolis
IN 46206

**Theodore Roosevelt
Birthplace**
28 E. 20th Street
New York
NY 10003

🏛 **Margaret Woodbury Strong Museum**
1 Manhattan Square
Rochester
NY 14607

🏛 **Teddy Bear Castle Museum**
431 Broad Street
Nevada City
CA 95959

🏛 **Teddy Bear Museum of Naples**
2511 Pine Ridge Road
Naples
FL 33942

📷 **American Teddy Bear Artists Guild**
PO Box 66823
Scotts Valley
CA 95067

📷 **Bill Boyd's Teddy Bear Jubilee MO-Kan Teddy Bear Society**
4922 State Line
Westwood Hills
KS 66205

📷 **Good Bears of the World**
PO Box 13097
Toledo
OH 43613

📷 **Robert Raikes Collectors Club**
PO Box 82
Mt. Shasta
CA 96067

📷 **Theodore Roosevelt Association**
PO Box 719
Oyster Bay
NY 11771

📷 **Teddy Bear Artists Association**
PO Box 905
Woodland Hills
CA 91365

📷 **Teddy Bear and Friends**
900 Frederick St.
Cumberland
MD 21502

📷 **The Teddy Bear Review**
PO Box 1239
Hanover
PA 17331

📷 **Teddy Bear Times**
3150 State Line Road
Cincinnati
North Bend
OH 45052

📷 **The Teddy Tribune**
254 W. Sidney Street
St. Paul
MN 55107

📷 **S.M.A.L.L. (The Society of Miniature Arctophiles Loving and Learning)**
951 S. Copper Key Ct.
Gilbert
AZ 85234

📷 **Muffy Vanderbear Club**
North American Bear Co. Inc.
401 N. Wabash
Suite 500
Chicago
IL 60611

MANUFACTURERS

Althans KG
Horberstrasse 4
8632 Neustadt Birkig
Germany

Les Créations Anima
Parc des Acqueducs
69230 Saint Genis Laual
France

Applause Inc.
6101 Variel Avenue
PO Box 4183
Woodland Hills
CA 91367-4183
USA

Baumann & Kienel KG
Coburger Strasse 53
D-8634 Roadach
(bei Coburg)
Germany

Berg Spielwaren Tiere mit Herz GmbH
Rosenegg 66
A-6391 Fieberbrunn
Austria

Russ Berrie & Co.
111 Bauer Drive
Oakland
NJ 07436
USA

Big Softies
Otley Mills
Ilkley Road
West Yorkshire LS21 3JP
England

Boulgom
Rue des Gilères, BP 91
74150 Rumilly
France

Bunjy Toys
PO Box 496
Estcourt 3310
Natal
Republic of South Africa

Canterbury Bears Ltd.
The Old Coach House
Court Hill
Littlebourne
Kent CT3 1XU
England

Hans Clemens GmbH
Waldstrasse 34–36
6926 Kirchardt/Heilbronn
Germany

Dakin Inc.
World Headquarters
7000 Marina Blvd.
Brisbane
CA 94005
USA

Dean's Company (1903)
Pontypool
Gwent NP4 6YY
Wales

Gabrielle Designs Ltd.
The Bear Garden
Great North Road
Adwick-le-Street
Doncaster
Yorkshire DN6 7EJ
England

Ganz Brothers Toys
One Pearce Road
Woodbridge
Ontario L4L 3T2
Canada

Golden Bear Products Ltd.
Rookery Road
Wrockwardine Wood
Telford
Shropshire TF2 9DW
England

Grisly Spielwaren GmbH & Co. KG
Beethoven Strasse 1
6719 Kichheimbolanden
Germany

Gund Inc.
PO Box H
Edison
NJ 08817
USA

Trudi Giocattoli spa
Via Angelo Angeli 120
33017 Tarcento (Udine)
Italy

Gebrüder Hermann KG
Postfach 1207
Amlingstadter Strasse 6
8606 Hirschaid
Germany

Hermann-Spielwaren GmbH
Im Grund 9–11
D-8630 Coburg-Cortendorf
Germany

Heunec Plüsch Speilwaren Fabrik KG
Strasse am Moos 11
Mörikestrasse 2 & 6
96465 Neustadt/Coburg
Germany

Jakas Soft Toys
85 Lewis Road
Wantirna
Victoria 3152
Australia

Lefray Toys Ltd./ Real Soft Toys
Glandwr Industrial Estate
Aberbeeg
Abertillery
Gwent NP3 2XF
Wales

Little Folk
3 Blackdown Park
Willand
Nr. Cullompton
Devon EX15 2QH
England

Mary Meyer Corporation
PO Box 275
Townsend
VT 05353
USA

Merrythought Ltd.
Ironbridge
Telford
Shropshire TF8 7NJ
England

Mighty Star Ltd.
2250 Boulevard de
Maisonneuve Est
Montreal
Quebec H2K 2E5
Canada

North American Bear Co.
Suite 500
401 N. Wabash
Chicago
IL 60611
USA

Nounours SA/ Aux Nations
Le Rocher Bidaine
F 35210 Chatillon en
Vendelais
France

H. Scharrer & Koch GmbH (Sigikid)
Am Wolfsgarten 8
8581 Mistelbach
Germany

Speciality Manufacturers
39 Richmond Road
Pinetown 3600
Republic of South Africa

Margarete Steiff GmbH
Alleenstrasse 2
Postfach 1560
D-7928 Giengen
Germany

Thiennot SA
BP 6 Rue du Stade
10220 Piney
France

GLOSSARY

• Acrilan
US tradename for an acrylic fibre invented by the Chemstrand Corporation, Decatur, Alabama. First introduced commercially in 1952; later woven into plush fabric for use in the soft-toy industry.

• Acrylic Plush
Fabric woven from acrylic fibres that are synthetically produced; the chemical, acryl-onitrile makes up 85% of content. Acrylic (polymethyl methacrylate) was invented in 1934, and was developed in the post-World War II period for fibres such as Acrilan, Courtelle, Dralon and Orlon, and other products such as paints. Acrylic fibres are fine and downy, making exceptionally soft and warm fabrics such as synthetic fur.

• Airbrushing
Painting by means of an airbrush – a device for spraying colour over a surface using compressed air, which enables an artist to work quickly and produce an even finish. Originally called an aerograph, it was first patented in Britain by US-born Charles L. Burdick in 1893. It is used in the soft-toy industry for applying non-toxic liquid dyes.

• Alpaca Plush
Originally imported from Bolivia and Peru, this plush is woven from alpaca yarn, spun from the long, strong fleece of the alpaca – a small llama. Extremely soft and woolly, it was often used to make baby toys.

• Artificial-silk Plush
Artificial silk was the first man-made fibre, and has been produced commercially from the 1880s. It is created from regenerated cellulose (wood pulp or cotton), which is chemically dissolved to form a viscose solution, then passed through spinnerets followed by mineral acid baths to produce a fibre. Often referred to as "art silk", it was introduced to the soft-toy industry in 1929.

• Boot Buttons
From the 19th to early 20th century, boots and shoes were often fastened with buttons. Being readily available and usually black and globular, they made perfect eyes for early teddy bears. The buttons were made from moulded wood pulp, resembling compressed paper (like hardboard); metal hooks were pushed into the flat backs.

• Broadcloth
A fine, dark-coloured cloth, usually in twill weave, originally for men's suits and later used in the US for teddy-bear noses.

• Brushed Nylon *see Nylon.*

• Buckram
A coarse, woven fabric that is stiffened with gum or paste.

• Burlap
Also described as hessian, a coarse, woven textile made from jute or hemp, used for making teddy bears in the very early years.

• Calico
A plain white, unprinted, bleached or un-bleached cotton cloth. The name derives from Calicut, a chief trading port between India and Europe in the 16th century.

• Celluloid
A semi-synthetic plastic composed of cellulose nitrate and camphor, which was first patented in 1869 by brothers, John and Isaiah Hyatt, in the US. It was particularly popular in the toy industry during the 1920s and 1930s, but was later banned because of its high flammability.

• Chamois Leather
Originally a leather prepared from the skin of the chamois – a European goat-like antelope. The name is now applied to any soft, pliable, yellowish brown leather.

• Composition
Also known as "compo", this is a mixture of various substances (similar to *papier mâché*) including plaster of Paris, bran, sawdust, and glue. It was used primarily in the doll and toy industry from the mid-19th century. While wet and still plastic, it was pressed into moulds and left until it hardened, when it could be painted.

• Cotter Pin
Double-pronged metal pin used to fasten the disc joints into place, enabling a teddy bear's limbs and head to swivel.

• Cotton Plush
A cheap quality plush, popular in the soft-toy industry during and immediately after World War II, woven entirely from cotton.

• Cotton Waste
A refuse yarn from the manufacture of cotton introduced as a stuffing material during World War II when kapok was unavailable. Such fillings were also known as white art wool, flock, and "sub". From the 1960s, waste from synthetic fabrics was also used – the darker the colour, the lower the grade of stuffing.

• Courtelle
Tradename for an acrylic fibre invented by the British company Courtaulds after World War II; the fibre was woven into plush and used in the soft-toy industry.

• Dacron
A teddy-bear stuffing material, bearing the US Du Pont Company's tradename for a polyester fibre patented in 1953.

• Distressed Plush
A plush, either alpaca or mohair, specially treated to resemble antique teddy-bear fur. The distressing process was invented in 1986 by Jack Wilson of the House of Nisbet in collaboration with Norton (Weaving) Ltd. of Yorkshire, using a 1904 "carricule" or velvet-crushing machine. Distressed plushes have become popular among bear artists and manufacturers attempting to produce old-looking bears.

• Dralon
Tradename for an acrylic staple fibre invented by the German company Farben Bayer AG at Dormagen near Leverkusen.

Naturally a light cream colour, it is woven and dyed into plush fabrics chiefly for the upholstery industry. It proved popular in the soft-toy industry from the 1960s for both fur and pads, as it is washable.

• Dual Plush
Refers to plush with pile dyed two colours, also known as tipped mohair. The process of tipping mohair involves laying the plush fabric out on a flat surface, brushing the tips of the pile with a contrasting dye, and leaving to dry. Dual plush was particularly popular during the 1920s.

• Duxeen
An imitation leathercloth like Rexine, used by bookbinders and toymakers, patented in 1920 by the Dux Chemical Solutions Co., Bromley-by-Bow, London, and produced by Messrs. Robert Williams & Sons (Gorton) Ltd. of Gorton, Manchester.

• Excelsior
Mid-19th century US tradename for fine wood shavings, or wood-wool, used for stuffing upholstery etc., and later teddy bears. The Latin motto for "higher", it was often used as a trademark.

• External Jointing
A primitive rod jointing system in which the ends of the rods running through the body of the teddy bear are visible at the shoulders and thighs.

• Fairy Foam
Mid-1960s British tradename for all-in-one foam-rubber stuffing material.

• Felt
Densely-matted, non-woven woollen fabric, which has been subjected to heat, steam, and pressure to compact it. It is the traditional material for the foot- and paw-pads of teddy bears.

• Fibrefill
Polyester fibres in the form of white, light-weight wadding, used as stuffing material in modern teddy-bear manufacture. It is also known by its US tradename, Dacron.

• Flannelette
A woven cotton textile with open weave, made to imitate flannel; brushed to give a slight nap. Also referred to as brushed cotton, it was popular with British teddy-bear manufacturers in the 1920s and 30s.

• Flock *see Cotton Waste.*

• Foam-rubber
Another term for polyurethane which has had pockets of inert gas introduced during its manufacture to form a light, foam-like material used in upholstery, cushions, and for artificial sponges, as well as a stuffing material in the soft-toy industry since the 1950s. It could be moulded to fit inside the outer casing or chopped into small pieces, sometimes described as poly-urethane foam chippings/chips/granules; shredded polyurethane; granulated foam rubber; latex foam; plastic foam; or synthetic foam stuffing. Tradenames such as "Fairy Foam" in the UK and "Sani-Foam" in the US have been patented.

• Glass Eyes
Originally made for taxidermists, blown glass eyes originating from Britain or Germany were introduced into teddy-bear manufacture around 1908. Early examples tended to be of clear glass with opaque black pupils; the backs were painted with brown enamel paint to appear life-like. Translucent amber glass with black pupils was one of the most popular designs for teddy bears' eyes.

• Googly Eyes
Also described as "Goo-Goo" eyes in the doll industry, this style of large, round, and staring eye was used from the early 1900s and throughout the 1920s, copying popular caricatures on postcards or in cartoons of the day. The term refers to bulbous opaque glass eyes with askance pupils. Sewn into a bear's face, they could be turned manually to give new comic expressions; or they were set in sockets, like those of a doll, to give a rolling action.

• Growler
An internal voice-box activated by tilting the toy, introduced to the teddy bear *c.*1908. Although modernized since, the mechanism's principle remains the same: weighted bellows force air through a reed, emitting a "growl". Pre-1930s examples consisted of hinged wood and oilcloth bellows with lead weights, a metal reed (sometimes with a double reed to create a two-tone growl), and card pipes, all contained in a cardboard tube with gauze protection at each open end. In the 1930s, the slide tilt-growler was introduced, with a weight consisting of a round tablet of bisque (unglazed porcelain) with the reed enclosed, joined to spiral oilcloth bellows. Upon tilting, the mechanism slid up and down in its card, tin, or plastic, container, with a perforated speaker at one end.

• Hardboard
Made from wood pulp, compressed in the drying process to form a stiff, dense type of fibreboard that was used by teddy-bear manufacturers to make joints.

• Joggle Eyes
Introduced after World War II, these eyes consisted of flat, white, plastic rounds with a clear plastic covering, each containing a loose, small, black circle representing the pupil. The pupils move in various directions to produce comical expressions when the bear is tilted or shaken.

• Kapok
A stuffing material popular in the soft-toy industry during the 1920s and 1930s, and still used to some degree after World War II because of its many ideal qualities: it is light, resilient, resistent to water, buoyant, and hygienic. The name derives from the Malayan word *kāpoq*, an off-white, vegetable fibre or fruit hair found in the seed pods of the tropical tree *Ceiba Pentandra*. Known since the 18th century, kapok was first imported into Europe in 1851.

• Kid Leather
Soft leather made from kid or lamb skins. It was originally employed for making gloves and shoes, but it is also used in the soft-toy industry for the production of paw-pads and foot-pads.

• Leathercloth
Imitation leather, woven or knitted fabric coated on one side with either cellulose nitrate, a vinyl such as polyvinyl chloride (PVC), or polyurethane, often embossed to simulate leather. Also known as leatherette, or by a tradename such as Rexine or Duxeen, it is used principally in the upholstery and bookbinding trade. It is also employed in the toy industry for teddies' paw-pads.

• Leatherette see Leathercloth.

• Modacrylic Plush
Woven from modacrylic fibres, similar to acrylic fibres, but with a content of only 35–85% of the chemical acrylonotrile.

• Mohair
Derived from the Arabic word muxayyar meaning "cloth of goat's hair", the term originally referred to yarn or cloth made from the fleece of the Turkish angora goat, although today it is generally a mixture of wool and cotton. In 1830, some angora goats were sent to South Africa, which is now one of the biggest mohair producers.

• Musical Movement
This term refers to the type of clockwork cylinder and comb musical mechanism invented in 1780 by Louis Favre of Switzerland. In teddy-bear manufacturing, the movements were originally encased either in squeeze-boxes, or in tin or wooden and tin boxes, activated through an external crank shaft or key. Later examples were produced in plastic boxes, sometimes activated through a pull-cord. Japanese manufacturers largely took over the Swiss monopoly of this product after World War II.

• Nylon
The first completely synthetic fibre, Nylon was invented by chemist W.H. Carothers in the laboratories of the Du Pont Company of Delaware, in the US. It was first introduced commercially in 1938, after 11 years' research. Also known as a polyamide, it is produced using amides, chemicals similar to those that make up proteins in animal fibres, derived from the petrochemical caprolactam. Nylon is tough, lightweight, and elastic, and since World War II has been used extensively in the toy industry. Brushed nylon is treated on one surface to give it a raised and soft-textured nap.

• Oilcloth
A cloth treated to render it waterproof; also a name for leathercloth.

• Orlon
US tradename for an acrylic fibre registered by the Du Pont Company in 1948, and first employed commercially in 1950. Orlon is frequently used in knitted fabrics such as imitation fur and in carpets, as well as in the soft-toy industry.

• Pile
Vertical threads which stand out from the surface of a fabric. Plush can be described as shaggy or short pile. Pile in loop form is known as "terry".

• Plastic
From the Greek word plastikos, meaning "able to be shaped", plastic is a general term describing a varied class of organic substances made up of long chains of molecules (or polymers), based on man-made chemicals (such as vinyls) or modified natural materials (such as celluloid). Under heat and pressure, they become plastic and can be cast in moulds to produce a permanent or rigid form.

• Plush
From the Latin word pilus, meaning "hair", and the old French word pluche, meaning "hairy fabric", plush is a cloth with a cut pile on one side, which is longer and less dense than velvet. It is usually woven, often by weaving two cloths together with a pile warp common to both, which is afterwards cut. Since World War II, cheaper plush made from synthetic yarns has been produced on a knitted backing.

• Polyester
A synthetic fibre that uses oil as raw material, and was invented in 1941 by J.R. Whinfield and J.T. Dickson at the Calico Printers Association in the UK. Its registered tradename in Britain is Terylene, whereas in the US it is known as Dacron. It is often mixed with natural fibres to make easily washable, woven fabrics, or to make strong sewing threads or a wadding known as fibrefill, a type of stuffing.

• Polystyrene
Developed in Germany in 1929, as one of the first synthetic plastics. Since World War II, it has been used as stuffing in the toy industry in the form of a lightweight, rigid foam, in granules, or pellets.

• Polyurethane
Describes a large class of synthetic resins and plastics first produced in 1937 and developed during World War II; it is used for making foam-rubber.

• Rayon
Term used generally since World War II for artificial silk. Since that period, modifications to equipment and chemicals used in the manufacturing process have resulted in a variety of rayons, such as viscose, acetate, and triacetate.

• Rexine
A tradename for a leathercloth or imitation leather used in upholstery and bookbinding, it was listed in the 1915 Trademarks Journal as belonging to the British Leather-cloth Manufacturing Co. Ltd. (later Rexine Ltd), Hyde, near Manchester. Rexine is formed by covering a woven cloth with several coatings of cellulose nitrate. The term is often used to describe the leather-cloth used on British and Australian bear pads from the late 1930s to early 1960s.

• Rod Jointing see External Jointing.

• Rubber
Originally commercial rubber was based on a natural substance, the milky viscous liquid or latex obtained from the tropical tree Hevea brasileinsis. During World War II, synthetic rubbers were extensively developed, and various types based on different chemicals are now produced for use in industry, including toy manufacture.

• Safe Eyes
Plastic eyes, each with an integral shank forming a screw and secured with a washer behind the plush; also referred to as "safe-lock" or "screw-lock" eyes; the recommended method of applying soft-toy eyes by toy safety standard laws worldwide.

• Satin
Originally described a silk fabric with a smooth glossy surface produced by a warp-faced weave. Now a term also used for other textiles resembling satin, but not necessarily of silk. Satinized fabric is that which has been treated to imitate satin.

• Sealing Wax
A man-made wax that was originally used for sealing documents, it was also employed in the early years of teddy manufacture, particularly in Germany, for making realistically moulded noses. Malleable when hot, it cooled to a hard finish, but was unsatisfactory as it often cracked.

• Shanks
The shaft or hook, usually of wire, protruding from the back of a glass or plastic eye, used for securing it inside the head. Later plastic eyes often had integral (all-in-one) shanks.

• "Sliced in" Ears
Term referring to a cheap method of securing ears to a teddy bear by cutting or "slicing" holes in the sides or top of the head and pushing in the gathered edge of the ear; no stitching is required.

• Slush Moulding
Also known as rotational moulding, this method of making hollow vinyl objects was used particularly for making doll and teddy bear heads of the post-World War II era. The mould is partially filled with a powdered resin, and then heated and spun rapidly. The centrifugal force pushing the melting resin against the moulded walls holds it there as the mould cools. The resin eventually solidifies.

• Squeaker
Internal voice box, used from the earliest days of teddy-bear manufacturing, made from two rounds or ovals of card or wood held together by a strip of oilcloth to form bellows, containing a coiled spring. When squeezed, a rush of air caused the internal or external reed to vibrate producing a squeak. Any old piece of card, including photographs, was used for their manufacture. Post-World War II versions of the squeaker use the same principle, but with soft vinyl bellows that are often in the form of a concertina.

• Styrofoam
US tradename for a type of polystyrene foam that was patented in 1950 by the Dow Chemical Company, and used in the soft-toy industry as a stuffing material.

• Sub see Cotton Waste.

• Suede
Derived from Suède (French for Sweden), this originally described undressed kid leather, but now applies to other kinds of leather (such as lamb skin or cowhide) resembling kid skin. Its special finish has a napped, velvety surface which is produced by buffing the flesh side with an emery wheel.

• Suedette
A type of cotton or rayon fabric with a velvety nap, dating from 1915, designed to imitate the texture of suede.

• Swing-tag
A paper, card, metal, or plastic tag usually bearing the manufacturer's tradename and/ or bear's name, and attached by thread either around the neck or arm, or sewn into the chest (also known as a chest -tag). Often lost or removed, it is thus named to differentiate it from the more permanent fabric label, usually sewn across a pad or into a seam.

• Tipped Mohair see Dual Plush.

• Twill
A woven fabric with diagonal ridges, created by passing the weft threads over one and under two or more of the warp threads (instead of over and under in regular succession as in plain weaving).

• Ultrasuede
US tradename for a synthetic, non-woven fabric that resembles suede, first used in 1971 and patented in 1973 by Spring Mills Inc., Fort Mill, South Carolina, US.

• Velcro
Registered tradename derived from the French velours croché, meaning "hooked velvet". Describes a revolutionary fastener consisting of two woven nylon strips, one with tiny loops, the other with hooks, which can be simply pressed together or pulled apart. It was first conceived by Swiss engineer, Georges de Mestral, in 1948.

• Velour
From the French word meaning "velvet", this describes a velvet-like plush fabric, with either a woven or a knitted backing, often synthetic in recent years.

• Velvet
A woven, silk fabric with a short, dense, and smooth-piled surface.

• Velveteen
A velvet-like fabric in appearance and texture, but woven from cotton instead of silk, which makes it cheaper to produce.

• Vinyl
Refers to various plastics that contain the chemical substance vinyl. Durable and inexpensive, vinyls are used both to make rigid products (such as toys) and flexible products (such as films) as well as vinyl coatings for fabrics. The most well known, polyvinyl chloride (PVC), was the first to be manufactured commercially.

• Wood-wool
Long, fine quality, soft wood (such as birch) shavings, originally a packing material for delicate objects but also used in upholstery and taxidermy. It is the traditional stuffing material for teddy-bears. Arriving in large bales, the material must be pulled apart and stuffed manually using rods.

• Yorkshire cloth
A term sometimes used for mohair plush, because it was spun in Yorkshire in the north of England, the traditional centre of the textile industry. Angora goats' hair was imported from Turkey and South Africa to be converted into yarn. It was then woven into plush in Yorkshire, or exported to one of the German mills such as Schulte's.

INDEX

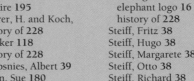

ACKNOWLEDGMENTS

Author's Acknowledgments
I am more than grateful for the assistance, support, and advice of Rosemary and Paul Volpp, George Black, Colin and Wendy Lewis, Brian Beacock, the curatorial staff of the Bethnal Green Museum of Childhood (especially Halina Pasierbska and Caroline Goodfellow), Pam Hebbs, and Gerry and Margaret Grey, without whom this book would not have been possible.

I am indebted to the numerous arctophiles, teddy-bear manufacturers, and artists who allowed their bears to be photographed, and particularly to those who put their trust in the postal service and mailed their teddies from various corners of the globe to London. I am also grateful to those people who spared the time to help me track down bears or information for this mammoth project. To all of these listed below, I offer a huge, heartfelt "thank you": **Australia:** Jacki Brooks; Jenny Marchionni (The Camperdown Children's Hospital Fund); Nancy Evans; Marjory Fainges; Jenny Laing; Pat Lovelock; Pol McCann; Wendy McDonald (Jakas Soft Toys); Joan McPherson; Lynn Riddell-Robertson (Numbat Books); Romy Roeder; Jenny Round; Keith Schneider (Russ Berrie [Australia] Pty. Ltd.); Tomoko Sato; Carole Williams (Teddy & Friends: The Bear Essentials); Gerry Warlow; Bob White. **Austria:** Udo Broschek (Berg Tiere mit Herz GmbH); Dr. Filek-Wittinghausen (Austrian Chamber of Commerce); Kurt Klaritsch and K. Koritnik (Steiermark Chamber of Commerce). **Canada:** John Cox (Ganz Toys); Dillon Goldsmith (Mighty Star Ltd.); Marcella Pittana; Joan Rankin; Mrs. S. Stratton (Cuddly Toys Ltd.); Trudi Teneycke. **France:** Philippe Mangon (Anima); O. Blanchet (Créations Blanchet); Patricia Braunstein (Boulgom); Aline Cousin; Marcelle Goffin; Marylou Jouet; Manera J-Jacques (sarl Maxi Jouet); Christophe Couvreur (Nounours Group). **Germany:** Roland Spindler (Althans KG); Jürgen and Marianne Cieslik; Peter Clemens and Elke Untch (Hans Clemens GmbH); Margot Drolshagen and Mrs. G. Lee (Gebrüder Hermann KG); Rolf and Dr. Ursula Hermann (Hermann-Spielwaren GmbH); H. Dransfeld (Heunec Plüsch Spielwaren Fabrik KG); Marion Hohmann (Käthe Kruse Puppen KG); Sabine Zoller and Simone Schneider ("Sigikid", H. Scharrer & Koch GmbH); Jörg Junginger (Margarete Steiff GmbH); Klaus and Jutta Hartmann (Teddybären & Plüsch); Walter Schubert (W. Walter KG). **Republic of Ireland**: Mairead Donlevy (National Museum of Ireland); Joan Hanna; Audrey Harris; Jagoda Mansfield. **Italy:** Bibija Garella (Lenci srl); Giuseppe Patriarca (Trudi Giocattoli spa). **The Netherlands:** Dorothée Wennink (Association of Benelux Toy Manufacturers); Jane Humme; Jonette Stabbert. **New Zealand:** Peggy Armstrong; Clive and Precille Harrison (Bear with Us); Allie and Nigel Hanton; Janis Harris; Nancy Hay (Maxwell Hay & Co. Ltd.); Denise Jackson; Heather Lyell; Frances McLeary; Dawn Nicholl; Denise Parsons; Sally Pearson; Robin Rive (Robbity Bob Ltd.); Peter and Valda McCombe (Sheepskin Products Ltd.); Cathy Philips (Teddies & Treasures); Michael and Judy Walton. **Republic of South Africa:** Annwen

Bates; George Allison (Bunjy Toys); Mary Kelly; Julian Pells (Prima Toys); G.A. and D.J. Weir (Speciality Manufacturers Division); Eunice Beaton (Thread Bears); Ken and Helen Wynne-Dyke. **Sweden:** Peter Pluntky; Agneta Thomson. **Switzerland:** Stephen Ernst; Stéphane Kaercher. **UK:** Margaret Jones (Alresford Crafts Ltd.); Paul Goble and Kim (Bears & Friends, Brighton); Kate Barringer; Valerie and Fred Lyle (Big Softies); Janice O'Dair (Bramwell Brown's Hug Shop); Deborah Canham; Maude and John Blackburn (Canterbury Bears Ltd.); Liz Carless; Marlene Couchman; Neil Miller and Michael Crane (The Dean's Company [1903]); Anna Dartnell; Gill Dutton; Faith Eaton Collection; Valerie (Especially Bears Shop); Mrs. Lawley (Golden Bear Products Ltd.); Katherine Grant; Jack Wilson (House of Nisbet); Pam Howells; Glenn and Irene Jackman (*Hugglets*); Staff of Imperial War Museum's Photographic Collection; Ray Jackson; Maddie Janes; Naomi Laight; Ben Lyford; Graham McBride (Little Folk); Deirdre Mackinnon; Felix Sear (Melrose Teddy Bear Museum); John Parkes and Oliver Holmes (Merrythought Ltd.); June Miller; Irene Moore; Jim Mulholland (Mulholland & Bailie Ltd.); Alan and Wendy Mullaney; Sue Nicoll; Belinda O'Brien; Anita Oliver; Eddie Owen; Ian Pout; Sue Quinn; John Radmall; Christina Revell; Sue Rixon; Pat Rush; Gwyneth Ashcroft and Curts Cooke (Russ Berrie [UK] Ltd.); Maureen and Alan Samuels; June Sanders; Sue Schoen; Ian Scott; Bunny Campione (Sotheby's); Judy and John Sparrow; Mr. and Mrs. Stubbs; C. A. Symon; Sylvia Coote (Teddy Bear Museum, Stratford-upon-Avon); Stacey Lee Terry; Rosemary Waterson; Coralie Wearing; Catherine While. **USA:** Art Husted; Alison Nielson and Julie Ruttenberg (Applause Inc.); Barbara Baldwin; Nick and Cassie Bisbikis; Loretta Botta; Ginger T. Brame; Sydney Charles; Audrey McFadden and Robyn Kutch (Dakin Inc.); Diane Gard; Shari J.K. Meltzer (Gund Inc.); Serieta Harrell; Marie Pamental (Hasbro Inc.); Dee Hockenberry; Linda Spiegel Lohre; Cindy Martin; Walter Meyer (Mary Meyer Corporation); Doris and Terry Michaud; Bev Miller; Joanne Mitchell; Linda Mullins; Barbara Isenberg and Bethany Pearlman (North Ameri can Bear Company Inc.); Russ Berrie & Company Inc; Sara Phillips; Carol-Lynn Rössel Waugh; Donna L. Saqui; Patricia Schoonmaker; Steve Schutt; Helen Sieverling; Barbara Sixby; Lisl Swinehart; Stephen Cronk (*Teddy Bear Review*); Susan Weiser; Susan Wiley.

I also wish to thank my editors, Irene and Helen, and designers Peter and Debbie for all their hard work and patience, particularly having to deal with an author 12,000 miles away; as well as photographer Peter for his tremendous skill and good humour throughout the many hours of "bear shoots".

Last but not least, I am deeply indebted to my mother Joan; my husband David; and friends Ruth Bottomley, Ruth Cornett, Janice Hunt, Ann and Jill Skinner, and Lynnet Wilson for all "bearing with me" throughout and keeping me sane. And to Medusa, who although tempted, did not chew up my text.

Publisher's Acknowledgments

DORLING KINDERSLEY WOULD LIKE TO THANK: Susie Behar, Polly Boyd, Lucinda Hawksley, Damien Moore, and Connie Novis for editorial assistance; Andrea Fair for keying-in the text; Sharon Moore for design assistance; Alastair Wardle and Adam Moore for computer support; Julia Pashley for picture research; Murdo Culver for organizing the transparencies; Michael Allaby for compiling the index; and Chris Elfes for additional photography in Australia.

PICTURE CREDITS

Photography by Peter Anderson: 1; 2; 3 c; 4 tr; 5 tl, bl, br; 9 br; 13 bl; 14 tr; 15 b; 16; 17 bl; 21 tr; 23 tr; 25 br; 26; 29 tl, br; 30; 31 tr, bl, br; 33 tr, bl, br; 35 tl, bl; 37 tr; 41 tr, bl; 42; 45 tr; 49 bl, tr; 50–51 all; 53 tr, tl, br; 54; 55 tr, bl, br; 56; 57 tl, bl; 61 tr, tl, bl; 63 tl, tr, bl; 64–65 all; 69 tl, tr, bl; 70; 71 br; 73 tl, bl, br; 74; 75 tl, tr bl; 76; 77 tl, bl; 78; 79 br; 83 tr, bl, br; 84; 85 tr, bl; 87 tr, bl, br; 88; 89 tl, br; 90; 91 tr, bl, br; 93 all; 95 tl, tr, bl; 96; 97 tr, bl 98; 99 tl, bl, br; 100–01 all; 103 tl, tr, br; 104; 105 tl, tr, br; 106; 107 tl, tr bl; 108; 109 tl, bl, br; 111 bl, br; 113 tl, tr, bl; 114; 115 tl; 117 tl, tr, bl; 118; 119 tl, tr; 121 tr, br; 123 all; 124–25 all; 126; 127 tl, tr, br; 129; 130; 131 tl, tr, bl; 133 tl, tr; 135 all; 136; 137 tr; 141 tl; 143 bl, br; 145 tl, tr, bl; 150; 151 tl, tr; 155 tl, br; 156; 157 tl, tr, br; 158; 159 tl, bl, br; 161 all; 163 tl, tr, bl; 164; 165 tl, bl, br; 166; 167 bl; 168; 169 br; 171 tr, bl, br; 173 bl, br; 177 bl, br; 178 tr, bl, br; 179 tl, bl; 180 tl, bl, br; 181 tr, bl, br; 182–83 all; 184 tl, tr, bl; 185 all; 186 br; 187 bl, br; 188 tm, m; 189 tl; 191 tl, ml, bl; 192 tl, bm, tr; 193 bl, cr, tr; 195 tr, cl; 196 tl, bl, cl; 197 tl, bl, mr; 198 tl; 199 tr; 201 cl.

Photography by Jim Coit: 3 tl; 4 bl; 5 tr, ml; 6 ml; 7 bl; 8 r; 9 tl; 10 br; 11 tr; 12 tl, mr, bl, tr, br; 13 br; 14 bl; 15 tl; 17 tl, tr; 18; 19 tr; 21 tl, bl; 23 tl, bl; 24; 25 tr, bl; 27 all; 32; 33 tl; 34; 37 tl, bl; 39 bl; 40; 41 bl; 43 tl, tr; 44; 45 tl, bl, br; 46–47 all; 49 tl, br; 55 tl; 59 tl, tr; 62; 63 br; 67 tr; 71 tl, tr; 73 tl; 75 br; 77 br;

79 tl, bl; 82; 83 tl; 85 tl, br; 86; 89 bl; 91 tl; 95 br; 97 tl; 103 bl; 105 bl; 109 tr; 110; 111 tl, tr; 112; 115 tr, bl, br; 116; 117 br; 119 bl, br; 120 127 bl; 129 tl, tr, bl; 133 br; 137 tl, bl, br; 138; 139 tr, bl, br; 140; 141 tr, bl, br; 142; 143 tl, tr; 145 br; 146–47 all; 151 br; 153 all; 154; 155 bl, tr; 157 bl; 159 tr; 160; 163 br; 165 tr; 167 tl, tr, br; 169 tl, tr, bl; 172 all; 173 tl, tr; 174 all; 175 all; 176 tl, bl, br; 177 tl, tr; 178 tl; 184 br; 186 tl, tr, bl; 187 tr, br; 188 tl, tr; 189 ml; 190 bl; 192 bl, br; 194 bl; 195 tr, bl-all; 196 mr; 197 tr; 198 bl; 199 bl; 200 bl, bm, br, tl br; 201 bl, bm, bl, tl.

Photography by Roland Kemp: 10 tl; 11 ml, br; 17 br; 19 tl, bl, br; 20; 21 br; 22; 23 br; 28; 29 bl; 31 tl; 35 tr; 36, 37 br; 38 bl; 39 br; 48; 52; 53 bl; 57 tr, br; 59 bl; 60; 61 br; 67 bl; 68; 69 br; 71 bl; 72; 79 tr; 89 cr; 92; 97 bl; 102; 107 br; 110; 113 br; 122; 128; 139 tl; 151; 152; 171 cl; 179 tr, br; 180 tr; 188 b; 198 tr, br; 199 tl.

Additional photography: Courtesy of Asquiths of Windsor 195 tl. Courtesy of Christie's 94 tr. Courtesy of Sotheby's 194 tl. Courtesy of the Trustees of the V&A, photographed by Pip Barnard: 38 bl; 41 tl; 43 bl; 99 tr; 131 br; 133 bl; 134; 144; 162. Chris Elfes (Australia): 58; 59 br; 80–81 all. Linda Mullins 191 tr. Private collection 13 tl. Matthew Ward 170. Paul Volpp 21 br; 87 tl; 132. Bear Care and Repair: 202–03 main bear Peter Anderson, others Jim Coit, Roland Kemp, Matthew Ward; 204–07 Peter Anderson, Matthew Ward, Roland Kemp; 208–09 Peter Anderson, Matthew Ward; 210–11 Peter Anderson, Matthew Ward, Roland Kemp; 212–13 Peter Anderson, Matthew Ward; 214 Jim Coit, Paul Volpp, Peter Anderson, Matthew Ward.

Library usage: 8 bl Mary Evans Picture Library; 8 bc T. Roosevelt Collection/ Harvard College Library; 10 Imperial War Museum; 11 Hulton Picture Company; 190 Rex Features; 169 tr ©1992 Hanna-Barbera Productions, Inc., licensed by Copyright Promotions Ltd. – Yogi 170

Factory archive material: 38–39 Margarete Steiff GmbH; 3 bl, 66–67 Merrythought Ltd; 94–95 Hermann-Spielwaren GmbH; Gebrüder Hermann KG; 148–49 Russ Berrie & Co. Inc.

BEAR CREDITS

- MRS. BAKER 202 br.
- KATE BARRINGER 23 tr.
- BRIAN BEACOCK 5 br; 65 br; 73 bl; 83 bl; 107 bl; 129 br; 156; 161 bl; 166; 188 c; 212; 213.
- RUSS BERRIE & COMPANY INC UK 170.
- BETHNAL GREEN MUSEUM OF CHILDHOOD (V&A) 38bl; 41 tl; 43 bl; 99 tr; 131 br; 133 bl; 134; 144; 162.
- NICK BISBIKIS JNR. 85 bl; 119 tr.
- HEATHER BISCHOFF 29 bl.
- GEORGE B. BLACK JNR. 77 bl.
- GYLES BRANDRETH 17 tr; 20; 21 br; 79 tr; 102; 179 tr, br; 198 br.
- BUNJY TOYS 169 br.
- GINA CAMPBELL 121 bl.
- CANTERBURY BEARS 5, 151 tl, bl.
- SYDNEY R. CHARLES 25 br; 26; 75 tl, tr, bl; 38 bl; 91 br; 97 bl; 107 br; 115 tl; 117 bl.
- JOAN COCKRILL 212 br.
- PAULINE COCKRILL 57 br; 157 br; 189 tl.
- MARLENE COUCHMAN 103 tl, tr; 159 tl.
- ANNA DARTNELL 157 tr.
- GILL DELLA CASA 212 CR; 214 br.
- FAITH EATON COLLECTION 31 tl, 165 br.
- NANCY EVANS 59 bl.
- PAUL GOBLE (BEARS & FRIENDS, BRIGHTON) 13 bl.
- JO GREENE 204.
- MARGARET & GERRY GREY 56; 106; 108; 183 br; 192 tr.
- GUND INC. 85 tl, bl.
- AUDREY HARRIS 159 br.
- KARIN HELLER 161 br.
- GEBRÜDER HERMANN 5 c; 31 bl, br; 95 tr; 97 br; 190 br.
- PAM HEBBS 9 br; 16; 19 bl, br; 22; 23 bl; 36; 39 br; 42; 48; 63 tl, bl; 73 bl; 103 br; 118; 130 tr; 135 bl; 177 bl, br; 178 tr, br; 186 br; 188 c; 191 tl, cl; 198 tr.
- HERMANN-SPIELWAREN 4 c; 10 tr; 30; 31 tr; 95 tl; 99 tl, bl. br.
- RAY JACKSON 124 tl.
- LEVER BROTHERS Snuggle courtesy of Lever Brothers Company 139 br.
- COLIN & WENDY LEWIS 1; 2; 4 tr; 5 bl; 11 bl; 14 tr; 15 b; 21 tr; 29 br; 33 tr, br; 37 tr; 41 tr; 49 tr, bl; 50 tl; 53 tr, br;

54; 55 tr, bl; 57 bl; 61 tl, tr, bl; 63 tr; 64; 65 tl, tr, bl; 69 tl, tr, bl; 70; 78; 88; 89 tl; 90; 91 tr; 93 all; 96; 97 tr; 101 tr, bl, br; 105 tl, tr, bl; 107 tl, tr; 109 tl, br; 111 bl; 113 tl, tr, bl; 114; 117 tl; 124; 125bl, br; 127 tl, tr, br; 130; 131 tl, bl; 132 tr; 135 tl; 155 tl; 163 tl; 171 tr; 180 tl, bl, br; 181 bl; 182 tl, bl, br; 192 tl; 192 cb 193 cr, bl; 214 c; 234; 239.
- GILLIAN LISTER 11 tl.
- BEN LYFORD 136; 210.
- DEIRDRE MacKINNON 17 bl; 55 tl.
- MERRYTHOUGHT LTD. 67 br; 121 tr, br.
- JUNE MILLER 123 tr, bl, br.
- CAREY MINHINNETT 104.
- BELINDA O'BRIEN 89 br.
- MRS. PEARCE 202 tr.
- IAN POUT 19 tl; 29 tr; 43 br; 69 br; 89 tr; 113 br.
- PRIVATE COLLECTION 35 br; 71 bl; 92, 139 tl, 152; 171 tl; 181 tl.
- JOHN RADMALL 10 tl, 51 br, 91 bl.
- CHRISTINA REVELL 109 bl.
- ROMY ROEDER 58; 59 br; 80-81.
- MR. & MRS. SAMUELS 135 tr; 143 bl; 145 tr, tl, bl; 150; 161 tl;163 tr, bl; 181 br; 195 cl; 196 tl; 197 cr; 199 tr; 203 bl; 214 r.
- JUNE SANDERS 51 bl.
- FELIX SEAR 50, 73.
- KIOK SIEM 37 br.
- HELEN SIEVERLING 35 tl; 76; 77 tl; 83 br; 84; 85 tr; 87 tr, bl, br; 98; 198 tl.
- ANN SKINNER 159 bl.
- JILL SKINNER 132.
- JUDY SPARROW 10 tl; 11 br; 28; 52; 53 bl; 57 tr; 60; 61 br; 67 bl; 68; 71 br; 72; 121tl; 123 tl; 125 br; 128; 135 br; 199 tr; 203 bl; 214 tr.
- LINDA SPIEGEL LOHRE 79 br.
- MR. & MRS. STUBBS 45 tr.
- SUDBURY HALL MUSEUM OF CHILDHOOD 29 tl.
- C.A. SYMON 158
- TEDDY BEAR MUSEUM OF NAPLES, FLORIDA 74; 83 tr; 95 bl; 100; 101 tl; 117 tr; 119 tl; 126; 137 tr; 141 tl; 151 tr; 155 br; 157 tl; 164; 165 tl; 167 bl; 168; 171 bl, br; 173 bl, br; 176 tr; 177 bl; 178 tr, br; 191 tl, cl.
- FRAUKE TOWNSEND 111 br.
- PAUL & ROSEMARY VOLPP 3 tl; 4 tl, bl, br; 5 cl; 6; 7; 8 r; 9 tl tr; 10 br; 11 tr; 12 all; 13 tr, bl; 14 bl; 15 tl; 17 tl, tr; 18; 19

t.r; 21 tl, bl; 23 tl, bl; 24; 25 tl, tr, bl; 27 all; 32; 33 tl; 34; 37 tl, bl; 39 bl; 40, bl, br; 41 bl, br; 43 tl, tr; 44; 45 tl, bl, br; 46; 47all; 49 tl, br; 55 tl; 59 tl, tr; 62; 63 br; 67 tr; 71 tl, tr; 73 tr; 75 br; 77 tr, br; 79 tr, bl; 82; 83 tl; 86; 87 tl; 89 bl; 91 tl; 95 br; 97 tl; 103 bl; 105 bl; 109 tr; 110; 111 tl, tr; 112; 115 tr, bl, br; 116; 117 br; 119 bl, br; 120; 127 bl; 129 tl, tr, bl; 133 br; 137 tl, bl; 138; 139 tr, bl, br; 140; 141 tr, bl, br; 142; 143 tl, tr; 145 br; 146–47; 151 br; 153 all; 154, tr, bl; 155 tr, bl; 157 bl; 159 tr; 160; 163 br; 165 tr; 167 tl, tr, br; 169 tl, tr, bl; 172 all; 173 tl, tr; 174–75 all; 176 tl, bl, br; 177 tl, tr; 178 tl; 184 br; 186 tl, tr, bl; 187 tr, br; 188 tl, tr; 189 c; 190 bl; 192 bl, br; 194 bl; 195 tr; 196 tr, cr; 197 tr; 198 bl; 199 bl, tl; 200; 201; 202 tl; 203 c; 214 bl; 236; 237; 238.
- WALSHAW & CO. 205.
- PENELOPE WARTON 212.
- CORALIE WEARING 35 bl.
- ANNA WHITE 161 tr.
- LISA WHITE 133 tl.
- ANKIE WILD, RIBCHESTER MUSEUM OF CHILDHOOD 193 tl.
- LYNNET WILSON 122.

- **BEAR ARTISTS**
Deborah Canham 182 tr.
Aline Cousin-Debrowolska 184 tr.
Marcelle Goffin 184 tl.
Joan Hanna 183 tr.
Allie & Nigel Hanton 185 br.
Janis Harris 185 tr.
Marylou Jouet 184 bl.
Mary Kelly 187 bl.
Frances McLeary 185 bl.
Irene Moore 183 tl.
Alan and Wendy Mullaney 181 tr.
Eddie Owen 179 bl
Joan Rankin 179 tl.
Jenny Round 187 tl.
Jonette Stabbert 183 bl.
Trudy Teneycke 178 br
Michael & Judy Walton 185 tl.